INSTANT VORTEX AIR FRYER OVEN

COOKBOOK

1000 Vibrant, Quick and Easy Recipes for
Mouthwatering and Affordable Homemade Meals

TIFFANY D. MORGAN

Copyright© 2022 By Tiffany D. Morgan All Rights Reserved

This book is copyright protected. It is only for personal use. You cannot amend, distribute, sell, use, quote or paraphrase any part of the content within this book, without the consent of the author or publisher.

Under no circumstances will any blame or legal responsibility be held against the publisher, or author, for any damages, reparation, or monetary loss due to the information contained within this book, either directly or indirectly.

Disclaimer Notice:

Please note the information contained within this document is for educational and entertainment purposes only. All effort has been executed to present accurate, up to date, reliable, complete information. No warranties of any kind are declared or implied. Readers acknowledge that the author is not engaged in the rendering of legal, financial, medical or professional advice. The content within this book has been derived from various sources. Please consult a licensed professional before attempting any techniques outlined in this book.

By reading this document, the reader agrees that under no circumstances is the author responsible for any losses, direct or indirect, that are incurred as a result of the use of the information contained within this document, including, but not limited to, errors, omissions, or inaccuracies.

Table of Contents

Introduction — 1

Chapter 1
Beginners Guide to the Vortex — 2
Step by Step Guide to the Usage of the Vortex — 3
Top 6 Instant Vortex Air Fryer Accessories — 4

Chapter 2
Cooking with the Instant Vortex Air Fryer — 5
Dos and Don'ts — 6
Choosing the Right Cooking Mode — 6
Tips and Tricks for Air Frying Success — 6
Best and Worst Ingredients — 7
How to Save Time Cooking — 7

Chapter 3
Breakfasts — 8
Sweet Banana Bread — 9
Low-Fat Buttermilk Biscuits — 9
Coffee Cake with Pecan — 9
Parmesan Ham and Egg Cups — 9
Mozzarella Tomato Salsa Rounds — 10
Almond, Coconut, and Apple Granola — 10
Corn Frittata with Avocado Dressing — 10
Egg in a Hole — 10
Avocado and Egg Burrito — 11
Cheese and Bacon Muffin Sandwiches — 11
Breakfast Raisins Bars — 11
Bell Pepper and Carrot Frittata — 11
Broccoli and Red Pepper Quiche — 12
Vanilla Banana Bread Pudding — 12
Baked Avocado with Eggs and Tomato — 12
Vanilla Pancake with Mixed Berries — 12
Chicken Breakfast Sausages — 13
Banana Chocolate Bread with Walnuts — 13
Shrimp and Spinach Frittata — 13
Cheddar Bacon Casserole — 13
Cheddar Hash Brown Casserole — 14
Mushroom and Spinach Frittata — 14
Breakfast Sausage Quiche — 14
Vanilla Pancake with Walnuts — 14
Half-and-Half Cinnamon Rolls — 15
Vanilla Blueberry Cobbler — 15
Asparagus Strata with Havarti Cheese — 15
Brown Rice Porridge with Dates — 15
Garlic Potatoes with Peppers and Onions — 16
Brown Rice Quiches with Pimiento — 16
Baked Eggs with Kale Pesto — 16
Blueberries Quesadillas — 16
Maple Banana Bread Pudding — 17
Spinach and Egg Florentine — 17
Banana Carrot Muffin — 17
Whole-Wheat Blueberries Muffins — 17
Orange Scones with Blueberries — 18
French Toast Sticks with Strawberries — 18
Blueberry Cake with Lemon — 18
Beef Hash with Eggs — 18
Maple French Toast Casserole — 19
Honey Cashew Granola with Cranberries — 19
Bacon and Egg Cup — 19
Italian Bacon Hot Dogs — 19
Creamy Sausage and Cauliflower — 19
Chicken Breakfast Sausage Biscuits — 20
French Toast Sticks — 20
Mozzarella Sausage Pizza — 20
Cheddar Egg and Bacon Muffins — 20
British Pumpkin Egg Bake — 20
Speedy Coffee Donuts — 21
Breaded Avocado — 21
Air-Fried Avocado Tempura — 21
Lush Veggie Omelet — 21
Mushroom and Yellow Squash Toast — 22

Chia Seeds Oat Porridge	22
Cheesy Onion Omelet	22
Ranch Risotto with Parmesan Cheese	22
Cheesy Italian Sausage Egg Muffins	23
Mozzarella Pepperoni Pizza	23
Simple Blueberry Muffins	23
Easy Cinnamon Toasts	23
Scotch Eggs	24
Warm Sourdough Croutons	24
Ricotta Spinach Omelet	24
Spinach and Tomato with Scrambled Eggs	24
Lime-Honey Grilled Fruit Salad	25
Bell Pepper, Onion, and Mushroom Frittata	25
Stuffed Bell Pepper with Cheddar Bacon	25
Glazed Strawberry Toast	25

Chapter 4
Vegan and Vegetarian — 26

Lemony-Honey Roasted Radishes	27
Stuffed Peppers with Cheese and Basil	27
Cheesy Eggplant with Chili Smoked Almonds	27
Butternut Squash with Goat Cheese	27
Double Cheese Roasted Asparagus	28
Golden Potato, Carrot and Onion	28
Potato Shells with Cheddar and Bacon	28
Butternut Squash and Parsnip with Thyme	28
Ginger-Pepper Broccoli	29
Parmesan Brussels Sprout	29
Roasted Veggie Rice with Eggs	29
Air Fried Tofu Sticks	29
Garlic Eggplant Slices with Parsley	30
Cayenne Green Beans	30
Honey Baby Carrots with Dill	30
Garlic Tofu with Basil	30
Zucchini Quesadilla with Gouda Cheese	31
Parmesan Fennel with Red Pepper	31
Curried Cauliflower with Cashews	31
Balsamic-Glazed Beets	31
Fried Root Veggies with Thyme	32
Halloumi Zucchinis and Eggplant	32
Red Chili Okra	32
Garlic Bell Peppers with Marjoram	32
Garlic Ratatouille	33
Cauliflower with Teriyaki Sauce	33
Onion-Stuffed Mushrooms	33
Garlic Turnip and Zucchini	33
Mozzarella Walnut Stuffed Mushrooms	34
Tomato-Stuffed Portobello Mushrooms	34
Spinach-Stuffed Beefsteak Tomatoes	34
Breaded Zucchini Chips with Parmesan	34
Rice and Olives Stuffed Peppers	35
Stuffed Bell Peppers with Cream Cheese	35
Chickpea-Stuffed Bell Peppers	35

Chapter 5
Vegetable Sides — 36

Garlic Potatoes with Heavy Cream	37
Maple Garlic Brussels Sprout	37
Garlic Butternut Squash Croquettes	37
Lime Sweet Potatoes with Allspice	37
Citrus Carrots with Balsamic Glaze	38
Sesame Green Beans with Sriracha	38
Corn Casserole with Swiss Cheese	38
Garlic Zucchini Crisps	38
Parmesan Corn on the Cob	39
Brown Sugar Acorn Squash	39
Garlic-Lime Shishito Peppers	39
Greek Potatoes with Chives	39
Breaded Asparagus Fries	40
Cheddar Broccoli Gratin	40
Garlic Zucchini Sticks	40
Roasted Potatoes with Rosemary	40
Balsamic Asparagus	41
Garlic Broccoli with Parmesan	41
Breaded Brussels Sprouts with Paprika	41
Garlicky Cabbage with Red Pepper	41
Balsamic-Maple Brussels Sprout	42
Mushroom Summer Rolls	42
Eggplant and Sushi Rice Bowl	42
Oyster Mushroom Pizza Squares	42
Crumbled Tofu with Sweet Potatoes	43
Cheddar and Basmati Rice Risotto	43
Avocado, Cauliflower, and Chickpea Mash	43
Air Fried Green Beans	43
Tomato and Black Bean Chili	44
Mediterranean Herbed Zucchini and Parsnip	44
Potato, Broccoli, and Zucchini Veg Bowl	44
Simple Air Fried Asparagus	44
Balsamic Chickpea and Fig Salad	44
Crispy Cauliflower	45
Roasted Broccoli	45
Breaded Gold Mushrooms	45
Bacon-Wrapped Jalapeño Poppers	45
Mushroom and Pepperoni Pizza	45
Beef and Cheese Stuffed Peppers	45

Chapter 6
Meats — 46

Juicy Bacon and Beef Cheeseburgers	47
Beef Meatloaf with Roasted Vegetables	47
Rump Roast with Bell Peppers	48
Mint-Roasted Boneless Lamb Leg	48
Rosemary-Balsamic Pork Loin Roast	48
Hoisin Roasted Pork Ribs	48
Brown Sugar-Mustard Glazed Ham	49
Bourbon Sirloin Steak	49
Pork Chops with Pickapeppa Sauce	49
Spicy Pepper Steak	49
Minted-Balsamic Lamb Chops	50
Dijon Pork Tenderloin	50
Prosciutto Tart with Asparagus	50
Teriyaki-Glazed Pork Ribs	50
Citrus Pork Ribs with Oregano	51
Vinegary Pork Schnitzel	51
Nut-Crusted Pork Rack	51
Garlic Pork Belly with Bay Leaves	51
Paprika Lamb Chops with Sage	52
Lemon Pork Loin Chop with Marjoram	52
Breaded Pork Loin Chops	52
Pork and Veggie Kebabs	52
Pork and Pineapple Kebabs	53
Bacon-Wrapped Pork Hot Dogs	53
BBQ Kielbasa Sausage	53
Pork Sausage Ratatouille	53

Garlic Pork Leg Roast with Candy Onions	54
Thyme Pork Chops with Carrots	54
Balsamic Italian Sausages and Red Grapes	54
Colby Pork Sausage with Cauliflower	54
Pork Chop Roast with Worcestershire	55
Pork Meatballs with Scallions	55
Breaded Calf's Liver Strips	55
Pork Chops and Apple Bake	55
Pork Tenderloin with Rice	56
Worcestershire Ribeye Steaks with Garlic	56
Beef Ravioli with Parmesan	56
Dijon-Honey Pork Tenderloin	56
Cheeseburgers with American Cheese	57
Roasted Pork Rib	57
Prosciutto-Wrapped Pork Tenderloin	57
Pork Tenderloin with Potatoes	57
Lamb Chops with Rosemary	58
Breaded Pork Chops	58
Bell Pepper and Sausage Rolls	58
Mozzarella Ham Stromboli	58
Beef Egg Rolls	59
Pork Chops with Rinds	59
Beef Cheeseburger Egg Rolls	59
Beef Chuck with Brussels Sprouts	59
Peppercorn Crusted Beef Tenderloin	60
BBQ Pork Steaks	60
Beef Chuck Cheeseburgers	60
Cheddar Bacon Burst with Spinach	60
Greek Lamb Rack	60
Cheese Crusted Chops	61
Crumbed Golden Filet Mignon	61
Air Fried Beef Ribs	61
Mexican Pork Chops	61
Mushroom and Beef Meatloaf	61
Orange Pork Tenderloin	62
Pepperoni and Bell Pepper Pockets	62
Potato and Prosciutto Salad	62
Char Siew	62
Citrus Pork Loin Roast	63
Barbecue Pork Ribs	63
Smoked Beef	63
Provolone Stuffed Beef and Pork Meatballs	63

Chapter 7
Fish and Seafood	**64**
Bacon-Wrapped Herb Rainbow Trout	65
Crab Cheese Enchiladas	65
Salmon Fillet with Spinach, and Beans	65
Marinated Catfish Fillet	65
Lemony Shrimp with Arugula	66
Broiled Lemony Salmon Steak	66
Fish Fillet with Poblano Sauce	66
Crispy Fish Fillet	66
Mediterranean Baked Fish Fillet	67
Curried Halibut Fillets with Parmesan	67
Flounder Fillet and Asparagus Rolls	67
Fish Fillet with Sun-Dried Tomato Pesto	67
Catfish, Toamto and Onion Kebabs	68
Clam Appetizers	68
Honey Halibut Steaks with Parsley	68
Catfish Fillets with Pecan Crust	68
Paprika Tilapia with Garlic Aioli	69

Lemon Tilapia Fillets with Garlic	69
Breaded Fish Sticks	69
Breaded Catfish Nuggets	69
Cayenne Prawns with Cumin	70
Orange Shrimp with Cayenne	70
Parmesan Fish Fillets with Tarragon	70
Paprika Tiger Shrimp	70
Old Bay Shrimp with Potatoes	71
Cajun Cod Fillets with Lemon Pepper	71
Cajun Catfish Cakes with Parmesan	71
Coconut Curried Fish with Chilies	71
Flounder Fillets with Lemon Pepper	72
Curried Prawns with Coconut	72
Shrimp Kebabs with Cherry Tomatoes	72
Shrimp Scampi with Garlic Butter	72
Parsley Shrimp with Lemon	73
Lemon Shrimp with Cumin	73
Hoisin Scallops with Sesame Seeds	73
Curried King Prawns with Cumin	73
Old Bay Crab Sticks with Mayo Sauce	74
Jumbo Shrimp with Dijon-Mayo Sauce	74
Shrimp and Artichoke Paella	74
Shrimp and Veggie Patties	74
Fried Breaded Scallops	75
Balsamic Ginger Scallops	75
Garlic Calamari Rings	75
Basil Scallops with Broccoli	75
Breaded Crab Cakes	76
Honey Halibut Steaks with Parsley	76
Balsamic Shrimp with Goat Cheese	76
Crab Ratatouille with Thyme	76
Lemon Crab Cakes with Mayo	77
Fried Bacon-Wrapped Scallops	77
Fried Scallops with Thyme	77

Chapter 8
Poultry	**78**
Chicken Pot Pie	79
Barbecue Drumsticks with Vegetable	79
Simple Chicken Cordon Bleu	79
Orange-Glazed Whole Chicken	79
Duck Breast with Potato	80
Sesame Balsamic Chicken Breast	80
Chicken Breast in Mango Sauce	80
Dijon-Rosemary Chicken Breasts	80
Chicken, Vegetable and Rice Casserole	81
Barbecue Turkey Burgers	81
Chicken and Veggies with 'Nduja	81
Tasty Meat and Vegetable Loaf	81
Garlicky Whole Chicken Bake	82
Garlic Chicken Wings	82
Five-Spice Turkey Thighs	82
Sweet-and-Sour Chicken Breasts	82
Turkey Breast with Strawberries	83
Chicken and Pepper Baguette with Mayo	83
Dijon Turkey Breast with Sage	83
Chicken Thighs with Mirin	83
Dijon Turkey with Carrots	84
Garlic Duck Leg Quarters	84
Curried Chicken and Brussels Sprouts	84
Balsamic Duck Breasts with Orange Marmalade	84
Balsamic Chicken Breast with Oregano	85

Paprika Hens in Wine	85
Vinegary Chicken with Pineapple	85
Peach Chicken with Dark Cherry	85
Turkey Meatloaves with Onion	86
Paprika Hens with Creole Seasoning	86
Paprika Whole Chicken Roast	86
Chicken Drumsticks with Green Beans	86
Teriyaki Chicken, Pepper, and Pineapple Kebabs	87
Rosemary Chicken Thighs	87
Lime Chicken Breast	87
Sriracha-Honey Chicken Thighs	87
Breaded Chicken Cutlets	88
Bacon-Wrapped and Cheese-Stuffed Chicken	88
Air Fried Chicken Wings with Buffalo Sauce	88
Bell Pepper Stuffed Chicken Roll-Ups	88
Bruschetta Chicken	89
Cheese-Encrusted Chicken Tenderloins with Peanuts	89
Air Fried Chicken Potatoes with Sun-Dried Tomato	89
Cheesy Pepperoni and Chicken Pizza	90
Drumsticks with Barbecue-Honey Sauce	90
Easy Chicken Fingers	90
Chicken Schnitzel	90
Crispy Chicken Skin	91
Gold Livers	91
Hawaiian Chicken Bites	91
Easy Cajun Chicken Drumsticks	91
Honey Glazed Chicken Breasts	92
Golden Chicken Cutlets	92
Spicy Tandoori Chicken Drumsticks	92
Lime Chicken with Cilantro	92
Nice Goulash	93
Simple Chicken Nuggets	93
Simple Whole Chicken Bake	93
Simple Air Fried Chicken Wings	93
Spanish Chicken and Pepper Baguette	94
Sweet-and-Sour Chicken Nuggets	94
China Spicy Turkey Thighs	94
Strawberry-Glazed Turkey	94
Turkey and Cauliflower Meatloaf	95
Deep Fried Duck Leg Quarters	95
Duck Breasts with Marmalade Balsamic Glaze	95
Rosemary Turkey Scotch Eggs	95

Chapter 9
Pizza	96
Simple Pizza Dough	97
No-Knead Pan Pizza Dough	97
Pro Dough	97
Garlic Tomato Pizza Sauce	98
Pepperoni Pizza with Mozzarella	98
Ham and Pineapple Pizza	98
Pear Pizza with Basil	98
Cheese Tomato Pizza with Basil	99
Arugula and Prosciutto Pizza	99
Prosciutto and Fig Pizza	99
Ricotta Margherita with Basil	99
Spring Pea Pizza with Ramps	100
Escarole and Radicchio Pizza with Walnuts	100
Zucchini Pizza with Pistachios	100
Mozzarella Brussels Sprout Pizza	101
Strawberry Pizza	101
Zucchini and Onion Pizza	101

Chapter 10
Casseroles, Frittatas, and Quiches	102
Cheddar Chicken Sausage Casserole	103
Corn Casserole with Bell Pepper	103
Asparagus Casserole with Grits	103
Parmesan Green Bean Casserole	103
Cheddar Pastrami Casserole	104
Spinach and Mushroom Frittata	104
Mushroom and Beef Casserole	104
Beef and Bean Casserole	104
Cheddar Broccoli Casserole	105
Cauliflower and Okra Casserole	105
Turkey Casserole with Almond Mayo	105
Tilapia and Rockfish Casserole	105
Cheddar and Egg Frittata with Parsley	106
Peppery Sausage Casserole with Cheddar	106
Chickpea and Spinach Casserole	106
Cheddar Chicken and Broccoli Divan	106
Kale and Egg Frittata with Feta	107
Swiss Chicken and Ham Casserole	107
Smoked Trout Frittata with Dill	107
Cheddar Broccoli and Carrot Quiche	107
Ricotta Pork Gratin with Mustard	108
Mexican Beef and Chile Casserole	108
Tomato and Olive Quiche	108
Potato and Chorizo Frittata	108
Asparagus Frittata with Goat Cheese	109
Spinach and Shrimp Frittata	109
Zucchini and Spinach Frittata	109

Chapter 11
Wraps and Sandwiches	110
Curried Shrimp and Zucchini Potstickers	111
Ricotta Spinach and Basil Pockets	111
Carrot and Mushroom Spring Rolls	112
Crispy Cream Cheese Wontons	112
Chicken Wraps with Ricotta Cheese	112
Avocado and Tomato Wraps	112
Chicken and Cabbage Wraps	113
Parmesan Eggplant Hoagies	113
Cream Cheese and Crab Wontons	113
Bacon and Egg Wraps with Salsa	113
Cajun Beef and Bell Pepper Fajitas	114
Potato Taquitos with Mexican Cheese	114
Chickpea and Mushroom Wraps	114
Mozzarella Chicken Taquitos	114
Lamb Hamburgers with Feta Cheese	115
Curried Pork Sliders	115
Pork Momos with Carrot	115
Pork and Cabbage Gyoza	115
Turkey and Pepper Hamburger	116
Beef Burgers with Seeds	116
Cheesy Bacon and Egg Wraps	116
Cheesy Spring Chicken Wraps	116
Avocado and Tomato Egg Rolls	117
Crispy Chicken Egg Rolls	117
Beef and Bell Pepper Fajitas	117
Cheesy Potato Taquitos	117
Eggplant Hoagies	118
Chicken and Yogurt Taquitos	118
Thai Pork Sliders	118
Lamb and Feta Hamburgers	118

Chapter 12
Holiday Specials — 119
- Balsamic Cherry Tomatoes — 120
- Vanilla Butter Cake — 120
- Chocolate Macaroons with Coconut — 120
- Pigs in a Blanket with Sesame Seeds — 120
- Cream-Glazed Cinnamon Rolls — 121
- Mozzarella Rice Arancini — 121
- Buttermilk Chocolate Cake — 122
- Teriyaki-Marinated Shrimp Skewers — 122
- Garlic Nuggets — 122
- Vanilla Cheese Blintzes — 122
- Asiago Balls — 123
- Sriracha Shrimp with Mayo — 123

Chapter 13
Rotisserie Recipes — 124
- Chicken Roast with Mustard Paste — 125
- Mustard Lamb Shoulder — 125
- Feta Stuffed Lamb Leg — 125
- Teriyaki Chicken — 126
- Chicken with Brown Sugar Brine — 126
- Turkey with Thyme-Sage Brine — 127
- Dried Fruit Stuffed Pork Loin — 127
- Bacon-Wrapped Sirloin Roast — 128

Chapter 14
Appetizers and Snacks — 129
- Sausage and Onion Rolls with Mustard — 130
- Parmesan Cauliflower with Turmeric — 130
- Roasted Mushrooms with Garlic — 130
- Cheddar Mushrooms with Pimientos — 131
- Jalapeño Poppers with Cheddar — 131
- Green Chiles and Cheese Nachos — 131
- Pepperoni Pizza Bites with Marinara — 131
- Cheddar Baked Potatoes with Chives — 132
- Honey Roasted Grapes with Basil — 132
- Lemon-Pepper Chicken Wings — 132
- Cheddar Sausage Balls — 132
- Sugar Roasted Walnuts — 133
- Balsamic Prosciutto-Wrapped Pears — 133
- Breaded Zucchini Tots — 133
- Ginger Shrimp with Sesame Seeds — 134
- Tuna Melts with Mayo — 134
- Paprika Polenta Fries with Chili-Lime Mayo — 135
- Lemon Ricotta with Capers — 135
- Fried Pickle Spears with Chili — 135
- Honey Snack Mix — 135
- Parmesan Snack Mix — 136
- Paprika Potato Chips — 136
- Hush Puppies with Jalapeño — 136
- Cinnamon Apple Chips — 136
- Avocado Chips with Lime — 137
- Ginger Apple Wedges — 137
- Cumin Tortilla Chips — 137
- Old Bay Fried Chicken Wings — 137
- Carrot Chips — 138
- Deviled Eggs with Mayo — 138
- Mushroom and Sausage Empanadas — 138
- Cumin Fried Chickpeas — 138
- Paprika Nut Mix — 139
- Garlic Fried Edamame — 139
- Nutmeg Apple Chips — 139
- Brie Pear Sandwiches — 139
- Parmesan Bruschetta with Tomato — 140
- Cheddar Black Bean and Corn Salsa — 140
- Italian Rice Balls with Olives — 140
- Buttermilk-Marinated Chicken Wings — 141
- Cinnamon Peach Wedges — 141
- BBQ Cheese Chicken Pizza — 141
- Breaded Artichoke Bites — 141
- Parmesan Crab Toasts — 142
- Pork and Turkey Sandwiches — 142
- Turkey-Wrapped Dates and Almonds — 142
- Muffuletta Sliders with Olive Mix — 142
- Ham and Cheese Stuffed Peppers — 143
- Cheese Stuffed Mushrooms — 143
- Cheesy Broccoli Bites — 143
- Green Beans with Cheese — 143
- Cauliflower with Cheese — 143
- Brussels Sprouts with Cheese — 144
- Chile Pork Ribs — 144
- Carrot with Butter — 144
- Syrupy Chicken Wings — 144
- Air Fried Yam Sticks — 145
- Potato Chips with Peppercorns — 145
- Zucchini with Cheese — 145
- Chicken Wings with Sriracha Sauce — 145
- Wax Beans with Cumin — 146
- Eggplant with Paprika — 146
- Tomato Chips with Cheese — 146
- Cinnamon Mixed Nuts — 146
- Paprika Beet Chips — 147
- Lime Avocado Chips — 147
- Sweet and Spicy Roasted Walnuts — 147
- Parma Prosciutto-Wrapped Pears — 147
- Ricotta Capers with Lemon Zest — 148
- Parmesan Ranch Snack Mix — 148
- Homemade Potato Chips — 148
- Cinnamon Apple Wedges with Yogurt — 148
- Air-Fried Old Bay Chicken Wings — 149
- Simple Carrot Chips — 149
- Sesame Kale Chips — 149

Chapter 15
Desserts — 150
- Rum-Plums with Brown Sugar Cream — 151
- Rhubarb with Sloe Gin and Rosemary — 151
- Easy Nutmeg Butter Cookies — 151
- Vanilla Coconut Cookies with Pecans — 152
- Peach and Apple Crisp with Oatmeal — 152
- Vanilla Walnuts Tart with Cloves — 152
- Mixed Berry Bake with Almond Topping — 152
- Peach and Blueberry Galette — 153
- Chocolate Blueberry Cupcakes — 153
- Vanilla Chocolate Cake — 154
- Coconut Orange Cake — 154
- Honey Apple-Peach Crumble — 154
- Honey-Glazed Peach and Plum Kebabs — 154
- Vanilla Chocolate Chip Cookies — 155
- Pineapple Sticks with Coconut — 155
- Vanilla Pound Cake — 155
- Pumpkin Pudding with Vanilla Wafers — 155
- Peanut Butter Bread Pudding — 156

Chocolate Cake with Blackberries	156
Vanilla Ricotta Cake with Lemon	156
Cinnamon Pineapple Rings	156
Apple Bake with Cinnamon	157
Vanilla Fudge Pie	157
Blackberry Cobbler	157
Vanilla Baked Peaches and Blueberries	157
Chocolate Chip Brownies	158
White Chocolate Cookies with Nutmeg	158
Mixed Berry Crisp with Cloves	158
Chocolate S'mores	158
Pecan Pie with Chocolate Chips	159
Banana Bread Pudding	159
Cookie Sundae with Chocolate Chips	159
Pumpkin Pudding	159
Apple Turnovers with Raisins	160
Brazilian Pineapple Bake	160
Ricotta Lemon Poppy Seed Cake	160
Cardamom and Vanilla Custard	160
Chickpea Brownies	161
Orange Cake	161
Cinnamon Almonds	161
Berry Crumble	161
Spice Cookies	162
Jelly Doughnuts	162
Chocolate and Peanut Butter Lava Cupcakes	162
Honey-Roasted Pears	162
Chocolate Croissants	163
Curry Peaches, Pears, and Plums	163
Apple, Peach, and Cranberry Crisp	163
Pecan and Cherry Stuffed Apples	163
Lemony Blackberry Crisp	164
Black Forest Pies	164

Chapter 16
Staples 165
Buttery Mushrooms	166
Shawarma Seasoning	166
Lemon Anchocy Dressing	166
Paprika-Oregano Seasoning	166
Baked White Rice	166
Ginger-Garlic Dipping Sauce	167
Garlic Tomato Sauce	167
Teriyaki Sauce	167
Creamy Grits	167
Poblano Garlic Sauce	167

Chapter 17
Dehydrate 168
Dehydrated Pineapple Slices	169
Pork Jerky	169
Beef Jerky	169
Strawberry Roll Ups	169
Cinnamon Orange Slices	169
Dehydrated Strawberries	170
Peach Fruit Leather	170
Dehydrated Zucchini Chips	170
Smoky Venison Jerky	170
Dried Mushrooms	170
Cinnamon Pear Chips	171
Dried Hot Peppers	171
Lemon-Pepper Salmon Jerky	171
Kiwi Chips	171
Dehydrated Onions	171
Candied Bacon	171

Appendix 1 Measurement Conversion Chart	172
Appendix 2: Air Fryer Cooking Chart	173
Appendix 3 The Dirty Dozen and Clean Fifteen	175
Appendix 4 Index	176

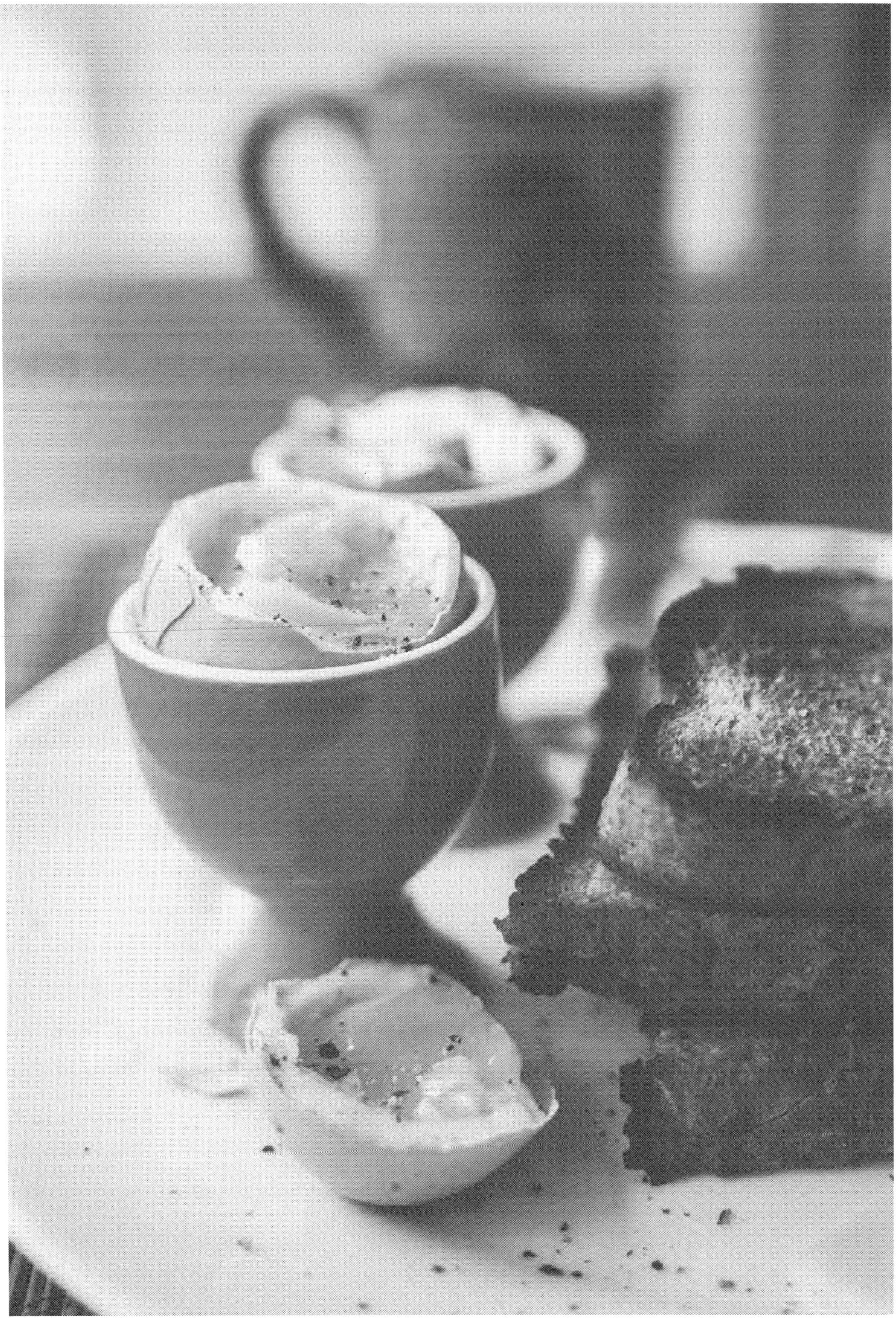

Introduction

HOW I MET MY VORTEX

The thought of a homemade meal cooked from scratch sounds lovely if only I had time! Who knew that it was possible to become so busy that one would forget to cook or simply be too exhausted to hover over pots that never seem to empty? The traditional lifestyle of cooking fresh foods—straight from the garden to the kitchen—seems like a fantasy in my fast-paced urban lifestyle; I know I am not the only one who feels this way. As many mothers enter the corporate environment and fill up 9-to-5 jobs, no one is left at home to prepare home-cooked meals that simmer for hours in a pot. Even for a foodie like myself, I find it nearly impossible to whip up delicious meals made from scratch while tending to my four children and answering a day's worth of emails in the evenings. For many years, I settled for unhealthy takeout meals that would appease the children and afford me the much needed time to work on other essential tasks. However, these quick and greasy takeout dinners were simply not sustainable in the long run for the health and well-being of my family. I knew that I had to find another convenient alternative that would meet all of my culinary and lifestyle needs.

Christmas came around, and guess what I received from my dear husband? An Instant Vortex Air Fryer oven with a note, "This might be what you were looking for." I did not know what to expect as I unwrapped this elegant and professional kitchen gadget. I realized that it was a modern rendition of an air fryer produced by one of my favorite brands, the Instant Pot. I should have known that any kitchen tool manufactured by Instant Pot would be phenomenal; however, I wanted to find out for myself. The first time I used my Instant Vortex Air Fryer was for a Sunday roast dinner. The Air Fryer assumed the role of kitchen chef, and this allowed me to take time out to read a book while the machine did all the work. This multifunctional appliance gave me the option of air frying, baking, roasting, broiling, reheating, dehydrating, and rotisserie cooking my food to make a fantastic dinner.

TRYING IT OUT

If you are going to make the A-Team, you have to ace the try-outs. I thought about experimenting on something that I cook lot, and that I have perfected cooking conventionally; something that I could run a direct comparison with. I thought about bacon – I confess that I think about bacon a lot!

Normally, I only to cook bacon on the weekend, when I do a big brunch for the fam. We all like our bacon crispy, and not greasy, so I cook it in the Vortex. Prep. time is around twenty to twenty-five minutes: first, I pre-heat the Vortex, and then I prepare a try with foil and a rack. For good results, it's a good twenty minutes cooking time. This is OK if I am doing a huge batch, for supper time BLTs, or to crumble on a salad later. But if it's just the four of us for breakfast or brunch, that process is just way too much effort, specially on a Sunday morning!

So, I tried out the Vortex Plus on bacon. The preheating feature is built in. Too easy! I pressed "Airfry" and set the simple timer dial for five minutes. Once pre-heated, the Vortex tells you to "ADD FOOD." That is when you insert the light-weight non-stick, easy-clean tray/s with your bacon on it. It took just two minutes to preheat. Once cooking is finished, the Vortex beeps, and displays "COOL DOWN" for a few seconds. Then it turns itself off, and you can take out the food. Seven minutes: easy start to perfect finish. I have to say, I was impressed. I am not readily impressed. The bacon was perfect. Did anyone in the fam. detect any difference in the flavour? Only to note: "This bacon's really crispy!" There was absolutely no greasiness to the meat either. All the grease dripped down below and collected in the drip tray. Top-notch results. Happy fam. Happy me.

Once the Vortex cooled down, I was able to clean it in my sink, with just a sponge and dish detergent. No fuss. Alternatively, it could have gone straight into the dishwasher. This was such a successful (and tasty!) try-out, that I made 2 trays of bacon, next day, for some quick tasty sandwiches: one tray on the top, and the other tray in the middle. The only difference: I set the timer to ten minutes, and half way through, the Vortex instructed me to turn the food, so I switched the position of the trays. The heating element and fan is at the top, so, naturally, it cooks the top tray quicker than the bottom tray. Both trays of bacon came out perfect and crispy.

Chapter 1
Beginners Guide to the Vortex

Step by Step Guide to the Usage of the Vortex

When you first get your Instant Vortex Air Fryer, it is essential that you do a test run to make sure everything is in working order. It won't take much of your time—approximately 25 minutes—and then you'll know if you're good to go!

Here are the steps to follow the test run and for general cooking:

1. Plug into a 120V power source. The air fryer should not be in Standby mode, and "OFF" should appear on the display. Press the dial button to wake the air fryer.
2. Remove the air fryer basket and place the cooking tray at the bottom of the basket. Look for the indicator arrows on the cooking tray and make sure these arrows point to the back or the front of the air fryer.
3. You can now put the air fryer basket back into the cooking chamber.
4. Press the Air Fry button, followed by Temp—use the dial to set the temperature to 400 degrees Fahrenheit. Press Time and adjust to 20 minutes using the dial.
5. Press start and cooking will begin. "On" will show on the display while the air fryer preheats. You can touch Time or Temp at any time during the cooking process to adjust the time and temperature using the dial.
6. As soon as the air fryer reaches the set temperature, "Add Food" will appear on the display. Since this is a test run, do not add any food.
7. After removing and reinserting the air fryer basket, the display will indicate the cooking time and temperature. It will also read "Cook."
8. Half-way through the selected Smart Program, the air fryer will beep to let you know that it is time to turn the food. You'll see "turn Food" on the display and can proceed to flip or shake the food items in the basket. When you remove the air fryer basket, the Smart Program will pause until 10 seconds after you put the basket back into the cooking chamber. It is only the Air Fry and Roast Smart Programs which will require this step—not all food will need to be turned.
9. Once the time has run out and your food is cooked, the display will indicate 'End' on the display. The fan will continue to blow in order to cool down the air fryer. If you don't remove the tray from the fryer immediately, you'll get a reminder at five, 30, and 60 minutes that the food is ready.
10. When you're done with this process, and everything runs accordingly to plan, then your Instant Vortex Air Fryer is in working order, and you're ready to use it for whatever culinary delights you can dream up!

Top 6 Instant Vortex Air Fryer Accessories

There are some tools I suggest you add to your kitchen arsenal so that you'll be able to cook anything your heart desires in your Vortex air fryer.

1. But before you go out looking for accessories, there are a few things you have to keep in mind.
2. Keep the size of the air fryer in mind. For the 4-1 Instant Vortex Air Fryer, I recommend not purchasing any pans or items larger than 8 ½ inches deep by 9 ½ inches wide. A square 8x8 pan will fit perfectly! If you own an Instant Pot, most of the items that are suitable for that appliance will work in the Vortex air fryer—my round springform cake pan meant for my Instant Pot fits absolutely fine in the air fryer.
3. Don't forget the air space. Before buying deep items, keep in mind that there should be space at the top and bottom of the item for air to circulate.
4. Pay attention to the materials. A lot of items claim to be oven-safe, but that is not always the case. The quick heating of the air and the speedy circulation may cause glass dishes to crack or break. Where possible, don't use glass as all but choose stainless steel, aluminum, or ceramic items. If you have to use glass, make sure it's from a reputable brand known for its oven safety.
5. Okay, let's look at the top six air fryer accessories I recommend.

Parchment Liners
Who has time to clean food stuck to the fry basket? Air fryer liners will cut your clean-up process in half. Don't use just any liners. Look for ones with holes in to help air circulate, and even then, you have to make sure the parchment paper is weighed down with something heavy, or the air will pick it up and whirl it around.

Baking Pan
You can bake sweet and savory dishes in a baking pan; cake, monkey bread, macaroni, and cheese, etc. The fact that you can cook so many dishes in a baking pan makes it one of those must-have accessories.

Grill Pan
Why not push your Instant Vortex Air Fryer's versatility up a notch further by turning it into a grill? With this basic item, you'll be able to make burgers, grill steak, chicken, seafood, and anything else you can toss onto a grill.

Cooking Rack With Skewers
A raised cooking rack is essential if you plan on using your air fryer for cooking larger foods. Air fryers work by circulating heat around the food—if you place something down on the surface, the air won't be able to move around it, leaving you with uneven crispness. By using a cooking rack, the food is elevated, and air can circulate freely; the result is an even, crips coating.

Silicone Oven Mitts
I suppose you can use traditional oven mitts, but I'd highly recommend getting the silicone kind. They're not bulky, do a better job of protecting you from heat, but most importantly, they have a better grip than fabric mitts. You don't want a basket with hot food slipping and falling on you, your child, or pet. Personally, I see these as essential.

Waffle Molds
Do your kids love waffles for breakfast each Saturday morning? The good news is, you can make them some in the air fryer in a fraction of the time it would take you, making it the traditional way. All you need are some air fryer waffle molds, and you're well on your way to winning the parent of the year award.

For those of you who use your air fryer the most out of all your other appliances, you may consider buying a full air fryer accessories pack. They include almost everything you need to ensure your air fryer success. You can also compare different versions to make sure you get one that contains items you think you'll use the most. With your kitchen all kitted out, there will be nothing you can't give a crispy coating.

Chapter 2
Cooking with the Instant Vortex Air Fryer

The air fryer is not a complicated appliance, but there are some tips I picked up that I want to share with you. But, before I do, let's look at things to keep in mind to ensure your safety.

Dos and Don'ts

Although your Instant Vortex Air Fryer comes with built-in safety features, here are some extra steps you can follow to ensure safe use.

1. The air fryer gets really hot while working its air frying magic, so don't touch it. Use oven mitts when you slide out the air fry basket or, better yet, wait for the appliance to cool down completely. Also, keep an eye out for steam escaping from the vents; you don't want to burn your hands or face.
2. You shouldn't let anyone with physical or mental disabilities use the air fryer without constant supervision. The same goes if a person has no idea to use an Instant Vortex Air Fryer; make sure you're there that they're not doing something wrong or dangerous.
3. Always place your air fryer out of reach of children. Make sure not to let the cord dangle from the countertop where a toddler can grab it and pull the warm appliance on to themselves.
4. Do not use your air fryer if you notice that its power cord is damaged.
5. Air Fryers are indoor appliances, so don't use it outside.
6. Never place your air fryer near a hot gas or an electric burner. It should be stable and secure on a dry, flat surface.
7. Make sure the air fry basket is locked in place before you use your fryer.
8. Don't tip the air fry basket to remove the food. The liquid inside may splash on you and cause burns.

Choosing the Right Cooking Mode

All cooking programs are essentially the same. The only difference is the temperature the mode heats to, as well as the cooking time. In the beginning, I didn't know this, and, unfortunately, the manual doesn't tell you. The different programs are only there for your convenience—you don't have to set the time and temperature manually; you just press one button.

Smart Programs

Here are some pre-sets to choose from to make your cooking as easy as possible.

Smart Program	Time Range	Temperature Range
Air Fry	1-60 minutes	180-400 F
Roast	1-60 minutes	180-400 F
Bake	1-60 minutes	180-400 F
Reheat	1-60 minutes	120-360 F
Broil*	1-40 minutes	400 F
Dehydrate*	1-72 hours	96-175 F

*You will only find the Broil and Dehydrate functions on the Vortex Plus 6 models, but I add them here to give you a better idea of the difference between the models.

Tips and Tricks for Air Frying Success

If you want your food to be extra crispy or you just want to ensure that none of your recipes flop, here are nine of my tips and tricks to help you succeed.

1. Use a kitchen spray bottle filled with oil to coat food. You'll end up using less than a teaspoon of oil, which makes it even healthier. It's also easier to cover more delicate foods this way. Extra-light olive oil should be your first choice since it has a higher smoking point and a milder taste than extra-virgin olive oil.
2. When cooking high-fat foods, empty some of the oil part way through cooking to avoid any smoking caused by excess fat.

3. Switch your Instant Vortex Air Fryer on four to five minutes before use.
4. Don't overfill the air fry basket. You should leave space for air to flow between the food. This will ensure everything is cooked evenly. I usually cook in batches when I have to make food for a lot of people, and I always stick to filling the basket only 2/3.
5. For food you want to crumb, always use the right order of breading. You'll first coat the food in flour, then dunk in egg, and lastly, roll in the bread crumbs. If you set up a dredging station beforehand—that means setting up the bowls in the correct order—it will take you less time to crumb your food. Another hint I can give you is to spray oil on food with crumbs gently. You don't want the breading to be too wet and fall off. Furthermore, the fan in the air fryer is mighty and if you don't press the crumbs onto the food firmly, it will get blown off.
6. When you cook food from frozen, you will need to adjust the cooking time. Check for doneness before removing from the air fryer.
7. As mentioned earlier, some food will need to be turned halfway through the cooking process. If you don't, then your food will not be crispy all around or cooked evenly.
8. Forget about your microwave and use your air fryer instead. A lot of the time, a microwave will leave your food soggy, but the air fryer will restore it to its former crunchy glory.
9. For extra crunch, spray your food with a second layer of oil.

Best and Worst Ingredients

I know it's obvious that you can air fry the foods that you always enjoyed deep-fried. It may even end up tasting better! But since the Instant Vortex Air Fryer is more than just a simple air fryer, you should experiment not only with the ingredients you air fry but also with the various mods.

Here are some things you need to keep in mind when it comes to ingredients.

THE BEST

- You can cook all vegetables in your air fryer. Cover it generously in batter and pop it in the air fryer. Crumbed beans with a tomato salsa is one of my favorite appetizers to serve to guests.
- You can cook meat, fish, and poultry in your air fryer any way you like—grill, roast, or fry; what are you in the mood for?
- Baking frozen foods in your air fryer will give it extra crunch than a standard convection oven would.
- If you fancy yourself a baker, you'd be happy to know that there won't be any temperature fluctuations in the air fryer. So, no more flopped souffle, cakes, or muffins.

THE WORST

The Instant Vortex Air Fryer is not meant for wet ingredients. The fan is mighty, and soups and sauces will just end up splattered all over. The same goes for food covered in wet batter. You'll end up with a ruined recipe and a big mess to clean.

Also, consider if the food you plan on making requires a lot of stirring. Pasta, for instance, will not cook well in an air fryer since it requires not only a lot of liquid to cook but also regular stirring.

How to Save Time Cooking

The Instant Vortex Air Fryer will already cut your cooking time in half, but there are ways that you can get out of the kitchen even quicker. I enjoy cooking mouth-watering meals, but some days I want to get in and out as quickly as possible to spend time with my friends and family.

Here are some things I do to save time in the kitchen.

- Prepare ingredients. This is also known as mise en place. It is where you dice, cut, marinate, and prep all your ingredients before you start cooking.
- Don't deviate from the recipe. I know there are times when you feel you know what to do next and forget to check the recipe. If you're new to the kitchen, there is a big chance that you'll end up using too much or little of something, and you'll end up doing something wrong. It will take extra time to fix your mistake or, worst-case scenario, start from scratch.
- Take your meat out of the fridge a few minutes before cooking. Room temperature meat will cook more evenly, and it may shorten the cooking time with a few minutes.

Chapter 3
Breakfasts

Sweet Banana Bread
Prep time: 10 minutes | Cook time: 40 minutes | Serves 6

2 ripe bananas
1 egg
½ cup skim milk
2 tablespoons honey
1 tablespoon vegetable oil
1 cup unbleached flour
¾ cup chopped trail mix
1 teaspoon baking powder
Salt, to taste

1. Process the bananas, egg, milk, honey, and oil in a blender or food processor until smooth and transfer to a mixing bowl.
2. Add the flour and trail mix, stirring to mix well. Add the baking powder and stir just enough to blend it into the batter. Add salt, to taste. Pour the mixture into an oiled or nonstick loaf pan.
3. Select Bake. Set temperature to 400°F (205°C) and set time to 40 minutes. Select Start to begin preheating.
4. Once preheated, slide the pan into the Vortex.
5. When done, a toothpick inserted in the center will come out clean.
6. Serve.

Low-Fat Buttermilk Biscuits
Prep time: 10 minutes | Cook time: 15 minutes | Makes 12 biscuits

2 cups unbleached flour
1 tablespoon baking powder
½ teaspoon baking soda
Salt, to taste
3 tablespoons margarine, at room temperature
1 cup low-fat buttermilk
Vegetable oil

1. Combine the flour, baking powder, baking soda, and salt in a medium bowl.
2. Cut in the margarine with 2 knives or a pastry blender until the mixture is crumbly.
3. Stir in the buttermilk, adding just enough so the dough will stay together when pinched.
4. Knead the dough on a floured surface for one minute, then pat or roll out the dough to ¾ inch thick. Cut out biscuit rounds with a 2½-inch biscuit cutter. Place the rounds on an oiled or nonstick baking sheet.
5. Select Bake. Set temperature to 400°F (205°C) and set time to 15 minutes. Select Start to begin preheating.
6. Once preheated, slide the baking sheet into the Vortex.
7. When done, the biscuits will be golden brown.
8. Serve.

Coffee Cake with Pecan
Prep time: 10 minutes | Cook time: 40 minutes | Serves 6

For the Cake:
2 cups unbleached flour
2 teaspoons baking powder
2 tablespoons vegetable oil
1 egg
1¼ cups skim milk
For the Topping:
½ cup brown sugar
1 tablespoon margarine, at room temperature
1 teaspoon ground cinnamon
¼ teaspoon grated nutmeg
¼ cup chopped pecans
Salt, to taste

1. Combine the ingredients for the cake in a medium bowl and mix thoroughly. Pour the batter into an oiled square baking (cake) pan and set aside.
2. Combine the topping ingredients in a small bowl, mashing the margarine into the dry ingredients with a fork until the mixture is crumbly. Sprinkle evenly on top of the batter.
3. Select Bake. Set temperature to 375°F (190°C) and set time to 40 minutes. Select Start to begin preheating.
4. Once preheated, slide the pan into the Vortex.
5. When done, a toothpick inserted in the center will come out clean. Cool and cut into squares.

Parmesan Ham and Egg Cups
Prep time: 5 minutes | Cook time: 12 minutes | Serves 6

Nonstick cooking spray
6 thin slices ham
6 large eggs
Kosher salt, to taste
Freshly ground black pepper, to taste
2 tablespoons finely grated Parmesan cheese

1. Spray the cups of a 6-cup muffin tin with cooking spray. Press a slice of ham into each cup, smoothing out the sides as much as possible. The ham should extend over the top of the cup by ¼ to ½ inch. Crack an egg into each cup and season with salt and pepper. Top each yolk with 1 teaspoon of the cheese.
2. Select Bake. Set temperature to 375°F (190°C) and set time to 10 minutes. Select Start to begin preheating.
3. Once preheated, slide the muffin tin into the Vortex.
4. After 5 minutes, slide out the muffin tin and check the eggs. They should just be starting to firm up and turn opaque. Rotate the muffin tin if the eggs are cooking unevenly.
5. Cook for another 5 minutes and check again; if the egg whites are cooked through, remove the tin from the Vortex. The total cook time is about 12 minutes for fully cooked whites and runny yolks; if you prefer the yolks more done, cook for an additional minute or two.
6. When the eggs are cooked as desired, remove the muffin tin and let cool for a couple of minutes. Run a thin knife around the ham and use a spoon to remove the cups.

Mozzarella Tomato Salsa Rounds
Prep time: 5 minutes | Cook time: 6 minutes | Makes 12 slices

1 French baguette, cut to make 12 1-inch slices (rounds)
¼ cup olive oil
1 cup tomato salsa
½ cup shredded low-fat Mozzarella
2 tablespoons finely chopped fresh cilantro

1. Brush both sides of each round with olive oil.
2. Spread one side of each slice with salsa and sprinkle each with Mozzarella. Place the rounds in an oiled or nonstick square baking (cake) pan.
3. Select Broil. Set temperature to 400°F (205°C) and set time to 6 minutes. Select Start to begin preheating.
4. Once preheated, slide the pan into the Vortex.
5. When done, the cheese will be melted and the rounds will be lightly browned. Garnish with the chopped cilantro and serve.

Almond, Coconut, and Apple Granola
Prep time: 10 minutes | Cook time: 12 minutes | Serves 6

3 cups gluten-free old-fashioned rolled oats
1 cup slivered almonds
1 cup unsweetened coconut chips
½ cup honey or pure maple syrup
⅓ cup packed light brown sugar
¼ cup vegetable oil
1 teaspoon ground cinnamon
¼ teaspoon kosher salt
2 cups chopped dried apples

1. In a large bowl, combine the oats, almonds, coconut, honey, brown sugar, oil, cinnamon, and salt and mix well. Spread the mixture in an even layer on a sheet pan.
2. Select Bake. Set temperature to 325°F (163°C) and set time to 12 minutes. Select Start to begin preheating.
3. Once preheated, slide the pan into the Vortex.
4. Bake for 6 minutes. Remove the pan and stir the granola. Return to the Vortex and continue baking until the nuts and oats are golden brown and crisp, another 6 minutes.
5. Let cool, then stir in the apples.

Corn Frittata with Avocado Dressing
Prep time: 10 minutes | Cook time: 20 minutes | Serves 2 or 3

½ cup cherry tomatoes, halved
Kosher salt and freshly ground black pepper, to taste
6 large eggs, lightly beaten
½ cup fresh corn kernels
¼ cup milk
1 tablespoon finely chopped fresh dill
½ cup shredded Monterey Jack cheese
Avocado Dressing:
1 ripe avocado, pitted and peeled
2 tablespoons fresh lime juice
¼ cup olive oil
1 scallion, finely chopped
8 fresh basil leaves, finely chopped

1. Put the tomato halves in a colander and lightly season with salt. Set aside for 10 minutes to drain well. Pour the tomatoes into a large bowl and fold in the eggs, corn, milk, and dill. Sprinkle with salt and pepper and stir until mixed.
2. Pour the egg mixture into a baking pan.
3. Select Bake. Set temperature to 300°F (150°C) and set time to 15 minutes. Press Start to begin preheating.
4. Once the Vortex has preheated, place the pan into the Vortex.
5. When done, remove the pan from the Vortex. Scatter the cheese on top.
6. Select Bake. Set temperature to 315°F (157°C) and set time to 5 minutes. Return the pan to the Vortex.
7. Meanwhile, make the avocado dressing: Mash the avocado with the lime juice in a medium bowl until smooth. Mix in the olive oil, scallion, and basil and stir until well incorporated.
8. When cooking is complete, the frittata will be puffy and set. Let the frittata cool for 5 minutes and serve alongside the avocado dressing.

Egg in a Hole
Prep time: 5 minutes | Cook time: 5 minutes | Serves 1

1 slice bread
1 teaspoon butter, softened
1 egg
Salt and pepper, to taste
1 tablespoon shredded Cheddar cheese
2 teaspoons diced ham

1. On a flat work surface, cut a hole in the center of the bread slice with a 2½-inch-diameter biscuit cutter.
2. Spread the butter evenly on each side of the bread slice and transfer to a baking dish.
3. Crack the egg into the hole and season as desired with salt and pepper. Scatter the shredded cheese and diced ham on top.
4. Select Bake, Super Convection, set temperature to 330°F (166°C), and set time to 5 minutes. Select Start/Stop to begin preheating.
5. Once preheated, place the baking dish on the bake position.
6. When cooking is complete, the bread should be lightly browned and the egg should be set. Remove from the Vortex and serve hot.

Avocado and Egg Burrito

Prep time: 10 minutes | Cook time: 4 minutes | Serves 4

4 low-sodium whole-wheat flour tortillas
Filling:
1 hard-boiled egg, chopped
2 hard-boiled egg whites, chopped
1 ripe avocado, peeled, pitted, and chopped
1 red bell pepper, chopped
1 (1.2-ounce / 34-g) slice low-sodium, low-fat American cheese, torn into pieces
3 tablespoons low-sodium salsa, plus additional for serving (optional)

Special Equipment:
4 toothpicks (optional) soaked in water for at least 30 minutes

1. Make the filling: Combine the egg, egg whites, avocado, red bell pepper, cheese, and salsa in a medium bowl and stir until blended.
2. Assemble the burritos: Arrange the tortillas on a clean work surface and place ¼ of the prepared filling in the middle of each tortilla, leaving about 1½-inch on each end unfilled. Fold in the opposite sides of each tortilla and roll up. Secure with toothpicks through the center, if needed.
3. Transfer the burritos to the perforated pan.
4. Select Air Fry. Set temperature to 390°F (199°C) and set time to 4 minutes. Press Start to begin preheating.
5. Once the Vortex has preheated, place the pan into the Vortex.
6. When cooking is complete, the burritos should be crisp and golden brown.
7. Allow to cool for 5 minutes and serve with salsa, if desired.

Cheese and Bacon Muffin Sandwiches

Prep time: 5 minutes | Cook time: 8 minutes | Serves 4

4 English muffins, split
8 slices Canadian bacon
4 slices cheese
Cooking spray

1. Make the sandwiches: Top each of 4 muffin halves with 2 slices of Canadian bacon, 1 slice of cheese, and finish with the remaining muffin half.
2. Put the sandwiches in the perforated pan and spritz the tops with cooking spray.
3. Select Bake. Set temperature to 370°F (188°C) and set time to 8 minutes. Press Start to begin preheating.
4. Once preheated, place the pan into the Vortex. Flip the sandwiches halfway through the cooking time.
5. When cooking is complete, remove the pan from the Vortex. Divide the sandwiches among four plates and serve warm.

Breakfast Raisins Bars

Prep time: 15 minutes | Cook time: 35 minutes | Makes 6 bars

1 cup unsweetened applesauce
1 carrot, peeled and grated
½ cup raisins
1 egg
1 tablespoon vegetable oil
2 tablespoons molasses
2 tablespoons brown sugar
¼ cup chopped walnuts
2 cups rolled oats
2 tablespoons sesame seeds
1 teaspoon ground cinnamon
¼ teaspoon grated nutmeg
¼ teaspoon ground ginger
Salt, to taste

1. Combine all the ingredients in a bowl, stirring well to blend. Press the mixture into an oiled or nonstick square baking (cake) pan.
2. Select Bake. Set temperature to 375°F (190°C) and set time to 35 minutes. Select Start to begin preheating.
3. Once preheated, slide the pan into the Vortex.
4. When done, the mixture will be golden brown. Cool and cut into squares.

Bell Pepper and Carrot Frittata

Prep time: 10 minutes | Cook time: 12 minutes | Serves 4

½ cup chopped red bell pepper
⅓ cup grated carrot
⅓ cup minced onion
1 teaspoon olive oil
1 egg
6 egg whites
⅓ cup 2% milk
1 tablespoon shredded Parmesan cheese

1. Mix together the red bell pepper, carrot, onion, and olive oil in a baking pan and stir to combine.
2. Select Bake. Set temperature to 350°F (180°C) and set time to 12 minutes. Press Start to begin preheating.
3. Once preheated, place the pan into the Vortex.
4. After 3 minutes, remove the pan from the Vortex. Stir the vegetables. Return the pan to the Vortex and continue cooking.
5. Meantime, whisk together the egg, egg whites, and milk in a medium bowl until creamy.
6. After 3 minutes, remove the pan from the Vortex. Pour the egg mixture over the top and scatter with the Parmesan cheese. Return the pan to the Vortex and continue cooking for additional 6 minutes.
7. When cooking is complete, the eggs will be set and the top will be golden around the edges.
8. Allow the frittata to cool for 5 minutes before slicing and serving.

Broccoli and Red Pepper Quiche
Prep time: 5 minutes | Cook time: 10 minutes | Serves 4

1 cup broccoli florets
¾ cup chopped roasted red peppers
1¼ cups grated Fontina cheese
6 eggs
¾ cup heavy cream
½ teaspoon salt
Freshly ground black pepper, to taste
Cooking spray

1. Spritz a baking pan with cooking spray
2. Add the broccoli florets and roasted red peppers to the pan and scatter the grated Fontina cheese on top.
3. In a bowl, beat together the eggs and heavy cream. Sprinkle with salt and pepper. Pour the egg mixture over the top of the cheese. Wrap the pan in foil.
4. Select Air Fry. Set temperature to 325°F (163°C) and set time to 10 minutes. Press Start to begin preheating.
5. Once preheated, place the pan into the Vortex.
6. After 8 minutes, remove the pan from the Vortex. Remove the foil. Return the pan to the Vortex and continue to cook another 2 minutes.
7. When cooked, the quiche should be golden brown.
8. Rest for 5 minutes before cutting into wedges and serve warm.

Vanilla Banana Bread Pudding
Prep time: 10 minutes | Cook time: 16 minutes | Serves 4

2 medium ripe bananas, mashed
½ cup low-fat milk
2 tablespoons maple syrup
2 tablespoons peanut butter
1 teaspoon vanilla extract
1 teaspoon ground cinnamon
2 slices whole-grain bread, cut into bite-sized cubes
¼ cup quick oats
Cooking spray

1. Spritz a baking dish lightly with cooking spray.
2. Mix the bananas, milk, maple syrup, peanut butter, vanilla, and cinnamon in a large mixing bowl and stir until well incorporated.
3. Add the bread cubes to the banana mixture and stir until thoroughly coated. Fold in the oats and stir to combine.
4. Transfer the mixture to the baking dish. Wrap the baking dish in aluminum foil.
5. Select Air Fry. Set temperature to 350°F (180°C) and set time to 16 minutes. Press Start to begin preheating.
6. Once the Vortex has preheated, place the pan into the Vortex.
7. After 10 minutes, remove the baking dish from the Vortex. Remove the foil. Return the baking dish to the Vortex and continue to cook another 6 minutes.
8. When done, the pudding should be set.
9. Let the pudding cool for 5 minutes before serving.

Baked Avocado with Eggs and Tomato
Prep time: 5 minutes | Cook time: 11 minutes | Serves 2

1 large avocado, halved and pitted
2 large eggs
2 tomato slices, divided
½ cup nonfat Cottage cheese, divided
½ teaspoon fresh cilantro, for garnish

1. Line the sheet pan with the aluminium foil.
2. Slice a thin piece from the bottom of each avocado half so they sit flat. Remove a small amount from each avocado half to make a bigger hole to hold the egg.
3. Arrange the avocado halves on the pan, hollow-side up. Break 1 egg into each half. Top each half with 1 tomato slice and ¼ cup of the Cottage cheese.
4. Select Bake. Set temperature to 400°F (205°C) and set time to 11 minutes. Press Start to begin preheating.
5. Once the unit has preheated, place the pan into the Vortex.
6. When cooking is complete, remove the pan from the Vortex. Garnish with the fresh cilantro and serve.

Vanilla Pancake with Mixed Berries
Prep time: 10 minutes | Cook time: 14 minutes | Serves 4

1 tablespoon unsalted butter, at room temperature
1 egg
2 egg whites
½ cup 2% milk
½ cup whole-wheat pastry flour
1 teaspoon pure vanilla extract
1 cup sliced fresh strawberries
½ cup fresh raspberries
½ cup fresh blueberries

1. Grease a baking pan with the butter.
2. Using a hand mixer, beat together the egg, egg whites, milk, pastry flour, and vanilla in a medium mixing bowl until well incorporated.
3. Pour the batter into the pan.
4. Select Bake. Set temperature to 330°F (166°C) and set time to 14 minutes. Press Start to begin preheating.
5. Once the Vortex has preheated, place the pan into the Vortex.
6. When cooked, the pancake should puff up in the center and the edges should be golden brown.
7. Allow the pancake to cool for 5 minutes and serve topped with the berries.

Chicken Breakfast Sausages

Prep time: 15 minutes | Cook time: 10 minutes | Makes 8 patties

1 Granny Smith apple, peeled and finely chopped
2 tablespoons apple juice
2 garlic cloves, minced
1 egg white
⅓ cup minced onion
3 tablespoons ground almonds
⅛ teaspoon freshly ground black pepper
1 pound (454 g) ground chicken breast

1. Combine all the ingredients except the chicken in a medium mixing bowl and stir well.
2. Add the chicken breast to the apple mixture and mix with your hands until well incorporated.
3. Divide the mixture into 8 equal portions and shape into patties. Arrange the patties in the perforated pan.
4. Select Air Fry. Set temperature to 330°F (166°C) and set time to 10 minutes. Press Start to begin preheating.
5. Once the Vortex has preheated, place the pan into the Vortex.
6. When done, a meat thermometer inserted in the center of the chicken should reach at least 165°F (74°C).
7. Remove from the Vortex to a plate. Let the chicken cool for 5 minutes and serve warm.

Banana Chocolate Bread with Walnuts

Prep time: 10 minutes | Cook time: 30 minutes | Serves 4

¼ cup cocoa powder
6 tablespoons plus 2 teaspoons all-purpose flour, divided
½ teaspoon kosher salt
¼ teaspoon baking soda
1½ ripe bananas
1 large egg, whisked
¼ cup vegetable oil
½ cup sugar
3 tablespoons buttermilk or plain yogurt (not Greek)
½ teaspoon vanilla extract
6 tablespoons chopped white chocolate
6 tablespoons chopped walnuts

1. Mix together the cocoa powder, 6 tablespoons of the flour, salt, and baking soda in a medium bowl.
2. Mash the bananas with a fork in another medium bowl until smooth. Fold in the egg, oil, sugar, buttermilk, and vanilla, and whisk until thoroughly combined. Add the wet mixture to the dry mixture and stir until well incorporated.
3. Combine the white chocolate, walnuts, and the remaining 2 tablespoons of flour in a third bowl and toss to coat. Add this mixture to the batter and stir until well incorporated. Pour the batter into a baking pan and smooth the top with a spatula.
4. Select Bake. Set temperature to 310°F (154°C) and set time to 30 minutes. Press Start to begin preheating.
5. Once the Vortex has preheated, place the pan into the Vortex.
6. When done, a toothpick inserted into the center of the bread should come out clean.
7. Remove from the Vortex and allow to cool on a wire rack for 10 minutes before serving.

Shrimp and Spinach Frittata

Prep time: 15 minutes | Cook time: 16 minutes | Serves 4

4 eggs
Pinch salt
½ cup cooked rice
½ cup chopped cooked shrimp
½ cup baby spinach
½ cup grated Monterey Jack cheese
Nonstick cooking spray

1. Spritz a baking pan with nonstick cooking spray.
2. Whisk the eggs and salt in a small bowl until frothy.
3. Place the cooked rice, shrimp, and baby spinach in the baking pan. Pour in the whisked eggs and scatter the cheese on top.
4. Select Bake. Set temperature to 320°F (160°C) and set time to 16 minutes. Press Start to begin preheating.
5. Once the Vortex has preheated, place the pan into the Vortex.
6. When cooking is complete, the frittata should be golden and puffy.
7. Let the frittata cool for 5 minutes before slicing to serve.

Cheddar Bacon Casserole

Prep time: 10 minutes | Cook time: 16 minutes | Serves 4

6 slices bacon
6 eggs
Salt and pepper, to taste
Cooking spray
½ cup chopped green bell pepper
½ cup chopped onion
¾ cup shredded Cheddar cheese

1. Place the bacon in a skillet over medium-high heat and cook each side for about 4 minutes until evenly crisp. Remove from the heat to a paper towel-lined plate to drain. Crumble it into small pieces and set aside.
2. Whisk the eggs with the salt and pepper in a medium bowl.
3. Spritz a baking pan with cooking spray.
4. Place the whisked eggs, crumbled bacon, green bell pepper, and onion in the prepared pan.
5. Select Bake. Set temperature to 400°F (205°C) and set time to 8 minutes. Press Start to begin preheating.
6. Once preheated, place the pan into the Vortex.
7. After 6 minutes, remove the pan from the Vortex. Scatter the Cheddar cheese all over. Return the pan to the Vortex and continue to cook another 2 minutes.
8. When cooking is complete, let sit for 5 minutes and serve on plates.

Cheddar Hash Brown Casserole

Prep time: 15 minutes | Cook time: 30 minutes | Serves 4

3½ cups frozen hash browns, thawed
1 teaspoon salt
1 teaspoon freshly ground black pepper
3 tablespoons butter, melted
1 (10.5-ounce / 298-g) can cream of chicken soup
½ cup sour cream
1 cup minced onion
½ cup shredded sharp Cheddar cheese
Cooking spray

1. Put the hash browns in a large bowl and season with salt and black pepper. Add the melted butter, cream of chicken soup, and sour cream and stir until well incorporated. Mix in the minced onion and cheese and stir well.
2. Spray a baking pan with cooking spray.
3. Spread the hash brown mixture evenly into the baking pan.
4. Select Bake. Set temperature to 325°F (163°C) and set time to 30 minutes. Press Start to begin preheating.
5. Once the Vortex has preheated, place the pan into the Vortex.
6. When cooked, the hash brown mixture will be browned.
7. Cool for 5 minutes before serving.

Mushroom and Spinach Frittata

Prep time: 10 minutes | Cook time: 22 minutes | Serves 2

4 large eggs
4 ounces (113 g) baby bella mushrooms, chopped
1 cup baby spinach, chopped
½ cup shredded Cheddar cheese
⅓ cup chopped leek, white part only
¼ cup halved grape tomatoes
1 tablespoon 2% milk
¼ teaspoon dried oregano
¼ teaspoon garlic powder
½ teaspoon kosher salt
Freshly ground black pepper, to taste
Cooking spray

1. Lightly spritz a baking dish with cooking spray.
2. Whisk the eggs in a large bowl until frothy. Add the mushrooms, baby spinach, cheese, leek, tomatoes, milk, oregano, garlic powder, salt, and pepper and stir until well blended. Pour the mixture into the prepared baking dish.
3. Select Bake. Set temperature to 300°F (150°C) and set time to 22 minutes. Press Start to begin preheating.
4. Once the Vortex has preheated, place the dish into the Vortex.
5. When cooked, the center will be puffed up and the top will be golden brown.
6. Let the frittata cool for 5 minutes before slicing to serve.

Breakfast Sausage Quiche

Prep time: 5 minutes | Cook time: 25 minutes | Serves 4

12 large eggs
1 cup heavy cream
Salt and black pepper, to taste
12 ounces (340 g) sugar-free breakfast sausage
2 cups shredded Cheddar cheese
Cooking spray

1. Coat a casserole dish with cooking spray.
2. Beat together the eggs, heavy cream, salt and pepper in a large bowl until creamy. Stir in the breakfast sausage and Cheddar cheese.
3. Pour the sausage mixture into the prepared casserole dish.
4. Select Bake. Set temperature to 375°F (190°C) and set time to 25 minutes. Press Start to begin preheating.
5. Once the Vortex has preheated, place the dish into the Vortex.
6. When done, the top of the quiche should be golden brown and the eggs will be set.
7. Remove from the Vortex and let sit for 5 to 10 minutes before serving.

Vanilla Pancake with Walnuts

Prep time: 10 minutes | Cook time: 20 minutes | Serves 4

3 tablespoons melted butter, divided
1 cup flour
2 tablespoons sugar
1½ teaspoons baking powder
¼ teaspoon salt
1 egg, beaten
¾ cup milk
1 teaspoon pure vanilla extract
½ cup roughly chopped walnuts
Maple syrup or fresh sliced fruit, for serving

1. Grease a baking pan with 1 tablespoon of melted butter.
2. Mix together the flour, sugar, baking powder, and salt in a medium bowl. Add the beaten egg, milk, the remaining 2 tablespoons of melted butter, and vanilla and stir until the batter is sticky but slightly lumpy.
3. Slowly pour the batter into the greased baking pan and scatter with the walnuts.
4. Select Bake. Set temperature to 330°F (166°C) and set time to 20 minutes. Press Start to begin preheating.
5. Once preheated, place the pan into the Vortex.
6. When cooked, the pancake should be golden brown and cooked through.
7. Let the pancake rest for 5 minutes and serve topped with the maple syrup or fresh fruit, if desired.

Half-and-Half Cinnamon Rolls

Prep time: 10 minutes | Cook time: 15 minutes | Makes 12 rolls and ½ cup icing

Cinnamon Mixture:
3 tablespoons dark brown sugar
3 tablespoons chopped pecans
2 tablespoons margarine
1 teaspoon ground cinnamon
Salt, to taste
Icing:
1 cup confectioners' sugar, sifted
1 tablespoon fat-free half-and-half
½ teaspoon vanilla extract
Salt, to taste

1. Make the buttermilk biscuit dough.
2. Roll out or pat the dough to ½ inch thick. In a small bowl, combine the cinnamon mixture ingredients. Spread the dough evenly with the cinnamon mixture and roll up like a jelly roll. With a sharp knife, cut the roll into 1-inch slices. Place on an oiled or nonstick baking sheet.
3. Select Bake. Set temperature to 400°F (205°C) and set time to 15 minutes. Select Start to begin preheating.
4. Once preheated, slide the pan into the Vortex.
5. When done, the rolls will be lightly browned. Let cool before frosting.
6. Combine the icing ingredients in a small bowl, adding more half-and-half or confectioners' sugar until the consistency is like thick cream. Drizzle over the tops of the cinnamon rolls and serve.

Vanilla Blueberry Cobbler

Prep time: 5 minutes | Cook time: 15 minutes | Serves 4

¾ teaspoon baking powder
⅓ cup whole-wheat pastry flour
Dash sea salt
⅓ cup unsweetened nondairy milk
2 tablespoons maple syrup
½ teaspoon vanilla
Cooking spray
½ cup blueberries
¼ cup granola
Nondairy yogurt, for topping (optional)

1. Spritz a baking pan with cooking spray.
2. Mix together the baking powder, flour, and salt in a medium bowl. Add the milk, maple syrup, and vanilla and whisk to combine.
3. Scrape the mixture into the prepared pan. Scatter the blueberries and granola on top.
4. Select Bake. Set temperature to 347°F (175°C) and set time to 15 minutes. Press Start to begin preheating.
5. Once preheated, place the pan into the Vortex.
6. When done, the top should begin to brown and a knife inserted in the center should come out clean.
7. Let the cobbler cool for 5 minutes and serve with a drizzle of nondairy yogurt.

Asparagus Strata with Havarti Cheese

Prep time: 10 minutes | Cook time: 17 minutes | Serves 4

6 asparagus spears, cut into 2-inch pieces
1 tablespoon water
2 slices whole-wheat bread, cut into ½-inch cubes
4 eggs
3 tablespoons whole milk
2 tablespoons chopped flat-leaf parsley
½ cup grated Havarti or Swiss cheese
Pinch salt
Freshly ground black pepper, to taste
Cooking spray

1. Add the asparagus spears and 1 tablespoon of water in a baking pan.
2. Select Bake. Set temperature to 330°F (166°C) and set time to 4 minutes. Press Start to begin preheating.
3. Once preheated, place the pan into the Vortex.
4. When cooking is complete, the asparagus spears will be crisp-tender.
5. Remove the asparagus from the pan and drain on paper towels.
6. Spritz the pan with cooking spray. Place the bread and asparagus in the pan.
7. Whisk together the eggs and milk in a medium mixing bowl until creamy. Fold in the parsley, cheese, salt, and pepper and stir to combine. Pour this mixture into the baking pan.
8. Select Bake and set time to 13 minutes. Place the pan back to the Vortex. When done, the eggs will be set and the top will be lightly browned.
9. Let cool for 5 minutes before slicing and serving.

Brown Rice Porridge with Dates

Prep time: 5 minutes | Cook time: 23 minutes | Serves 1 or 2

½ cup cooked brown rice
1 cup canned coconut milk
¼ cup unsweetened shredded coconut
¼ cup packed dark brown sugar
4 large Medjool dates, pitted and roughly chopped
½ teaspoon kosher salt
¼ teaspoon ground cardamom
Heavy cream, for serving (optional)

1. Place all the ingredients except the heavy cream in a baking pan and stir until blended.
2. Select Bake. Set temperature to 375°F (190°C) and set time to 23 minutes. Press Start to begin preheating.
3. Once the Vortex has preheated, place the pan into the Vortex. Stir the porridge halfway through the cooking time.
4. When cooked, the porridge will be thick and creamy.
5. Remove from the Vortex and ladle the porridge into bowls.
6. Serve hot with a drizzle of the cream, if desired.

Garlic Potatoes with Peppers and Onions
Prep time: 10 minutes | Cook time: 35 minutes | Serves 4

1 pound (454 g) red potatoes, cut into ½-inch dices
1 large red bell pepper, cut into ½-inch dices
1 large green bell pepper, cut into ½-inch dices
1 medium onion, cut into ½-inch dices
1½ tablespoons extra-virgin olive oil
1¼ teaspoons kosher salt
¾ teaspoon sweet paprika
¾ teaspoon garlic powder
Freshly ground black pepper, to taste

1. Mix together the potatoes, bell peppers, onion, oil, salt, paprika, garlic powder, and black pepper in a large mixing and toss to coat.
2. Transfer the potato mixture to the perforated pan.
3. Select Air Fry. Set temperature to 350°F (180°C) and set time to 35 minutes. Press Start to begin preheating.
4. Once preheated, place the pan into the Vortex. Stir the potato mixture three times during cooking.
5. When done, the potatoes should be nicely browned.
6. Remove from the Vortex to a plate and serve warm.

Brown Rice Quiches with Pimiento
Prep time: 10 minutes | Cook time: 14 minutes | Serves 6

4 ounces (113 g) diced green chilies
3 cups cooked brown rice
1 cup shredded reduced-fat Cheddar cheese, divided
½ cup egg whites
⅓ cup fat-free milk
¼ cup diced pimiento
½ teaspoon cumin
1 small eggplant, cubed
1 bunch fresh cilantro, finely chopped
Cooking spray

1. Spritz a 12-cup muffin pan with cooking spray.
2. In a large bowl, stir together all the ingredients, except for ½ cup of the cheese.
3. Scoop the mixture evenly into the muffin cups and sprinkle the remaining ½ cup of the cheese on top.
4. Select Bake. Set temperature to 400°F (205°C) and set time to 14 minutes. Press Start to begin preheating.
5. Once the unit has preheated, place the pan into the Vortex.
6. When cooking is complete, remove the pan and check the quiches. They should be set.
7. Carefully transfer the quiches to a platter and serve immediately.

Baked Eggs with Kale Pesto
Prep time: 5 minutes | Cook time: 11 minutes | Serves 2

1 cup roughly chopped kale leaves, stems and center ribs removed
¼ cup grated pecorino cheese
¼ cup olive oil
1 garlic clove, peeled
3 tablespoons whole almonds
Kosher salt and freshly ground black pepper, to taste
4 large eggs
2 tablespoons heavy cream
3 tablespoons chopped pitted mixed olives

1. Place the kale, pecorino, olive oil, garlic, almonds, salt, and pepper in a small blender and blitz until well incorporated.
2. One at a time, crack the eggs in a baking pan. Drizzle the kale pesto on top of the egg whites. Top the yolks with the cream and swirl together the yolks and the pesto.
3. Select Bake. Set temperature to 300°F (150°C) and set time to 11 minutes. Press Start to begin preheating.
4. Once preheated, place the pan into the Vortex.
5. When cooked, the top should begin to brown and the eggs should be set.
6. Allow the eggs to cool for 5 minutes. Scatter the olives on top and serve warm.

Blueberries Quesadillas
Prep time: 5 minutes | Cook time: 4 minutes | Serves 2

¼ cup nonfat Ricotta cheese
¼ cup plain nonfat Greek yogurt
2 tablespoons finely ground flaxseeds
1 tablespoon granulated stevia
½ teaspoon cinnamon
¼ teaspoon vanilla extract
2 (8-inch) low-carb whole-wheat tortillas
½ cup fresh blueberries, divided

1. Line the sheet pan with the aluminum foil.
2. In a small bowl, whisk together the Ricotta cheese, yogurt, flaxseeds, stevia, cinnamon and vanilla.
3. Place the tortillas on the sheet pan. Spread half of the yogurt mixture on each tortilla, almost to the edges. Top each tortilla with ¼ cup of blueberries. Fold the tortillas in half.
4. Select Bake. Set temperature to 400°F (205°C) and set time to 4 minutes. Press Start to begin preheating.
5. Once the unit has preheated, place the pan into the Vortex.
6. When cooking is complete, remove the pan from the Vortex. Serve immediately.

Maple Banana Bread Pudding
Prep time: 10 minutes | Cook time: 18 minutes | Serves 4

2 medium ripe bananas, mashed
½ cup low-fat milk
2 tablespoons maple syrup
2 tablespoons peanut butter
1 teaspoon vanilla extract
1 teaspoon ground cinnamon
2 slices whole-grain bread, torn into bite-sized pieces
¼ cup quick oats
Cooking spray

1. Spritz the sheet pan with cooking spray.
2. In a large bowl, combine the bananas, milk, maple syrup, peanut butter, vanilla extract and cinnamon. Use an immersion blender to mix until well combined.
3. Stir in the bread pieces to coat well. Add the oats and stir until everything is combined.
4. Transfer the mixture to the sheet pan. Cover with the aluminum foil.
5. Select Air Fry. Set temperature to 375°F (190°C) and set time to 18 minutes. Press Start to begin preheating.
6. Once the unit has preheated, place the pan into the Vortex.
7. After 10 minutes, remove the foil and continue to cook for 8 minutes.
8. Serve immediately.

Spinach and Egg Florentine
Prep time: 10 minutes | Cook time: 15 minutes | Serves 4

3 cups frozen spinach, thawed and drained
2 tablespoons heavy cream
¼ teaspoon kosher salt
⅛ teaspoon freshly ground black pepper
4 ounces (113 g) Ricotta cheese
2 garlic cloves, minced
½ cup panko bread crumbs
3 tablespoons grated Parmesan cheese
2 teaspoons unsalted butter, melted
4 large eggs

1. In a medium bowl, whisk together the spinach, heavy cream, salt, pepper, Ricotta cheese and garlic.
2. In a small bowl, whisk together the bread crumbs, Parmesan cheese and butter. Set aside.
3. Spoon the spinach mixture on the sheet pan and form four even circles.
4. Select Roast. Set temperature to 375°F (190°C) and set time to 15 minutes. Press Start to begin preheating.
5. Once the unit has preheated, place the pan into the Vortex.
6. After 8 minutes, remove the pan from the Vortex. The spinach should be bubbling. With the back of a large spoon, make indentations in the spinach for the eggs. Crack the eggs into the indentations and sprinkle the panko mixture over the surface of the eggs. Return the pan to the Vortex to continue cooking.
7. When cooking is complete, remove the pan from the Vortex. Serve hot.

Banana Carrot Muffin
Prep time: 10 minutes | Cook time: 20 minutes | Serves 12

1½ cups whole-wheat flour
1 cup grated carrot
1 cup mashed banana
½ cup bran
½ cup low-fat buttermilk
2 tablespoons agave nectar
2 teaspoons baking powder
1 teaspoon vanilla
1 teaspoon baking soda
½ teaspoon nutmeg
Pinch cloves
2 egg whites

1. Line a muffin pan with 12 paper liners.
2. In a large bowl, stir together all the ingredients. Mix well, but do not over beat.
3. Scoop the mixture into the muffin cups.
4. Select Bake. Set temperature to 400°F (205°C) and set time to 20 minutes. Press Start to begin preheating.
5. Once the unit has preheated, place the pan into the Vortex.
6. When cooking is complete, remove the pan and let rest for 5 minutes.
7. Serve warm or at room temperature.

Whole-Wheat Blueberries Muffins
Prep time: 5 minutes | Cook time: 25 minutes | Makes 8 muffins

½ cup unsweetened applesauce
½ cup plant-based milk
½ cup maple syrup
1 teaspoon vanilla extract
2 cups whole-wheat flour
½ teaspoon baking soda
1 cup blueberries
Cooking spray

1. Spritz a 8-cup muffin pan with cooking spray.
2. In a large bowl, stir together the applesauce, milk, maple syrup and vanilla extract. Whisk in the flour and baking soda until no dry flour is left and the batter is smooth. Gently mix in the blueberries until they are evenly distributed throughout the batter.
3. Spoon the batter into the muffin cups, three-quarters full.
4. Select Bake. Set temperature to 375°F (190°C) and set time to 25 minutes. Press Start to begin preheating.
5. Once preheated, place the pan into the Vortex.
6. When cooking is complete, remove the pan and check the muffins. You can stick a knife into the center of a muffin and it should come out clean.
7. Let rest for 5 minutes before serving.

Orange Scones with Blueberries
Prep time: 5 minutes | Cook time: 20 minutes | Serves 14

½ cup low-fat buttermilk
¾ cup orange juice
Zest of 1 orange
2¼ cups whole-wheat pastry flour
⅓ cup agave nectar
¼ cup canola oil
1 teaspoon baking soda
1 teaspoon cream of tartar
1 cup fresh blueberries

1. In a small bowl, stir together the buttermilk, orange juice and orange zest.
2. In a large bowl, whisk together the flour, agave nectar, canola oil, baking soda and cream of tartar.
3. Add the buttermilk mixture and blueberries to the bowl with the flour mixture. Mix gently by hand until well combined.
4. Transfer the batter onto a lightly floured baking sheet. Pat into a circle about ¾ inch thick and 8 inches across. Use a knife to cut the circle into 14 wedges, cutting almost all the way through.
5. Select Bake. Set temperature to 375°F (190°C) and set time to 20 minutes. Press Start to begin preheating.
6. Once the unit has preheated, place the baking sheet into the Vortex.
7. When cooking is complete, remove the baking sheet and check the scones. They should be lightly browned.
8. Let rest for 5 minutes and cut completely through the wedges before serving.

French Toast Sticks with Strawberries
Prep time: 5 minutes | Cook time: 12 minutes | Serves 4

3 slices low-sodium whole-wheat bread, each cut into 4 strips
1 tablespoon unsalted butter, melted
1 tablespoon 2 percent milk
1 tablespoon sugar
1 egg, beaten
1 egg white
1 cup sliced fresh strawberries
1 tablespoon freshly squeezed lemon juice

1. Arrange the bread strips on a plate and drizzle with the melted butter.
2. In a bowl, whisk together the milk, sugar, egg and egg white.
3. Dredge the bread strips into the egg mixture and place on a wire rack to let the batter drip off. Arrange half the coated bread strips on the sheet pan.
4. Select Air Fry. Set temperature to 380°F (193°C) and set time to 6 minutes. Press Start to begin preheating.
5. Once preheated, place the pan into the Vortex.
6. After 3 minutes, remove the pan from the Vortex. Use tongs to turn the strips over. Rotate the pan and return the pan to the Vortex to continue cooking.
7. When cooking is complete, the strips should be golden brown.
8. In a small bowl, mash the strawberries with a fork and stir in the lemon juice. Serve the French toast sticks with the strawberry sauce.

Blueberry Cake with Lemon
Prep time: 5 minutes | Cook time: 10 minutes | Serves 8

1½ cups Bisquick
¼ cup granulated sugar
2 large eggs, beaten
¾ cup whole milk
1 teaspoon vanilla extract
½ teaspoon lemon zest
Cooking spray
2 cups blueberries

1. Stir together the Bisquick and sugar in a medium bowl. Stir together the eggs, milk, vanilla and lemon zest. Add the wet ingredients to the dry ingredients and stir until well combined.
2. Spritz the sheet pan with cooking spray and line with the parchment paper, pressing it into place. Spray the parchment paper with cooking spray. Pour the batter on the pan and spread it out evenly. Sprinkle the blueberries evenly over the top.
3. Select Bake. Set temperature to 375°F (190°C) and set time to 10 minutes. Press Start to begin preheating.
4. Once the unit has preheated, place the pan into the Vortex.
5. When cooking is complete, the cake should be pulling away from the edges of the pan and the top should be just starting to turn golden brown.
6. Let the cake rest for a minute before cutting into 16 squares. Serve immediately.

Beef Hash with Eggs
Prep time: 10 minutes | Cook time: 25 minutes | Serves 4

2 medium Yukon Gold potatoes, peeled and cut into ¼-inch cubes
1 medium onion, chopped
⅓ cup diced red bell pepper
3 tablespoons vegetable oil
½ teaspoon dried thyme
½ teaspoon kosher salt, divided
½ teaspoon freshly ground black pepper, divided
¾ pound (340 g) corned beef, cut into ¼-inch pieces
4 large eggs

1. In a large bowl, stir together the potatoes, onion, red pepper, vegetable oil, thyme, ¼ teaspoon of the salt and ¼ teaspoon of the pepper. Spread the vegetable mixture on the sheet pan in an even layer.
2. Select Roast. Set temperature to 375°F (190°C) and set time to 25 minutes. Press Start to begin preheating.
3. Once the unit has preheated, place the pan into the Vortex.
4. After 15 minutes, remove the pan from the Vortex and add the corned beef. Stir the mixture to incorporate the corned beef. Return the pan to the Vortex and continue cooking.
5. After 5 minutes, remove the pan from the Vortex. Using a large spoon, create 4 circles in the hash to hold the eggs. Gently crack an egg into each circle. Season the eggs with the remaining ¼ teaspoon of the salt and ¼ teaspoon of the pepper. Return the pan to the Vortex. Continue cooking for 3 to 5 minutes, depending on how you like your eggs.
6. When cooking is complete, remove the pan from the Vortex. Serve immediately.

Maple French Toast Casserole
Prep time: 5 minutes | Cook time: 12 minutes | Serves 6

3 large eggs, beaten
1 cup whole milk
1 tablespoon pure maple syrup
1 teaspoon vanilla extract
¼ teaspoon cinnamon
¼ teaspoon kosher salt
3 cups stale bread cubes
1 tablespoon unsalted butter, at room temperature

1. In a medium bowl, whisk together the eggs, milk, maple syrup, vanilla extract, cinnamon and salt. Stir in the bread cubes to coat well.
2. Grease the bottom of the sheet pan with the butter. Spread the bread mixture into the pan in an even layer.
3. Select Roast. Set temperature to 350°F (180°C) and set time to 12 minutes. Press Start to begin preheating.
4. Once the unit has preheated, place the pan into the Vortex.
5. After about 10 minutes, remove the pan and check the casserole. The top should be browned and the middle of the casserole just set. If more time is needed, return the pan to the Vortex and continue cooking.
6. When cooking is complete, serve warm.

Honey Cashew Granola with Cranberries
Prep time: 5 minutes | Cook time: 12 minutes | Serves 6

3 cups old-fashioned rolled oats
2 cups raw cashews
1 cup unsweetened coconut chips
½ cup honey
¼ cup vegetable oil
⅓ cup packed light brown sugar
¼ teaspoon kosher salt
1 cup dried cranberries

1. In a large bowl, stir together all the ingredients, except for the cranberries. Spread the mixture on the sheet pan in an even layer.
2. Select Bake. Set temperature to 325°F (163°C) and set time to 12 minutes. Press Start to begin preheating.
3. Once the unit has preheated, place the pan into the Vortex.
4. After 5 to 6 minutes, remove the pan and stir the granola. Return the pan to the Vortex and continue cooking.
5. When cooking is complete, remove the pan. Let the granola cool to room temperature. Stir in the cranberries before serving.

Bacon and Egg Cup
Prep time: 5 minutes | Cook time: 15 minutes | Serves 1

2 eggs
4 ounces (113 g) bacon, cooked
Salt and ground black pepper, to taste

1. Select the BAKE function and preheat VORTEX to 400°F (204°C).
2. Put liners in a regular cupcake tin. Crack an egg into each of the cups and add the bacon.
3. Season with some pepper and salt. Bake in the preheated air fryer oven for 15 minutes, or until the eggs are set. Serve warm.

Italian Bacon Hot Dogs
Prep time: 5 minutes | Cook time: 15 minutes | Serves 4

3 brazilian sausages, cut into 3 equal pieces
9 slices bacon
1 tablespoon Italian herbs
Salt and ground black pepper, to taste

1. Take each slice of bacon and wrap around each piece of sausage.
2. Sprinkle with Italian herbs, salt and pepper. Select the AIR FRY function and cook the sausages in the air fryer oven at 355°F (179°C) for 15 minutes.
3. Serve warm.

Creamy Sausage and Cauliflower
Prep time: 5 minutes | Cook time: 45 minutes | Serves 4

1 pound (454 g) sausage, cooked and crumbled
2 cups heavy whipping cream
1 head cauliflower, chopped
1 cup grated Cheddar cheese, plus more for topping
8 eggs, beaten
Salt and ground black pepper, to taste

1. Select the BAKE function and preheat VORTEX to 350°F (177°C).
2. In a large bowl, mix the sausage, heavy whipping cream, chopped cauliflower, cheese and eggs. Sprinkle with salt and ground black pepper.
3. Pour the mixture into a greased casserole dish.
4. Bake in the preheated air fryer oven for 45 minutes or until firm.
5. Top with more Cheddar cheese and serve.

Chicken Breakfast Sausage Biscuits
Prep time: 5 minutes | Cook time: 15 minutes | Serves 5

12 ounces (340 g) chicken breakfast sausage
1 (6-ounce / 170-g) can biscuits
⅛ cup cream cheese

1. Form the sausage into 5 small patties. Place the sausage patties in the air fryer oven.
2. Select the AIR FRY function and cook at 370°F (188°C) for 5 minutes.
3. Open the air fryer oven. Flip the patties. Air fry for an additional 5 minutes.
4. Remove the cooked sausages from the air fryer oven. Separate the biscuit dough into 5 biscuits.
5. Place the biscuits in the air fryer oven. Air fry for 3 minutes.
6. Open the air fryer oven. Flip the biscuits. Air fry for an additional 2 minutes.
7. Remove the cooked biscuits from the air fryer oven. Split each biscuit in half. Spread 1 teaspoon of cream cheese onto the bottom of each biscuit.
8. Top with a sausage patty and the other half of the biscuit, and serve.

French Toast Sticks
Prep time: 10 minutes | Cook time: 6 minutes | Serves 4

2 eggs
½ cup milk
⅛ teaspoon salt
½ teaspoon pure vanilla extract
¾ cup crushed cornflakes
6 slices sandwich bread, each slice cut into 4 strips
Maple syrup, for dipping
Cooking spray

1. In a small bowl, beat together the eggs, milk, salt, and vanilla.
2. Put crushed cornflakes on a plate or in a shallow dish. Dip bread strips in egg mixture, shake off excess, and roll in cornflake crumbs.
3. Spray both sides of bread strips with oil. Put bread strips in air fryer basket in a single layer.
4. Select the AIR FRY function and cook at 390°F (199°C) for 6 minutes, or until golden brown.
5. Repeat with the remaining French toast sticks. Serve with maple syrup.

Mozzarella Sausage Pizza
Prep time: 10 minutes | Cook time: 6 minutes | Serves 4

2 tablespoons ketchup
1 pita bread
⅓ cup sausage
½ pound (227 g) Mozzarella cheese
1 teaspoon garlic powder
1 tablespoon olive oil

1. Select the BAKE function and preheat VORTEX to 340°F (171°C).
2. Spread the ketchup over the pita bread. Top with the sausage and cheese.
3. Sprinkle with the garlic powder and olive oil.
4. Put the pizza in the air fryer basket and bake for 6 minutes. Serve warm.

Cheddar Egg and Bacon Muffins
Prep time: 5 minutes | Cook time: 15 minutes | Serves 1

2 eggs
Salt and ground black pepper, to taste
1 tablespoon green pesto
3 ounces (85 g) shredded Cheddar cheese
5 ounces (142 g) cooked bacon
1 scallion, chopped

1. Select the BAKE function and preheat VORTEX to 350°F (177°C). Line a cupcake tin with parchment paper.
2. Beat the eggs with pepper, salt, and pesto in a bowl. Mix in the cheese. Pour the eggs into the cupcake tin and top with the bacon and scallion.
3. Bake in the preheated air fryer oven for 15 minutes, or until the egg is set. Serve immediately.

British Pumpkin Egg Bake
Prep time: 10 minutes | Cook time: 10 minutes | Serves 2

2 eggs
½ cup milk
2 cups flour
2 tablespoons cider vinegar
2 teaspoons baking powder
1 tablespoon sugar
1 cup pumpkin purée
1 teaspoon cinnamon powder
1 teaspoon baking soda
1 tablespoon olive oil

1. Select the BAKE function and preheat VORTEX to 300°F (149°C).
2. Crack the eggs into a bowl and beat with a whisk.
3. Combine with the milk, flour, cider vinegar, baking powder, sugar, pumpkin purée, cinnamon powder, and baking soda, mixing well.
4. Grease a baking tray with oil. Add the mixture and transfer into the air fryer oven. Bake for 10 minutes. Serve warm.

Speedy Coffee Donuts
Prep time: 5 minutes | Cook time: 6 minutes | Serves 6

¼ cup sugar
½ teaspoon salt
1 cup flour
1 teaspoon baking powder
¼ cup coffee
1 tablespoon aquafaba
1 tablespoon sunflower oil

1. In a large bowl, combine the sugar, salt, flour, and baking powder.
2. Add the coffee, aquafaba, and sunflower oil and mix until a dough is formed. Leave the dough to rest in and the refrigerator.
3. Remove the dough from the fridge and divide up, kneading each section into a doughnut.
4. Put the doughnuts inside the air fryer oven.
5. Select the AIR FRY function and cook at 400°F (204°C) for 6 minutes. Serve immediately.

Breaded Avocado
Prep time: 5 minutes | Cook time: 6 minutes | Serves 4

2 large avocados, sliced
¼ teaspoon paprika
Salt and ground black pepper, to taste
½ cup flour
2 eggs, beaten
1 cup bread crumbs

1. Sprinkle paprika, salt and pepper on the slices of avocado.
2. Lightly coat the avocados with flour. Dredge them in the eggs, before covering with bread crumbs. Transfer to the air fryer oven.
3. Select the AIR FRY function and cook at 400°F (204°C) for 6 minutes.
4. Serve warm.

Air-Fried Avocado Tempura
Prep time: 5 minutes | Cook time: 10 minutes | Serves 4

½ cup bread crumbs
½ teaspoons salt
1 Haas avocado, pitted, peeled and sliced
Liquid from 1 can white beans

1. Mix the bread crumbs and salt in a shallow bowl until well-incorporated.
2. Dip the avocado slices in the bean liquid, then into the bread crumbs.
3. Put the avocados in the air fryer oven, taking care not to overlap any slices.
4. Select the AIR FRY function and cook at 350°F (177°C) for 10 minutes, giving the basket a good shake at the halfway point.
5. Serve immediately.

Lush Veggie Omelet
Prep time: 10 minutes | Cook time: 13 minutes | Serves 2

2 teaspoons canola oil
4 eggs, whisked
3 tablespoons plain milk
1 teaspoon melted butter
1 red bell pepper, seeded and chopped
1 green bell pepper, seeded and chopped
1 white onion, finely chopped
½ cup baby spinach leaves, roughly chopped
½ cup Halloumi cheese, shaved
Kosher salt and freshly ground black pepper, to taste

1. Select the BAKE function and preheat VORTEX to 350°F (177°C).
2. Grease a baking pan with canola oil.
3. Put the remaining ingredients in the baking pan and stir well.
4. Transfer to the air fryer oven and bake for 13 minutes.
5. Serve warm.

Mushroom and Yellow Squash Toast
Prep time: 10 minutes | Cook time: 10 minutes | Serves 4

1 tablespoon olive oil
1 red bell pepper, cut into strips
2 green onions, sliced
1 cup sliced button or cremini mushrooms
1 small yellow squash, sliced
2 tablespoons softened butter
4 slices bread
½ cup soft goat cheese

1. Brush the air fryer basket with the olive oil. Put the red pepper, green onions, mushrooms, and squash inside the air fryer oven and give them a stir.
2. Select the AIR FRY function and cook at 350°F (177°C) for 7 minutes, or until the vegetables are tender, shaking the basket once throughout the cooking time.
3. Remove the vegetables and set them aside. Spread the butter on the slices of bread and transfer to the air fryer oven, butter-side up. Brown for 3 minutes.
4. Remove the toast from the air fryer oven and top with goat cheese and vegetables.
5. Serve warm.

Chia Seeds Oat Porridge
Prep time: 10 minutes | Cook time: 5 minutes | Serves 4

2 tablespoons peanut butter
4 tablespoons honey
1 tablespoon butter, melted
4 cups milk
2 cups oats
1 cup chia seeds

1. Select the BAKE function and preheat VORTEX to 390°F (199°C).
2. Put the peanut butter, honey, butter, and milk in a bowl and stir to mix.
3. Add the oats and chia seeds and stir.
4. Transfer the mixture to a bowl and bake in the air fryer oven for 5 minutes. Give another stir before serving.

Cheesy Onion Omelet
Prep time: 10 minutes | Cook time: 12 minutes | Serves 2

3 eggs
Salt and ground black pepper, to taste
½ teaspoons soy sauce
1 large onion, chopped
2 tablespoons grated Cheddar cheese
Cooking spray

1. Select the BAKE function and preheat VORTEX to 355°F (179°C).
2. In a bowl, whisk together the eggs, salt, pepper, and soy sauce.
3. Spritz a small pan with cooking spray. Spread the chopped onion across the bottom of the pan, then transfer the pan to the air fryer oven.
4. Bake in the preheated air fryer oven for 6 minutes or until the onion is translucent.
5. Add the egg mixture on top of the onions to coat well.
6. Add the cheese on top, then continue baking for another 6 minutes.
7. Allow to cool before serving.

Ranch Risotto with Parmesan Cheese
Prep time: 10 minutes | Cook time: 30 minutes | Serves 2

1 tablespoon olive oil
1 clove garlic, minced
1 tablespoon unsalted butter
1 onion, diced
¾ cup Arborio rice
2 cups chicken stock, boiling
½ cup Parmesan cheese, grated

1. Select the BAKE function and preheat VORTEX to 390°F (199°C).
2. Grease a round baking tin with olive oil and stir in the garlic, butter, and onion.
3. Transfer the tin to the air fryer oven and bake for 4 minutes. Add the rice and bake for 4 more minutes.
4. Turn the air fryer oven to 320°F (160°C) and pour in the chicken stock. Cover and bake for 22 minutes. Scatter with cheese and serve.

Cheesy Italian Sausage Egg Muffins
Prep time: 5 minutes | Cook time: 20 minutes | Serves 4

6 ounces (170 g) Italian sausage, sliced
6 eggs
⅛ cup heavy cream
Salt and ground black pepper, to taste
3 ounces (85 g) Parmesan cheese, grated
Cooking spray

1. Select the BAKE function and preheat VORTEX to 350°F (177°C).
2. Spritz a muffin pan with cooking spray. Put the sliced sausage in the muffin pan.
3. Beat the eggs with the cream in a bowl and season with salt and pepper.
4. Pour half of the mixture over the sausages in the pan.
5. Sprinkle with cheese and the remaining egg mixture.
6. Bake in the preheated air fryer oven for 20 minutes or until set.
7. Serve immediately.

Mozzarella Pepperoni Pizza
Prep time: 10 minutes | Cook time: 6 minutes | Serves 1

1 teaspoon olive oil
1 tablespoon pizza sauce
1 pita bread
6 pepperoni slices
¼ cup grated Mozzarella cheese
¼ teaspoon garlic powder
¼ teaspoon dried oregano

1. Select the BAKE function and preheat VORTEX to 350°F (177°C).
2. Grease the air fryer basket with olive oil.
3. Spread the pizza sauce on top of the pita bread.
4. Put the pepperoni slices over the sauce, followed by the Mozzarella cheese. Season with garlic powder and oregano.
5. Put the pita pizza inside the air fryer oven and place a trivet on top.
6. Bake in the preheated air fryer oven for 6 minutes and serve.

Simple Blueberry Muffins
Prep time: 10 minutes | Cook time: 12 minutes | Makes 8 muffins

1⅓ cups flour
½ cup sugar
2 teaspoons baking powder
¼ teaspoon salt
⅓ cup canola oil
1 egg
½ cup milk
⅔ cup blueberries, fresh or frozen and thawed

1. Select the BAKE function and preheat VORTEX to 330°F (166°C).
2. In a medium bowl, stir together flour, sugar, baking powder, and salt. In a separate bowl, combine oil, egg, and milk and mix well.
3. Add egg mixture to dry ingredients and stir just until moistened. Gently stir in the blueberries.
4. Spoon batter evenly into parchment paper-lined muffin cups. Put 4 muffin cups in air fryer basket and bake for 12 minutes or until tops spring back when touched lightly.
5. Repeat with the remaining muffins.
6. Serve immediately.

Easy Cinnamon Toasts
Prep time: 5 minutes | Cook time: 4 minutes | Serves 4

1 tablespoon salted butter
2 teaspoons ground cinnamon
4 tablespoons sugar
½ teaspoon vanilla extract
10 bread slices

1. Select the BAKE function and preheat VORTEX to 380°F (193°C).
2. In a bowl, combine the butter, cinnamon, sugar, and vanilla extract.
3. Spread onto the slices of bread.
4. Put the bread inside the air fryer oven and bake for 4 minutes or until golden brown.
5. Serve warm.

Scotch Eggs

Prep time: 5 minutes | Cook time: 25 minutes | Serves 4

4 large hard boiled eggs
1 (12-ounce / 340-g) package pork sausage
8 slices thick-cut bacon

Special Equipment:
4 wooden toothpicks, soaked in water for at least 30 minutes

1. Slice the sausage into four parts and place each part into a large circle.
2. Put an egg into each circle and wrap it in the sausage.
3. Put in the refrigerator for 1 hour. Make a cross with two pieces of thick-cut bacon.
4. Put a wrapped egg in the center, fold the bacon over top of the egg, and secure with a toothpick.
5. Select the AIR FRY function and cook at 450°F (235°C) for 25 minutes.
6. Serve immediately.

Warm Sourdough Croutons

Prep time: 5 minutes | Cook time: 6 minutes | Makes 4 cups

4 cups cubed sourdough bread, 1-inch cubes
1 tablespoon olive oil
1 teaspoon fresh thyme leaves
¼ teaspoon salt
Freshly ground black pepper, to taste

1. Combine all ingredients in a bowl.
2. Toss the bread cubes into the air fryer oven.
3. Select the AIR FRY function and cook at 400°F (204°C) for 6 minutes, shaking the basket once or twice while they cook.
4. Serve warm.

Ricotta Spinach Omelet

Prep time: 10 minutes | Cook time: 10 minutes | Serves 1

1 teaspoon olive oil
3 eggs
Salt and ground black pepper, to taste
1 tablespoon ricotta cheese
¼ cup chopped spinach
1 tablespoon chopped parsley

1. Grease the air fryer basket with olive oil.
2. Select the BAKE function and preheat VORTEX to 330°F (166°C).
3. In a bowl, beat the eggs with a fork and sprinkle salt and pepper.
4. Add the ricotta, spinach, and parsley and then transfer to the air fryer oven.
5. Bake for 10 minutes or until the egg is set.
6. Serve warm.

Spinach and Tomato with Scrambled Eggs

Prep time: 10 minutes | Cook time: 10 minutes | Serves 2

2 tablespoons olive oil
4 eggs, whisked
5 ounces (142 g) fresh spinach, chopped
1 medium tomato, chopped
1 teaspoon fresh lemon juice
½ teaspoon coarse salt
½ teaspoon ground black pepper
½ cup of fresh basil, roughly chopped

1. Grease a baking pan with the oil, tilting it to spread the oil around.
2. Select the BAKE function and preheat VORTEX to 280°F (138°C).
3. Mix the remaining ingredients, apart from the basil leaves, whisking well until everything is completely combined.
4. Bake in the air fryer oven for 10 minutes.
5. Top with fresh basil leaves before serving.

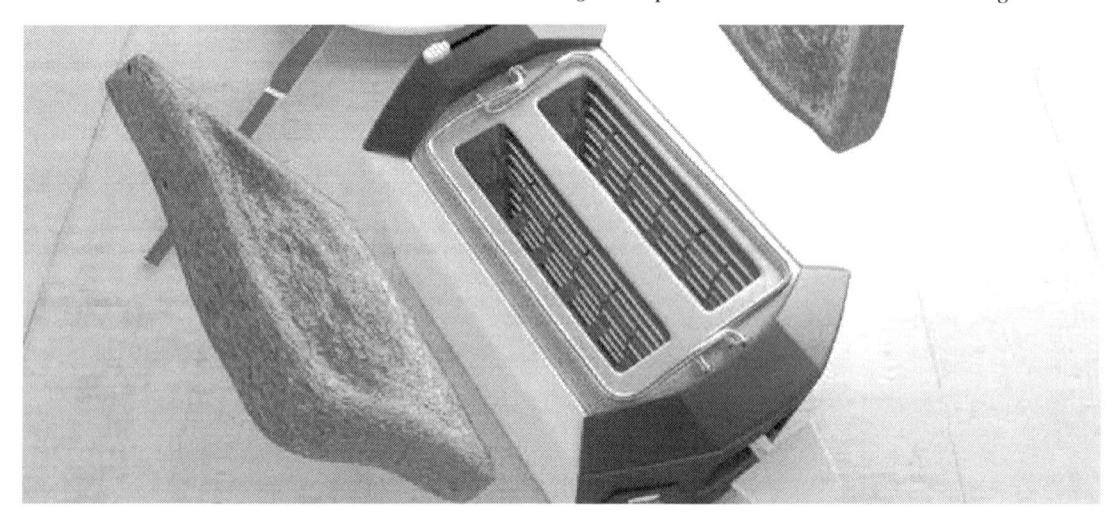

Lime-Honey Grilled Fruit Salad
Prep time: 5 minutes | Cook time: 4 minutes | Serves 4

½ pound (227 g) strawberries, washed, hulled and halved
1 (9-ounce / 255-g) can pineapple chunks, drained, juice reserved
2 peaches, pitted and sliced
6 tablespoons honey, divided
1 tablespoon freshly squeezed lime juice

1. Insert the Grill Grate and close the hood. Select GRILL, set the temperature to MAX, and set the time to 4 minutes. Select START/STOP to begin preheating.
2. While the unit is preheating, combine the strawberries, pineapple, and peaches in a large bowl with 3 tablespoons of honey. Toss to coat evenly.
3. When the unit beeps to signify it has preheated, place the fruit on the Grill Grate. Gently press the fruit down to maximize grill marks. Close the hood and grill for 4 minutes without flipping.
4. Meanwhile, in a small bowl, combine the remaining 3 tablespoons of honey, lime juice, and 1 tablespoon of reserved pineapple juice.
5. When cooking is complete, place the fruit in a large bowl and toss with the honey mixture. Serve immediately.

Bell Pepper, Onion, and Mushroom Frittata
Prep time: 10 minutes | Cook time: 10 minutes | Serves 4

4 large eggs
¼ cup whole milk
Sea salt, to taste
Freshly ground black pepper, to taste
½ bell pepper, seeded and diced
½ onion, chopped
4 cremini mushrooms, sliced
½ cup shredded Cheddar cheese

1. In a medium bowl, whisk together the eggs and milk. Season with the salt and pepper. Add the bell pepper, onion, mushrooms, and cheese. Mix until well combined.
2. Select BAKE, set the temperature to 400°F (205°C), and set the time to 10 minutes. Select START/STOP to begin preheating.
3. Meanwhile, pour the egg mixture into the Ninja Multi-Purpose Pan or baking pan, spreading evenly.
4. When the unit beeps to signify it has preheated, place the pan directly in the pot. Close the hood and cook for 10 minutes, or until lightly golden.

Stuffed Bell Pepper with Cheddar Bacon
Prep time: 10 minutes | Cook time: 10 minutes | Serves 4

1 cup shredded Cheddar cheese
4 slices bacon, cooked and chopped
4 bell peppers, seeded and tops removed
4 large eggs
Sea salt, to taste
Freshly ground black pepper, to taste
Chopped fresh parsley, for garnish

1. Insert the Crisper Basket and close the hood. Select AIR CRISP, set the temperature to 390°F (199°C), and set the time to 15 minutes. Select START/STOP to begin preheating.
2. Meanwhile, divide the cheese and bacon between the bell peppers. Crack one of the eggs into each bell pepper, and season with salt and pepper.
3. When the unit beeps to signify it has preheated, place each bell pepper in the basket. Close the hood and cook for 10 to 15 minutes, until the egg whites are cooked and the yolks are slightly runny.
4. Remove the peppers from the basket, garnish with parsley, and serve.

Glazed Strawberry Toast
Prep time: 5 minutes | Cook time: 8 minutes | Makes 4 toasts

4 slices bread, ½-inch thick
1 cup sliced strawberries
1 teaspoon sugar
Cooking spray

1. On a clean work surface, lay the bread slices and spritz one side of each slice of bread with cooking spray.
2. Place the bread slices in the air fryer basket, sprayed side down. Top with the strawberries and a sprinkle of sugar.
3. Select Air Fry, Super Convection, set temperature to 375°F (190°C), and set time to 8 minutes. Select Start/Stop to begin preheating.
4. Once preheated, place the basket on the air fry position.
5. When cooking is complete, the toast should be well browned on each side. Remove from the Vortex to a plate and serve.

Chapter 4
Vegan and Vegetarian

Lemony-Honey Roasted Radishes
Prep time: 10 minutes | Cook time: 17 minutes | Serves 4

1 pound (454 g) radishes, with green leaves attached
1 tablespoon extra-virgin olive oil
1 tablespoon white balsamic vinegar
1 preserved lemon, flesh discarded, rind cut into shreds, plus 2 tablespoons brine from the jar, plus more if needed
1 tablespoon unsalted butter
Sea salt flakes and freshly ground black pepper, to taste
1½ tablespoons clear honey
Leaves from 6 mint sprigs, torn

1. Wash the radishes well and remove their leaves.
2. Halve the radishes lengthwise. Put them in a baking pan with the olive oil, white balsamic, half the preserved lemon brine, and all the butter. Season.
3. Select Bake. Set temperature to 400°F (205°C) and set time to 17 minutes. Select Start to begin preheating.
4. Once preheated, slide the pan into the Vortex.
5. After 7 minutes, add the remaining tablespoon of brine and the honey. Shake the pan around and return to the Vortex for a final 10 minutes.
6. Transfer to a warmed serving dish and mix in the reserved radish leaves; they will wilt in the heat. Stir in the shredded preserved lemon rind and taste for seasoning. Scatter on the mint leaves and serve.

Stuffed Peppers with Cheese and Basil
Prep time: 10 minutes | Cook time: 40 minutes | Serves 6

6 medium bell peppers
A little extra-virgin olive oil
5½ ounces (156 g) ricotta (fresh rather than ultra-pasteurized, if possible)
10½ ounces (297 g) soft goat cheese
1 cup finely grated Parmesan cheese
Sea salt flakes and freshly ground black pepper, to taste
1 cup basil leaves, torn
1 large egg
1 garlic clove, crushed
1 tablespoon toasted pine nuts (optional)

1. Halve the peppers, deseed them, brush them with olive oil, and put them into a gratin dish from which they can be served.
2. Drain the ricotta and the goat cheese. Mix together all three cheeses with seasoning, the basil, egg, and garlic, gently mashing. Add the pine nuts if you are using them.
3. Spoon the mixture into the pepper halves and transfer the stuffed peppers to a baking pan.
4. Select Bake. Set temperature to 375°F (190°C) and set time to 40 minutes. Select Start to begin preheating.
5. Once preheated, slide the pan into the Vortex. When done, the filling should be golden and souffléd and the peppers completely tender when pierced with a sharp knife. If they're not ready, return them to the Vortex for an extra 5 to 10 minutes, then test again.

Cheesy Eggplant with Chili Smoked Almonds
Prep time: 10 minutes | Cook time: 45 minutes | Serves 6

3¾ pounds (1.7 kg) globe eggplants
5 tablespoons extra-virgin olive oil
2 teaspoons harissa
Sea salt flakes and freshly ground black pepper, to taste
2 garlic cloves, finely grated
Juice of ½ lemon, or to taste
3½ ounces (99 g) goat curd or soft creamy goat cheese
1 tablespoon smoked almonds, roughly chopped (you want quite big bits)
2 red Fresno chilies, halved, seeded, and very thinly sliced
Leaves from 1 rosemary sprig, chopped
Warm flatbread or toasted sourdough bread, to serve

1. Put the eggplants in a baking pan and brush lightly with some of the olive oil. Pierce each a few times with the tines of a fork.
2. Select Bake. Set temperature to 400°F (205°C) and set time to 45 minutes. Select Start to begin preheating.
3. Once preheated, slide the pan into the Vortex.
4. When done, the eggplants will be completely soft and look a bit deflated.
5. Leave until cool enough to handle, then slit the skins and scoop the flesh out into a bowl. Chop the flesh. Mash, and add about 3½ tablespoons of the oil, the harissa, salt, pepper, garlic, and lemon juice to taste. Put this into a warmed serving bowl and scatter the goat cheese on top.
6. Heat the remaining extra-virgin olive oil in a frying pan and quickly fry the smoked almonds, chilies, and rosemary together. Pour this over the roast eggplants and serve with bread.

Butternut Squash with Goat Cheese
Prep time: 5 minutes | Cook time: 20 minutes | Serves 2

1 pound (454 g) butternut squash, cut into wedges
2 tablespoons olive oil
1 tablespoon dried rosemary
Salt, to salt
1 cup crumbled goat cheese
1 tablespoon maple syrup

1. Toss the squash wedges with the olive oil, rosemary, and salt in a large bowl until well coated.
2. Transfer the squash wedges to the perforated pan, spreading them out in as even a layer as possible.
3. Select Air Fry. Set temperature to 350°F (180°C) and set time to 20 minutes. Press Start to begin preheating.
4. Once preheated, place the pan into the Vortex.
5. After 10 minutes, remove from the Vortex and flip the squash. Return the pan to the Vortex and continue cooking for 10 minutes.
6. When cooking is complete, the squash should be golden brown. Remove the pan from the Vortex. Sprinkle the goat cheese on top and serve drizzled with the maple syrup.

Double Cheese Roasted Asparagus

Prep time: 5 minutes | Cook time: 10 minutes | Serves 4

⅔ pound (302 g) asparagus spears, of medium thickness
Extra-virgin olive oil
Sea salt flakes and freshly ground black pepper, to taste
4½ ounces (127 g) ricotta cheese (fresh rather than ultra-pasteurized, if possible)
Pecorino cheese, or Parmesan cheese, shaved

1. Trim the woody ends from the asparagus spears, put them on an sheet pan with a slight lip, and drizzle with olive oil. Season with salt.
2. Select Bake. Set temperature to 400°F (205°C) and set time to 10 minutes. Select Start to begin preheating.
3. Once preheated, slide the pan into the Vortex.
4. When done, the asparagus spears will be tender.
5. Put the asparagus on a serving plate. Scatter the ricotta in nuggets over the top, followed by the shaved pecorino or Parmesan cheese. Season with salt and pepper, pour on more olive oil, and serve immediately.

Golden Potato, Carrot and Onion

Prep time: 10 minutes | Cook time: 38 minutes | Serves 4

2 cups peeled and shredded potatoes
½ cup peeled and shredded carrots
¼ cup shredded onion
1 teaspoon salt
1 teaspoon dried rosemary
1 teaspoon dried cumin
3 tablespoons vegetable oil
Salt and freshly ground black pepper, to taste

1. Mix all the ingredients together in an ovenproof baking dish. Adjust the seasonings to taste. Cover the dish with aluminum foil.
2. Select Bake. Set temperature to 400°F (205°C) and set time to 30 minutes. Select Start to begin preheating.
3. Once preheated, slide the baking dish into the Vortex. When done, the vegetables will be tender. Remove the cover.
4. Select Broil. Set temperature to 400°F (205°C) and set time to 8 minutes. Slide the pan into the Vortex. When done, the top will be browned.

Potato Shells with Cheddar and Bacon

Prep time: 5 minutes | Cook time: 8 minutes | Serves 4

4 tablespoons shredded reduced-fat Cheddar cheese
4 slices lean turkey bacon, cooked and crumbled
4 potato shells
4 tablespoons nonfat sour cream
4 teaspoons chopped fresh or frozen chives
Salt and freshly ground black pepper, to taste

1. Sprinkle 1 tablespoon Cheddar cheese and 1 tablespoon crumbled bacon into each potato shell. Place the shells on a broiling rack with a pan underneath.
2. Select Broil. Set temperature to 400°F (205°C) and set time to 8 minutes. Select Start to begin preheating.
3. Once preheated, slide the pan into the Vortex.
4. When done, the cheese will be melted and the shells lightly browned. Spoon 1 tablespoon sour cream into each shell and sprinkle with 1 teaspoon chives. Add salt and pepper to taste.

Butternut Squash and Parsnip with Thyme

Prep time: 5 minutes | Cook time: 16 minutes | Serves 2

1 parsnip, sliced
1 cup sliced butternut squash
1 small red onion, cut into wedges
½ chopped celery stalk
1 tablespoon chopped fresh thyme
2 teaspoons olive oil
Salt and black pepper, to taste

1. Toss all the ingredients in a large bowl until the vegetables are well coated.
2. Transfer the vegetables to the perforated pan.
3. Select Air Fry. Set temperature to 380°F (193°C) and set time to 16 minutes. Press Start to begin preheating.
4. Once preheated, place the pan into the Vortex. Stir the vegetables halfway through the cooking time.
5. When cooking is complete, the vegetables should be golden brown and tender. Remove from the Vortex and serve warm.

Ginger-Pepper Broccoli

Prep time: 5 minutes | Cook time: 10 minutes | Serves 2

12 ounces (340 g) broccoli florets
2 tablespoons Asian hot chili oil
1 teaspoon ground Sichuan peppercorns (or black pepper)
2 garlic cloves, finely chopped
1 (2-inch) piece fresh ginger, peeled and finely chopped
Kosher salt and freshly ground black pepper

1. Toss the broccoli florets with the chili oil, Sichuan peppercorns, garlic, ginger, salt, and pepper in a mixing bowl until thoroughly coated.
2. Transfer the broccoli florets to the perforated pan.
3. Select Air Fry. Set temperature to 375°F (190°C) and set time to 10 minutes. Press Start to begin preheating.
4. Once preheated, place the pan into the Vortex. Stir the broccoli florets halfway through the cooking time.
5. When cooking is complete, the broccoli florets should be lightly browned and tender. Remove the broccoli from the Vortex and serve on a plate.

Parmesan Brussels Sprout

Prep time: 10 minutes | Cook time: 20 minutes | Serves 4

1 pound (454 g) fresh Brussels sprouts, trimmed
1 tablespoon olive oil
½ teaspoon salt
⅛ teaspoon pepper
¼ cup grated Parmesan cheese

1. In a large bowl, combine the Brussels sprouts with olive oil, salt, and pepper and toss until evenly coated.
2. Spread the Brussels sprouts evenly in the perforated pan.
3. Select Air Fry. Set temperature to 330°F (166°C) and set time to 20 minutes. Press Start to begin preheating.
4. Once preheated, place the pan into the Vortex. Stir the Brussels sprouts twice during cooking.
5. When cooking is complete, the Brussels sprouts should be golden brown and crisp. Remove the pan from the Vortex. Sprinkle the grated Parmesan cheese on top and serve warm.

Roasted Veggie Rice with Eggs

Prep time: 5 minutes | Cook time: 12 minutes | Serves 4

2 teaspoons melted butter
1 cup chopped mushrooms
1 cup cooked rice
1 cup peas
1 carrot, chopped
1 red onion, chopped
1 garlic clove, minced
Salt and black pepper, to taste
2 hard-boiled eggs, grated
1 tablespoon soy sauce

1. Coat a baking dish with melted butter.
2. Stir together the mushrooms, cooked rice, peas, carrot, onion, garlic, salt, and pepper in a large bowl until well mixed. Pour the mixture into the prepared baking dish.
3. Select Roast. Set temperature to 380°F (193°C) and set time to 12 minutes. Press Start to begin preheating.
4. Once preheated, place the baking dish into the Vortex.
5. When cooking is complete, remove from the Vortex. Divide the mixture among four plates. Serve warm with a sprinkle of grated eggs and a drizzle of soy sauce.

Air Fried Tofu Sticks

Prep time: 5 minutes | Cook time: 14 minutes | Serves 4

2 tablespoons olive oil, divided
½ cup flour
½ cup crushed cornflakes
Salt and black pepper, to taste
14 ounces (397 g) firm tofu, cut into ½-inch-thick strips

1. Grease the perforated pan with 1 tablespoon of olive oil.
2. Combine the flour, cornflakes, salt, and pepper on a plate.
3. Dredge the tofu strips in the flour mixture until they are completely coated. Transfer the tofu strips to the greased pan.
4. Drizzle the remaining 1 tablespoon of olive oil over the top of tofu strips.
5. Select Air Fry. Set temperature to 360°F (182°C) and set time to 14 minutes. Press Start to begin preheating.
6. Once preheated, place the pan into the Vortex. Flip the tofu strips halfway through the cooking time.
7. When cooking is complete, the tofu strips should be crispy. Remove from the Vortex and serve warm.

Garlic Eggplant Slices with Parsley
Prep time: 5 minutes | Cook time: 12 minutes | Serves 4

1 cup flour
4 eggs
Salt, to taste
2 cups bread crumbs
1 teaspoon Italian seasoning
2 eggplants, sliced
2 garlic cloves, sliced
2 tablespoons chopped parsley
Cooking spray

1. Spritz the perforated pan with cooking spray. Set aside.
2. On a plate, place the flour. In a shallow bowl, whisk the eggs with salt. In another shallow bowl, combine the bread crumbs and Italian seasoning.
3. Dredge the eggplant slices, one at a time, in the flour, then in the whisked eggs, finally in the bread crumb mixture to coat well.
4. Lay the coated eggplant slices in the perforated pan.
5. Select Air Fry. Set temperature to 390°F (199°C) and set time to 12 minutes. Press Start to begin preheating.
6. Once preheated, place the pan into the Vortex. Flip the eggplant slices halfway through the cooking time.
7. When cooking is complete, the eggplant slices should be golden brown and crispy. Transfer the eggplant slices to a plate and sprinkle the garlic and parsley on top before serving.

Cayenne Green Beans
Prep time: 5 minutes | Cook time: 15 minutes | Serves 4

½ cup flour
2 eggs
1 cup panko bread crumbs
½ cup grated Parmesan cheese
1 teaspoon cayenne pepper
Salt and black pepper, to taste
1½ pounds (680 g) green beans

1. In a bowl, place the flour. In a separate bowl, lightly beat the eggs. In a separate shallow bowl, thoroughly combine the bread crumbs, cheese, cayenne pepper, salt, and pepper.
2. Dip the green beans in the flour, then in the beaten eggs, finally in the bread crumb mixture to coat well. Transfer the green beans to the perforated pan.
3. Select Air Fry. Set temperature to 400°F (205°C) and set time to 15 minutes. Press Start to begin preheating.
4. Once preheated, place the pan into the Vortex. Stir the green beans halfway through the cooking time.
5. When cooking is complete, remove from the Vortex to a bowl and serve.

Honey Baby Carrots with Dill
Prep time: 5 minutes | Cook time: 12 minutes | Serves 4

1 pound (454 g) baby carrots
2 tablespoons olive oil
1 tablespoon honey
1 teaspoon dried dill
Salt and black pepper, to taste

1. Place the carrots in a large bowl. Add the olive oil, honey, dill, salt, and pepper and toss to coat well.
2. Transfer the carrots to the perforated pan.
3. Select Roast. Set temperature to 350°F (180°C) and set time to 12 minutes. Press Start to begin preheating.
4. Once preheated, place the pan into the Vortex. Stir the carrots once during cooking.
5. When cooking is complete, the carrots should be crisp-tender. Remove from the Vortex and serve warm.

Garlic Tofu with Basil
Prep time: 5 minutes | Cook time: 10 minutes | Serves 2

1 tablespoon soy sauce
1 tablespoon water
⅓ teaspoon garlic powder
⅓ teaspoon onion powder
⅓ teaspoon dried oregano
⅓ teaspoon dried basil
Black pepper, to taste
6 ounces (170 g) extra firm tofu, pressed and cubed

1. In a large mixing bowl, whisk together the soy sauce, water, garlic powder, onion powder, oregano, basil, and black pepper. Add the tofu cubes, stirring to coat, and let them marinate for 10 minutes.
2. Arrange the tofu in the perforated pan.
3. Select Bake. Set temperature to 390°F (199°C) and set time to 10 minutes. Press Start to begin preheating.
4. Once preheated, place the pan into the Vortex. Flip the tofu halfway through the cooking time.
5. When cooking is complete, the tofu should be crisp.
6. Remove from the Vortex to a plate and serve.

Zucchini Quesadilla with Gouda Cheese
Prep time: 5 minutes | Cook time: 10 minutes | Serves 1

1 teaspoon olive oil
2 flour tortillas
¼ zucchini, sliced
¼ yellow bell pepper, sliced
¼ cup shredded Gouda cheese
1 tablespoon chopped cilantro
½ green onion, sliced

1. Coat the perforated pan with 1 teaspoon of olive oil.
2. Arrange a flour tortilla in the perforated pan and scatter the top with zucchini, bell pepper, Gouda cheese, cilantro, and green onion. Place the other flour tortilla on top.
3. Select Air Fry. Set temperature to 390°F (199°C) and set time to 10 minutes. Press Start to begin preheating.
4. Once preheated, place the pan into the Vortex.
5. When cooking is complete, the tortillas should be lightly browned and the vegetables should be tender. Remove from the Vortex and cool for 5 minutes before slicing into wedges.

Parmesan Fennel with Red Pepper
Prep time: 10 minutes | Cook time: 30 minutes | Serves 6 to 8

4 fennel bulbs
3 tablespoons extra-virgin olive oil
2 garlic cloves, finely grated
3 teaspoons fennel seeds, coarsely crushed in a mortar
3 teaspoons crushed red pepper
Sea salt flakes and freshly ground black pepper, to taste
½ cup finely grated Parmesan cheese

1. Trim the tips of the fennel bulbs, halve the bulbs and remove any thicker or discolored outer leaves. Cut each half into ¾-in thick wedges, keeping them intact at the base. Toss in a bowl with the olive oil, garlic, fennel seeds, crushed red pepper, any reserved fennel fronds, and plenty of seasoning. Put into a gratin dish and cover tightly with foil.
2. Select Bake. Set temperature to 400°F (205°C) and set time to 30 minutes. Select Start to begin preheating.
3. Once preheated, slide the pan into the Vortex.
4. Bake for about 20 minutes, then remove the foil, sprinkle on the Parmesan, and return to the Vortex for a final 10 minutes, or until the fennel is tender (check it by piercing a piece with a sharp knife) and the top is golden.

Curried Cauliflower with Cashews
Prep time: 5 minutes | Cook time: 12 minutes | Serves 2

4 cups cauliflower florets (about half a large head)
1 tablespoon olive oil
1 teaspoon curry powder
Salt, to taste
½ cup toasted, chopped cashews, for garnish
Yogurt Sauce:
¼ cup plain yogurt
2 tablespoons sour cream
1 teaspoon honey
1 teaspoon lemon juice
Pinch cayenne pepper
Salt, to taste
1 tablespoon chopped fresh cilantro, plus leaves for garnish

1. In a large mixing bowl, toss the cauliflower florets with the olive oil, curry powder, and salt.
2. Place the cauliflower florets in the perforated pan.
3. Select Air Fry. Set temperature to 400°F (205°C) and set time to 12 minutes. Press Start to begin preheating.
4. Once preheated, place the pan into the Vortex. Stir the cauliflower florets twice during cooking.
5. When cooking is complete, the cauliflower should be golden brown.
6. Meanwhile, mix all the ingredients for the yogurt sauce in a small bowl and whisk to combine.
7. Remove the cauliflower from the Vortex and drizzle with the yogurt sauce. Scatter the toasted cashews and cilantro on top and serve immediately.

Balsamic-Glazed Beets
Prep time: 5 minutes | Cook time: 10 minutes | Serves 2

Beet:
2 beets, cubed
2 tablespoons olive oil
2 springs rosemary, chopped
Salt and black pepper, to taste
Balsamic Glaze:
⅓ cup balsamic vinegar
1 tablespoon honey

1. Combine the beets, olive oil, rosemary, salt, and pepper in a mixing bowl and toss until the beets are completely coated.
2. Place the beets in the perforated pan.
3. Select Air Fry. Set temperature to 400°F (205°C) and set time to 10 minutes. Press Start to begin preheating.
4. Once preheated, place the pan into the Vortex. Stir the vegetables halfway through.
5. When cooking is complete, the beets should be crisp and browned at the edges.
6. Meanwhile, make the balsamic glaze: Place the balsamic vinegar and honey in a small saucepan and bring to a boil over medium heat. When the sauce boils, reduce the heat to medium-low heat and simmer until the liquid is reduced by half.
7. When ready, remove the beets from the Vortex to a platter. Pour the balsamic glaze over the top and serve immediately.

Fried Root Veggies with Thyme
Prep time: 10 minutes | Cook time: 22 minutes | Serves 4

2 carrots, sliced
2 potatoes, cut into chunks
1 rutabaga, cut into chunks
1 turnip, cut into chunks
1 beet, cut into chunks
8 shallots, halved
2 tablespoons olive oil
Salt and black pepper, to taste
2 tablespoons tomato pesto
2 tablespoons water
2 tablespoons chopped fresh thyme

1. Toss the carrots, potatoes, rutabaga, turnip, beet, shallots, olive oil, salt, and pepper in a large mixing bowl until the root vegetables are evenly coated.
2. Place the root vegetables in the perforated pan.
3. Select Air Fry. Set temperature to 400°F (205°C) and set time to 22 minutes. Press Start to begin preheating.
4. Once preheated, place the pan into the Vortex. Stir the vegetables twice during cooking.
5. When cooking is complete, the vegetables should be tender.
6. Meanwhile, in a small bowl, whisk together the tomato pesto and water until smooth.
7. When ready, remove the root vegetables from the Vortex to a platter. Drizzle with the tomato pesto mixture and sprinkle with the thyme. Serve immediately.

Halloumi Zucchinis and Eggplant
Prep time: 5 minutes | Cook time: 14 minutes | Serves 2

2 zucchinis, cut into even chunks
1 large eggplant, peeled, cut into chunks
1 large carrot, cut into chunks
6 ounces (170 g) halloumi cheese, cubed
2 teaspoons olive oil
Salt and black pepper, to taste
1 teaspoon dried mixed herbs

1. Combine the zucchinis, eggplant, carrot, cheese, olive oil, salt, and pepper in a large bowl and toss to coat well.
2. Spread the mixture evenly in the perforated pan.
3. Select Air Fry. Set temperature to 340°F (171°C) and set time to 14 minutes. Press Start to begin preheating.
4. Once preheated, place the pan into the Vortex. Stir the mixture once during cooking.
5. When cooking is complete, they should be crispy and golden. Remove from the Vortex and serve topped with mixed herbs.

Red Chili Okra
Prep time: 5 minutes | Cook time: 10 minutes | Serves 4

3 tablespoons sour cream
2 tablespoons flour
2 tablespoons semolina
½ teaspoon red chili powder
Salt and black pepper, to taste
1 pound (454 g) okra, halved
Cooking spray

1. Spray the perforated pan with cooking spray. Set aside.
2. In a shallow bowl, place the sour cream. In another shallow bowl, thoroughly combine the flour, semolina, red chili powder, salt, and pepper.
3. Dredge the okra in the sour cream, then roll in the flour mixture until evenly coated. Transfer the okra to the perforated pan.
4. Select Air Fry. Set temperature to 400°F (205°C) and set time to 10 minutes. Press Start to begin preheating.
5. Once preheated, place the pan into the Vortex. Flip the okra halfway through the cooking time.
6. When cooking is complete, the okra should be golden brown and crispy. Remove the pan from the Vortex. Cool for 5 minutes before serving.

Garlic Bell Peppers with Marjoram
Prep time: 10 minutes | Cook time: 22 minutes | Serves 4

1 green bell pepper, sliced into 1-inch strips
1 red bell pepper, sliced into 1-inch strips
1 orange bell pepper, sliced into 1-inch strips
1 yellow bell pepper, sliced into 1-inch strips
2 tablespoons olive oil, divided
½ teaspoon dried marjoram
Pinch salt
Freshly ground black pepper, to taste
1 head garlic

1. Toss the bell peppers with 1 tablespoon of olive oil in a large bowl until well coated. Season with the marjoram, salt, and pepper. Toss again and set aside.
2. Cut off the top of a head of garlic. Place the garlic cloves on a large square of aluminum foil. Drizzle the top with the remaining 1 tablespoon of olive oil and wrap the garlic cloves in foil.
3. Transfer the garlic to the perforated pan.
4. Select Roast. Set temperature to 330°F (166°C) and set time to 15 minutes. Press Start to begin preheating.
5. Once preheated, place the pan into the Vortex.
6. After 15 minutes, remove the perforated pan from the Vortex and add the bell peppers. Return to the Vortex and set time to 7 minutes.
7. When cooking is complete or until the garlic is soft and the bell peppers are tender.
8. Transfer the cooked bell peppers to a plate. Remove the garlic and unwrap the foil. Let the garlic rest for a few minutes. Once cooled, squeeze the roasted garlic cloves out of their skins and add them to the plate of bell peppers. Stir well and serve immediately.

Garlic Ratatouille

Prep time: 15 minutes | Cook time: 16 minutes | Serves 2

2 Roma tomatoes, thinly sliced
1 zucchini, thinly sliced
2 yellow bell peppers, sliced
2 garlic cloves, minced
2 tablespoons olive oil
2 tablespoons herbes de Provence
1 tablespoon vinegar
Salt and black pepper, to taste

1. Place the tomatoes, zucchini, bell peppers, garlic, olive oil, herbes de Provence, and vinegar in a large bowl and toss until the vegetables are evenly coated. Sprinkle with salt and pepper and toss again. Pour the vegetable mixture into a baking dish.
2. Select Roast. Set temperature to 390°F (199°C) and set time to 16 minutes. Press Start to begin preheating.
3. Once preheated, place the baking dish into the Vortex. Stir the vegetables halfway through.
4. When cooking is complete, the vegetables should be tender.
5. Let the vegetable mixture stand for 5 minutes in the Vortex before removing and serving.

Cauliflower with Teriyaki Sauce

Prep time: 5 minutes | Cook time: 14 minutes | Serves 4

½ cup soy sauce
⅓ cup water
1 tablespoon brown sugar
1 teaspoon sesame oil
1 teaspoon cornstarch
2 cloves garlic, chopped
½ teaspoon chili powder
1 big cauliflower head, cut into florets

1. Make the teriyaki sauce: In a small bowl, whisk together the soy sauce, water, brown sugar, sesame oil, cornstarch, garlic, and chili powder until well combined.
2. Place the cauliflower florets in a large bowl and drizzle the top with the prepared teriyaki sauce and toss to coat well.
3. Put the cauliflower florets in the perforated pan.
4. Select Air Fry. Set temperature to 340°F (171°C) and set time to 14 minutes. Press Start to begin preheating.
5. Once preheated, place the pan into the Vortex. Stir the cauliflower halfway through.
6. When cooking is complete, the cauliflower should be crisp-tender.
7. Let the cauliflower cool for 5 minutes before serving.

Onion-Stuffed Mushrooms

Prep time: 5 minutes | Cook time: 12 minutes | Serves 2

18 medium-sized white mushrooms
1 small onion, peeled and chopped
4 garlic cloves, peeled and minced
2 tablespoons olive oil
2 teaspoons cumin powder
A pinch ground allspice
Fine sea salt and freshly ground black pepper, to taste

1. On a clean work surface, remove the mushroom stems. Using a spoon, scoop out the mushroom gills and discard.
2. Thoroughly combine the onion, garlic, olive oil, cumin powder, allspice, salt, and pepper in a mixing bowl. Stuff the mushrooms evenly with the mixture.
3. Place the stuffed mushrooms in the perforated pan.
4. Select Roast. Set temperature to 345°F (174°C) and set time to 12 minutes. Press Start to begin preheating.
5. Once preheated, place the pan into the Vortex.
6. When cooking is complete, the mushroom should be browned.
7. Cool for 5 minutes before serving.

Garlic Turnip and Zucchini

Prep time: 5 minutes | Cook time: 18 minutes | Serves 4

3 turnips, sliced
1 large zucchini, sliced
1 large red onion, cut into rings
2 cloves garlic, crushed
1 tablespoon olive oil
Salt and black pepper, to taste

1. Put the turnips, zucchini, red onion, and garlic in a baking pan. Drizzle the olive oil over the top and sprinkle with the salt and pepper.
2. Select Bake. Set temperature to 330°F (166°C) and set time to 18 minutes. Press Start to begin preheating.
3. Once preheated, place the pan into the Vortex.
4. When cooking is complete, the vegetables should be tender. Remove from the Vortex and serve on a plate.

Mozzarella Walnut Stuffed Mushrooms
Prep time: 5 minutes | Cook time: 10 minutes | Serves 4

4 large portobello mushrooms
1 tablespoon canola oil
½ cup shredded Mozzarella cheese
⅓ cup minced walnuts
2 tablespoons chopped fresh parsley
Cooking spray

1. Spritz the perforated pan with cooking spray.
2. On a clean work surface, remove the mushroom stems. Scoop out the gills with a spoon and discard. Coat the mushrooms with canola oil. Top each mushroom evenly with the shredded Mozzarella cheese, followed by the minced walnuts.
3. Arrange the mushrooms in the perforated pan.
4. Select Roast. Set temperature to 350°F (180°C) and set time to 10 minutes. Press Start to begin preheating.
5. Once preheated, place the pan into the Vortex.
6. When cooking is complete, the mushroom should be golden brown.
7. Transfer the mushrooms to a plate and sprinkle the parsley on top for garnish before serving.

Tomato-Stuffed Portobello Mushrooms
Prep time: 5 minutes | Cook time: 8 minutes | Serves 4

4 portobello mushrooms, stem removed
1 tablespoon olive oil
1 tomato, diced
½ green bell pepper, diced
½ small red onion, diced
½ teaspoon garlic powder
Salt and black pepper, to taste
½ cup grated Mozzarella cheese

1. Using a spoon to scoop out the gills of the mushrooms and discard them. Brush the mushrooms with the olive oil.
2. In a mixing bowl, stir together the remaining ingredients except the Mozzarella cheese. Using a spoon to stuff each mushroom with the filling and scatter the Mozzarella cheese on top.
3. Arrange the mushrooms in the perforated pan.
4. Select Roast. Set temperature to 330°F (166°C) and set time to 8 minutes. Press Start to begin preheating.
5. Once preheated, place the pan into the Vortex.
6. When cooking is complete, the cheese should be melted.
7. Serve warm.

Spinach-Stuffed Beefsteak Tomatoes
Prep time: 10 minutes | Cook time: 18 minutes | Serves 4

4 medium beefsteak tomatoes, rinsed
½ cup grated carrot
1 medium onion, chopped
1 garlic clove, minced
2 teaspoons olive oil
2 cups fresh baby spinach
¼ cup crumbled low-sodium feta cheese
½ teaspoon dried basil

1. On your cutting board, cut a thin slice off the top of each tomato. Scoop out a ¼- to ½-inch-thick tomato pulp and place the tomatoes upside down on paper towels to drain. Set aside.
2. Stir together the carrot, onion, garlic, and olive oil in a baking pan.
3. Select Bake. Set temperature to 350°F (180°C) and set time to 5 minutes. Press Start to begin preheating.
4. Once preheated, place the pan into the Vortex. Stir the vegetables halfway through.
5. When cooking is complete, the carrot should be crisp-tender.
6. Remove the pan from the Vortex and stir in the spinach, feta cheese, and basil.
7. Spoon ¼ of the vegetable mixture into each tomato and transfer the stuffed tomatoes to the Vortex. Set time to 13 minutes on Bake.
8. When cooking is complete, the filling should be hot and the tomatoes should be lightly caramelized.
9. Let the tomatoes cool for 5 minutes and serve.

Breaded Zucchini Chips with Parmesan
Prep time: 5 minutes | Cook time: 14 minutes | Serves 4

2 egg whites
Salt and black pepper, to taste
½ cup seasoned bread crumbs
2 tablespoons grated Parmesan cheese
¼ teaspoon garlic powder
2 medium zucchini, sliced
Cooking spray

1. Spritz the perforated pan with cooking spray.
2. In a bowl, beat the egg whites with salt and pepper. In a separate bowl, thoroughly combine the bread crumbs, Parmesan cheese, and garlic powder.
3. Dredge the zucchini slices in the egg white, then coat in the bread crumb mixture.
4. Arrange the zucchini slices in the perforated pan.
5. Select Air Fry. Set temperature to 400°F (205°C) and set time to 14 minutes. Press Start to begin preheating.
6. Once preheated, place the pan into the Vortex. Flip the zucchini halfway through.
7. When cooking is complete, the zucchini should be tender.
8. Remove from the Vortex to a plate and serve.

Rice and Olives Stuffed Peppers
Prep time: 5 minutes | Cook time: 16 to 17 minutes | Serves 4

4 red bell peppers, tops sliced off
2 cups cooked rice
1 cup crumbled feta cheese
1 onion, chopped
¼ cup sliced kalamata olives
¾ cup tomato sauce
1 tablespoon Greek seasoning
Salt and black pepper, to taste
2 tablespoons chopped fresh dill, for serving

1. Microwave the red bell peppers for 1 to 2 minutes until tender.
2. When ready, transfer the red bell peppers to a plate to cool.
3. Mix the cooked rice, feta cheese, onion, kalamata olives, tomato sauce, Greek seasoning, salt, and pepper in a medium bowl and stir until well combined.
4. Divide the rice mixture among the red bell peppers and transfer to a greased baking dish.
5. Select Bake. Set temperature to 360°F (182°C) and set time to 15 minutes. Press Start to begin preheating.
6. Once preheated, place the baking dish into the Vortex.
7. When cooking is complete, the rice should be heated through and the vegetables should be soft.
8. Remove from the Vortex and serve with the dill sprinkled on top.

Stuffed Bell Peppers with Cream Cheese
Prep time: 5 minutes | Cook time: 15 minutes | Serves 2

2 bell peppers, tops and seeds removed
Salt and pepper, to taste
⅔ cup cream cheese
2 tablespoons mayonnaise
1 tablespoon chopped fresh celery stalks
Cooking spray

1. Spritz the perforated pan with cooking spray.
2. Place the peppers in the perforated pan.
3. Select Roast. Set temperature to 400°F (205°C) and set time to 10 minutes. Press Start to begin preheating.
4. Once preheated, place the pan into the Vortex. Flip the peppers halfway through.
5. When cooking is complete, the peppers should be crisp-tender.
6. Remove from the Vortex to a plate and season with salt and pepper.
7. Mix the cream cheese, mayo, and celery in a small bowl and stir to incorporate. Evenly stuff the roasted peppers with the cream cheese mixture with a spoon. Serve immediately.

Chickpea-Stuffed Bell Peppers
Prep time: 10 minutes | Cook time: 18 minutes | Serves 4

4 medium red, green, or yellow bell peppers, halved and deseeded
4 tablespoons extra-virgin olive oil, divided
½ teaspoon kosher salt, divided
1 (15-ounce / 425-g) can chickpeas
1½ cups cooked white rice
½ cup diced roasted red peppers
¼ cup chopped parsley
½ small onion, finely chopped
3 garlic cloves, minced
½ teaspoon cumin
¼ teaspoon freshly ground black pepper
¾ cup panko bread crumbs

1. Brush the peppers inside and out with 1 tablespoon of olive oil. Season the insides with ¼ teaspoon of kosher salt. Arrange the peppers on the sheet pan, cut side up.
2. Place the chickpeas with their liquid into a large bowl. Lightly mash the beans with a potato masher. Sprinkle with the remaining ¼ teaspoon of kosher salt and 1 tablespoon of olive oil. Add the rice, red peppers, parsley, onion, garlic, cumin, and black pepper to the bowl and stir to incorporate.
3. Divide the mixture among the bell pepper halves.
4. Stir together the remaining 2 tablespoons of olive oil and panko in a small bowl. Top the pepper halves with the panko mixture.
5. Select Roast. Set temperature to 375°F (190°C) and set time to 18 minutes. Press Start to begin preheating.
6. Once preheated, place the pan into the Vortex.
7. When done, the peppers should be slightly wrinkled, and the panko should be golden brown.
8. Remove from the Vortex and serve on a plate.

Chapter 5
Vegetable Sides

Garlic Potatoes with Heavy Cream
Prep time: 5 minutes | Cook time: 15 to 20 minutes | Serves 4

2 cup sliced frozen potatoes, thawed
3 cloves garlic, minced
Pinch salt
Freshly ground black pepper, to taste
¾ cup heavy cream

1. Toss the potatoes with the garlic, salt, and black pepper in a baking pan until evenly coated. Pour the heavy cream over the top.
2. Select Bake. Set temperature to 380°F (193°C) and set time to 15 minutes. Press Start to begin preheating.
3. Once preheated, place the pan into the Vortex.
4. When cooking is complete, the potatoes should be tender and the top golden brown. Check for doneness and bake for another 5 minutes if needed. Remove from the Vortex and serve hot.

Maple Garlic Brussels Sprout
Prep time: 10 minutes | Cook time: 11 minutes | Serves 4

2½ cups trimmed Brussels sprouts
Sauce:
1½ teaspoons mellow white miso
1½ tablespoons maple syrup
1 teaspoon toasted sesame oil
1 teaspoons tamari or shoyu
1 teaspoon grated fresh ginger
2 large garlic cloves, finely minced
¼ to ½ teaspoon red chili flakes
Cooking spray

1. Spritz the perforated pan with cooking spray.
2. Arrange the Brussels sprouts in the perforated pan and spray them with cooking spray.
3. Select Air Fry. Set temperature to 392°F (200°C) and set time to 11 minutes. Press Start to begin preheating.
4. Once preheated, place the pan into the Vortex.
5. After 6 minutes, remove the pan from the Vortex. Flip the Brussels sprouts and spritz with cooking spray again. Return to the Vortex and continue cooking for 5 minutes more.
6. Meanwhile, make the sauce: Stir together the miso and maple syrup in a medium bowl. Add the sesame oil, tamari, ginger, garlic, and red chili flakes and whisk to combine.
7. When cooking is complete, the Brussels sprouts should be crisp-tender. Transfer the Brussels sprouts to the bowl of sauce, tossing to coat well. If you prefer a saltier taste, you can add additional ½ teaspoon tamari to the sauce. Serve immediately.

Garlic Butternut Squash Croquettes
Prep time: 5 minutes | Cook time: 17 minutes | Serves 4

⅓ butternut squash, peeled and grated
⅓ cup all-purpose flour
2 eggs, whisked
4 cloves garlic, minced
1½ tablespoons olive oil
1 teaspoon fine sea salt
⅓ teaspoon freshly ground black pepper, or more to taste
⅓ teaspoon dried sage
A pinch of ground allspice

1. Line the perforated pan with parchment paper. Set aside.
2. In a mixing bowl, stir together all the ingredients until well combined.
3. Make the squash croquettes: Use a small cookie scoop to drop tablespoonfuls of the squash mixture onto a lightly floured surface and shape into balls with your hands. Transfer them to the perforated pan.
4. Select Air Fry. Set temperature to 345°F (174°C) and set time to 17 minutes. Press Start to begin preheating.
5. Once preheated, place the pan into the Vortex.
6. When cooking is complete, the squash croquettes should be golden brown. Remove from the Vortex to a plate and serve warm.

Lime Sweet Potatoes with Allspice
Prep time: 5 minutes | Cook time: 22 minutes | Serves 4

5 garnet sweet potatoes, peeled and diced
1½ tablespoons fresh lime juice
1 tablespoon butter, melted
2 teaspoons tamarind paste
1½ teaspoon ground allspice
⅓ teaspoon white pepper
½ teaspoon turmeric powder
A few drops liquid stevia

1. In a large mixing bowl, combine all the ingredients and toss until the sweet potatoes are evenly coated. Place the sweet potatoes in the perforated pan.
2. Select Air Fry. Set temperature to 400°F (205°C) and set time to 22 minutes. Press Start to begin preheating.
3. Once preheated, place the pan into the Vortex. Stir the potatoes twice during cooking.
4. When cooking is complete, the potatoes should be crispy on the outside and soft on the inside. Let the potatoes cool for 5 minutes before serving.

Citrus Carrots with Balsamic Glaze
Prep time: 5 minutes | Cook time: 18 minutes | Serves 3

3 medium-size carrots, cut into 2-inch × ½-inch sticks
1 tablespoon orange juice
2 teaspoons balsamic vinegar
1 teaspoon maple syrup
1 teaspoon avocado oil
½ teaspoon dried rosemary
¼ teaspoon sea salt
¼ teaspoon lemon zest

1. Put the carrots in a baking pan and sprinkle with the orange juice, balsamic vinegar, maple syrup, avocado oil, rosemary, sea salt, finished by the lemon zest. Toss well.
2. Select Roast. Set temperature to 392°F (200°C) and set time to 18 minutes. Press Start to begin preheating.
3. Once preheated, place the pan into the Vortex. Stir the carrots several times during the cooking process.
4. When cooking is complete, the carrots should be nicely glazed and tender. Remove from the Vortex and serve hot.

Sesame Green Beans with Sriracha
Prep time: 5 minutes | Cook time: 8 minutes | Serves 4

1 tablespoon reduced-sodium soy sauce or tamari
½ tablespoon Sriracha sauce
4 teaspoons toasted sesame oil, divided
12 ounces (340 g) trimmed green beans
½ tablespoon toasted sesame seeds

1. Whisk together the soy sauce, Sriracha sauce, and 1 teaspoon of sesame oil in a small bowl until smooth. Set aside.
2. Toss the green beans with the remaining sesame oil in a large bowl until evenly coated.
3. Place the green beans in the perforated pan in a single layer.
4. Select Air Fry. Set temperature to 375°F (190°C) and set time to 8 minutes. Press Start to begin preheating.
5. Once preheated, place the pan into the Vortex. Stir the green beans halfway through the cooking time.
6. When cooking is complete, the green beans should be lightly charred and tender. Remove from the Vortex to a platter. Pour the prepared sauce over the top of green beans and toss well. Serve sprinkled with the toasted sesame seeds.

Corn Casserole with Swiss Cheese
Prep time: 5 minutes | Cook time: 15 minutes | Serves 4

2 cups frozen yellow corn
1 egg, beaten
3 tablespoons flour
½ cup grated Swiss or Havarti cheese
½ cup light cream
¼ cup milk
Pinch salt
Freshly ground black pepper, to taste
2 tablespoons butter, cut into cubes
Nonstick cooking spray

1. Spritz a baking pan with nonstick cooking spray.
2. Stir together the remaining ingredients except the butter in a medium bowl until well incorporated. Transfer the mixture to the prepared baking pan and scatter with the butter cubes.
3. Select Bake. Set temperature to 320°F (160°C) and set time to 15 minutes. Press Start to begin preheating.
4. Once preheated, place the pan into the Vortex.
5. When cooking is complete, the top should be golden brown and a toothpick inserted in the center should come out clean. Remove the pan from the Vortex. Let the casserole cool for 5 minutes before slicing into wedges and serving.

Garlic Zucchini Crisps
Prep time: 5 minutes | Cook time: 14 minutes | Serves 4

2 zucchini, sliced into ¼- to ½-inch-thick rounds (about 2 cups)
¼ teaspoon garlic granules
⅛ teaspoon sea salt
Freshly ground black pepper, to taste (optional)
Cooking spray

1. Spritz the perforated pan with cooking spray.
2. Put the zucchini rounds in the perforated pan, spreading them out as much as possible. Top with a sprinkle of garlic granules, sea salt, and black pepper (if desired). Spritz the zucchini rounds with cooking spray.
3. Select Roast. Set temperature to 392°F (200°C) and set time to 14 minutes. Press Start to begin preheating.
4. Once preheated, place the pan into the Vortex. Flip the zucchini rounds halfway through.
5. When cooking is complete, the zucchini rounds should be crisp-tender. Remove from the Vortex. Let them rest for 5 minutes and serve.

Parmesan Corn on the Cob
Prep time: 10 minutes | Cook time: 15 minutes | Serves 4

2 tablespoon olive oil, divided
2 tablespoons grated Parmesan cheese
1 teaspoon garlic powder
1 teaspoon chili powder
1 teaspoon ground cumin
1 teaspoon paprika
1 teaspoon salt
¼ teaspoon cayenne pepper (optional)
4 ears fresh corn, shucked

1. Grease the perforated pan with 1 tablespoon of olive oil. Set aside.
2. Combine the Parmesan cheese, garlic powder, chili powder, cumin, paprika, salt, and cayenne pepper (if desired) in a small bowl and stir to mix well.
3. Lightly coat the ears of corn with the remaining 1 tablespoon of olive oil. Rub the cheese mixture all over the ears of corn until completely coated.
4. Arrange the ears of corn in the greased pan in a single layer.
5. Select Air Fry. Set temperature to 400°F (205°C) and set time to 15 minutes. Press Start to begin preheating.
6. Once preheated, place the pan into the Vortex. Flip the ears of corn halfway through the cooking time.
7. When cooking is complete, they should be lightly browned. Remove from the Vortex and let them cool for 5 minutes before serving.

Brown Sugar Acorn Squash
Prep time: 5 minutes | Cook time: 15 minutes | Serves 2

1 medium acorn squash, halved crosswise and deseeded
1 teaspoon coconut oil
1 teaspoon light brown sugar
Few dashes of ground cinnamon
Few dashes of ground nutmeg

1. On a clean work surface, rub the cut sides of the acorn squash with coconut oil. Scatter with the brown sugar, cinnamon, and nutmeg.
2. Put the squash halves in the perforated pan, cut-side up.
3. Select Air Fry. Set temperature to 325°F (163°C) and set time to 15 minutes. Press Start to begin preheating.
4. Once preheated, place the pan into the Vortex.
5. When cooking is complete, the squash halves should be just tender when pierced in the center with a paring knife. Remove the pan from the Vortex. Rest for 5 to 10 minutes and serve warm.

Garlic-Lime Shishito Peppers
Prep time: 5 minutes | Cook time: 9 minutes | Serves 3

½ pound (227 g) shishito peppers, rinsed
Cooking spray
Sauce:
1 tablespoon tamari or shoyu
2 teaspoons fresh lime juice
2 large garlic cloves, minced

1. Spritz the perforated pan with cooking spray.
2. Place the shishito peppers in the perforated pan and spritz them with cooking spray.
3. Select Roast. Set temperature to 392°F (200°C) and set time to 9 minutes. Press Start to begin preheating.
4. Once preheated, place the pan into the Vortex.
5. Meanwhile, whisk together all the ingredients for the sauce in a large bowl. Set aside.
6. After 3 minutes, remove the pan from the Vortex. Flip the peppers and spritz them with cooking spray. Return to the Vortex and continue cooking.
7. After another 3 minutes, remove the pan from the Vortex. Flip the peppers and spray with cooking spray. Return to the Vortex and continue roasting for 3 minutes more, or until the peppers are blistered and nicely browned.
8. When cooking is complete, remove the peppers from the Vortex to the bowl of sauce. Toss to coat well and serve immediately.

Greek Potatoes with Chives
Prep time: 5 minutes | Cook time: 35 minutes | Serves 4

4 (7-ounce / 198-g) russet potatoes, rinsed
Olive oil spray
½ teaspoon kosher salt, divided
½ cup 2% plain Greek yogurt
¼ cup minced fresh chives
Freshly ground black pepper, to taste

1. Pat the potatoes dry and pierce them all over with a fork. Spritz the potatoes with olive oil spray. Sprinkle with ¼ teaspoon of the salt.
2. Transfer the potatoes to the perforated pan.
3. Select Bake. Set temperature to 400°F (205°C) and set time to 35 minutes. Press Start to begin preheating.
4. Once preheated, place the pan into the Vortex.
5. When cooking is complete, the potatoes should be fork-tender. Remove from the Vortex and split open the potatoes. Top with the yogurt, chives, the remaining ¼ teaspoon of salt, and finish with the black pepper. Serve immediately.

Breaded Asparagus Fries
Prep time: 15 minutes | Cook time: 6 minutes | Serves 4

2 egg whites
¼ cup water
¼ cup plus 2 tablespoons grated Parmesan cheese, divided
¾ cup panko bread crumbs
¼ teaspoon salt
12 ounces (340 g) fresh asparagus spears, woody ends trimmed
Cooking spray

1. In a shallow dish, whisk together the egg whites and water until slightly foamy. In a separate shallow dish, thoroughly combine ¼ cup of Parmesan cheese, bread crumbs, and salt.
2. Dip the asparagus in the egg white, then roll in the cheese mixture to coat well.
3. Place the asparagus in the perforated pan in a single layer, leaving space between each spear. Spritz the asparagus with cooking spray.
4. Select Air Fry. Set temperature to 390°F (199°C) and set time to 6 minutes. Press Start to begin preheating.
5. Once preheated, place the pan into the Vortex.
6. When cooking is complete, the asparagus should be golden brown and crisp. Remove the pan from the Vortex. Sprinkle with the remaining 2 tablespoons of cheese and serve hot.

Cheddar Broccoli Gratin
Prep time: 5 minutes | Cook time: 14 minutes | Serves 2

⅓ cup fat-free milk
1 tablespoon all-purpose or gluten-free flour
½ tablespoon olive oil
½ teaspoon ground sage
¼ teaspoon kosher salt
⅛ teaspoon freshly ground black pepper
2 cups roughly chopped broccoli florets
6 tablespoons shredded Cheddar cheese
2 tablespoons panko bread crumbs
1 tablespoon grated Parmesan cheese
Olive oil spray

1. Spritz a baking dish with olive oil spray.
2. Mix the milk, flour, olive oil, sage, salt, and pepper in a medium bowl and whisk to combine. Stir in the broccoli florets, Cheddar cheese, bread crumbs, and Parmesan cheese and toss to coat.
3. Pour the broccoli mixture into the prepared baking dish.
4. Select Bake. Set temperature to 330°F (166°C) and set time to 14 minutes. Press Start to begin preheating.
5. Once preheated, place the baking dish into the Vortex.
6. When cooking is complete, the top should be golden brown and the broccoli should be tender. Remove from the Vortex and serve immediately.

Garlic Zucchini Sticks
Prep time: 5 minutes | Cook time: 14 minutes | Serves 4

2 small zucchini, cut into 2-inch × ½-inch sticks
3 tablespoons chickpea flour
2 teaspoons arrowroot (or cornstarch)
½ teaspoon garlic granules
¼ teaspoon sea salt
⅛ teaspoon freshly ground black pepper
1 tablespoon water
Cooking spray

1. Combine the zucchini sticks with the chickpea flour, arrowroot, garlic granules, salt, and pepper in a medium bowl and toss to coat. Add the water and stir to mix well.
2. Spritz the perforated pan with cooking spray and spread out the zucchini sticks in the pan. Mist the zucchini sticks with cooking spray.
3. Select Air Fry. Set temperature to 392°F (200°C) and set time to 14 minutes. Press Start to begin preheating.
4. Once preheated, place the pan into the Vortex. Stir the sticks halfway through the cooking time.
5. When cooking is complete, the zucchini sticks should be crispy and nicely browned. Remove from the Vortex and serve warm.

Roasted Potatoes with Rosemary
Prep time: 5 minutes | Cook time: 20 minutes | Serves 4

1½ pounds (680 g) small red potatoes, cut into 1-inch cubes
2 tablespoons olive oil
2 tablespoons minced fresh rosemary
1 tablespoon minced garlic
1 teaspoon salt, plus additional as needed
½ teaspoon freshly ground black pepper, plus additional as needed

1. Toss the potato cubes with the olive oil, rosemary, garlic, salt, and pepper in a large bowl until thoroughly coated.
2. Arrange the potato cubes in the perforated pan in a single layer.
3. Select Roast. Set temperature to 400°F (205°C) and set time to 20 minutes. Press Start to begin preheating.
4. Once preheated, place the pan into the Vortex. Stir the potatoes a few times during cooking for even cooking.
5. When cooking is complete, the potatoes should be tender. Remove from the Vortex to a plate. Taste and add additional salt and pepper as needed.

Balsamic Asparagus

Prep time: 5 minutes | Cook time: 10 minutes | Serves 4

1 pound (454 g) asparagus, woody ends trimmed
2 tablespoons olive oil
1 tablespoon balsamic vinegar
2 teaspoons minced garlic
Salt and freshly ground black pepper, to taste

1. In a large shallow bowl, toss the asparagus with the olive oil, balsamic vinegar, garlic, salt, and pepper until thoroughly coated. Put the asparagus in the perforated pan.
2. Select Roast. Set temperature to 400°F (205°C) and set time to 10 minutes. Press Start to begin preheating.
3. Once preheated, place the pan into the Vortex. Flip the asparagus with tongs halfway through the cooking time.
4. When cooking is complete, the asparagus should be crispy. Remove the pan from the Vortex and serve warm.

Garlic Broccoli with Parmesan

Prep time: 5 minutes | Cook time: 4 minutes | Serves 4

1 pound (454 g) broccoli florets
1 medium shallot, minced
2 tablespoons olive oil
2 tablespoons unsalted butter, melted
2 teaspoons minced garlic
¼ cup grated Parmesan cheese

1. Combine the broccoli florets with the shallot, olive oil, butter, garlic, and Parmesan cheese in a medium bowl and toss until the broccoli florets are thoroughly coated.
2. Place the broccoli florets in the perforated pan in a single layer.
3. Select Roast. Set temperature to 360°F (182°C) and set time to 4 minutes. Press Start to begin preheating.
4. Once preheated, place the pan into the Vortex.
5. When cooking is complete, the broccoli florets should be crisp-tender. Remove from the Vortex and serve warm.

Breaded Brussels Sprouts with Paprika

Prep time: 5 minutes | Cook time: 15 minutes | Serves 4

1 pound (454 g) Brussels sprouts, halved
1 cup bread crumbs
2 tablespoons grated Grana Padano cheese
1 tablespoon paprika
2 tablespoons canola oil
1 tablespoon chopped sage

1. Line the perforated pan with parchment paper. Set aside.
2. In a small bowl, thoroughly mix the bread crumbs, cheese, and paprika. In a large bowl, place the Brussels sprouts and drizzle the canola oil over the top. Sprinkle with the bread crumb mixture and toss to coat.
3. Transfer the Brussels sprouts to the prepared pan.
4. Select Roast. Set temperature to 400°F (205°C) and set time to 15 minutes. Press Start to begin preheating.
5. Once preheated, place the pan into the Vortex. Stir the Brussels a few times during cooking.
6. When cooking is complete, the Brussels sprouts should be lightly browned and crisp. Transfer the Brussels sprouts to a plate and sprinkle the sage on top before serving.

Garlicky Cabbage with Red Pepper

Prep time: 5 minutes | Cook time: 7 minutes | Serves 4

1 head cabbage, sliced into 1-inch-thick ribbons
1 tablespoon olive oil
1 teaspoon garlic powder
1 teaspoon red pepper flakes
1 teaspoon salt
1 teaspoon freshly ground black pepper

1. Toss the cabbage with the olive oil, garlic powder, red pepper flakes, salt, and pepper in a large mixing bowl until well coated.
2. Transfer the cabbage to the perforated pan.
3. Select Roast. Set temperature to 350°F (180°C) and set time to 7 minutes. Press Start to begin preheating.
4. Once preheated, place the pan into the Vortex. Flip the cabbage with tongs halfway through the cooking time.
5. When cooking is complete, the cabbage should be crisp. Remove from the Vortex to a plate and serve warm.

Balsamic-Maple Brussels Sprout
Prep time: 5 minutes | Cook time: 13 minutes | Serves 2

2 cups Brussels sprouts, halved
1 tablespoon olive oil
1 tablespoon balsamic vinegar
1 tablespoon maple syrup
¼ teaspoon sea salt

1. Preheat the air fryer to 375°F (191°C).
2. Evenly coat the Brussels sprouts with the olive oil, balsamic vinegar, maple syrup, and salt.
3. Transfer to the air fryer basket and air fry for 5 minutes. Give the basket a good shake, turn the heat to 400°F (204°C) and continue to air fry for another 8 minutes.
4. Serve hot.

Mushroom Summer Rolls
Prep time: 15 minutes | Cook time: 15 minutes | Serves 4

1 cup shiitake mushroom, sliced thinly
1 celery stalk, chopped
1 medium carrot, shredded
½ teaspoon finely chopped ginger
1 teaspoon sugar
1 tablespoon soy sauce
1 teaspoon nutritional yeast
8 spring roll sheets
1 teaspoon corn starch
2 tablespoons water

1. In a bowl, combine the ginger, soy sauce, nutritional yeast, carrots, celery, mushroom, and sugar.
2. Mix the cornstarch and water to create an adhesive for the spring rolls.
3. Scoop a tablespoonful of the vegetable mixture into the middle of the spring roll sheets. Brush the edges of the sheets with the cornstarch adhesive and enclose around the filling to make spring rolls.
4. Preheat the air fryer to 400°F (204°C). When warm, place the rolls inside and air fry for 15 minutes or until crisp.
5. Serve hot.

Eggplant and Sushi Rice Bowl
Prep time: 15 minutes | Cook time: 10 minutes | Serves 4

¼ cup sliced cucumber
1 teaspoon salt
1 tablespoon sugar
7 tablespoons Japanese rice vinegar
3 medium eggplants, sliced
3 tablespoons sweet white miso paste
1 tablespoon mirin rice wine
4 cups cooked sushi rice
4 spring onions
1 tablespoon toasted sesame seeds

1. Coat the cucumber slices with the rice wine vinegar, salt, and sugar.
2. Put a dish on top of the bowl to weight it down completely.
3. In a bowl, mix the eggplants, mirin rice wine, and miso paste. Allow to marinate for half an hour.
4. Preheat the air fryer to 400°F (204°C).
5. Put the eggplant slices in the air fryer and air fry for 10 minutes.
6. Fill the bottom of a serving bowl with rice and top with the eggplants and pickled cucumbers.
7. Add the spring onions and sesame seeds for garnish. Serve immediately.

Oyster Mushroom Pizza Squares
Prep time: 10 minutes | Cook time: 10 minutes | Serves 10

1 pizza dough, cut into squares
1 cup chopped oyster mushrooms
1 shallot, chopped
¼ red bell pepper, chopped
2 tablespoons parsley
Salt and ground black pepper, to taste

1. Preheat the air fryer to 400°F (204°C).
2. In a bowl, combine the oyster mushrooms, shallot, bell pepper and parsley. Sprinkle some salt and pepper as desired.
3. Spread this mixture on top of the pizza squares.
4. Bake in the air fryer for 10 minutes.
5. Serve warm.

Crumbled Tofu with Sweet Potatoes
Prep time: 15 minutes | Cook time: 35 minutes | Serves 8

8 sweet potatoes, scrubbed
2 tablespoons olive oil
1 large onion, chopped
2 green chilies, deseeded and chopped
8 ounces (227 g) tofu, crumbled
2 tablespoons Cajun seasoning
1 cup chopped tomatoes
1 can kidney beans, drained and rinsed
Salt and ground black pepper, to taste

1. Preheat the air fryer to 400°F (204°C).
2. With a knife, pierce the skin of the sweet potatoes and air fry in the air fryer for 30 minutes or until soft.
3. Remove from the air fryer, halve each potato, and set to one side.
4. Over a medium heat, fry the onions and chilies in the olive oil in a skillet for 2 minutes until fragrant.
5. Add the tofu and Cajun seasoning and air fry for a further 3 minutes before incorporating the kidney beans and tomatoes. Sprinkle some salt and pepper as desire.
6. Top each sweet potato halve with a spoonful of the tofu mixture and serve.

Cheddar and Basmati Rice Risotto
Prep time: 10 minutes | Cook time: 30 minutes | Serves 2

1 onion, diced
1 small carrot, diced
2 cups vegetable broth, boiling
½ cup grated Cheddar cheese
1 clove garlic, minced
¾ cup long-grain basmati rice
1 tablespoon olive oil
1 tablespoon unsalted butter

1. Preheat the air fryer to 390°F (199°C).
2. Grease a baking tin with oil and stir in the butter, garlic, carrot, and onion.
3. Put the tin in the air fryer and bake for 4 minutes.
4. Pour in the rice and bake for a further 4 minutes, stirring three times throughout the baking time.
5. Turn the temperature down to 320°F (160°C).
6. Add the vegetable broth and give the dish a gentle stir. Bake for 22 minutes, leaving the air fryer uncovered.
7. Pour in the cheese, stir once more and serve.

Avocado, Cauliflower, and Chickpea Mash
Prep time: 10 minutes | Cook time: 25 minutes | Serves 4

1 medium head cauliflower, cut into florets
1 can chickpeas, drained and rinsed
1 tablespoon extra-virgin olive oil
2 tablespoons lemon juice
Salt and ground black pepper, to taste
4 flatbreads, toasted
2 ripe avocados, mashed

1. Preheat the air fryer to 425°F (218°C).
2. In a bowl, mix the chickpeas, cauliflower, lemon juice and olive oil. Sprinkle salt and pepper as desired.
3. Put inside the air fryer basket and air fry for 25 minutes.
4. Spread on top of the flatbread along with the mashed avocado. Sprinkle with more pepper and salt and serve.

Air Fried Green Beans
Prep time: 10 minutes | Cook time: 10 minutes | Serves 4

1½ pounds (680 g) French green beans, stems removed and blanched
1 tablespoon salt
½ pound (227 g) shallots, peeled and cut into quarters
½ teaspoon ground white pepper
2 tablespoons olive oil

1. Preheat the air fryer to 400°F (204°C).
2. Coat the vegetables with the rest of the ingredients in a bowl.
3. Transfer to the air fryer basket and air fry for 10 minutes, making sure the green beans achieve a light brown color.
4. Serve hot.

Tomato and Black Bean Chili
Prep time: 15 minutes | Cook time: 23 minutes | Serves 6

1 tablespoon olive oil
1 medium onion, diced
3 garlic cloves, minced
1 cup vegetable broth
3 cans black beans, drained and rinsed
2 cans diced tomatoes
2 chipotle peppers, chopped
2 teaspoons cumin
2 teaspoons chili powder
1 teaspoon dried oregano
½ teaspoon salt

1. Over a medium heat, fry the garlic and onions in the olive oil for 3 minutes.
2. Add the remaining ingredients, stirring constantly and scraping the bottom to prevent sticking.
3. Preheat the air fryer to 400°F (204°C).
4. Take a dish and place the mixture inside. Put a sheet of aluminum foil on top.
5. Transfer to the air fryer and bake for 20 minutes.
6. When ready, plate up and serve immediately.

Mediterranean Herbed Zucchini and Parsnip
Prep time: 10 minutes | Cook time: 6 minutes | Serves 4

1 large zucchini, sliced
1 cup cherry tomatoes, halved
1 parsnip, sliced
1 green pepper, sliced
1 carrot, sliced
1 teaspoon mixed herbs
1 teaspoon mustard
1 teaspoon garlic purée
6 tablespoons olive oil
Salt and ground black pepper, to taste

1. Preheat the air fryer to 400°F (204°C).
2. Combine all the ingredients in a bowl, making sure to coat the vegetables well.
3. Transfer to the air fryer and air fry for 6 minutes, ensuring the vegetables are tender and browned.
4. Serve immediately.

Potato, Broccoli, and Zucchini Veg Bowl
Prep time: 10 minutes | Cook time: 45 minutes | Serves 4

2 potatoes, peeled and cubed
4 carrots, cut into chunks
1 head broccoli, cut into florets
4 zucchinis, sliced thickly
Salt and ground black pepper, to taste
¼ cup olive oil
1 tablespoon dry onion powder

1. Preheat the air fryer to 400°F (204°C).
2. In a baking dish, add all the ingredients and combine well.
3. Bake for 45 minutes in the air fryer, ensuring the vegetables are soft and the sides have browned before serving.

Simple Air Fried Asparagus
Prep time: 5 minutes | Cook time: 5 minutes | Serves 4

1 pound (454 g) fresh asparagus spears, trimmed
1 tablespoon olive oil
Salt and ground black pepper, to taste

1. Preheat the air fryer to 375°F (191°C).
2. Combine all the ingredients and transfer to the air fryer basket.
3. Air fry for 5 minutes or until soft.
4. Serve hot.

Balsamic Chickpea and Fig Salad
Prep time: 15 minutes | Cook time: 20 minutes | Serves 4

8 fresh figs, halved
1½ cups cooked chickpeas
1 teaspoon crushed roasted cumin seeds
4 tablespoons balsamic vinegar
2 tablespoons extra-virgin olive oil, plus more for greasing
Salt and ground black pepper, to taste
3 cups arugula rocket, washed and dried

1. Preheat the air fryer to 375°F (191°C).
2. Cover the air fryer basket with aluminum foil and grease lightly with oil. Put the figs in the air fryer basket and air fry for 10 minutes.
3. In a bowl, combine the chickpeas and cumin seeds.
4. Remove the air fried figs from the air fryer and replace with the chickpeas. Air fry for 10 minutes. Leave to cool.
5. In the meantime, prepare the dressing. Mix the balsamic vinegar, olive oil, salt and pepper.
6. In a salad bowl, combine the arugula rocket with the cooled figs and chickpeas.
7. Toss with the sauce and serve.

Crispy Cauliflower
Prep time: 5 minutes | Cook time: 17 minutes | Serves 4

¼ cup vegan butter, melted
¼ cup sriracha sauce
4 cups cauliflower florets
1 cup bread crumbs
1 teaspoon salt

1. Preheat the air fryer to 375°F (191°C).
2. Mix the sriracha and vegan butter in a bowl and pour this mixture over the cauliflower, taking care to cover each floret entirely.
3. In a separate bowl, combine the bread crumbs and salt.
4. Dip the cauliflower florets in the bread crumbs, coating each one well. Air fry in the air fryer for 17 minutes.
5. Serve hot.

Roasted Broccoli
Prep time: 5 minutes | Cook time: 15 minutes | Serves 6

2 heads broccoli, cut into florets
2 teaspoons extra-virgin olive oil, plus more for coating
1 teaspoon salt
½ teaspoon black pepper
1 clove garlic, minced
½ teaspoon lemon juice

1. Cover the air fryer basket with aluminum foil and coat with a light brushing of oil.
2. Preheat the air fryer to 375°F (191°C).
3. In a bowl, combine all ingredients, save for the lemon juice, and transfer to the air fryer basket. Roast for 15 minutes.
4. Serve with the lemon juice.

Breaded Gold Mushrooms
Prep time: 10 minutes | Cook time: 10 minutes | Serves 4

6 small mushrooms
1 tablespoon bread crumbs
1 tablespoon olive oil
1 ounce (28 g) onion, peeled and diced
1 teaspoon parsley
1 teaspoon garlic purée
Salt and ground black pepper, to taste

1. Preheat the air fryer to 350°F (177°C).
2. Combine the bread crumbs, oil, onion, parsley, salt, pepper and garlic in a bowl. Cut out the mushrooms' stalks and stuff each cap with the crumb mixture.
3. Air fry in the air fryer for 10 minutes.
4. Serve hot.

Bacon-Wrapped Jalapeño Poppers
Prep time: 5 minutes | Cook time: 33 minutes | Serves 4

8 medium jalapeño peppers
5 ounces (142 g) cream cheese
¼ cup grated Mozzarella cheese
½ teaspoon Italian seasoning mix
8 slices bacon

1. Preheat the air fryer to 400°F (204°C).
2. Cut the jalapeños in half.
3. Use a spoon to scrape out the insides of the peppers.
4. In a bowl, add together the cream cheese, Mozzarella cheese and Italian seasoning.
5. Pack the cream cheese mixture into the jalapeño halves and place the other halves on top.
6. Wrap each pepper in 1 slice of bacon, starting from the bottom and working up.
7. Bake for 33 minutes.
8. Serve!

Mushroom and Pepperoni Pizza
Prep time: 5 minutes | Cook time: 18 minutes | Serves 4

4 large portobello mushrooms, stems removed
4 teaspoons olive oil
1 cup marinara sauce
1 cup shredded Mozzarella cheese
10 slices sugar-free pepperoni

1. Preheat the air fryer to 375°F (191°C).
2. Brush each mushroom cap with the olive oil, one teaspoon for each cap.
3. Put on a baking sheet and bake, stem-side down, for 8 minutes.
4. Air fry for another 10 minutes until browned.
5. Serve hot.

Beef and Cheese Stuffed Peppers
Prep time: 10 minutes | Cook time: 30 minutes | Serves 4

1 pound (454 g) ground beef
1 tablespoon taco seasoning mix
1 can diced tomatoes and green chilis
4 green bell peppers
1 cup shredded Monterey jack cheese, divided

1. Preheat the air fryer to 350°F (177°C).
2. Set a skillet over a high heat and cook the ground beef for 8 minutes. Make sure it is cooked through and browned all over. Drain the fat.
3. Stir in the taco seasoning mix, and the diced tomatoes and green chilis. Allow the mixture to cook for a further 4 minutes.
4. In the meantime, slice the tops off the green peppers and remove the seeds and membranes.
5. When the meat mixture is fully cooked, spoon equal amounts of it into the peppers and top with the Monterey jack cheese. Then place the peppers into the air fryer. Air fry for 15 minutes.
6. The peppers are ready when they are soft, and the cheese is bubbling and brown. Serve warm.

Chapter 6
Meats

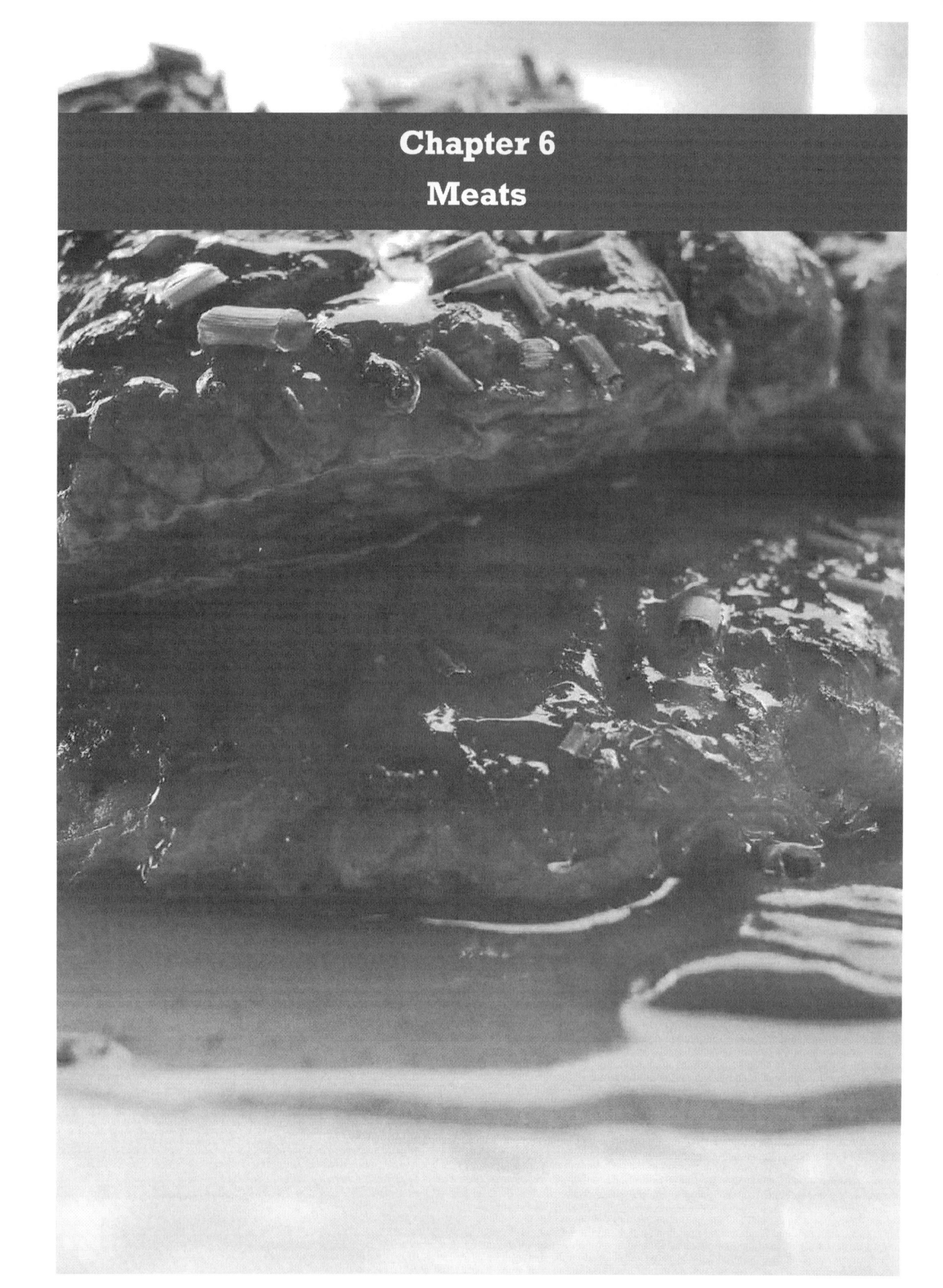

Juicy Bacon and Beef Cheeseburgers
Prep time: 10 minutes | Cook time: 18 minutes | Serves 4

1½ pounds (680 g) ground beef
1 tablespoon Worcestershire sauce
1 teaspoon kosher salt
½ teaspoon freshly ground black pepper
½ teaspoon garlic powder
¾ cup grated sharp Cheddar cheese
4 bacon slices, halved crosswise so you have 8 short strips
4 hamburger buns
Burger fixings as desired: sliced tomatoes, pickles, onions, ketchup, mustard, relish, mayonnaise, etc., for serving

1. Line a baking sheet with aluminum foil and place a wire rack on top.
2. In a medium bowl, mix together the ground beef, Worcestershire sauce, salt, pepper, and garlic powder. Shape the mixture into 8 very thin patties. Top 4 patties with Cheddar, dividing the cheese equally, and top each with 1 of the remaining 4 patties. Press the patties together, sealing the cheese inside. The patties should be equal sizes, about ½ inch thick and 4 to 5 inches across. Place the patties on the wire rack on top of the baking sheet.
3. Arrange the bacon slices on the rack around the patties.
4. Select Bake. Set temperature to 400°F (205°C) and set time to 18 minutes. Select Start to begin preheating.
5. Once preheated, slide the baking sheet into the Vortex.
6. When done, the burgers will be cooked through and the bacon will be browned and crisp.
7. Remove the patties immediately and place them on the buns.
8. Pat the bacon strips with a paper towel to remove excess fat and lay 2 pieces on top of each burger. Garnish as desired and serve immediately.

Beef Meatloaf with Roasted Vegetables
Prep time: 15 minutes | Cook time: 45 minutes | Serves 4

1½ pounds (680 g) ground beef
¼ cup finely diced onion
1 large egg, lightly beaten
½ cup dried bread crumbs, or panko bread crumbs
2 tablespoons tomato paste
2 tablespoons Worcestershire sauce
1½ teaspoons kosher salt, divided
1 teaspoon freshly ground black pepper, divided
2 cups small Brussels sprouts, halved
1 large red onion, halved and sliced
2 cups small new potatoes, halved or quartered
2 tablespoons olive oil

1. Line one or two rimmed baking sheets with aluminum foil or parchment paper.
2. In a medium bowl, mix together the ground beef, onion, egg, bread crumbs, tomato paste, Worcestershire sauce, 1 teaspoon of salt, and ½ teaspoon of pepper until well combined. Form the mixture into a loaf on the prepared sheet.
3. In a large bowl, toss together the Brussels sprouts, red onion, potatoes, olive oil, and the remaining ½ teaspoon of salt and ½ teaspoon of pepper. Arrange the vegetables either around the meatloaf or on a separate baking sheet.
4. Select Bake. Set temperature to 350°F (180°C) and set time to 45 minutes. Select Start to begin preheating.
5. Once preheated, slide the baking sheet into the Vortex.
6. When done, the vegetables will be tender and browned and the meat will be cooked through. Remove from the Vortex, tent the meatloaf loosely with foil, and let stand for 10 minutes before serving.

Rump Roast with Bell Peppers
Prep time: 10 minutes | Cook time: 40 minutes | Serves 6 to 8

2 red bell peppers, stemmed, seeded, and cut into 1-inch-wide strips
2 yellow bell peppers, stemmed, seeded, and cut into 1-inch-wide strips
2 green bell peppers, stemmed, seeded, and cut into 1-inch-wide strips
6 garlic cloves, peeled and left whole
4 tablespoons olive oil, divided
2 teaspoons kosher salt, divided
1½ teaspoons freshly ground black pepper, divided
1 (3- to 3½-pound / 1.4- to 1.6-kg) boneless rump roast, at room temperature
1 tablespoon chopped fresh thyme leaves

1. In a baking dish, toss together the red, yellow, and green bell peppers, garlic, 2 tablespoons of olive oil, ½ teaspoon of salt, and ½ teaspoon of pepper. Spread the peppers out to the sides of the pan, leaving space in the middle for the roast.
2. Rub the remaining 2 tablespoons of olive oil all over the roast and season it with the remaining 1½ teaspoons of salt and 1 teaspoon of pepper.
3. Select Bake. Set temperature to 375°F (190°C) and set time to 40 minutes. Select Start to begin preheating.
4. Once preheated, slide the baking dish into the Vortex.
5. When done, the outside of the roast will be browned and it will be cooked to an internal temperature of 135°F (57°C).
6. Remove the roast from the Vortex, tent loosely with aluminum foil, and let rest for 10 minutes. Carve the roast thinly and serve hot, with the roasted peppers and garlic alongside, garnished with the thyme.

Mint-Roasted Boneless Lamb Leg
Prep time: 10 minutes | Cook time: 30 minutes | Serves 8

2 tablespoons olive oil
6 garlic cloves, minced
¼ cup chopped fresh mint leaves
1 tablespoon chopped fresh flat-leaf parsley leaves
1 teaspoon kosher salt
¾ teaspoon freshly ground black pepper
1 (3- to 3½-pound / 1.4- to 1.6-kg) boneless leg of lamb, at room temperature

1. In a small bowl, stir together the olive oil, garlic, mint, parsley, salt, and pepper. Rub the herb mixture all over the meat. Place the meat in a shallow baking pan.
2. Select Bake. Set temperature to 400°F (205°C) and set time to 30 minutes. Select Start to begin preheating.
3. Once preheated, slide the pan into the Vortex.
4. When done, the meat will be reach the desired internal temperature to 130°F (54°C) for medium-rare, 140°F (60°C) for medium, and 145°F (63°C) for medium-well.
5. Remove the roast from the Vortex, tent with aluminum foil, and let rest for at least 15 minutes.
6. To serve, carve the meat thinly across the grain and serve with the pan juices drizzled over the top.

Rosemary-Balsamic Pork Loin Roast
Prep time: 10 minutes | Cook time: 35 minutes | Serves 4

¼ cup olive oil
3 tablespoons balsamic vinegar
5 garlic cloves, minced
½ cup chopped fresh rosemary leaves
1 teaspoon kosher salt
½ teaspoon freshly ground black pepper
1 (2-pound / 907-g) boneless pork loin roast

1. In a small bowl, stir together the olive oil, vinegar, garlic, rosemary, salt, and pepper. Rub the mixture all over the pork loin and place it in a baking dish.
2. Select Bake. Set temperature to 400°F (205°C) and set time to 18 minutes. Select Start to begin preheating.
3. Once preheated, slide the pan into the Vortex.
4. When done, lower the temperature to 350°F (180°C) and continue to roast the pork for 20 to 30 minutes more, until the internal temperature is around 145°F (63°C). Remove from the Vortex, tent loosely with aluminum foil, and let rest for 10 minutes before slicing and serving.

Hoisin Roasted Pork Ribs
Prep time: 10 minutes | Cook time: 1 hour | Serves 4 to 6

2 pounds (907 g) baby back pork ribs
⅓ cup hoisin sauce
2 tablespoons soy sauce
2 tablespoons light brown sugar
1 tablespoon minced peeled fresh ginger
2 garlic cloves, minced
1 tablespoon toasted sesame oil
¼ teaspoon ground cinnamon
¼ teaspoon ground fennel
¼ teaspoon cayenne pepper
¼ teaspoon freshly ground black pepper

1. Place the ribs in a large baking pan. Pierce the meat with a fork.
2. In a small bowl, whisk the hoisin sauce, soy sauce, brown sugar, ginger, garlic, sesame oil, cinnamon, fennel, cayenne, and pepper. Brush the mixture over the meat. Reserve any extra marinade for basting.
3. Select Bake. Set temperature to 350°F (180°C) and set time to 1 hour. Select Start to begin preheating.
4. Once preheated, slide the pan into the Vortex. Baste the ribs with the reserved seasoning mixture every 20 minutes.
5. Cut between the bones to separate the ribs and serve immediately.

Brown Sugar-Mustard Glazed Ham

Prep time: 5 minutes | **Cook time:** 1½ hours | **Serves** 14 to 16

1 (10- to 12-pound / 4.5- to 5.4-kg) bone-in spiral-sliced ham
1 cup brown sugar
2 tablespoons honey
2 tablespoons Dijon mustard
2 tablespoons apple cider vinegar

1. Place the ham in a shallow baking pan.
2. Select Bake. Set temperature to 325°F (163°C) and set time to 1½ hours. Select Start to begin preheating.
3. Once preheated, slide the pan into the Vortex.
4. In a small bowl, stir together the brown sugar, honey, mustard, and vinegar.
5. After 1 hour, spoon the brown sugar mixture all over the ham. Return the ham to the Vortex and bake for 30 minutes more, until heated through and the glaze is bubbling and browned.

Bourbon Sirloin Steak

Prep time: 5 minutes | **Cook time:** 14 minutes | **Serves** 2

2 (6- to 8-ounce / 170- to 227-g) sirloin steaks, ¾ inch thick
Brushing Mixture:
¼ cup bourbon
1 teaspoon garlic powder
1 tablespoon olive oil
1 teaspoon soy sauce

1. Combine the brushing mixture ingredients in a small bowl. Brush the steaks on both sides with the mixture and place on the broiling rack with a pan underneath.
2. Select Broil. Set temperature to 400°F (205°C) and set time to 14 minutes. Select Start to begin preheating.
3. Once preheated, slide the pan into the Vortex.
4. After 4 minutes, remove from the Vortex, turn with tongs, brush the top and sides, and broil again for 4 minutes, or until done to your preference. To use the brushing mixture as a sauce or gravy, pour the mixture into a baking pan.
5. Broil the mixture for 6 minutes, or until it begins to bubble.

Pork Chops with Pickapeppa Sauce

Prep time: 10 minutes | **Cook time:** 16 minutes | **Serves** 2

½ to ¾ pound (227- to 340-g) boneless lean pork sirloin chops
Seasoning Mixture:
½ teaspoon ground cumin
¼ teaspoon turmeric
Pinch of ground cardamom
Pinch of grated nutmeg
1 teaspoon vegetable oil
1 teaspoon Pickapeppa sauce

1. Combine the seasoning mixture ingredients in a small bowl and brush on both sides of the chops. Place the chops on the broiling rack with a pan underneath.
2. Select Broil. Set temperature to 400°F (205°C) and set time to 16 minutes. Select Start to begin preheating.
3. Once preheated, slide the pan into the Vortex.
4. After 8 minutes, remove the chops, turn, and brush with the mixture. Broil again for 8 minutes, or until the chops are done to your preference.

Spicy Pepper Steak

Prep time: 10 minutes | **Cook time:** 12 minutes | **Serves** 2

½ to ¾ pound (227- to 340-g) pepper steaks, cut into 3 × 4-inch strips
Spicy Mixture:
1 tablespoon olive oil
1 tablespoon brown mustard
1 teaspoon chili powder
1 teaspoon garlic powder
1 teaspoon hot sauce
1 tablespoon barbecue sauce or salsa
Salt and freshly ground black pepper, to taste

1. Blend the spicy mixture ingredients in a small bowl and brush both sides of the beef strips.
2. Roll up the strips lengthwise and fasten with toothpicks near each end. Place the beef rolls in an oiled or nonstick square baking (cake) pan.
3. Select Broil. Set temperature to 400°F (205°C) and set time to 12 minutes. Select Start to begin preheating.
4. Once preheated, slide the pan into the Vortex.
5. After 6 minutes, remove from the Vortex, and turn with tongs. Brush with the spicy mixture and broil again for 6 minutes, or until done to your preference.

Minted-Balsamic Lamb Chops

Prep time: 5 minutes | Cook time: 15 minutes | Serves 4

4 lean lamb chops, fat trimmed, approximately ¾ inch thick
1 tablespoon balsamic vinegar
Mint Mixture:
4 tablespoons finely chopped fresh mint
2 tablespoons nonfat yogurt
1 tablespoon olive oil
Salt and freshly ground black pepper, to taste

1. Combine the mint mixture ingredients in a small bowl, stirring well to blend. Set aside. Place the lamp chops on a broiling rack with a pan underneath.
2. Select Broil. Set temperature to 400°F (205°C) and set time to 15 minutes. Select Start to begin preheating.
3. Once preheated, slide the pan into the Vortex.
4. Broil the lamb chops for 10 minutes, or until they are slightly pink. Remove from the Vortex and brush one side liberally with balsamic vinegar. Turn the chops over with tongs and spread with the mint mixture, using all of the mixture.
5. Broil again for 5 minutes, or until lightly browned.

Dijon Pork Tenderloin

Prep time: 5 minutes | Cook time: 10 minutes | Serves 6

2 large egg whites
1½ tablespoons Dijon mustard
2 cups crushed pretzel crumbs
1½ pounds (680 g) pork tenderloin, cut into ¼-pound (113-g) sections
Cooking spray

1. Spritz the perforated pan with cooking spray.
2. Whisk the egg whites with Dijon mustard in a bowl until bubbly. Pour the pretzel crumbs in a separate bowl.
3. Dredge the pork tenderloin in the egg white mixture and press to coat. Shake the excess off and roll the tenderloin over the pretzel crumbs.
4. Arrange the well-coated pork tenderloin in the pan and spritz with cooking spray.
5. Select Air Fry. Set temperature to 350°F (180°C) and set time to 10 minutes. Press Start to begin preheating.
6. Once preheated, place the pan into the Vortex.
7. After 5 minutes, remove the pan from the Vortex. Flip the pork. Return the pan to the Vortex and continue cooking.
8. When cooking is complete, the pork should be golden brown and crispy.
9. Serve immediately.

Prosciutto Tart with Asparagus

Prep time: 10 minutes | Cook time: 25 minutes | Serves 4

All-purpose flour, for dusting
1 sheet (½ package) frozen puff pastry, thawed
½ cup grated Parmesan cheese
1 pound (454 g) (or more) asparagus, trimmed
8 ounces (227 g) thinly sliced prosciutto, sliced into ribbons about ½-inch wide
2 teaspoons aged balsamic vinegar

1. On a lightly floured cutting board, unwrap and unfold the puff pastry and roll it lightly with a rolling pin so as to press the folds together. Place it on the sheet pan.
2. Roll about ½ inch of the pastry edges up to form a ridge around the perimeter. Crimp the corners together to create a solid rim around the pastry. Using a fork, pierce the bottom of the pastry all over. Scatter the cheese over the bottom of the pastry.
3. Arrange the asparagus spears on top of the cheese in a single layer with 4 or 5 spears pointing one way, the next few pointing the opposite direction. You may need to trim them so they fit within the border of the pastry shell. Lay the prosciutto on top more or less evenly.
4. Select Bake. Set temperature to 375°F (190°C) and set time to 25 minutes. Press Start to begin preheating.
5. Once the unit has preheated, place the pan into the Vortex.
6. After about 15 minutes, check the tart, rotating the pan if the crust is not browning evenly and continue cooking until the pastry is golden brown and the edges of the prosciutto pieces are browned.
7. Remove the pan from the Vortex. Allow to cool for 5 minutes before slicing.
8. Drizzle with the balsamic vinegar just before serving.

Teriyaki-Glazed Pork Ribs

Prep time: 5 minutes | Cook time: 30 minutes | Serves 4

¼ cup soy sauce
¼ cup honey
1 teaspoon garlic powder
1 teaspoon ground dried ginger
4 (8-ounce / 227-g) boneless country-style pork ribs
Cooking spray

1. Spritz the perforated pan with cooking spray.
2. Make the teriyaki sauce: combine the soy sauce, honey, garlic powder, and ginger in a bowl. Stir to mix well.
3. Brush the ribs with half of the teriyaki sauce, then arrange the ribs in the pan. Spritz with cooking spray.
4. Select Air Fry. Set temperature to 350°F (180°C) and set time to 30 minutes. Press Start to begin preheating.
5. Once preheated, place the pan into the Vortex.
6. After 15 minutes, remove the pan from the Vortex. Flip the ribs and brush with remaining teriyaki sauce. Return the pan to the Vortex and continue cooking.
7. When cooking is complete, the internal temperature of the ribs should reach at least 145°F (63°C).
8. Serve immediately.

Citrus Pork Ribs with Oregano
Prep time: 10 minutes | Cook time: 25 minutes | Serves 6

2½ pounds (1.1 kg) boneless country-style pork ribs, cut into 2-inch pieces
3 tablespoons olive brine
1 tablespoon minced fresh oregano leaves
⅓ cup orange juice
1 teaspoon ground cumin
1 tablespoon minced garlic
1 teaspoon salt
1 teaspoon ground black pepper
Cooking spray

1. Combine all the ingredients in a large bowl. Toss to coat the pork ribs well. Wrap the bowl in plastic and refrigerate for at least an hour to marinate.
2. Spritz the perforated pan with cooking spray.
3. Arrange the marinated pork ribs in the pan and spritz with cooking spray.
4. Select Air Fry. Set temperature to 400°F (205°C) and set time to 25 minutes. Press Start to begin preheating.
5. Once preheated, place the pan into the Vortex. Flip the ribs halfway through.
6. When cooking is complete, the ribs should be well browned.
7. Serve immediately.

Vinegary Pork Schnitzel
Prep time: 5 minutes | Cook time: 14 minutes | Serves 2

½ cup pork rinds
½ tablespoon fresh parsley
½ teaspoon fennel seed
½ teaspoon mustard
⅓ tablespoon cider vinegar
1 teaspoon garlic salt
⅓ teaspoon ground black pepper
2 eggs
2 pork schnitzel, halved
Cooking spray

1. Spritz the perforated pan with cooking spray.
2. Put the pork rinds, parsley, fennel seeds, and mustard in a food processor. Pour in the vinegar and sprinkle with salt and ground black pepper. Pulse until well combined and smooth.
3. Pour the pork rind mixture in a large bowl. Whisk the eggs in a separate bowl.
4. Dunk the pork schnitzel in the whisked eggs, then dunk in the pork rind mixture to coat well. Shake the excess off.
5. Arrange the schnitzel in the pan and spritz with cooking spray.
6. Select Air Fry. Set temperature to 350°F (180°C) and set time to 14 minutes. Press Start to begin preheating.
7. Once preheated, place the pan into the Vortex.
8. After 7 minutes, remove the pan from the Vortex. Flip the schnitzel. Return the pan to the Vortex and continue cooking.
9. When cooking is complete, the schnitzel should be golden and crispy.
10. Serve immediately.

Nut-Crusted Pork Rack
Prep time: 5 minutes | Cook time: 35 minutes | Serves 2

1 clove garlic, minced
2 tablespoons olive oil
1 pound (454 g) rack of pork
1 cup chopped macadamia nuts
1 tablespoon bread crumbs
1 tablespoon rosemary, chopped
1 egg
Salt and ground black pepper, to taste

1. Combine the garlic and olive oil in a small bowl. Stir to mix well.
2. On a clean work surface, rub the pork rack with the garlic oil and sprinkle with salt and black pepper on both sides.
3. Combine the macadamia nuts, bread crumbs, and rosemary in a shallow dish. Whisk the egg in a large bowl.
4. Dredge the pork in the egg, then roll the pork over the macadamia nut mixture to coat well. Shake the excess off.
5. Arrange the pork in the perforated pan.
6. Select Air Fry. Set temperature to 350°F (180°C) and set time to 30 minutes. Press Start to begin preheating.
7. Once preheated, place the pan into the Vortex.
8. After 30 minutes, remove the pan from the Vortex. Flip the pork rack. Return the pan to the Vortex and increase temperature to 390°F (199°C) and set time to 5 minutes. Keep cooking.
9. When cooking is complete, the pork should be browned.
10. Serve immediately.

Garlic Pork Belly with Bay Leaves
Prep time: 10 minutes | Cook time: 30 minutes | Serves 4

1 pound (454 g) pork belly, cut into three thick chunks
6 garlic cloves
2 bay leaves
2 tablespoons soy sauce
1 teaspoon kosher salt
1 teaspoon ground black pepper
3 cups water
Cooking spray

1. Put all the ingredients in a pressure cooker, then put the lid on and cook on high for 15 minutes.
2. Natural release the pressure and release any remaining pressure, transfer the tender pork belly on a clean work surface. Allow to cool under room temperature until you can handle.
3. Generously Spritz the perforated pan with cooking spray.
4. Cut each chunk into two slices, then put the pork slices in the pan.
5. Select Air Fry. Set temperature to 400°F (205°C) and set time to 15 minutes. Press Start to begin preheating.
6. Once preheated, place the pan into the Vortex.
7. After 7 minutes, remove the pan from the Vortex. Flip the pork. Return the pan to the Vortex and continue cooking.
8. When cooking is complete, the pork fat should be crispy.
9. Serve immediately.

Paprika Lamb Chops with Sage
Prep time: 5 minutes | Cook time: 25 minutes | Serves 4

1 cup all-purpose flour
2 teaspoons dried sage leaves
2 teaspoons garlic powder
1 tablespoon mild paprika
1 tablespoon salt
4 (6-ounce / 170-g) bone-in lamb shoulder chops, fat trimmed
Cooking spray

1. Spritz the perforated pan with cooking spray.
2. Combine the flour, sage leaves, garlic powder, paprika, and salt in a large bowl. Stir to mix well. Dunk in the lamb chops and toss to coat well.
3. Arrange the lamb chops in the pan and spritz with cooking spray.
4. Select Air Fry. Set temperature to 375°F (190°C) and set time to 25 minutes. Press Start to begin preheating.
5. Once preheated, place the pan into the Vortex. Flip the chops halfway through.
6. When cooking is complete, the chops should be golden brown and reaches your desired doneness.
7. Serve immediately.

Lemon Pork Loin Chop with Marjoram
Prep time: 15 minutes | Cook time: 15 minutes | Serves 4

4 thin boneless pork loin chops
2 tablespoons lemon juice
½ cup flour
¼ teaspoon marjoram
1 teaspoon salt
1 cup panko bread crumbs
2 eggs
Lemon wedges, for serving
Cooking spray

1. On a clean work surface, drizzle the pork chops with lemon juice on both sides.
2. Combine the flour with marjoram and salt on a shallow plate. Pour the bread crumbs on a separate shallow dish. Beat the eggs in a large bowl.
3. Dredge the pork chops in the flour, then dunk in the beaten eggs to coat well. Shake the excess off and roll over the bread crumbs. Arrange the pork chops in the perforated pan and spritz with cooking spray.
4. Select Air Fry. Set temperature to 400°F (205°C) and set time to 15 minutes. Press Start to begin preheating.
5. Once preheated, place the pan into the Vortex.
6. After 7 minutes, remove the pan from the Vortex. Flip the pork. Return the pan to the Vortex and continue cooking.
7. When cooking is complete, the pork should be crispy and golden.
8. Squeeze the lemon wedges over the fried chops and serve immediately.

Breaded Pork Loin Chops
Prep time: 5 minutes | Cook time: 10 minutes | Serves 4

⅔ cup all-purpose flour
2 large egg whites
1 cup panko bread crumbs
4 (4-ounce / 113-g) center-cut boneless pork loin chops (about ½ inch thick)
Cooking spray

1. Pour the flour in a bowl. Whisk the egg whites in a separate bowl. Spread the bread crumbs on a large plate.
2. Dredge the pork loin chops in the flour first, press to coat well, then shake the excess off and dunk the chops in the eggs whites, and then roll the chops over the bread crumbs. Shake the excess off.
3. Arrange the pork chops in the perforated pan and spritz with cooking spray.
4. Select Air Fry. Set temperature to 375°F (190°C) and set time to 10 minutes. Press Start to begin preheating.
5. Once preheated, place the pan into the Vortex.
6. After 5 minutes, remove the pan from the Vortex. Flip the pork chops. Return the pan to the Vortex and continue cooking.
7. When cooking is complete, the pork chops should be crunchy and lightly browned.
8. Serve immediately.

Pork and Veggie Kebabs
Prep time: 25 minutes | Cook time: 15 minutes | Serves 4

1 pound (454 g) pork tenderloin, cubed
1 teaspoon smoked paprika
Salt and ground black pepper, to taste
1 green bell pepper, cut into chunks
1 zucchini, cut into chunks
1 red onion, sliced
1 tablespoon oregano
Cooking spray

Special Equipment:
Small bamboo skewers, soaked in water for 20 minutes to keep them from burning while cooking

1. Spritz the perforated pan with cooking spray.
2. Add the pork to a bowl and season with the smoked paprika, salt and black pepper. Thread the seasoned pork cubes and vegetables alternately onto the soaked skewers. Arrange the skewers in the pan.
3. Select Air Fry. Set temperature to 350°F (180°C) and set time to 15 minutes. Press Start to begin preheating.
4. Once preheated, place the pan into the Vortex.
5. After 7 minutes, remove the pan from the Vortex. Flip the pork skewers. Return the pan to the Vortex and continue cooking.
6. When cooking is complete, the pork should be browned and vegetables are tender.
7. Transfer the skewers to the serving dishes and sprinkle with oregano. Serve hot.

Pork and Pineapple Kebabs
Prep time: 10 minutes | Cook time: 12 minutes | Serves 4

¼ teaspoon kosher salt or ⅛ teaspoon fine salt
1 medium pork tenderloin (about 1 pound / 454 g) cut into 1½-inch chunks
1 green bell pepper, seeded and cut into 1-inch pieces
1 red bell pepper, seeded and cut into 1-inch pieces
2 cups fresh pineapple chunks
¾ cup Teriyaki Sauce or store-bought variety, divided
Special Equipment:
12 (9- to 12-inch) wooden skewers, soaked in water for about 30 minutes

1. Sprinkle the pork cubes with the salt.
2. Thread the pork, bell peppers, and pineapple onto a skewer. Repeat until all skewers are complete. Brush the skewers generously with about half of the Teriyaki Sauce. Place them on the sheet pan.
3. Select Roast. Set temperature to 375°F (190°C) and set time to 10 minutes. Press Start to begin preheating.
4. Once the unit has preheated, place the pan into the Vortex.
5. After about 5 minutes, remove the pan from the Vortex. Turn over the skewers and brush with the remaining half of Teriyaki Sauce. Transfer the pan back to the Vortex and continue cooking until the vegetables are tender and browned in places and the pork is browned and cooked through.
6. Remove the pan from the Vortex and serve.

Bacon-Wrapped Pork Hot Dogs
Prep time: 5 minutes | Cook time: 10 minutes | Serves 5

10 thin slices of bacon
5 pork hot dogs, halved
1 teaspoon cayenne pepper
Sauce:
¼ cup mayonnaise
4 tablespoons low-carb ketchup
1 teaspoon rice vinegar
1 teaspoon chili powder

1. Arrange the slices of bacon on a clean work surface. One by one, place the halved hot dog on one end of each slice, season with cayenne pepper and wrap the hot dog with the bacon slices and secure with toothpicks as needed.
2. Place wrapped hot dogs in the perforated pan.
3. Select Air Fry. Set temperature to 390°F (199°C) and set time to 10 minutes. Press Start to begin preheating.
4. Once preheated, place the pan into the Vortex. Flip the bacon-wrapped hot dogs halfway through.
5. When cooking is complete, the bacon should be crispy and browned.
6. Make the sauce: Stir all the ingredients for the sauce in a small bowl. Wrap the bowl in plastic and set in the refrigerator until ready to serve.
7. Transfer the hot dogs to a platter and serve hot with the sauce.

BBQ Kielbasa Sausage
Prep time: 15 minutes | Cook time: 10 minutes | Serves 2 to 4

¾ pound (340 g) kielbasa sausage, cut into ½-inch slices
1 (8-ounce / 227-g) can pineapple chunks in juice, drained
1 cup bell pepper chunks
1 tablespoon barbecue seasoning
1 tablespoon soy sauce
Cooking spray

1. Spritz the perforated pan with cooking spray.
2. Combine all the ingredients in a large bowl. Toss to mix well.
3. Pour the sausage mixture in the perforated pan.
4. Select Air Fry. Set temperature to 390°F (199°C) and set time to 10 minutes. Press Start to begin preheating.
5. Once preheated, place the pan into the Vortex.
6. After 5 minutes, remove the pan from the Vortex. Stir the sausage mixture. Return the pan to the Vortex and continue cooking.
7. When cooking is complete, the sausage should be lightly browned and the bell pepper and pineapple should be soft.
8. Serve immediately.

Pork Sausage Ratatouille
Prep time: 10 minutes | Cook time: 25 minutes | Serves 4

4 pork sausages
Ratatouille:
2 zucchinis, sliced
1 eggplant, sliced
15 ounces (425 g) tomatoes, sliced
1 red bell pepper, sliced
1 medium red onion, sliced
1 cup canned butter beans, drained
1 tablespoon balsamic vinegar
2 garlic cloves, minced
1 red chili, chopped
2 tablespoons fresh thyme, chopped
2 tablespoons olive oil

1. Place the sausages in the perforated pan.
2. Select Air Fry. Set temperature to 390°F (199°C) and set time to 10 minutes. Press Start to begin preheating.
3. Once preheated, place the pan into the Vortex.
4. After 7 minutes, remove the pan from the Vortex. Flip the sausages. Return the pan to the Vortex and continue cooking.
5. When cooking is complete, the sausages should be lightly browned.
6. Meanwhile, make the ratatouille: arrange the vegetable slices on the prepared pan alternatively, then add the remaining ingredients on top.
7. Transfer the air fried sausage to a plate, then place the pan into the Vortex.
8. Select Bake. Set time to 15 minutes and bake until the vegetables are tender. Give the vegetables a stir halfway through the baking.
9. Serve the ratatouille with the sausage on top.

Garlic Pork Leg Roast with Candy Onions
Prep time: 10 minutes | Cook time: 52 minutes | Serves 4

2 teaspoons sesame oil
1 teaspoon dried sage, crushed
1 teaspoon cayenne pepper
1 rosemary sprig, chopped
1 thyme sprig, chopped
Sea salt and ground black pepper, to taste
2 pounds (907 g) pork leg roast, scored
½ pound (227 g) candy onions, sliced
4 cloves garlic, finely chopped
2 chili peppers, minced

1. In a mixing bowl, combine the sesame oil, sage, cayenne pepper, rosemary, thyme, salt and black pepper until well mixed. In another bowl, place the pork leg and brush with the seasoning mixture.
2. Place the seasoned pork leg in a baking pan. Select Air Fry. Set temperature to 400°F (205°C) and set time to 40 minutes. Press Start to begin preheating.
3. Once preheated, place the pan into the Vortex.
4. After 20 minutes, remove the pan from the Vortex. Flip the pork leg. Return the pan to the Vortex and continue cooking.
5. After another 20 minutes, add the candy onions, garlic, and chili peppers to the pan and air fry for another 12 minutes.
6. When cooking is complete, the pork leg should be browned.
7. Transfer the pork leg to a plate. Let cool for 5 minutes and slice. Spread the juices left in the pan over the pork and serve warm with the candy onions.

Thyme Pork Chops with Carrots
Prep time: 10 minutes | Cook time: 15 minutes | Serves 4

2 carrots, cut into sticks
1 cup mushrooms, sliced
2 garlic cloves, minced
2 tablespoons olive oil
1 pound (454 g) boneless pork chops
1 teaspoon dried oregano
1 teaspoon dried thyme
Salt and ground black pepper, to taste
Cooking spray

1. In a mixing bowl, toss together the carrots, mushrooms, garlic, olive oil and salt until well combined.
2. Add the pork chops to a different bowl and season with oregano, thyme, cayenne pepper, salt and black pepper.
3. Lower the vegetable mixture in the greased pan. Place the seasoned pork chops on top.
4. Select Air Fry. Set temperature to 360°F (182°C) and set time to 15 minutes. Press Start to begin preheating.
5. Once preheated, place the pan into the Vortex.
6. After 7 minutes, remove the pan from the Vortex. Flip the pork and stir the vegetables. Return the pan to the Vortex and continue cooking.
7. When cooking is complete, the pork chops should be browned and the vegetables should be tender.
8. Transfer the pork chops to the serving dishes and let cool for 5 minutes. Serve warm with vegetable on the side.

Balsamic Italian Sausages and Red Grapes
Prep time: 10 minutes | Cook time: 20 minutes | Serves 6

2 pounds (905 g) seedless red grapes
3 shallots, sliced
2 teaspoons fresh thyme
2 tablespoons olive oil
½ teaspoon kosher salt
Freshly ground black pepper, to taste
6 links (about 1½ pounds / 680 g) hot Italian sausage
3 tablespoons balsamic vinegar

1. Place the grapes in a large bowl. Add the shallots, thyme, olive oil, salt, and pepper. Gently toss. Place the grapes in a baking pan. Arrange the sausage links evenly in the pan.
2. Select Roast. Set temperature to 375°F (190°C) and set time to 20 minutes. Press Start to begin preheating.
3. Once preheated, place the pan into the Vortex.
4. After 10 minutes, remove the pan. Turn over the sausages and sprinkle the vinegar over the sausages and grapes. Gently toss the grapes and move them to one side of the pan. Return the pan to the Vortex and continue cooking.
5. When cooking is complete, the grapes should be very soft and the sausages browned. Serve immediately.

Colby Pork Sausage with Cauliflower
Prep time: 5 minutes | Cook time: 27 minutes | Serves 6

1 pound (454 g) cauliflower, chopped
6 pork sausages, chopped
½ onion, sliced
3 eggs, beaten
⅓ cup Colby cheese
1 teaspoon cumin powder
½ teaspoon tarragon
½ teaspoon sea salt
½ teaspoon ground black pepper
Cooking spray

1. Spritz the baking pan with cooking spray.
2. In a saucepan over medium heat, boil the cauliflower until tender. Place the boiled cauliflower in a food processor and pulse until puréed. Transfer to a large bowl and combine with remaining ingredients until well blended.
3. Pour the cauliflower and sausage mixture into the pan.
4. Select Bake. Set temperature to 365°F (185°C) and set time to 27 minutes. Press Start to begin preheating.
5. Once preheated, place the pan into the Vortex.
6. When cooking is complete, the sausage should be lightly browned.
7. Divide the mixture among six serving dishes and serve warm.

Pork Chop Roast with Worcestershire
Prep time: 5 minutes | Cook time: 20 minutes | Serves 2

2 (10-ounce / 284-g) bone-in, center cut pork chops, 1-inch thick
2 teaspoons Worcestershire sauce
Salt and ground black pepper, to taste
Cooking spray

1. Rub the Worcestershire sauce on both sides of pork chops.
2. Season with salt and pepper to taste.
3. Spritz the perforated pan with cooking spray and place the chops in the perforated pan side by side.
4. Select Roast. Set temperature to 350°F (180°C) and set time to 20 minutes. Press Start to begin preheating.
5. Once preheated, place the pan into the Vortex.
6. After 10 minutes, remove the pan from the Vortex. Flip the pork chops with tongs. Return the pan to the Vortex and continue cooking.
7. When cooking is complete, the pork should be well browned on both sides.
8. Let rest for 5 minutes before serving.

Pork Meatballs with Scallions
Prep time: 5 minutes | Cook time: 15 minutes | Serves 4

1 pound (454 g) ground pork
2 cloves garlic, finely minced
1 cup scallions, finely chopped
1½ tablespoons Worcestershire sauce
½ teaspoon freshly grated ginger root
1 teaspoon turmeric powder
1 tablespoon oyster sauce
1 small sliced red chili, for garnish
Cooking spray

1. Spritz the perforated pan with cooking spray.
2. Combine all the ingredients, except for the red chili in a large bowl. Toss to mix well.
3. Shape the mixture into equally sized balls, then arrange them in the perforated pan and spritz with cooking spray.
4. Select Air Fry. Set temperature to 350°F (180°C) and set time to 15 minutes. Press Start to begin preheating.
5. Once preheated, place the pan into the Vortex.
6. After 7 minutes, remove the pan from the Vortex. Flip the balls. Return the pan to the Vortex and continue cooking.
7. When cooking is complete, the balls should be lightly browned.
8. Serve the pork meatballs with red chili on top.

Breaded Calf's Liver Strips
Prep time: 15 minutes | Cook time: 4 to 5 minutes | Serves 4

1 pound (454 g) sliced calf's liver, cut into about ½-inch-wide strips
Salt and ground black pepper, to taste
2 eggs
2 tablespoons milk
½ cup whole wheat flour
1½ cups panko bread crumbs
½ cup plain bread crumbs
½ teaspoon salt
¼ teaspoon ground black pepper
Cooking spray

1. Sprinkle the liver strips with salt and pepper.
2. Beat together the egg and milk in a bowl. Place wheat flour in a shallow dish. In a second shallow dish, mix panko, plain bread crumbs, ½ teaspoon salt, and ¼ teaspoon pepper.
3. Dip liver strips in flour, egg wash, and then bread crumbs, pressing in coating slightly to make crumbs stick.
4. Spritz the perforated pan with cooking spray. Place strips in a single layer in the perforated pan.
5. Select Air Fry. Set temperature to 400°F (205°C) and set time to 4 minutes. Press Start to begin preheating.
6. Once preheated, place the pan into the Vortex.
7. After 2 minutes, remove the pan from the Vortex. Flip the strips with tongs. Return the pan to the Vortex and continue cooking.
8. When cooking is complete, the liver strips should be crispy and golden.
9. Serve immediately.

Pork Chops and Apple Bake
Prep time: 10 minutes | Cook time: 45 minutes | Serves 4

2 apples, peeled, cored, and sliced
1 teaspoon ground cinnamon, divided
4 boneless pork chops (½-inch thick)
Salt and freshly ground black pepper, to taste
3 tablespoons brown sugar
¾ cup water
1 tablespoon olive oil

1. Layer apples in bottom of a baking pan. Sprinkle with ½ teaspoon of cinnamon.
2. Trim fat from pork chops. Lay on top of the apple slices. Sprinkle with salt and pepper.
3. In a small bowl, combine the brown sugar, water, and remaining cinnamon. Pour the mixture over the chops. Drizzle chops with 1 tablespoon of olive oil.
4. Select Bake. Set temperature to 375°F (190°C) and set time to 45 minutes. Press Start to begin preheating.
5. Once preheated, place the pan into the Vortex.
6. When cooking is complete, an instant-read thermometer inserted in the pork should register 165°F (74°C).
7. Allow to rest for 3 minutes before serving.

Pork Tenderloin with Rice
Prep time: 10 minutes | Cook time: 12 minutes | Serves 4

3 scallions, diced (about ½ cup)
½ red bell pepper, diced (about ½ cup)
2 teaspoons sesame oil
½ pound (227 g) pork tenderloin, diced
½ cup frozen peas, thawed
½ cup roasted mushrooms
½ cup soy sauce
2 cups cooked rice
1 egg, beaten

1. Place the scallions and red pepper on a baking pan. Drizzle with the sesame oil and toss the vegetables to coat them in the oil.
2. Select Roast. Set temperature to 375°F (190°C) and set time to 12 minutes. Press Start to begin preheating.
3. Once preheated, place the pan into the Vortex.
4. While the vegetables are cooking, place the pork in a large bowl. Add the peas, mushrooms, soy sauce, and rice and toss to coat the ingredients with the sauce.
5. After about 4 minutes, remove the pan from the Vortex. Place the pork mixture on the pan and stir the scallions and peppers into the pork and rice. Return the pan to the Vortex and continue cooking.
6. After another 6 minutes, remove the pan from the Vortex. Move the rice mixture to the sides to create an empty circle in the middle of the pan. Pour the egg in the circle. Return the pan to the Vortex and continue cooking.
7. When cooking is complete, remove the pan from the Vortex and stir the egg to scramble it. Stir the egg into the fried rice mixture. Serve immediately.

Worcestershire Ribeye Steaks with Garlic
Prep time: 15 minutes | Cook time: 10 to 12 minutes | Serves 2 to 4

2 (8-ounce / 227-g) boneless ribeye steaks
4 teaspoons Worcestershire sauce
½ teaspoon garlic powder
Salt and ground black pepper, to taste
4 teaspoons olive oil

1. Brush the steaks with Worcestershire sauce on both sides. Sprinkle with garlic powder and coarsely ground black pepper. Drizzle the steaks with olive oil. Allow steaks to marinate for 30 minutes.
2. Transfer the steaks in the perforated pan.
3. Select Roast. Set temperature to 400°F (205°C) and set time to 4 minutes. Press Start to begin preheating.
4. Once preheated, place the pan into the Vortex.
5. After 2 minutes, remove the pan from the Vortex. Flip the steaks. Return the pan to the Vortex and continue cooking.
6. When cooking is complete, the steaks should be well browned.
7. Remove the steaks from the perforated pan and let sit for 5 minutes. Salt and serve.

Beef Ravioli with Parmesan
Prep time: 10 minutes | Cook time: 12 minutes | Serves 4

1 (20-ounce / 567-g) package frozen cheese ravioli
1 teaspoon kosher salt
1¼ cups water
6 ounces (170 g) cooked ground beef
2½ cups Marinara sauce
¼ cup grated Parmesan cheese, for garnish

1. Place the ravioli in an even layer on a baking pan. Stir the salt into the water until dissolved and pour it over the ravioli.
2. Select Bake. Set temperature to 400°F (205°C) and set time to 12 minutes. Press Start to begin preheating.
3. Once preheated, place the pan into the Vortex.
4. While the ravioli is cooking, mix the ground beef into the marinara sauce in a medium bowl.
5. After 6 minutes, remove the pan from the Vortex. Blot off any remaining water, or drain the ravioli and return them to the pan. Pour the meat sauce over the ravioli. Return the pan to the Vortex and continue cooking.
6. When cooking is complete, remove the pan from the Vortex. The ravioli should be tender and sauce heated through. Gently stir the ingredients. Serve the ravioli with the Parmesan cheese, if desired.

Dijon-Honey Pork Tenderloin
Prep time: 15 minutes | Cook time: 18 minutes | Serves 4

3 tablespoons Dijon mustard
3 tablespoons honey
1 teaspoon dried rosemary
1 tablespoon olive oil
1 pound (454 g) pork tenderloin, rinsed and drained
Salt and freshly ground black pepper, to taste

1. In a small bowl, combine the Dijon mustard, honey, and rosemary. Stir to combine.
2. Rub the pork tenderloin with salt and pepper on all sides on a clean work surface.
3. Heat the olive oil in an oven-safe skillet over high heat. Sear the pork loin on all sides in the skillet for 6 minutes or until golden brown. Flip the pork halfway through.
4. Remove from the heat and spread honey-mustard mixture evenly to coat the pork loin. Transfer the pork to a sheet pan.
5. Select Bake. Set temperature to 400°F (205°C) and set time to 18 minutes. Press Start to begin preheating.
6. Once preheated, place the pan into the Vortex.
7. When cooking is complete, an instant-read thermometer inserted in the pork should register at least 145°F (63°C).
8. Remove from the Vortex and allow to rest for 3 minutes. Slice the pork into ½-inch slices and serve.

Cheeseburgers with American Cheese
Prep time: 10 minutes | Cook time: 19 minutes | Serves 2

½ slice hearty white sandwich bread, crust removed, torn into ¼-inch pieces
1 tablespoon milk
½ teaspoon garlic powder
½ teaspoon onion powder
12 ounces (340 g) 85% lean ground beef
Salt and pepper
2 slices American cheese (2 ounces / 57 g)
2 hamburger buns, toasted if desired

1. Mash bread, milk, garlic powder, and onion powder into paste in medium bowl using fork. Break up ground beef into small pieces over bread mixture in bowl and lightly knead with hands until well combined. Divide mixture into 2 lightly packed balls, then gently flatten each into 1-inch-thick patty. Press center of each patty with fingertips to create ¼-inch-deep depression. Season with salt and pepper.
2. Arrange patties in air fryer basket, spaced evenly apart. Place basket in air fryer oven. Select the AIR FRY function and cook at 350°F (180°C) for 18 to 21 minutes, or until burgers are lightly browned and register 140°F (60°C) to 145°F (63°C) (for medium-well) or 150°F (66°C) to 155°F (68°C) (for well-done), flipping and rotating burgers halfway through cooking.
3. Top each burger with 1 slice cheese. Return basket to air fryer oven and cook until cheese is melted, about 30 seconds. Serve burgers on buns.

Roasted Pork Rib
Prep time: 5 minutes | Cook time: 20 minutes | Serves 2

1 (1-pound / 454-g) bone-in pork rib or center-cut chop, 1½ to 1¾ inches thick, trimmed
1 teaspoon vegetable oil
Salt and pepper

1. Select the ROAST function and preheat VORTEX to 350°F (180°C).
2. Pat chop dry with paper towels. Using sharp knife, cut 2 slits, about 2 inches apart, through fat on edge of chop. Rub with oil and season with salt and pepper.
3. Place chop in air fryer basket, then place basket in air fryer oven. Roast until pork registers 140°F (60°C), 20 to 25 minutes, flipping and rotating chop halfway through cooking.
4. Transfer chop to cutting board, tent with aluminum foil, and let rest for 5 minutes. Carve pork from bone and slice ½ inch thick. Serve.

Prosciutto-Wrapped Pork Tenderloin
Prep time: 5 minutes | Cook time: 20 minutes | Serves 4

2 (1-pound / 454-g) pork tenderloins, trimmed and halved crosswise
6 tablespoons unsalted butter, melted
¼ teaspoon pepper
12 thin slices prosciutto (6 ounces / 170 g)
8 large fresh sage leaves
Lemon wedges

1. Pat pork dry with paper towels, brush with 3 tablespoons melted butter, and season with pepper. For each piece of pork, shingle 3 slices of prosciutto on cutting board, overlapping edges slightly, and lay pork in center. (Tuck thinner tail ends of tenderloins under themselves as needed to create uniform bundles.) Top with 2 sage leaves, then fold prosciutto around pork, pressing on overlapping ends to secure. Brush pork bundles with remaining 3 tablespoons melted butter and arrange seam side down in air fryer basket.
2. Place basket in air fryer oven. Select the AIR FRY function and cook at 400°F (205°C) for 20 to 25 minutes, or until pork registers 140°F (60°C). Transfer pork to cutting board, tent with aluminum foil, and let rest for 5 minutes. Slice pork ½ inch thick and serve with lemon wedges.

Pork Tenderloin with Potatoes
Prep time: 10 minutes | Cook time: 28 minutes | Serves 4 to 6

3 tablespoons ground cumin
1 teaspoon chili powder
1 teaspoon kosher salt
¼ teaspoon black pepper
2 cloves garlic, minced
1 pound (454 g) pork tenderloin, cut into 2 pieces
Vegetable oil for spraying
1 pound (454 g) Yukon gold potatoes, quartered
1 tablespoon extra-virgin olive oil

1. Combine the spices and garlic in a small bowl. Transfer 1 tablespoon of the spice mixture to another bowl and set it aside to season the potatoes. Rub both pieces of the tenderloin with the remaining seasoning mixture. Set aside.
2. Select the ROAST function and preheat VORTEX to 350°F (180°C). Spray the air fryer basket with oil. Place both pieces of tenderloin in the air fryer basket and spray lightly with oil. Roast the tenderloin for approximately 20 minutes, turning halfway through, until a thermometer inserted in the center of the tenderloin reads 145°F (63°C). While the tenderloin cooks, place the potatoes in a medium bowl. Add the reserved tablespoon of seasoning mixture and the olive oil. Toss gently to coat the potatoes.
3. Transfer the tenderloin pieces to a platter and tent with foil to rest for 10 minutes. While the tenderloin rests, place the potatoes in the air fryer oven. Select the AIR FRY function and cook at 400°F (205°C) for 8 to 10 minutes, tossing once halfway through cooking, until golden brown. Serve immediately alongside the pork tenderloin.

Lamb Chops with Rosemary
Prep time: 5 minutes | Cook time: 15 minutes | Serves 4

8 (3-ounce / 85-g) lamb chops
2 teaspoons extra-virgin olive oil
1½ teaspoons chopped fresh rosemary
1 garlic clove, minced
Salt
Pepper

1. Select the ROAST function and preheat VORTEX to 390°F (199°C).
2. Drizzle the lamb chops with olive oil.
3. In a small bowl, combine the rosemary, garlic, and salt and pepper to taste. Rub the seasoning onto the front and back of each lamb chop.
4. Place the lamb chops in the air fryer oven. It is okay to stack them. Roast for 10 minutes.
5. Open the air fryer oven. Flip the lamb chops. Roast for an additional 5 minutes.
6. Cool before serving.

Breaded Pork Chops
Prep time: 5 minutes | Cook time: 15 minutes | Serves 5

5 (3½- to 5-ounce / 99- to 142-g) pork chops (bone-in or boneless)
Seasoning salt
Pepper
¼ cup all-purpose flour
2 tablespoons panko bread crumbs
Cooking oil

1. Season the pork chops with the seasoning salt and pepper to taste.
2. Sprinkle the flour on both sides of the pork chops, then coat both sides with panko bread crumbs.
3. Place the pork chops in the air fryer oven. Spray the pork chops with cooking oil. Select the AIR FRY function and cook at 380°F (193°C) for 6 minutes.
4. Open the air fryer oven and flip the pork chops. Air fry for an additional 6 minutes
5. Cool before serving.

Bell Pepper and Sausage Rolls
Prep time: 5 minutes | Cook time: 15 minutes | Serves 5

5 Italian sausages
1 green bell pepper, seeded and cut into strips
1 red bell pepper, seeded and cut into strips
½ onion, cut into strips
1 teaspoon dried oregano
½ teaspoon garlic powder
5 Italian rolls or buns

1. Place the sausages in the air fryer oven. No cooking oil is needed as the sausages will produce oil during the cooking process. The sausages should fit in the basket without stacking. If not, stacking is okay.
2. Select the AIR FRY function and cook at 360°F (182°C) for 10 minutes.
3. Season the green and red bell peppers and the onion with the oregano and garlic powder.
4. Open the air fryer oven and flip the sausages. Add the peppers and onion to the basket. Air fry for an additional 3 to 5 minutes, until the vegetables are soft and the sausages are no longer pink on the inside.
5. Serve the sausages (sliced or whole) on buns with the peppers and onion.

Mozzarella Ham Stromboli
Prep time: 10 minutes | Cook time: 20 minutes | Serves 6

1 teaspoon all-purpose flour
1 (13-ounce / 369-g) can refrigerated pizza dough
6 slices provolone cheese
½ cup shredded Mozzarella cheese
12 slices deli ham
½ red bell pepper, seeded and sliced
½ teaspoon dried basil
½ teaspoon oregano
Pepper
Cooking oil

1. Sprinkle the flour on a flat work surface. Roll out the pizza dough. Cut the dough into 6 equal-sized rectangles.
2. Add 1 slice of provolone, 1 tablespoon of Mozzarella, 2 slices of ham, and a few slices of red bell pepper to each of the rectangles.
3. Season each with dried basil, oregano, and pepper to taste.
4. Fold up each crust to close the stromboli. Using the back of a fork, press along the open edges to seal.
5. Place the stromboli in the air fryer oven. Do not stack. Work in batches. Spray the stromboli with cooking oil. Select the AIR FRY function and cook at 400°F (205°C) for 10 minutes.
6. Remove the cooked stromboli from the air fryer oven, then repeat with the remaining stromboli.
7. Cool before serving.

Beef Egg Rolls

Prep time: 15 minutes | Cook time: 12 minutes | Makes 8 egg rolls

½ chopped onion
2 garlic cloves, chopped
½ packet taco seasoning
Salt and ground black pepper, to taste
1 pound (454 g) lean ground beef
½ can cilantro lime rotel
16 egg roll wrappers
1 cup shredded Mexican cheese
1 tablespoon olive oil
1 teaspoon cilantro

1. Add onions and garlic to a skillet, cooking until fragrant. Then add taco seasoning, pepper, salt, and beef, cooking until beef is broke up into tiny pieces and cooked thoroughly.
2. Add rotel and stir well.
3. Lay out egg wrappers and brush with a touch of water to soften a bit.
4. Load wrappers with beef filling and add cheese to each.
5. Fold diagonally to close and use water to secure edges.
6. Brush filled egg wrappers with olive oil and add to the air fryer oven.
7. Select the AIR FRY function and cook at 400°F (205°C) for 8 minutes. Flip, and air fry for another 4 minutes.
8. Serve sprinkled with cilantro.

Pork Chops with Rinds

Prep time: 5 minutes | Cook time: 15 minutes | Serves 4

1 teaspoon chili powder
½ teaspoon garlic powder
1½ ounces (43 g) pork rinds, finely ground
4 (4-ounce / 113-g) pork chops
1 tablespoon coconut oil, melted

1. Combine the chili powder, garlic powder, and ground pork rinds.
2. Coat the pork chops with the coconut oil, followed by the pork rind mixture, taking care to cover them completely. Then place the chops in the air fryer basket.
3. Select the AIR FRY function and cook at 400°F (204°C) for 15 minutes, or until the internal temperature of the chops reaches at least 145°F (63°C), turning halfway through.
4. Serve immediately.

Beef Cheeseburger Egg Rolls

Prep time: 15 minutes | Cook time: 8 minutes | Makes 6 egg rolls

8 ounces (227 g) raw lean ground beef
½ cup chopped onion
½ cup chopped bell pepper
¼ teaspoon onion powder
¼ teaspoon garlic powder
3 tablespoons cream cheese
1 tablespoon yellow mustard
3 tablespoons shredded Cheddar cheese
6 chopped dill pickle chips
6 egg roll wrappers

1. In a skillet, add the beef, onion, bell pepper, onion powder, and garlic powder. Stir and crumble beef until fully cooked, and vegetables are soft.
2. Take skillet off the heat and add cream cheese, mustard, and Cheddar cheese, stirring until melted.
3. Pour beef mixture into a bowl and fold in pickles.
4. Lay out egg wrappers and divide the beef mixture into each one. Moisten egg roll wrapper edges with water. Fold sides to the middle and seal with water.
5. Repeat with all other egg rolls.
6. Put rolls into air fryer oven, one batch at a time. Select the AIR FRY function and cook at 392°F (200°C) for 8 minutes.
7. Serve immediately.

Beef Chuck with Brussels Sprouts

Prep time: 20 minutes | Cook time: 15 minutes | Serves 4

1 pound (454 g) beef chuck shoulder steak
2 tablespoons vegetable oil
1 tablespoon red wine vinegar
1 teaspoon fine sea salt
½ teaspoon ground black pepper
1 teaspoon smoked paprika
1 teaspoon onion powder
½ teaspoon garlic powder
½ pound (227 g) Brussels sprouts, cleaned and halved
½ teaspoon fennel seeds
1 teaspoon dried basil
1 teaspoon dried sage

1. Massage the beef with the vegetable oil, wine vinegar, salt, black pepper, paprika, onion powder, and garlic powder, coating it well.
2. Allow to marinate for a minimum of 3 hours.
3. Remove the beef from the marinade and put in the air fryer oven. Select the AIR FRY function and cook at 390°F (199°C) for 10 minutes. Flip the beef halfway through.
4. Put the prepared Brussels sprouts in the air fryer oven along with the fennel seeds, basil, and sage.
5. Lower the heat to 380°F (193°C) and air fry everything for another 5 minutes.
6. Give them a good stir. Air fry for an additional 10 minutes.
7. Serve immediately.

Peppercorn Crusted Beef Tenderloin
Prep time: 5 minutes | Cook time: 25 minutes | Serves 6

2 pounds (907 g) beef tenderloin
2 teaspoons roasted garlic, minced
2 tablespoons salted butter, melted
3 tablespoons ground 4 peppercorn blend

1. Remove any surplus fat from the beef tenderloin.
2. Combine the roasted garlic and melted butter to apply to the tenderloin with a brush.
3. On a plate, spread out the peppercorns and roll the tenderloin in them, making sure they are covering and clinging to the meat. Transfer the tenderloin to the air fryer basket.
4. Select the AIR FRY function and cook at 400°F (204°C) for 25 minutes, turning halfway through cooking.
5. Let the tenderloin rest for ten minutes before slicing and serving.

BBQ Pork Steaks
Prep time: 5 minutes | Cook time: 15 minutes | Serves 4

4 pork steaks
1 tablespoon Cajun seasoning
2 tablespoons BBQ sauce
1 tablespoon vinegar
1 teaspoon soy sauce
½ cup brown sugar
½ cup ketchup

1. Sprinkle pork steaks with Cajun seasoning.
2. Combine remaining ingredients and brush onto steaks.
3. Add coated steaks to air fryer oven. Select the AIR FRY function and cook at 290°F (143°C) for 15 minutes, or until just browned.
4. Serve immediately.

Beef Chuck Cheeseburgers
Prep time: 10 minutes | Cook time: 15 minutes | Serves 4

¾ pound (340 g) ground beef chuck
1 envelope onion soup mix
Kosher salt and freshly ground black pepper, to taste
1 teaspoon paprika
4 slices Monterey Jack cheese
4 ciabatta rolls

1. In a bowl, stir together the ground chuck, onion soup mix, salt, black pepper, and paprika to combine well.
2. Take four equal portions of the mixture and mold each one into a patty. Transfer to the air fryer oven. Select the AIR FRY function and cook at 385°F (196°C) for 10 minutes.
3. Put the slices of cheese on the top of the burgers.
4. Air fry for another minute before serving on ciabatta rolls.

Cheddar Bacon Burst with Spinach
Prep time: 5 minutes | Cook time: 60 minutes | Serves 8

30 slices bacon
1 tablespoon Chipotle seasoning
2 teaspoons Italian seasoning
2½ cups Cheddar cheese
4 cups raw spinach

1. Select the BAKE function and preheat VORTEX to 375°F (191°C).
2. Weave the bacon into 15 vertical pieces and 12 horizontal pieces. Cut the extra 3 in half to fill in the rest, horizontally.
3. Season the bacon with Chipotle seasoning and Italian seasoning.
4. Add the cheese to the bacon.
5. Add the spinach and press down to compress.
6. Tightly roll up the woven bacon.
7. Line a baking sheet with kitchen foil and add plenty of salt to it.
8. Put the bacon on top of a cooling rack and put that on top of the baking sheet.
9. Bake for 60 minutes.
10. Let cool for 15 minutes before slicing and serving.

Greek Lamb Rack
Prep time: 5 minutes | Cook time: 10 minutes | Serves 4

¼ cup freshly squeezed lemon juice
1 teaspoon oregano
2 teaspoons minced fresh rosemary
1 teaspoon minced fresh thyme
2 tablespoons minced garlic
Salt and freshly ground black pepper, to taste
2 to 4 tablespoons olive oil
1 lamb rib rack (7 to 8 ribs)

1. Select the ROAST function and preheat VORTEX to 360°F (182°C).
2. In a small mixing bowl, combine the lemon juice, oregano, rosemary, thyme, garlic, salt, pepper, and olive oil and mix well.
3. Rub the mixture over the lamb, covering all the meat. Put the rack of lamb in the air fryer oven. Roast for 10 minutes. Flip the rack halfway through.
4. After 10 minutes, measure the internal temperature of the rack of lamb reaches at least 145°F (63°C).
5. Serve immediately.

Cheese Crusted Chops
Prep time: 10 minutes | Cook time: 12 minutes | Serves 4 to 6

¼ teaspoon pepper
½ teaspoons salt
4 to 6 thick boneless pork chops
1 cup pork rind crumbs
¼ teaspoon chili powder
½ teaspoons onion powder
1 teaspoon smoked paprika
2 beaten eggs
3 tablespoons grated Parmesan cheese
Cooking spray

1. Rub the pepper and salt on both sides of pork chops.
2. In a food processor, pulse pork rinds into crumbs. Mix crumbs with chili powder, onion powder, and paprika in a bowl.
3. Beat eggs in another bowl.
4. Dip pork chops into eggs then into pork rind crumb mixture.
5. Spritz the air fryer basket with cooking spray and add pork chops to the basket.
6. Select the AIR FRY function and cook at 400°F (205°C) for 12 minutes.
7. Serve garnished with the Parmesan cheese.

Crumbed Golden Filet Mignon
Prep time: 15 minutes | Cook time: 12 minutes | Serves 4

½ pound (227 g) filet mignon
Sea salt and ground black pepper, to taste
½ teaspoon cayenne pepper
1 teaspoon dried basil
1 teaspoon dried rosemary
1 teaspoon dried thyme
1 tablespoon sesame oil
1 small egg, whisked
½ cup bread crumbs

1. Cover the filet mignon with the salt, black pepper, cayenne pepper, basil, rosemary, and thyme. Coat with sesame oil.
2. Put the egg in a shallow plate.
3. Pour the bread crumbs in another plate.
4. Dip the filet mignon into the egg. Roll it into the crumbs.
5. Transfer the steak to the air fryer oven. Select the AIR FRY function and cook at 360°F (182°C) for 12 minutes, or until it turns golden.
6. Serve immediately.

Air Fried Beef Ribs
Prep time: 20 minutes | Cook time: 8 minutes | Serves 4

1 pound (454 g) meaty beef ribs, rinsed and drained
3 tablespoons apple cider vinegar
1 cup coriander, finely chopped
1 tablespoon fresh basil leaves, chopped
2 garlic cloves, finely chopped
1 chipotle powder
1 teaspoon fennel seeds
1 teaspoon hot paprika
Kosher salt and black pepper, to taste
½ cup vegetable oil

1. Coat the ribs with the remaining ingredients and refrigerate for at least 3 hours.
2. Separate the ribs from the marinade and put them in the air fryer basket.
3. Select the AIR FRY function and cook at 360°F (182°C) for 8 minutes.
4. Pour the remaining marinade over the ribs before serving.

Mexican Pork Chops
Prep time: 5 minutes | Cook time: 15 minutes | Serves 2

¼ teaspoon dried oregano
1½ teaspoons taco seasoning mix
2 (4-ounce / 113-g) boneless pork chops
2 tablespoons unsalted butter, divided

1. Combine the dried oregano and taco seasoning in a small bowl and rub the mixture into the pork chops. Brush the chops with 1 tablespoon butter. Transfer to the air fryer basket.
2. Select the AIR FRY function and cook at 400°F (204°C) for 15 minutes, turning them over halfway through to air fry on the other side.
3. When the chops are a brown color, check the internal temperature has reached 145°F (63°C) and remove from the air fryer oven. Serve with a garnish of remaining butter.

Mushroom and Beef Meatloaf
Prep time: 10 minutes | Cook time: 25 minutes | Serves 4

1 pound (454 g) ground beef
1 egg, beaten
1 mushrooms, sliced
1 tablespoon thyme
1 small onion, chopped
3 tablespoons bread crumbs
Ground black pepper, to taste

1. Select the BAKE function and preheat VORTEX to 400°F (204°C).
2. Put all the ingredients into a large bowl and combine entirely.
3. Transfer the meatloaf mixture into the loaf pan and move it to the air fryer basket.
4. Bake for 25 minutes. Slice up before serving.

Orange Pork Tenderloin
Prep time: 15 minutes | Cook time: 23 minutes | Serves 3 to 4

2 tablespoons brown sugar
2 teaspoons cornstarch
2 teaspoons Dijon mustard
½ cup orange juice
½ teaspoon soy sauce
2 teaspoons grated fresh ginger
¼ cup white wine
Zest of 1 orange
1 pound (454 g) pork tenderloin
Salt and freshly ground black pepper, to taste
Oranges, halved, for garnish
Fresh parsley, for garnish

1. Combine the brown sugar, cornstarch, Dijon mustard, orange juice, soy sauce, ginger, white wine and orange zest in a small saucepan and bring the mixture to a boil on the stovetop. Lower the heat and simmer while you air fry the pork tenderloin or until the sauce has thickened.
2. Season all sides of the pork tenderloin with salt and freshly ground black pepper. Transfer the tenderloin to the air fryer basket.
3. Select the AIR FRY function and cook at 370°F (188°C) for 20 to 23 minutes, or until the internal temperature reaches 145°F (63°C). Flip the tenderloin over halfway through the cooking process and baste with the sauce.
4. Transfer the tenderloin to a cutting board and let it rest for 5 minutes. Slice the pork at a slight angle and serve immediately with orange halves and fresh parsley.

Pepperoni and Bell Pepper Pockets
Prep time: 5 minutes | Cook time: 8 minutes | Serves 4

4 bread slices, 1-inch thick
Olive oil, for misting
24 slices pepperoni
1 ounce (28 g) roasted red peppers, drained and patted dry
1 ounce (28 g) Pepper Jack cheese, cut into 4 slices

1. Spray both sides of bread slices with olive oil.
2. Stand slices upright and cut a deep slit in the top to create a pocket (almost to the bottom crust, but not all the way through).
3. Stuff each bread pocket with 6 slices of pepperoni, a large strip of roasted red pepper, and a slice of cheese.
4. Put bread pockets in air fryer basket, standing up. Select the AIR FRY function and cook at 360°F (182°C) for 8 minutes, until filling is heated through and bread is lightly browned.
5. Serve hot.

Potato and Prosciutto Salad
Prep time: 10 minutes | Cook time: 7 minutes | Serves 8

Salad:
4 pounds (1.8 kg) potatoes, boiled and cubed
15 slices prosciutto, diced
2 cups shredded Cheddar cheese
Dressing:
15 ounces (425 g) sour cream
2 tablespoons mayonnaise
1 teaspoon salt
1 teaspoon black pepper
1 teaspoon dried basil

1. Put the potatoes, prosciutto, and Cheddar in a baking dish. Put it in the air fryer oven.
2. Select the AIR FRY function and cook at 350°F (177°C) for 7 minutes.
3. In a separate bowl, mix the sour cream, mayonnaise, salt, pepper, and basil using a whisk.
4. Coat the salad with the dressing and serve.

Char Siew
Prep time: 10 minutes | Cook time: 20 minutes | Serves 4 to 6

1 strip of pork shoulder butt with a good amount of fat marbling
Olive oil, for brushing the pan
Marinade:
1 teaspoon sesame oil
4 tablespoons raw honey
1 teaspoon low-sodium dark soy sauce
1 teaspoon light soy sauce
1 tablespoon rose wine
2 tablespoons Hoisin sauce

1. Combine all the marinade ingredients together in a Ziploc bag. Put pork in bag, making sure all sections of pork strip are engulfed in the marinade. Chill for 3 to 24 hours.
2. Take out the strip 30 minutes before planning to roast.
3. Select the ROAST function and preheat VORTEX to 350°F (177°C).
4. Put foil on small pan and brush with olive oil. Put marinated pork strip onto prepared pan.
5. Roast in the preheated air fryer oven for 20 minutes.
6. Glaze with marinade every 5 to 10 minutes.
7. Remove strip and leave to cool a few minutes before slicing.
8. Serve immediately.

Citrus Pork Loin Roast
Prep time: 10 minutes | Cook time: 45 minutes | Serves 8

1 tablespoon lime juice
1 tablespoon orange marmalade
1 teaspoon coarse brown mustard
1 teaspoon curry powder
1 teaspoon dried lemongrass
2 pound (907 g) boneless pork loin roast
Salt and ground black pepper, to taste
Cooking spray

1. Mix the lime juice, marmalade, mustard, curry powder, and lemongrass.
2. Rub mixture all over the surface of the pork loin. Season with salt and pepper.
3. Spray air fryer basket with cooking spray and place pork roast diagonally in the basket.
4. Select the AIR FRY function and cook at 360°F (182°C) for 45 minutes, until the internal temperature reaches at least 145°F (63°C).
5. Wrap roast in foil and let rest for 10 minutes before slicing.
6. Serve immediately.

Barbecue Pork Ribs
Prep time: 5 minutes | Cook time: 30 minutes | Serves 4

1 tablespoon barbecue dry rub
1 teaspoon mustard
1 tablespoon apple cider vinegar
1 teaspoon sesame oil
1 pound (454 g) pork ribs, chopped

1. Combine the dry rub, mustard, apple cider vinegar, and sesame oil, then coat the ribs with this mixture. Refrigerate the ribs for 20 minutes.
2. When the ribs are ready, place them in the air fryer oven. Select the AIR FRY function and cook at 360°F (182°C) for 15 minutes. Flip them and air fry on the other side for a further 15 minutes.
3. Serve immediately.

Smoked Beef
Prep time: 10 minutes | Cook time: 45 minutes | Serves 8

2 pounds (907 g) roast beef, at room temperature
2 tablespoons extra-virgin olive oil
1 teaspoon sea salt flakes
1 teaspoon ground black pepper
1 teaspoon smoked paprika
Few dashes of liquid smoke
2 jalapeño peppers, thinly sliced

1. Select the ROAST function and preheat VORTEX to 330°F (166°C).
2. With kitchen towels, pat the beef dry.
3. Massage the extra-virgin olive oil, salt, black pepper, and paprika into the meat. Cover with liquid smoke.
4. Put the beef in the air fryer oven and roast for 30 minutes. Flip the roast over and allow to roast for another 15 minutes.
5. When cooked through, serve topped with sliced jalapeños.

Provolone Stuffed Beef and Pork Meatballs
Prep time: 15 minutes | Cook time: 12 minutes | Serves 4 to 6

1 tablespoon olive oil
1 small onion, finely chopped
1 to 2 cloves garlic, minced
¾ pound (340 g) ground beef
¾ pound (340 g) ground pork
¾ cup bread crumbs
¼ cup grated Parmesan cheese
¼ cup finely chopped fresh parsley
½ teaspoon dried oregano
1½ teaspoons salt
Freshly ground black pepper, to taste
2 eggs, lightly beaten
5 ounces (142 g) sharp or aged provolone cheese, cut into 1-inch cubes

1. Preheat a skillet over medium-high heat. Add the oil and cook the onion and garlic until tender, but not browned.
2. Transfer the onion and garlic to a large bowl and add the beef, pork, bread crumbs, Parmesan cheese, parsley, oregano, salt, pepper and eggs. Mix well until all the ingredients are combined. Divide the mixture into 12 evenly sized balls. Make one meatball at a time, by pressing a hole in the meatball mixture with the finger and pushing a piece of provolone cheese into the hole. Mold the meat back into a ball, enclosing the cheese.
3. Working in two batches, transfer six of the meatballs to the air fryer basket. Select the AIR FRY function and cook at 380°F (193°C) for 12 minutes, shaking the basket and turning the meatballs twice during the cooking process. Repeat with the remaining 6 meatballs. Serve warm.

Chapter 7
Fish and Seafood

Bacon-Wrapped Herb Rainbow Trout
Prep time: 10 minutes | Cook time: 20 minutes | Serves 4

4 (8- to 10-ounce / 227- to 283-g) rainbow trout, butterflied and boned
2 teaspoons kosher salt, divided
1 tablespoon extra-virgin olive oil, divided
1 tablespoon freshly squeezed lemon juice, divided
2 tablespoons chopped fresh parsley, divided
2 tablespoons chopped fresh chives, divided
8 thin bacon slices
Lemon wedges, for serving

1. Lightly oil a sheet pan.
2. Sprinkle the inside and outside of each trout with the salt. Brush the inside with the oil and drizzle with the lemon juice. Scatter the parsley and chives on one side of each butterflied trout. Fold the trout closed and wrap each one with two slices of bacon. Transfer to the sheet pan.
3. Select Bake. Set temperature to 400°F (205°C) and set time to 20 minutes. Select Start to begin preheating.
4. Once preheated, slide the pan into the Vortex. Flip the trout halfway through the cooking time.
5. When done, the bacon will be crisp.
6. Serve with lemon wedges.

Crab Cheese Enchiladas
Prep time: 10 minutes | Cook time: 25 minutes | Serves 4

8 (6-inch) corn tortillas
Nonstick cooking spray or vegetable oil, for brushing
2 cups mild tomatillo salsa or green enchilada sauce
½ cup heavy (whipping) cream
8 ounces (227 g) lump crab meat, picked through to remove any shells
3 or 4 scallions, chopped
8 ounces (227 g) Monterey Jack cheese, shredded

1. Spray the tortillas on both sides with cooking spray or brush lightly with oil. Arrange on a sheet pan, overlapping as little as possible.
2. Select Bake. Set temperature to 350°F (180°C) and set time to 5 minutes. Select Start to begin preheating.
3. Once preheated, slide the pan into the Vortex.
4. When done, the tortillas will be warm and flexible.
5. Meanwhile, stir together the salsa and cream in a shallow, microwave-safe bowl and heat in the microwave until very warm, about 45 seconds.
6. Pour a quarter of the salsa mixture into a baking pan. Place a tortilla in the sauce, turning it over to coat thoroughly. Spoon a heaping tablespoon of crab down the middle of the tortilla, then top with a teaspoon of scallions and a heaping tablespoon of cheese. Roll up the tortilla and place it seam-side down at one end of the pan. Repeat with the remaining tortillas, forming a row of enchiladas in the pan. Spoon most or all of the remaining sauce over the enchiladas so they are nicely coated but not drowning. Sprinkle the remaining cheese over the top.
7. Bake for 18 to 20 minutes, until the cheese is melted and the sauce is bubbling.

Salmon Fillet with Spinach, and Beans
Prep time: 10 minutes | Cook time: 35 minutes | Serves 4

2 tablespoons olive oil, divided
1 garlic clove, thinly sliced
1 (9- to 10-ounce / 255- to 283-g) bag baby spinach
1 (15-ounce / 425-g) can cannellini or navy beans, rinsed and drained
1½ teaspoons kosher salt, divided
½ teaspoon ground cumin
½ teaspoon ground coriander
¼ teaspoon red pepper flakes
4 (6-ounce / 170-g) skinless salmon fillets

1. Heat 1 tablespoon of oil in a large, oven-safe skillet over medium-high heat. Add the garlic and cook, stirring, until fragrant, about 30 seconds. Add the spinach a handful at a time and cook, tossing, until slightly wilted, adding more as you have room. Stir in the beans, ¾ teaspoon of salt, cumin, coriander, and red pepper flakes.
2. Season the salmon with the remaining ¾ teaspoon of salt. Place the fillets in a single layer on top of the spinach mixture and drizzle with the remaining 1 tablespoon of oil.
3. Select Bake. Set temperature to 300°F (150°C) and set time to 35 minutes. Select Start to begin preheating.
4. Once preheated, put the skillet in the Vortex.
5. When done, the salmon will be opaque in the center.

Marinated Catfish Fillet
Prep time: 10 minutes | Cook time: 15 minutes | Serves 4

4 (6-ounce / 170-g) catfish fillets
Marinade Ingredients:
1 tablespoon olive oil
1 tablespoon lemon juice
¼ dry white wine
1 tablespoon garlic powder
1 tablespoon soy sauce

1. Combine the marinade ingredients in an ovenproof baking dish. Add the fillets and let stand for 10 minutes, spooning the marinade over the fillets every 2 minutes.
2. Select Broil. Set temperature to 400°F (205°C) and set time to 15 minutes. Select Start to begin preheating.
3. Once preheated, place the baking dish in the Vortex.
4. When done, the fish will flake easily with a fork.

Lemony Shrimp with Arugula

Prep time: 10 minutes | Cook time: 10 minutes | Serves 4

4 tablespoons unsalted butter, melted
2 tablespoons extra-virgin olive oil
1 teaspoon kosher salt
6 garlic cloves, minced
¼ cup chopped fresh parsley, divided
2 pounds (907 g) large shrimp, peeled and deveined
2 tablespoons freshly squeezed lemon juice
1 (9- to 10-ounce / 255- to 283-g) bag arugula

1. In a baking pan, add the butter, oil, salt, garlic, and half the parsley. Stir well. Add the shrimp and toss to coat, then arrange the shrimp in a single layer.
2. Select Bake. Set temperature to 375°F (190°C) and set time to 5 minutes. Select Start to begin preheating.
3. Once preheated, slide the pan into the Vortex.
4. When done, the shrimp will be opaque and pink.
5. Remove the pan from the Vortex. Add the lemon juice, arugula, and remaining parsley. Toss well to wilt the arugula. Serve immediately.

Broiled Lemony Salmon Steak

Prep time: 10 minutes | Cook time: 20 minutes | Serves 2

2 (6-ounce / 170-g) salmon steaks
Brushing Mixture:
2 tablespoons lemon juice
2 tablespoons olive oil
1 tablespoon soy sauce
1 teaspoon dried dill or dill weed
½ teaspoon garlic powder
1 teaspoon soy sauce

1. Combine the brushing mixture ingredients in a small bowl and brush the salmon steak tops, skin side down, liberally, reserving the remaining mixture. Let the steaks sit at room temperature for 10 minutes, then place on a broiling rack with a pan underneath.
2. Select Broil. Set temperature to 400°F (205°C) and set time to 20 minutes. Select Start to begin preheating.
3. Once preheated, slide the pan into the Vortex.
4. After 15 minutes, remove from the Vortex, and brush the steaks with the remaining mixture. Broil again for 5 minutes, or until the meat flakes easily with a fork.

Fish Fillet with Poblano Sauce

Prep time: 10 minutes | Cook time: 20 minutes | Makes 4 fillets

4 (5-ounce / 142-g) thin fish fillets—perch, scrod, catfish, or flounder
1 tablespoon olive oil
Poblano Sauce:
1 poblano chili, seeded and chopped
1 bell pepper, seeded and chopped
2 tablespoons chopped onion
5 garlic cloves, peeled
1 tablespoon flour
1 cup fat-free half-and-half
Salt, to taste

1. Brush the fillets with olive oil and transfer to an oiled or nonstick square baking (cake) pan. Set aside.
2. Combine the poblano sauce ingredients and process in a blender or food processor until smooth. Spoon the poblano sauce over the fillets, covering them well.
3. Select Bake. Set temperature to 350°F (180°C) and set time to 20 minutes. Select Start to begin preheating.
4. Once preheated, slide the pan into the Vortex.
5. When done, the fish will flake easily with a fork.

Crispy Fish Fillet

Prep time: 10 minutes | Cook time: 14 minutes | Serves 4

4 (6-ounce / 170-g) fish fillets, approximately ¼- to ½-inch thick
2 tablespoons vegetable oil
Coating Ingredients:
1 cup cornmeal
1 teaspoon garlic powder
1 teaspoon ground cumin
1 teaspoon paprika
Salt, to taste

1. Combine the coating ingredients in a small bowl, blending well. Transfer to a large plate, spreading evenly over the surface. Brush the fillets with vegetable oil and press both sides of each fillet into the coating.
2. Place the fillets in an oiled or nonstick square baking (cake) pan, laying them flat.
3. Select Broil. Set temperature to 400°F (205°C) and set time to 14 minutes. Select Start to begin preheating.
4. Once preheated, slide the pan into the Vortex.
5. Broil for 7 minutes, then remove the pan from the Vortex and carefully turn the fillets with a spatula. Broil for another 7 minutes, or until the fish flakes easily with a fork and the coating is crisped to your preference. Serve immediately.

Mediterranean Baked Fish Fillet
Prep time: 10 minutes | Cook time: 25 minutes | Serves 4

4 (6-ounce / 170-g) fish fillets (red snapper, cod, whiting, sole, or mackerel)
Mixture Ingredients:
1 tablespoon olive oil
2 tablespoons tomato paste
3 plum tomatoes, chopped
2 garlic cloves, minced
2 tablespoons capers
2 tablespoons pitted and chopped black olives
2 tablespoons chopped fresh basil leaves
2 tablespoons chopped fresh parsley

1. Combine the baking mixture ingredients in a small bowl. Set aside.
2. Layer the fillets in an oiled or nonstick square baking (cake) pan, overlapping them if necessary, and spoon the baking mixture over the fish.
3. Select Bake. Set temperature to 350°F (180°C) and set time to 25 minutes. Select Start to begin preheating.
4. Once preheated, slide the pan into the Vortex.
5. When done, the fish will flake easily with a fork.

Curried Halibut Fillets with Parmesan
Prep time: 5 minutes | Cook time: 10 minutes | Serves 4

2 medium-sized halibut fillets
Dash of tabasco sauce
1 teaspoon curry powder
½ teaspoon ground coriander
½ teaspoon hot paprika
Kosher salt and freshly cracked mixed peppercorns, to taste
2 eggs
1½ tablespoons olive oil
½ cup grated Parmesan cheese

1. On a clean work surface, drizzle the halibut fillets with the tabasco sauce. Sprinkle with the curry powder, coriander, hot paprika, salt, and cracked mixed peppercorns. Set aside.
2. In a shallow bowl, beat the eggs until frothy. In another shallow bowl, combine the olive oil and Parmesan cheese.
3. One at a time, dredge the halibut fillets in the beaten eggs, shaking off any excess, then roll them over the Parmesan cheese until evenly coated.
4. Arrange the halibut fillets in the perforated pan in a single layer.
5. Select Roast. Set temperature to 365°F (185°C) and set time to 10 minutes. Press Start to begin preheating.
6. Once preheated, place the pan into the Vortex.
7. When cooking is complete, the fish should be golden brown and crisp. Cool for 5 minutes before serving.

Flounder Fillet and Asparagus Rolls
Prep time: 10 minutes | Cook time: 30 minutes | Serves 4

1 dozen asparagus stalks, tough stem part cut off
4 (6-ounce / 170-g) flounder fillets
4 tablespoons chopped scallions
4 tablespoons shredded carrots
4 tablespoons finely chopped Almonds
1 teaspoon dried dill weed
Salt and freshly ground black pepper, to taste
1 lemon, cut into wedges

1. Place 3 asparagus stalks lengthwise on a flounder fillet. Add 1 tablespoon scallions, 1 tablespoon carrots, 1 tablespoon almonds, and a sprinkling of dill. Season to taste with salt and pepper and roll the fillet together so that the long edges overlap. Secure the edges with toothpicks or tie with cotton string. Carefully place the rolled fillet in an oiled or nonstick square baking (cake) pan. Repeat the process for the remaining ingredients. Cover the pan with aluminum foil.
2. Select Bake. Set temperature to 400°F (205°C) and set time to 20 minutes. Select Start to begin preheating.
3. Once preheated, slide the pan into the Vortex, covered.
4. When done, the asparagus will be tender. Remove the cover.
5. Select Broil. Set temperature to 400°F (205°C) and set time to 10 minutes. Slide the pan into the Vortex. When done, the fish will be lightly browned.
6. Remove and discard the toothpicks or string. Serve the rolled fillets with lemon wedges.

Fish Fillet with Sun-Dried Tomato Pesto
Prep time: 10 minutes | Cook time: 31 minutes | Serves 4

4 (6-ounce / 170-g) fish fillets (trout, catfish, flounder, or tilapia)
1 tablespoon reduced-fat mayonnaise
2 tablespoons chopped fresh cilantro Olive oil
Tomato Sauce:
¼ cup chopped sun-dried tomatoes
2 tablespoons chopped fresh basil
⅔ cup dry white wine
2 tablespoons grated Parmesan cheese
2 tablespoons olive oil
1 tablespoon pine nuts
Salt and freshly ground black pepper, to taste

1. Process the tomato sauce ingredients in a blender or food processor until smooth.
2. Layer the fish fillets in an oiled or nonstick square baking (cake) pan. Spoon the sauce over the fish, spreading evenly.
3. Select Bake. Set temperature to 400°F (205°C) and set time to 25 minutes. Select Start to begin preheating.
4. Once preheated, slide the pan into the Vortex, uncovered.
5. When done, the fish will flake easily with a fork. Remove from the Vortex, spread the mayonnaise on top of the fish, and garnish with the cilantro.
6. Select Broil. Set temperature to 400°F (205°C) and set time to 6 minutes. Slide the pan into the Vortex. When done, the fish will be lightly browned.

Catfish, Toamto and Onion Kebabs
Prep time: 10 minutes | Cook time: 20 minutes | Serves 4

4 (5-ounce / 142-g) catfish fillets
4 (9-inch) metal skewers
2 plum tomatoes, quartered
1 onion, cut into 1 × 1-inch pieces
Marinade:
3 tablespoons lemon juice
3 tablespoons tomato juice
2 garlic cloves, minced
2 tablespoons olive oil
1 teaspoon soy sauce

1. Combine the marinade ingredients in a small bowl. Set aside.
2. Cut the fillets into 2 by 3-inch strips and place in a shallow glass or ceramic dish. Add the marinade and refrigerate, covered, for at least 20 minutes. Remove the strips from the marinade, roll, and skewer, alternating the rolled strips with the tomatoes and onion.
3. Brush the kebabs with marinade, reserving the remaining marinade for brushing again later. Place the skewers on a broiling rack with a pan underneath.
4. Select Broil. Set temperature to 400°F (205°C) and set time to 20 minutes. Select Start to begin preheating.
5. Once preheated, slide the pan into the Vortex.
6. Broil for 10 minutes, then remove the pan from the Vortex and carefully turn the skewers. Brush the kebabs with the marinade and broil again for 10 minutes, or until browned.

Clam Appetizers
Prep time: 10 minutes | Cook time: 15 minutes | Makes 12 appetizers

1 (6-ounce / 170-g) can minced clams, well drained
1 cup multigrain bread crumbs
1 tablespoon minced onion
1 teaspoon garlic powder
1 teaspoon Worcestershire sauce
1 tablespoon chopped fresh parsley
2 tablespoons olive oil
Salt and freshly ground black pepper, to taste
Lemon wedges

1. Combine all the ingredients in a medium bowl and fill 12 scrubbed clamshells or small baking dishes with equal portions of the mixture. Place in an oiled or nonstick square (cake) pan.
2. Select Bake. Set temperature to 400°F (205°C) and set time to 15 minutes. Select Start to begin preheating.
3. Once preheated, slide the pan into the Vortex.
4. When done, the clam will be lightly browned.

Honey Halibut Steaks with Parsley
Prep time: 5 minutes | Cook time: 10 minutes | Serves 4

1 pound (454 g) halibut steaks
¼ cup vegetable oil
2½ tablespoons Worcester sauce
2 tablespoons honey
2 tablespoons vermouth
1 tablespoon freshly squeezed lemon juice
1 tablespoon fresh parsley leaves, coarsely chopped
Salt and pepper, to taste
1 teaspoon dried basil

1. Put all the ingredients in a large mixing dish and gently stir until the fish is coated evenly. Transfer the fish to the perforated pan.
2. Select Roast. Set temperature to 390°F (199°C) and set time to 10 minutes. Press Start to begin preheating.
3. Once preheated, place the pan into the Vortex. Flip the fish halfway through cooking time.
4. When cooking is complete, the fish should reach an internal temperature of at least 145°F (63°C) on a meat thermometer. Remove from the Vortex and let the fish cool for 5 minutes before serving.

Catfish Fillets with Pecan Crust
Prep time: 5 minutes | Cook time: 12 minutes | Serves 4

½ cup pecan meal
1 teaspoon fine sea salt
¼ teaspoon ground black pepper
4 (4-ounce / 113-g) catfish fillets
Avocado oil spray
For Garnish (Optional):
Fresh oregano
Pecan halves

1. Spray the perforated pan with avocado oil spray.
2. Combine the pecan meal, sea salt, and black pepper in a large bowl. Dredge each catfish fillet in the meal mixture, turning until well coated. Spritz the fillets with avocado oil spray, then transfer to the perforated pan.
3. Select Air Fry. Set temperature to 375°F (190°C) and set time to 12 minutes. Press Start to begin preheating.
4. Once preheated, place the pan into the Vortex. Flip the fillets halfway through the cooking time.
5. When cooking is complete, the fish should be cooked through and no longer translucent. Remove from the Vortex and sprinkle the oregano sprigs and pecan halves on top for garnish, if desired. Serve immediately.

Paprika Tilapia with Garlic Aioli
Prep time: 5 minutes | Cook time: 15 minutes | Serves 4

Tilapia:
4 tilapia fillets
1 tablespoon extra-virgin olive oil
1 teaspoon garlic powder
1 teaspoon paprika
1 teaspoon dried basil
A pinch of lemon-pepper seasoning
Garlic Aioli:
2 garlic cloves, minced
1 tablespoon mayonnaise
Juice of ½ lemon
1 teaspoon extra-virgin olive oil
Salt and pepper, to taste

1. On a clean work surface, brush both sides of each fillet with the olive oil. Sprinkle with the garlic powder, paprika, basil, and lemon-pepper seasoning. Place the fillets in the perforated pan.
2. Select Bake. Set temperature to 400°F (205°C) and set time to 15 minutes. Press Start to begin preheating.
3. Once preheated, place the pan into the Vortex. Flip the fillets halfway through.
4. Meanwhile, make the garlic aioli: Whisk together the garlic, mayo, lemon juice, olive oil, salt, and pepper in a small bowl until smooth.
5. When cooking is complete, the fish should flake apart with a fork and no longer translucent in the center. Remove the fish from the Vortex and serve with the garlic aioli on the side.

Lemon Tilapia Fillets with Garlic
Prep time: 10 minutes | Cook time: 12 minutes | Serves 4

1 tablespoon olive oil
1 tablespoon lemon juice
1 teaspoon minced garlic
½ teaspoon chili powder
4 tilapia fillets

1. Line a baking pan with parchment paper.
2. In a shallow bowl, stir together the olive oil, lemon juice, garlic, and chili powder to make a marinade. Put the tilapia fillets in the bowl, turning to coat evenly.
3. Place the fillets in the baking pan in a single layer.
4. Select Air Fry. Set temperature to 375°F (190°C) and set time to 12 minutes. Press Start to begin preheating.
5. Once preheated, slide the pan into the Vortex.
6. When cooked, the fish will flake apart with a fork. Remove from the Vortex to a plate and serve hot.

Breaded Fish Sticks
Prep time: 10 minutes | Cook time: 8 minutes | Makes 8 fish sticks

8 ounces (227 g) fish fillets (pollock or cod) cut into ½×3-inch strips
Salt, to taste (optional)
½ cup plain bread crumbs
Cooking spray

1. Season the fish strips with salt to taste, if desired.
2. Place the bread crumbs on a plate. Roll the fish strips in the bread crumbs to coat. Spritz the fish strips with cooking spray.
3. Arrange the fish strips in the perforated pan in a single layer.
4. Select Air Fry. Set temperature to 390°F (199°C) and set time to 8 minutes. Press Start to begin preheating.
5. Once preheated, place the pan into the Vortex.
6. When cooking is complete, they should be golden brown. Remove from the Vortex and cool for 5 minutes before serving.

Breaded Catfish Nuggets
Prep time: 10 minutes | Cook time: 7 to 8 minutes | Serves 4

2 medium catfish fillets, cut into chunks (approximately 1 × 2 inch)
Salt and pepper, to taste
2 eggs
2 tablespoons skim milk
½ cup cornstarch
1 cup panko bread crumbs
Cooking spray

1. In a medium bowl, season the fish chunks with salt and pepper to taste.
2. In a small bowl, beat together the eggs with milk until well combined.
3. Place the cornstarch and bread crumbs into separate shallow dishes.
4. Dredge the fish chunks one at a time in the cornstarch, coating well on both sides, then dip in the egg mixture, shaking off any excess, finally press well into the bread crumbs. Spritz the fish chunks with cooking spray.
5. Arrange the fish chunks in the perforated pan in a single layer.
6. Select Air Fry. Set temperature to 390°F (199°C) and set time to 8 minutes. Press Start to begin preheating.
7. Once preheated, place the pan into the Vortex. Flip the fish chunks halfway through the cooking time.
8. When cooking is complete, they should be no longer translucent in the center and golden brown. Remove the fish chunks from the Vortex to a plate. Serve warm.

Cayenne Prawns with Cumin
Prep time: 10 minutes | Cook time: 8 minutes | Serves 2

8 prawns, cleaned
Salt and black pepper, to taste
½ teaspoon ground cayenne pepper
½ teaspoon garlic powder
½ teaspoon ground cumin
½ teaspoon red chili flakes
Cooking spray

1. Spritz the perforated pan with cooking spray.
2. Toss the remaining ingredients in a large bowl until the prawns are well coated.
3. Spread the coated prawns evenly in the perforated pan and spray them with cooking spray.
4. Select Air Fry. Set temperature to 340°F (171°C) and set time to 8 minutes. Press Start to begin preheating.
5. Once preheated, place the pan into the Vortex. Flip the prawns halfway through the cooking time.
6. When cooking is complete, the prawns should be pink. Remove the prawns from the Vortex to a plate

Orange Shrimp with Cayenne
Prep time: 40 minutes | Cook time: 12 minutes | Serves 4

⅓ cup orange juice
3 teaspoons minced garlic
1 teaspoon Old Bay seasoning
¼ to ½ teaspoon cayenne pepper
1 pound (454 g) medium shrimp, thawed, deveined, peeled, with tails off, and patted dry
Cooking spray

1. Stir together the orange juice, garlic, Old Bay seasoning, and cayenne pepper in a medium bowl. Add the shrimp to the bowl and toss to coat well.
2. Cover the bowl with plastic wrap and marinate in the refrigerator for 30 minutes.
3. Spritz the perforated pan with cooking spray. Place the shrimp in the pan and spray with cooking spray.
4. Select Air Fry. Set temperature to 400°F (205°C) and set time to 12 minutes. Press Start to begin preheating.
5. Once preheated, place the pan into the Vortex. Flip the shrimp halfway through the cooking time.
6. When cooked, the shrimp should be opaque and crisp. Remove from the Vortex and serve hot.

Parmesan Fish Fillets with Tarragon
Prep time: 8 minutes | Cook time: 17 minutes | Serves 4

⅓ cup grated Parmesan cheese
½ teaspoon fennel seed
½ teaspoon tarragon
⅓ teaspoon mixed peppercorns
2 eggs, beaten
4 (4-ounce / 113-g) fish fillets, halved
2 tablespoons dry white wine
1 teaspoon seasoned salt

1. Place the grated Parmesan cheese, fennel seed, tarragon, and mixed peppercorns in a food processor and pulse for about 20 seconds until well combined. Transfer the cheese mixture to a shallow dish.
2. Place the beaten eggs in another shallow dish.
3. Drizzle the dry white wine over the top of fish fillets. Dredge each fillet in the beaten eggs on both sides, shaking off any excess, then roll them in the cheese mixture until fully coated. Season with the salt.
4. Arrange the fillets in the perforated pan.
5. Select Air Fry. Set temperature to 345°F (174°C) and set time to 17 minutes. Press Start to begin preheating.
6. Once preheated, place the pan into the Vortex. Flip the fillets once halfway through the cooking time.
7. When cooking is complete, the fish should be cooked through no longer translucent. Remove from the Vortex and cool for 5 minutes before serving.

Paprika Tiger Shrimp
Prep time: 5 minutes | Cook time: 10 minutes | Serves 4

1 pound (454 g) tiger shrimp
2 tablespoons olive oil
½ tablespoon Old Bay seasoning
¼ tablespoon smoked paprika
¼ teaspoon cayenne pepper
A pinch of sea salt

1. Toss all the ingredients in a large bowl until the shrimp are evenly coated.
2. Arrange the shrimp in the perforated pan.
3. Select Air Fry. Set temperature to 380°F (193°C) and set time to 10 minutes. Press Start to begin preheating.
4. Once preheated, place the pan into the Vortex.
5. When cooking is complete, the shrimp should be pink and cooked through. Remove from the Vortex and serve hot.

Old Bay Shrimp with Potatoes
Prep time: 10 minutes | Cook time: 15 minutes | Serves 4

1 pound (454 g) small red potatoes, halved
2 ears corn, shucked and cut into rounds, 1 to 1½ inches thick
2 tablespoons Old Bay or similar seasoning
½ cup unsalted butter, melted
1 (12- to 13-ounce / 340- to 369-g) package kielbasa or other smoked sausages
3 garlic cloves, minced
1 pound (454 g) medium shrimp, peeled and deveined

1. Place the potatoes and corn in a large bowl.
2. Stir together the butter and Old Bay seasoning in a small bowl. Drizzle half the butter mixture over the potatoes and corn, tossing to coat. Spread out the vegetables on a sheet pan.
3. Select Roast. Set temperature to 350°F (180°C) and set time to 15 minutes. Press Start to begin preheating.
4. Once the Vortex has preheated, place the pan into the Vortex.
5. Meanwhile, cut the sausages into 2-inch lengths, then cut each piece in half lengthwise. Put the sausages and shrimp in a medium bowl and set aside.
6. Add the garlic to the bowl of remaining butter mixture and stir well.
7. After 10 minutes, remove the sheet pan and pour the vegetables into the large bowl. Drizzle with the garlic butter and toss until well coated. Arrange the vegetables, sausages, and shrimp on the sheet pan.
8. Return to the Vortex and continue cooking. After 5 minutes, check the shrimp for doneness. The shrimp should be pink and opaque. If they are not quite cooked through, roast for an additional 1 minute.
9. When done, remove from the Vortex and serve on a plate.

Cajun Cod Fillets with Lemon Pepper
Prep time: 5 minutes | Cook time: 12 minutes | Makes 2 cod fillets

1 tablespoon Cajun seasoning
1 teaspoon salt
½ teaspoon lemon pepper
½ teaspoon freshly ground black pepper
2 (8-ounce / 227-g) cod fillets, cut to fit into the perforated pan
Cooking spray
2 tablespoons unsalted butter, melted
1 lemon, cut into 4 wedges

1. Spritz the perforated pan with cooking spray.
2. Thoroughly combine the Cajun seasoning, salt, lemon pepper, and black pepper in a small bowl. Rub this mixture all over the cod fillets until completely coated.
3. Put the fillets in the perforated pan and brush the melted butter over both sides of each fillet.
4. Select Bake. Set temperature to 360°F (182°C) and set time to 12 minutes. Press Start to begin preheating.
5. Once preheated, place the pan into the Vortex. Flip the fillets halfway through the cooking time.
6. When cooking is complete, the fish should flake apart with a fork. Remove the fillets from the Vortex and serve with fresh lemon wedges.

Cajun Catfish Cakes with Parmesan
Prep time: 5 minutes | Cook time: 15 minutes | Serves 4

2 catfish fillets
3 ounces (85 g) butter
1 cup shredded Parmesan cheese
1 cup shredded Swiss cheese
½ cup buttermilk
1 teaspoon baking powder
1 teaspoon baking soda
1 teaspoon Cajun seasoning

1. Bring a pot of salted water to a boil. Add the catfish fillets to the boiling water and let them boil for 5 minutes until they become opaque.
2. Remove the fillets from the pot to a mixing bowl and flake them into small pieces with a fork.
3. Add the remaining ingredients to the bowl of fish and stir until well incorporated.
4. Divide the fish mixture into 12 equal portions and shape each portion into a patty. Place the patties in the perforated pan.
5. Select Air Fry. Set temperature to 380°F (193°C) and set time to 15 minutes. Press Start to begin preheating.
6. Once preheated, place the pan into the Vortex. Flip the patties halfway through the cooking time.
7. When cooking is complete, the patties should be golden brown and cooked through. Remove from the Vortex. Let the patties sit for 5 minutes and serve.

Coconut Curried Fish with Chilies
Prep time: 10 minutes | Cook time: 22 minutes | Serves 4

2 tablespoons sunflower oil, divided
1 pound (454 g) fish, chopped
1 ripe tomato, pureéd
2 red chilies, chopped
1 shallot, minced
1 garlic clove, minced
1 cup coconut milk
1 tablespoon coriander powder
1 teaspoon red curry paste
½ teaspoon fenugreek seeds
Salt and white pepper, to taste

1. Coat the perforated pan with 1 tablespoon of sunflower oil. Place the fish in the perforated pan.
2. Select Air Fry. Set temperature to 380°F (193°C) and set time to 10 minutes. Press Start to begin preheating.
3. Once preheated, place the pan into the Vortex. Flip the fish halfway through the cooking time.
4. When cooking is complete, transfer the cooked fish to a baking pan greased with the remaining 1 tablespoon of sunflower oil. Stir in the remaining ingredients.
5. Select Air Fry. Set temperature to 350°F (180°C) and set time to 12 minutes. Place the pan into the Vortex.
6. When cooking is complete, they should be heated through. Cool for 5 to 8 minutes before serving.

Flounder Fillets with Lemon Pepper
Prep time: 8 minutes | Cook time: 12 minutes | Serves 2

2 flounder fillets, patted dry
1 egg
½ teaspoon Worcestershire sauce
¼ cup almond flour
¼ cup coconut flour
½ teaspoon coarse sea salt
½ teaspoon lemon pepper
¼ teaspoon chili powder
Cooking spray

1. In a shallow bowl, beat together the egg with Worcestershire sauce until well incorporated.
2. In another bowl, thoroughly combine the almond flour, coconut flour, sea salt, lemon pepper, and chili powder.
3. Dredge the fillets in the egg mixture, shaking off any excess, then roll in the flour mixture to coat well.
4. Select Bake. Set temperature to 390°F (199°C) and set time to 12 minutes. Press Start to begin preheating.
5. Once preheated, place the pan into the Vortex.
6. After 7 minutes, remove from the Vortex and flip the fillets and spray with cooking spray. Return the pan to the Vortex and continue cooking for 5 minutes, or until the fish is flaky.
7. When cooking is complete, remove from the Vortex and serve warm.

Curried Prawns with Coconut
Prep time: 15 minutes | Cook time: 8 minutes | Serves 4

12 prawns, cleaned and deveined
1 teaspoon fresh lemon juice
½ teaspoon cumin powder
Salt and ground black pepper, to taste
1 medium egg
⅓ cup beer
½ cup flour, divided
1 tablespoon curry powder
1 teaspoon baking powder
½ teaspoon grated fresh ginger
1 cup flaked coconut

1. In a large bowl, toss the prawns with the lemon juice, cumin powder, salt, and pepper until well coated. Set aside.
2. In a shallow bowl, whisk together the egg, beer, ¼ cup of flour, curry powder, baking powder, and ginger until combined.
3. In a separate shallow bowl, put the remaining ¼ cup of flour, and on a plate, place the flaked coconut.
4. Dip the prawns in the flour, then in the egg mixture, finally roll in the flaked coconut to coat well. Transfer the prawns to a baking sheet.
5. Select Air Fry. Set temperature to 350°F (180°C) and set time to 8 minutes. Press Start to begin preheating.
6. Once preheated, place the baking sheet into the Vortex.
7. After 5 minutes, remove from the Vortex and flip the prawns. Return to the Vortex and continue cooking for 3 minutes more.
8. When cooking is complete, remove from the Vortex and serve warm.

Shrimp Kebabs with Cherry Tomatoes
Prep time: 15 minutes | Cook time: 5 minutes | Serves 4

1½ pounds (680 g) jumbo shrimp, cleaned, shelled and deveined
1 pound (454 g) cherry tomatoes
2 tablespoons butter, melted
1 tablespoons Sriracha sauce
Sea salt and ground black pepper, to taste
1 teaspoon dried parsley flakes
½ teaspoon dried basil
½ teaspoon dried oregano
½ teaspoon mustard seeds
½ teaspoon marjoram

Special Equipment:
4 to 6 wooden skewers, soaked in water for 30 minutes

1. Put all the ingredients in a large bowl and toss to coat well.
2. Make the kebabs: Thread, alternating jumbo shrimp and cherry tomatoes, onto the wooden skewers. Place the kebabs in the perforated pan.
3. Select Air Fry. Set temperature to 400°F (205°C) and set time to 5 minutes. Press Start to begin preheating.
4. Once preheated, place the pan into the Vortex.
5. When cooking is complete, the shrimp should be pink and the cherry tomatoes should be softened. Remove from the Vortex. Let the shrimp and cherry tomato kebabs cool for 5 minutes and serve hot.

Shrimp Scampi with Garlic Butter
Prep time: 5 minutes | Cook time: 8 minutes | Serves 4

Sauce:
¼ cup unsalted butter
2 tablespoons fish stock or chicken broth
2 cloves garlic, minced
2 tablespoons chopped fresh basil leaves
1 tablespoon lemon juice
1 tablespoon chopped fresh parsley, plus more for garnish
1 teaspoon red pepper flakes
Shrimp:
1 pound (454 g) large shrimp, peeled and deveined, tails removed
Fresh basil sprigs, for garnish

1. Put all the ingredients for the sauce in a baking pan and stir to incorporate.
2. Select Air Fry. Set temperature to 350°F (180°C) and set time to 8 minutes. Press Start to begin preheating.
3. Once preheated, place the baking pan into the Vortex.
4. After 3 minutes, remove from the Vortex and add the shrimp to the baking pan, flipping to coat in the sauce. Return the pan to the Vortex and continue cooking for 5 minutes until the shrimp are pink and opaque. Stir the shrimp twice during cooking.
5. When cooking is complete, remove the pan from the Vortex. Serve garnished with the parsley and basil sprigs.

Parsley Shrimp with Lemon
Prep time: 10 minutes | Cook time: 8 minutes | Serves 4

1 pound (454 g) shrimp, deveined
4 tablespoons olive oil
1½ tablespoons lemon juice
1½ tablespoons fresh parsley, roughly chopped
2 cloves garlic, finely minced
1 teaspoon crushed red pepper flakes, or more to taste
Garlic pepper, to taste
Sea salt flakes, to taste

1. Toss all the ingredients in a large bowl until the shrimp are coated on all sides.
2. Arrange the shrimp in the perforated pan.
3. Select Air Fry. Set temperature to 385°F (196°C) and set time to 8 minutes. Press Start to begin preheating.
4. Once preheated, place the pan into the Vortex.
5. When cooking is complete, the shrimp should be pink and cooked through. Remove from the Vortex and serve warm.

Lemon Shrimp with Cumin
Prep time: 10 minutes | Cook time: 5 minutes | Serves 4

18 shrimp, shelled and deveined
2 garlic cloves, peeled and minced
2 tablespoons extra-virgin olive oil
2 tablespoons freshly squeezed lemon juice
½ cup fresh parsley, coarsely chopped
1 teaspoon onion powder
1 teaspoon lemon-pepper seasoning
½ teaspoon hot paprika
½ teaspoon salt
¼ teaspoon cumin powder

1. Toss all the ingredients in a mixing bowl until the shrimp are well coated.
2. Cover and allow to marinate in the refrigerator for 30 minutes.
3. When ready, transfer the shrimp to the perforated pan.
4. Select Air Fry. Set temperature to 400°F (205°C) and set time to 5 minutes. Press Start to begin preheating.
5. Once preheated, place the pan into the Vortex.
6. When cooking is complete, the shrimp should be pink on the outside and opaque in the center. Remove from the Vortex and serve warm.

Hoisin Scallops with Sesame Seeds
Prep time: 10 minutes | Cook time: 8 minutes | Serves 4

1 pound (454 g) sea scallops
3 tablespoons hoisin sauce
½ cup toasted sesame seeds
6 ounces (170 g) snow peas, trimmed
3 teaspoons vegetable oil, divided
1 teaspoon soy sauce
1 teaspoon sesame oil
1 cup roasted mushrooms

1. Brush the scallops with the hoisin sauce. Put the sesame seeds in a shallow dish. Roll the scallops in the sesame seeds until evenly coated.
2. Combine the snow peas with 1 teaspoon of vegetable oil, the sesame oil, and soy sauce in a medium bowl and toss to coat.
3. Grease the sheet pan with the remaining 2 teaspoons of vegetable oil. Put the scallops in the middle of the pan and arrange the snow peas around the scallops in a single layer.
4. Select Roast. Set temperature to 375°F (190°C) and set time to 8 minutes. Press Start to begin preheating.
5. Once the Vortex has preheated, place the pan into the Vortex.
6. After 5 minutes, remove the pan and flip the scallops. Fold in the mushrooms and stir well. Return the pan to the Vortex and continue cooking.
7. When done, remove the pan from the Vortex and cool for 5 minutes. Serve warm.

Curried King Prawns with Cumin
Prep time: 10 minutes | Cook time: 8 minutes | Serves 2

12 king prawns, rinsed
1 tablespoon coconut oil
Salt and ground black pepper, to taste
1 teaspoon onion powder
1 teaspoon garlic paste
1 teaspoon curry powder
½ teaspoon piri piri powder
½ teaspoon cumin powder

1. Combine all the ingredients in a large bowl and toss until the prawns are completely coated. Place the prawns in the perforated pan.
2. Select Air Fry. Set temperature to 360°F (182°C) and set time to 8 minutes. Press Start to begin preheating.
3. Once preheated, place the pan into the Vortex. Flip the prawns halfway through the cooking time.
4. When cooking is complete, the prawns will turn pink. Remove from the Vortex and serve hot.

Old Bay Crab Sticks with Mayo Sauce
Prep time: 5 minutes | Cook time: 12 minutes | Serves 4

Crab Sticks:
2 eggs
1 cup flour
⅓ cup panko bread crumbs
1 tablespoon Old Bay seasoning
1 pound (454 g) crab sticks
Cooking spray
Mayo Sauce:
½ cup mayonnaise
1 lime, juiced
2 garlic cloves, minced

1. In a bowl, beat the eggs. In a shallow bowl, place the flour. In another shallow bowl, thoroughly combine the panko bread crumbs and Old Bay seasoning.
2. Dredge the crab sticks in the flour, shaking off any excess, then in the beaten eggs, finally press them in the bread crumb mixture to coat well.
3. Arrange the crab sticks in the perforated pan and spray with cooking spray.
4. Select Air Fry. Set temperature to 390°F (199°C) and set time to 12 minutes. Press Start to begin preheating.
5. Once preheated, place the pan into the Vortex. Flip the crab sticks halfway through the cooking time.
6. Meanwhile, make the sauce by whisking together the mayo, lime juice, and garlic in a small bowl.
7. When cooking is complete, remove the pan from the Vortex. Serve the crab sticks with the mayo sauce on the side.

Jumbo Shrimp with Dijon-Mayo Sauce
Prep time: 5 minutes | Cook time: 7 minutes | Serves 4

Shrimp:
12 jumbo shrimp
½ teaspoon garlic salt
¼ teaspoon freshly cracked mixed peppercorns
Sauce:
4 tablespoons mayonnaise
1 teaspoon grated lemon rind
1 teaspoon Dijon mustard
1 teaspoon chipotle powder
½ teaspoon cumin powder

1. In a medium bowl, season the shrimp with garlic salt and cracked mixed peppercorns.
2. Place the shrimp in the perforated pan.
3. Select Air Fry. Set temperature to 395°F (202°C) and set time to 7 minutes. Press Start to begin preheating.
4. Once preheated, place the pan into the Vortex.
5. After 5 minutes, remove from the Vortex and flip the shrimp. Return the pan to the Vortex and continue cooking for 2 minutes more, or until they are pink and no longer opaque.
6. Meanwhile, stir together all the ingredients for the sauce in a small bowl until well mixed.
7. When cooking is complete, remove the shrimp from the Vortex and serve alongside the sauce.

Shrimp and Artichoke Paella
Prep time: 5 minutes | Cook time: 16 minutes | Serves 4

1 (10-ounce / 284-g) package frozen cooked rice, thawed
1 (6-ounce / 170-g) jar artichoke hearts, drained and chopped
¼ cup vegetable broth
½ teaspoon dried thyme
½ teaspoon turmeric
1 cup frozen cooked small shrimp
½ cup frozen baby peas
1 tomato, diced

1. Mix together the cooked rice, chopped artichoke hearts, vegetable broth, thyme, and turmeric in a baking pan and stir to combine.
2. Select Bake. Set temperature to 340°F (171°C) and set time to 16 minutes. Press Start to begin preheating.
3. Once preheated, place the pan into the Vortex.
4. After 9 minutes, remove from the Vortex and add the shrimp, baby peas, and diced tomato to the baking pan. Mix well. Return the pan to the Vortex and continue cooking for 7 minutes more, or until the shrimp are done and the paella is bubbling.
5. When cooking is complete, remove the pan from the Vortex. Cool for 5 minutes before serving.

Shrimp and Veggie Patties
Prep time: 15 minutes | Cook time: 12 minutes | Serves 4

½ pound (227 g) raw shrimp, shelled, deveined, and chopped finely
2 cups cooked sushi rice
¼ cup chopped red bell pepper
¼ cup chopped celery
¼ cup chopped green onion
2 teaspoons Worcestershire sauce
½ teaspoon salt
½ teaspoon garlic powder
½ teaspoon Old Bay seasoning
½ cup plain bread crumbs
Cooking spray

1. Put all the ingredients except the bread crumbs and oil in a large bowl and stir to incorporate.
2. Scoop out the shrimp mixture and shape into 8 equal-sized patties with your hands, no more than ½-inch thick. Roll the patties in the bread crumbs on a plate and spray both sides with cooking spray. Place the patties in the perforated pan.
3. Select Air Fry. Set temperature to 390°F (199°C) and set time to 12 minutes. Press Start to begin preheating.
4. Once preheated, place the pan into the Vortex. Flip the patties halfway through the cooking time.
5. When cooking is complete, the outside should be crispy brown. Remove the pan from the Vortex. Divide the patties among four plates and serve warm.

Fried Breaded Scallops
Prep time: 5 minutes | Cook time: 7 minutes | Serves 4

1 egg
3 tablespoons flour
1 cup bread crumbs
1 pound (454 g) fresh scallops
2 tablespoons olive oil
Salt and black pepper, to taste

1. In a bowl, lightly beat the egg. Place the flour and bread crumbs into separate shallow dishes.
2. Dredge the scallops in the flour and shake off any excess. Dip the flour-coated scallops in the beaten egg and roll in the bread crumbs.
3. Brush the scallops generously with olive oil and season with salt and pepper, to taste. Transfer the scallops to the perforated pan.
4. Select Air Fry. Set temperature to 360°F (182°C) and set time to 7 minutes. Press Start to begin preheating.
5. Once preheated, place the pan into the Vortex. Flip the scallops halfway through the cooking time.
6. When cooking is complete, the scallops should reach an internal temperature of just 145°F (63°C) on a meat thermometer. Remove the pan from the Vortex. Let the scallops cool for 5 minutes and serve.

Balsamic Ginger Scallops
Prep time: 10 minutes | Cook time: 12 minutes | Serves 2

1/3 cup shallots, chopped
1½ tablespoons olive oil
1½ tablespoons coconut aminos
1 tablespoon Mediterranean seasoning mix
½ tablespoon balsamic vinegar
½ teaspoon ginger, grated
1 clove garlic, chopped
1 pound (454 g) scallops, cleaned
Cooking spray
Belgian endive, for garnish

1. Place all the ingredients except the scallops and Belgian endive in a small skillet over medium heat and stir to combine. Let this mixture simmer for about 2 minutes.
2. Remove the mixture from the skillet to a large bowl and set aside to cool.
3. Add the scallops, coating them all over, then transfer to the refrigerator to marinate for at least 2 hours.
4. When ready, place the scallops in the perforated pan in a single layer and spray with cooking spray.
5. Select Air Fry. Set temperature to 345°F (174°C) and set time to 10 minutes. Press Start to begin preheating.
6. Once preheated, place the pan into the Vortex. Flip the scallops halfway through the cooking time.
7. When cooking is complete, the scallops should be tender and opaque. Remove from the Vortex and serve garnished with the Belgian endive.

Garlic Calamari Rings
Prep time: 5 minutes | Cook time: 12 minutes | Serves 4

2 large eggs
2 garlic cloves, minced
½ cup cornstarch
1 cup bread crumbs
1 pound (454 g) calamari rings
Cooking spray
1 lemon, sliced

1. In a small bowl, whisk the eggs with minced garlic. Place the cornstarch and bread crumbs into separate shallow dishes.
2. Dredge the calamari rings in the cornstarch, then dip in the egg mixture, shaking off any excess, finally roll them in the bread crumbs to coat well. Let the calamari rings sit for 10 minutes in the refrigerator.
3. Spritz the perforated pan with cooking spray. Transfer the calamari rings to the pan.
4. Select Air Fry. Set temperature to 390°F (199°C) and set time to 12 minutes. Press Start to begin preheating.
5. Once preheated, place the pan into the Vortex. Stir the calamari rings once halfway through the cooking time.
6. When cooking is complete, remove the pan from the Vortex. Serve the calamari rings with the lemon slices sprinkled on top.

Basil Scallops with Broccoli
Prep time: 15 minutes | Cook time: 9 minutes | Serves 4

1 cup frozen peas
1 cup green beans
1 cup frozen chopped broccoli
2 teaspoons olive oil
½ teaspoon dried oregano
½ teaspoon dried basil
12 ounces (340 g) sea scallops, rinsed and patted dry

1. Put the peas, green beans, and broccoli in a large bowl. Drizzle with the olive oil and toss to coat well. Transfer the vegetables to the perforated pan.
2. Select Air Fry. Set temperature to 400°F (205°C) and set time to 5 minutes. Press Start to begin preheating.
3. Once preheated, place the pan into the Vortex.
4. When cooking is complete, the vegetables should be fork-tender. Transfer the vegetables to a serving bowl. Scatter with the oregano and basil and set aside.
5. Place the scallops in the perforated pan.
6. Select Air Fry. Set temperature to 400°F (205°C) and set time to 4 minutes. Place the pan into the Vortex.
7. When cooking is complete, the scallops should be firm and just opaque in the center. Remove from the Vortex to the bowl of vegetables and toss well. Serve warm.

Breaded Crab Cakes

Prep time: 10 minutes | Cook time: 30 minutes | Serves 6

1 pound (454 g) fresh lump crab meat, drained and chopped
1 cup bread crumbs
½ cup plain nonfat yogurt
1 tablespoon olive oil
2 tablespoons capers
1 tablespoon garlic powder
1 teaspoon hot sauce
1 egg, beaten
1 tablespoon Worcestershire sauce
Salt and freshly ground black pepper, to taste

1. Combine all the ingredients in a bowl. Shape the mixture into patties approximately 2½ inches wide, adding more bread crumbs if the mixture is too wet and sticky and more yogurt if the mixture is too dry and crumbly. Place the patties in an oiled or non-stick square (cake) pan.
2. Select Bake. Set temperature to 350°F (180°C) and set time to 25 minutes. Select Start to begin preheating.
3. Once preheated, slide the pan into the Vortex, uncovered.
4. After 25 minutes, select Broil. Set temperature to 400°F (205°C) and set time to 5 minutes.
5. When done, the patties will be golden brown.

Honey Halibut Steaks with Parsley

Prep time: 5 minutes | Cook time: 10 minutes | Serves 4

1 pound (454 g) halibut steaks
¼ cup vegetable oil
2½ tablespoons Worcester sauce
2 tablespoons honey
2 tablespoons vermouth
1 tablespoon freshly squeezed lemon juice
1 tablespoon fresh parsley leaves, coarsely chopped
Salt and pepper, to taste
1 teaspoon dried basil

1. Put all the ingredients in a large mixing dish and gently stir until the fish is coated evenly. Transfer the fish to the perforated pan.
2. Select Roast. Set temperature to 390°F (199°C) and set time to 10 minutes. Press Start to begin preheating.
3. Once preheated, place the pan into the Vortex. Flip the fish halfway through cooking time.
4. When cooking is complete, the fish should reach an internal temperature of at least 145°F (63°C) on a meat thermometer. Remove from the Vortex and let the fish cool for 5 minutes before serving.

Balsamic Shrimp with Goat Cheese

Prep time: 15 minutes | Cook time: 8 minutes | Serves 2

1 pound (454 g) shrimp, deveined
1½ tablespoons olive oil
1½ tablespoons balsamic vinegar
1 tablespoon coconut aminos
½ tablespoon fresh parsley, roughly chopped
Sea salt flakes, to taste
1 teaspoon Dijon mustard
½ teaspoon smoked cayenne pepper
½ teaspoon garlic powder
Salt and ground black peppercorns, to taste
1 cup shredded goat cheese

1. Except for the cheese, stir together all the ingredients in a large bowl until the shrimp are evenly coated.
2. Place the shrimp in the perforated pan.
3. Select Roast. Set temperature to 385°F (196°C) and set time to 8 minutes. Press Start to begin preheating.
4. Once preheated, place the pan into the Vortex.
5. When cooking is complete, the shrimp should be pink and cooked through. Remove from the Vortex and serve with the shredded goat cheese sprinkled on top.

Crab Ratatouille with Thyme

Prep time: 15 minutes | Cook time: 13 minutes | Serves 4

1½ cups peeled and cubed eggplant
2 large tomatoes, chopped
1 red bell pepper, chopped
1 onion, chopped
1 tablespoon olive oil
½ teaspoon dried basil
½ teaspoon dried thyme
Pinch salt
Freshly ground black pepper, to taste
1½ cups cooked crab meat

1. In a metal bowl, stir together the eggplant, tomatoes, bell pepper, onion, olive oil, basil and thyme. Season with salt and pepper.
2. Select Roast. Set temperature to 400°F (205°C) and set time to 13 minutes. Press Start to begin preheating.
3. Once preheated, place the metal bowl into the Vortex.
4. After 9 minutes, remove the bowl from the Vortex. Add the crab meat and stir well and continue roasting for another 4 minutes, or until the vegetables are softened and the ratatouille is bubbling.
5. When cooking is complete, remove from the Vortex and serve warm.

Lemon Crab Cakes with Mayo
Prep time: 5 minutes | Cook time: 10 minutes | Serves 4

8 ounces (227 g) jumbo lump crab meat
1 egg, beaten
Juice of ½ lemon
⅓ cup bread crumbs
¼ cup diced green bell pepper
¼ cup diced red bell pepper
¼ cup mayonnaise
1 tablespoon Old Bay seasoning
1 teaspoon flour
Cooking spray

1. Make the crab cakes: Place all the ingredients except the flour and oil in a large bowl and stir until well incorporated.
2. Divide the crab mixture into four equal portions and shape each portion into a patty with your hands. Top each patty with a sprinkle of ¼ teaspoon of flour.
3. Arrange the crab cakes in the perforated pan and spritz them with cooking spray.
4. Select Air Fry. Set temperature to 375°F (190°C) and set time to 10 minutes. Press Start to begin preheating.
5. Once preheated, place the pan into the Vortex. Flip the crab cakes halfway through.
6. When cooking is complete, the cakes should be cooked through. Remove the pan from the Vortex. Divide the crab cakes among four plates and serve.

Fried Bacon-Wrapped Scallops
Prep time: 5 minutes | Cook time: 10 minutes | Serves 4

8 slices bacon, cut in half
16 sea scallops, patted dry
Cooking spray
Salt and freshly ground black pepper, to taste
16 toothpicks, soaked in water for at least 30 minutes

1. On a clean work surface, wrap half of a slice of bacon around each scallop and secure with a toothpick.
2. Lay the bacon-wrapped scallops in the perforated pan in a single layer.
3. Spritz the scallops with cooking spray and sprinkle the salt and pepper to season.
4. Select Air Fry. Set temperature to 370°F (188°C) and set time to 10 minutes. Press Start to begin preheating.
5. Once preheated, place the pan into the Vortex. Flip the scallops halfway through the cooking time.
6. When cooking is complete, the bacon should be cooked through and the scallops should be firm. Remove the scallops from the Vortex to a plate Serve warm.

Fried Scallops with Thyme
Prep time: 5 minutes | Cook time: 4 minutes | Serves 2

12 medium sea scallops, rinsed and patted dry
1 teaspoon fine sea salt
¾ teaspoon ground black pepper, plus more for garnish
Fresh thyme leaves, for garnish (optional)
Avocado oil spray

1. Coat the perforated pan with avocado oil spray.
2. Place the scallops in a medium bowl and spritz with avocado oil spray. Sprinkle the salt and pepper to season.
3. Transfer the seasoned scallops to the perforated pan, spacing them apart.
4. Select Air Fry. Set temperature to 390°F (199°C) and set time to 4 minutes. Press Start to begin preheating.
5. Once preheated, place the pan into the Vortex. Flip the scallops halfway through the cooking time.
6. When cooking is complete, the scallops should reach an internal temperature of just 145°F (63°C) on a meat thermometer. Remove the pan from the Vortex. Sprinkle the pepper and thyme leaves on top for garnish, if desired. Serve immediately.

Chapter 8
Poultry

Chicken Pot Pie
Prep time: 10 minutes | Cook time: 45 minutes | Serves 4

4 tablespoons (½ stick) unsalted butter
½ cup chopped onion
¼ cup all-purpose flour
½ teaspoon kosher salt
¼ teaspoon freshly ground black pepper
1¾ cups low-sodium chicken broth
½ cup whole milk
2½ cups shredded cooked chicken
2 cups frozen mixed vegetables, thawed
1 (9-inch) refrigerated piecrust

1. In a large cast-iron skillet, melt the butter over medium heat. Add the onion and cook, stirring, until softened. Stir in the flour, salt, and pepper until well blended. Gradually stir in the broth and milk, and cook, stirring occasionally, until bubbly and thickened, about 5 minutes.
2. Stir in the chicken and mixed vegetables. Remove from the heat. Top with the crust, pressing the dough over the edges of the skillet to seal. Cut 3 or 4 slits into the crust.
3. Select Bake. Set temperature to 400°F (205°C) and set time to 40 minutes. Select Start to begin preheating.
4. Once preheated, put the skillet in the Vortex.
5. When done, the crust will be golden brown and the filling will be bubbling. Let stand for 5 minutes before serving.

Barbecue Drumsticks with Vegetable
Prep time: 10 minutes | Cook time: 30 minutes | Serves 4

8 chicken drumsticks
1 teaspoon kosher salt, divided
1 pound (454 g) sweet potatoes, peeled and cut into 1-inch chunks
3 tablespoons vegetable oil, divided
1 cup barbecue sauce, plus more if desired
8 ounces (227 g) green beans, trimmed

1. Season the drumsticks on all sides with ½ teaspoon of salt. Let sit for a few minutes, then blot dry with a paper towel.
2. Put the sweet potato chunks on a sheet pan and drizzle with 2 tablespoons of oil. Move them to one side of the pan.
3. Place the drumsticks on the other side of the pan. Brush all sides of the chicken with half the barbecue sauce.
4. Select Bake. Set temperature to 375°F (190°C) and set time to 30 minutes. Select Start to begin preheating.
5. Once preheated, slide the pan into the Vortex.
6. Bake for 15 minutes. Brush the drumsticks with the remaining barbecue sauce. Add the beans to the sweet potatoes and drizzle with the remaining 1 tablespoon of oil. Add the remaining ½ teaspoon of salt, and toss the beans and potatoes together. Bake for another 15 minutes, until the vegetables are sizzling and browned in spots and the chicken is cooked through.
7. If you like, brush the drumsticks with additional barbecue sauce, and serve with the beans and sweet potatoes on the side.

Simple Chicken Cordon Bleu
Prep time: 10 minutes | Cook time: 30 minutes | Serves 4

Nonstick cooking spray
2 (10- to 12-ounce / 283- to 340-g) boneless, skinless chicken breasts
½ teaspoon kosher salt
4 teaspoons Dijon mustard
4 thin slices prosciutto
4 thin slices Gruyère, Emmental, or other Swiss-style cheese
⅔ cup panko bread crumbs (gluten-free if necessary)
2 tablespoons unsalted butter, melted
¼ cup grated Parmesan cheese

1. Spray a baking pan with cooking spray.
2. Lay the chicken breasts flat on a cutting board. With your knife parallel to the board, slice each breast across, for a total of four flat pieces. Sprinkle the chicken with the salt. Lay a piece of plastic wrap over the chicken pieces, and use the heel of your hand to press the chicken into a more even thickness.
3. Transfer the chicken pieces to the prepared baking pan. Spread 1 teaspoon of mustard on each chicken piece. Layer one slice of ham and one slice of cheese evenly over each chicken piece.
4. In a small bowl, mix together the bread crumbs, melted butter, and Parmesan cheese. Sprinkle the mixture over the top of each piece.
5. Select Bake. Set temperature to 375°F (190°C) and set time to 30 minutes. Select Start to begin preheating.
6. Once preheated, slide the pan into the Vortex.
7. When done, the topping will be browned and the chicken will be done—slide a paring knife into one of the chicken pieces to be sure.

Orange-Glazed Whole Chicken
Prep time: 5 minutes | Cook time: 1 hours 40 minutes | Serves 6

1 (3-pound / 1.4-kg) whole chicken, rinsed and patted dry with paper towels
Brushing Mixture:
2 tablespoons orange juice concentrate
1 tablespoon soy sauce
1 tablespoon toasted sesame oil
1 teaspoon ground ginger
Salt and freshly ground black pepper, to taste

1. Place the chicken, breast side up, in an oiled or nonstick square (cake) pan and brush with the mixture, which has been combined in a small bowl, reserving the remaining mixture. Cover with aluminum foil.
2. Select Bake. Set temperature to 400°F (205°C) and set time to 1 hour and 40 minutes. Select Start to begin preheating.
3. Once preheated, slide the pan into the Vortex.
4. Bake for 1 hour 20 minutes. Uncover and brush the chicken with remaining mixture.
5. Bake, uncovered, for 20 minutes, or until the breast is tender when pierced with a fork and golden brown.

Duck Breast with Potato
Prep time: 5 minutes | Cook time: 12 minutes | Serves 4

2 (1-pound / 454-g) boneless, skin-on duck breast halves
2 teaspoons kosher salt
1 pound (454 g) russet potatoes, peeled and cut into very thin sticks

1. With a very sharp knife, gently score the skin side of each duck breast, cutting through the skin and fat but not into the flesh. Space the scores ¼ to ½ inch apart. Turn the breast 90 degrees and score at right angles to the first series of scores. You'll have a diamond pattern of cuts over the skin. Sprinkle both sides with 1 teaspoon of salt.
2. Arrange the breasts on a baking pan, skin-side down.
3. Select Bake. Set temperature to 400°F (205°C) and set time to 4 minutes. Select Start to begin preheating.
4. Once preheated, slide the pan into the Vortex.
5. When done, the skin will be light brown and beginning to crisp and most of the fat has rendered
6. Remove the pan from the Vortex and arrange the potatoes around the breasts. Toss them to coat with the rendered duck fat and sprinkle with the remaining 1 teaspoon of salt. Bake for another 3 to 4 minutes, until the duck skin is dark golden brown.
7. Turn the breasts over and toss the potatoes. Continue to bake until the duck reaches an internal temperature of 150°F (66°C). This can take anywhere from 4 to 8 minutes, depending on the type of duck and the size of the breasts.
8. Remove the pan from the Vortex and let it rest for 5 minutes before slicing the duck. Serve with the fries.

Sesame Balsamic Chicken Breast
Prep time: 5 minutes | Cook time: 20 minutes | Serves 2

2 skinless, boneless chicken breast filets
3 tablespoons sesame seeds
Mixture:
2 tablespoons sesame oil
2 teaspoons soy sauce
2 teaspoons balsamic vinegar

1. Combine the mixture ingredients in a small bowl and brush the fillets liberally. Reserve the mixture. Place the fillets on a broiling rack with a pan underneath.
2. Select Broil. Set temperature to 400°F (205°C) and set time to 15 minutes. Select Start to begin preheating.
3. Once preheated, slide the pan into the Vortex.
4. When done, the meat will be tender and the juices will run clear when the meat is pierced. Remove from the Vortex and brush the fillets with the remaining mixture. Place the sesame seeds on a plate and press the chicken breast halves into the seeds, coating well.
5. Broil for 5 minutes, or until the sesame seeds are browned.

Chicken Breast in Mango Sauce
Prep time: 10 minutes | Cook time: 40 minutes | Serves 2

2 skinless and boneless chicken breast halves
1 tablespoon capers
1 tablespoon raisins
Mango Mixture:
1 cup mango pieces
1 teaspoon balsamic vinegar
½ teaspoon garlic powder
1 teaspoon fresh ginger, peeled and minced
½ teaspoon soy sauce
½ teaspoon curry powder
1 tablespoon pimientos, minced
Salt and pepper, to taste

1. Process the mango mixture ingredients in a food processor or blender until smooth. Transfer to an oiled or nonstick square (cake) pan and add the capers, raisins, and pimientos, stirring well to blend. Add the chicken breasts and spoon the mixture over the breasts to coat well.
2. Select Bake. Set temperature to 375°F (190°C) and set time to 40 minutes. Select Start to begin preheating.
3. Once preheated, slide the pan into the Vortex.
4. When done, serve the breasts with the sauce.

Dijon-Rosemary Chicken Breasts
Prep time: 5 minutes | Cook time: 30 minutes | Serves 2

2 skinless, boneless chicken breast halves
Sauce:
3 tablespoons dry white wine
1 tablespoon Dijon mustard
2 tablespoons nonfat plain yogurt
Salt and freshly ground black pepper, to taste
2 rosemary sprigs

1. Place each breast on a 12 × 12-inch square of heavy-duty aluminum foil (or regular foil doubled) and turn up the edges of the foil.
2. Mix together the sauce ingredients and spoon over the chicken breasts. Lay a rosemary sprig on each breast. Bring up the edges of the foil and fold to form a sealed packet. Transfer to a baking pan.
3. Select Bake. Set temperature to 400°F (205°C) and set time to 25 minutes. Select Start to begin preheating.
4. Once preheated, slide the pan into the Vortex.
5. Bake for 25 minutes or until juices run clear when the meat is pierced with a fork. Remove the rosemary sprigs.
6. Broil for 5 minutes, or until lightly browned. Replace the sprigs and serve.

Chicken, Vegetable and Rice Casserole
Prep time: 10 minutes | Cook time: 52 minutes | Serves 4

4 skinless, boneless chicken thighs, cut into 1-inch cubes
½ cup brown rice
4 scallions, chopped
1 plum tomato, chopped
1 cup frozen peas
1 cup frozen corn
1 cup peeled and chopped carrots
2 tablespoons chopped fresh parsley
1 teaspoon mustard seed
1 teaspoon dried dill weed
¼ teaspoon celery seed
Salt and freshly ground black pepper, to taste
½ cup finely chopped pecans

1. Combine all the ingredients, except the pecans, with 2½ cups water in an ovenproof baking dish. Adjust the seasonings to taste. Cover with aluminum foil.
2. Select Bake. Set temperature to 400°F (205°C) and set time to 45 minutes. Select Start to begin preheating.
3. Once preheated, slide the baking dish into the Vortex.
4. When done, the rice will be tender. Uncover and sprinkle the top with the pecans.
5. Broil for 7 minutes, or until the pecans are browned.

Barbecue Turkey Burgers
Prep time: 5 minutes | Cook time: 20 minutes | Serves 4

1 pound (454 g) lean ground turkey breast
2 tablespoons bread crumbs
2 tablespoons barbecue sauce
½ teaspoon garlic powder
½ teaspoon chili powder
Salt and freshly ground black pepper, to taste

1. Combine all ingredients in a bowl, mixing well. Divide into 4 portions and shape into patties. Transfer to a baking pan.
2. Select Broil. Set temperature to 400°F (205°C) and set time to 20 minutes. Select Start to begin preheating.
3. Once preheated, slide the pan into the Vortex.
4. When done, the meat will be browned and the juice will run clear when pierced with a fork.

Chicken and Veggies with 'Nduja
Prep time: 10 minutes | Cook time: 40 minutes | Serves 4

8 good-sized skin-on, bone-in chicken thighs, excess skin neatly trimmed
1 pound (454 g) head cauliflower, broken into florets
1 pound (454 g) baby waxy potatoes, scrubbed, then halved or quartered, depending on size
2¾ ounces (78 g) 'nduja, broken into nuggets
6 thyme sprigs
3 tablespoons olive oil
Sea salt flakes and freshly ground black pepper, to taste
Green salad, or bitter greens, to serve

1. Put all the ingredients in a baking pan, season, and toss around with your hands. The chicken should end up skin-side up. Make sure the nuggets of 'nduja aren't lying on top, or they'll burn.
2. Select Bake. Set temperature to 400°F (205°C) and set time to 40 minutes. Select Start to begin preheating.
3. Once preheated, slide the pan into the Vortex. Stir the mixture three times during cooking. The 'nduja partly melts and you need to ensure it gets well mixed in.
4. Towards the end of the cooking time, it's good to spoon the bits of 'nduja over the chicken, as it gives it a lovely color. The potatoes should be tender when pierced with a sharp knife and the chicken cooked through. Serve with a green salad or bitter greens.

Tasty Meat and Vegetable Loaf
Prep time: 10 minutes | Cook time: 35 minutes | Serves 4

1 to 1½ pounds (454- to 680-g) ground turkey or chicken breast
1 egg
1 tablespoon chopped fresh parsley
2 tablespoons chopped bell pepper
3 tablespoons chopped canned mushrooms
2 tablespoons chopped onion
2 garlic cloves, minced
½ cup multigrain bread crumbs
1 tablespoon Worcestershire sauce
1 tablespoon ketchup
Freshly ground black pepper, to taste

1. Combine all the ingredients in a large bowl and press into a loaf pan.
2. Select Bake. Set temperature to 400°F (205°C) and set time to 35 minutes. Select Start to begin preheating.
3. Once preheated, slide the pan into the Vortex.
4. When done, the loaf will be browned on top.

Garlicky Whole Chicken Bake
Prep time: 10 minutes | Cook time: 1 hour | Serves 2 to 4

½ cup melted butter
3 tablespoons garlic, minced
Salt, to taste
1 teaspoon ground black pepper
1 (1-pound / 454-g) whole chicken

1. Combine the butter with garlic, salt, and ground black pepper in a small bowl.
2. Brush the butter mixture over the whole chicken, then place the chicken in the perforated pan, skin side down.
3. Select Bake. Set temperature to 350°F (180°C) and set time to 60 minutes. Press Start to begin preheating.
4. Once preheated, place the pan into the Vortex. Flip the chicken halfway through.
5. When cooking is complete, an instant-read thermometer inserted in the thickest part of the chicken should register at least 165°F (74°C).
6. Remove the chicken from the Vortex and allow to cool for 15 minutes before serving.

Garlic Chicken Wings
Prep time: 10 minutes | Cook time: 15 minutes | Serves 4

1 tablespoon olive oil
8 whole chicken wings
Chicken seasoning or rub, to taste
1 teaspoon garlic powder
Freshly ground black pepper, to taste

1. Grease the perforated pan with olive oil.
2. On a clean work surface, rub the chicken wings with chicken seasoning and rub, garlic powder, and ground black pepper.
3. Arrange the well-coated chicken wings in the perforated pan.
4. Select Air Fry. Set temperature to 400°F (205°C) and set time to 15 minutes. Press Start to begin preheating.
5. Once preheated, place the pan into the Vortex. Flip the chicken wings halfway through.
6. When cooking is complete, the internal temperature of the chicken wings should reach at least 165°F (74°C).
7. Remove the chicken wings from the Vortex. Serve immediately.

Five-Spice Turkey Thighs
Prep time: 10 minutes | Cook time: 25 minutes | Serves 6

2 pounds (907 g) turkey thighs
1 teaspoon Chinese five-spice powder
¼ teaspoon Sichuan pepper
1 teaspoon pink Himalayan salt
1 tablespoon Chinese rice vinegar
1 tablespoon mustard
1 tablespoon chili sauce
2 tablespoons soy sauce
Cooking spray

1. Spritz the perforated pan with cooking spray.
2. Rub the turkey thighs with five-spice powder, Sichuan pepper, and salt on a clean work surface.
3. Put the turkey thighs in the perforated pan and spritz with cooking spray.
4. Select Air Fry. Set temperature to 360°F (182°C) and set time to 22 minutes. Press Start to begin preheating.
5. Once preheated, place the pan into the Vortex. Flip the thighs at least three times during the cooking.
6. When cooking is complete, the thighs should be well browned.
7. Meanwhile, heat the remaining ingredients in a saucepan over medium-high heat. Cook for 3 minutes or until the sauce is thickened and reduces to two thirds.
8. Transfer the thighs onto a plate and baste with sauce before serving.

Sweet-and-Sour Chicken Breasts
Prep time: 15 minutes | Cook time: 15 minutes | Serves 4

1 cup cornstarch
Chicken seasoning or rub, to taste
Salt and ground black pepper, to taste
2 eggs
2 (4-ounce/ 113-g) boneless, skinless chicken breasts, cut into 1-inch pieces
1½ cups sweet-and-sour sauce
Cooking spray

1. Spritz the perforated pan with cooking spray.
2. Combine the cornstarch, chicken seasoning, salt, and pepper in a large bowl. Stir to mix well. Whisk the eggs in a separate bowl.
3. Dredge the chicken pieces in the bowl of cornstarch mixture first, then in the bowl of whisked eggs, and then in the cornstarch mixture again.
4. Arrange the well-coated chicken pieces in the perforated pan. Spritz with cooking spray.
5. Select Air Fry. Set temperature to 360°F (182°C) and set time to 15 minutes. Press Start to begin preheating.
6. Once preheated, place the pan into the Vortex. Flip the chicken halfway through.
7. When cooking is complete, the chicken should be golden brown and crispy.
8. Transfer the chicken pieces on a large serving plate, then baste with sweet-and-sour sauce before serving.

Turkey Breast with Strawberries
Prep time: 15 minutes | Cook time: 37 minutes | Serves 2

2 pounds (907 g) turkey breast
1 tablespoon olive oil
Salt and ground black pepper, to taste
1 cup fresh strawberries

1. Rub the turkey bread with olive oil on a clean work surface, then sprinkle with salt and ground black pepper.
2. Transfer the turkey in the perforated pan and spritz with cooking spray.
3. Select Air Fry. Set temperature to 375°F (190°C) and set time to 30 minutes. Press Start to begin preheating.
4. Once preheated, place the pan into the Vortex. Flip the turkey breast halfway through.
5. Meanwhile, put the strawberries in a food processor and pulse until smooth.
6. When cooking is complete, spread the puréed strawberries over the turkey and cook for 7 more minutes.
7. Serve immediately.

Chicken and Pepper Baguette with Mayo
Prep time: 10 minutes | Cook time: 20 minutes | Serves 2

1¼ pounds (567 g) assorted small chicken parts, breasts cut into halves
¼ teaspoon salt
¼ teaspoon ground black pepper
2 teaspoons olive oil
½ pound (227 g) mini sweet peppers
¼ cup light mayonnaise
¼ teaspoon smoked paprika
½ clove garlic, crushed
Baguette, for serving
Cooking spray

1. Spritz the perforated pan with cooking spray.
2. Toss the chicken with salt, ground black pepper, and olive oil in a large bowl.
3. Arrange the sweet peppers and chicken in the perforated pan.
4. Select Air Fry. Set temperature to 375°F (190°C) and set time to 20 minutes. Press Start to begin preheating.
5. Once preheated, place the pan into the Vortex. Flip the chicken and transfer the peppers on a plate halfway through.
6. When cooking is complete, the chicken should be well browned.
7. Meanwhile, combine the mayo, paprika, and garlic in a small bowl. Stir to mix well.
8. Assemble the baguette with chicken and sweet pepper, then spread with mayo mixture and serve.

Dijon Turkey Breast with Sage
Prep time: 5 minutes | Cook time: 30 minutes | Serves 4

1 teaspoon chopped fresh sage
1 teaspoon chopped fresh tarragon
1 teaspoon chopped fresh thyme leaves
1 teaspoon chopped fresh rosemary leaves
1½ teaspoons sea salt
1 teaspoon ground black pepper
1 (2-pound / 907-g) turkey breast
3 tablespoons Dijon mustard
3 tablespoons butter, melted
Cooking spray

1. Spritz the perforated pan with cooking spray.
2. Combine the herbs, salt, and black pepper in a small bowl. Stir to mix well. Set aside.
3. Combine the Dijon mustard and butter in a separate bowl. Stir to mix well.
4. Rub the turkey with the herb mixture on a clean work surface, then brush the turkey with Dijon mixture.
5. Arrange the turkey in the perforated pan.
6. Select Air Fry. Set temperature to 390°F (199°C) and set time to 30 minutes. Press Start to begin preheating.
7. Once preheated, place the pan into the Vortex. Flip the turkey breast halfway through.
8. When cooking is complete, an instant-read thermometer inserted in the thickest part of the turkey breast should reach at least 165°F (74°C).
9. Transfer the cooked turkey breast on a large plate and slice to serve.

Chicken Thighs with Mirin
Prep time: 10 minutes | Cook time: 15 minutes | Serves 4

½ cup mirin
¼ cup dry white wine
½ cup soy sauce
1 tablespoon light brown sugar
1½ pounds (680 g) boneless, skinless chicken thighs, cut
4 medium scallions, trimmed, cut into 1½-inch pieces
Cooking spray
Special Equipment:
4 (4-inch) bamboo skewers, soaked in water for at least 30 minutes

1. Combine the mirin, dry white wine, soy sauce, and brown sugar in a saucepan. Bring to a boil over medium heat. Keep stirring.
2. Boil for another 2 minutes or until it has a thick consistency. Turn off the heat.
3. Spritz the perforated pan with cooking spray.
4. Run the bamboo skewers through the chicken pieces and scallions alternatively.
5. Arrange the skewers in the perforated pan, then brush with mirin mixture on both sides. Spritz with cooking spray.
6. Select Air Fry. Set temperature to 400°F (205°C) and set time to 10 minutes. Press Start to begin preheating.
7. Once preheated, place the pan into the Vortex. Flip the skewers halfway through.
8. When cooking is complete, the chicken and scallions should be glossy.
9. Serve immediately.

Dijon Turkey with Carrots

Prep time: 10 minutes | Cook time: 25 minutes | Serves 4

2 (12-ounce / 340-g) turkey tenderloins
1 teaspoon kosher salt, divided
6 slices bacon
3 tablespoons balsamic vinegar
2 tablespoons honey
1 tablespoon Dijon mustard
½ teaspoon dried thyme
6 large carrots, peeled and cut into ¼-inch rounds
1 tablespoon olive oil

1. Sprinkle the turkey with ¾ teaspoon of the salt. Wrap each tenderloin with 3 strips of bacon, securing the bacon with toothpicks. Place the turkey in a baking pan.
2. In a small bowl, mix the balsamic vinegar, honey, mustard, and thyme.
3. Place the carrots in a medium bowl and drizzle with the oil. Add 1 tablespoon of the balsamic mixture and ¼ teaspoon of kosher salt and toss to coat. Place these on the pan around the turkey tenderloins. Baste the tenderloins with about one-half of the remaining balsamic mixture.
4. Select Roast. Set temperature to 375°F (190°C) and set time to 25 minutes. Press Start to begin preheating.
5. Once preheated, place the pan into the Vortex.
6. After 13 minutes, remove the pan from the Vortex. Gently stir the carrots. Flip the tenderloins and baste with the remaining balsamic mixture. Return the pan to the Vortex and continue cooking.
7. When cooking is complete, the carrots should tender and the center of the tenderloins should register 165°F (74°C) on a meat thermometer. Remove the pan from the Vortex. Slice the turkey and serve with the carrots.

Garlic Duck Leg Quarters

Prep time: 5 minutes | Cook time: 45 minutes | Serves 4

4 (½-pound / 227-g) skin-on duck leg quarters
2 medium garlic cloves, minced
½ teaspoon salt
½ teaspoon ground black pepper

1. Spritz the perforated pan with cooking spray.
2. On a clean work surface, rub the duck leg quarters with garlic, salt, and black pepper.
3. Arrange the leg quarters in the perforated pan and spritz with cooking spray.
4. Select Air Fry. Set temperature to 300°F (150°C) and set time to 30 minutes. Press Start to begin preheating.
5. Once preheated, place the pan into the Vortex.
6. After 30 minutes, remove the pan from the Vortex. Flip the leg quarters. Increase temperature to 375°F (190°C) and set time to 15 minutes. Return the pan to the Vortex and continue cooking.
7. When cooking is complete, the leg quarters should be well browned and crispy.
8. Remove the duck leg quarters from the Vortex and allow to cool for 10 minutes before serving.

Curried Chicken and Brussels Sprouts

Prep time: 10 minutes | Cook time: 20 minutes | Serves 4

1 pound (454 g) boneless, skinless chicken thighs
1 teaspoon kosher salt, divided
¼ cup unsalted butter, melted
1 tablespoon curry powder
2 medium sweet potatoes, peeled and cut in 1-inch cubes
12 ounces (340 g) Brussels sprouts, halved

1. Sprinkle the chicken thighs with ½ teaspoon of kosher salt. Place them in the single layer on a baking pan.
2. In a small bowl, stir together the butter and curry powder.
3. Place the sweet potatoes and Brussels sprouts in a large bowl. Drizzle half the curry butter over the vegetables and add the remaining kosher salt. Toss to coat. Transfer the vegetables to the baking pan and place in a single layer around the chicken. Brush half of the remaining curry butter over the chicken.
4. Select Roast. Set temperature to 400°F (205°C) and set time to 20 minutes. Press Start to begin preheating.
5. Once preheated, place the pan into the Vortex.
6. After 10 minutes, remove the pan from the Vortex and turn over the chicken thighs. Baste them with the remaining curry butter. Return the pan to the Vortex and continue cooking.
7. Cooking is complete when the sweet potatoes are tender and the chicken is cooked through and reads 165°F (74°C) on a meat thermometer.

Balsamic Duck Breasts with Orange Marmalade

Prep time: 5 minutes | Cook time: 13 minutes | Serves 4

4 (6-ounce / 170-g) skin-on duck breasts
1 teaspoon salt
¼ cup orange marmalade
1 tablespoon white balsamic vinegar
¾ teaspoon ground black pepper

1. Cut 10 slits into the skin of the duck breasts, then sprinkle with salt on both sides.
2. Place the breasts in the perforated pan, skin side up.
3. Select Air Fry. Set temperature to 400°F (205°C) and set time to 10 minutes. Press Start to begin preheating.
4. Once preheated, place the pan into the Vortex.
5. Meanwhile, combine the remaining ingredients in a small bowl. Stir to mix well.
6. When cooking is complete, brush the duck skin with the marmalade mixture. Flip the breast and air fry for 3 more minutes or until the skin is crispy and the breast is well browned.
7. Serve immediately.

Balsamic Chicken Breast with Oregano
Prep time: 35 minutes | Cook time: 40 minutes | Serves 2

¼ cup balsamic vinegar
2 teaspoons dried oregano
2 garlic cloves, minced
1 tablespoon olive oil
⅛ teaspoon salt
½ teaspoon freshly ground black pepper
2 (4-ounce / 113-g) boneless, skinless, chicken-breast halves
Cooking spray

1. In a small bowl, add the vinegar, oregano, garlic, olive oil, salt, and pepper. Mix to combine.
2. Put the chicken in a resealable plastic bag. Pour the vinegar mixture in the bag with the chicken, seal the bag, and shake to coat the chicken. Refrigerate for 30 minutes to marinate.
3. Spritz a baking pan with cooking spray. Put the chicken in the prepared baking pan and pour the marinade over the chicken.
4. Select Bake. Set temperature to 400°F (205°C) and set time to 40 minutes. Press Start to begin preheating.
5. Once preheated, place the pan into the Vortex.
6. After 20 minutes, remove the pan from the Vortex. Flip the chicken. Return the pan to the Vortex and continue cooking.
7. When cooking is complete, the internal temperature of the chicken should registers at least 165°F (74°C).
8. Let sit for 5 minutes, then serve.

Paprika Hens in Wine
Prep time: 2 hours 15 minutes | Cook time: 30 minutes | Serves 8

4 (1¼-pound / 567-g) Cornish hens, giblets removed, split lengthwise
2 cups white wine, divided
2 garlic cloves, minced
1 small onion, minced
½ teaspoon celery seeds
½ teaspoon poultry seasoning
½ teaspoon paprika
½ teaspoon dried oregano
¼ teaspoon freshly ground black pepper

1. Place the hens, cavity side up, on a rack in a baking pan. Pour 1½ cups of the wine over the hens; set aside.
2. In a shallow bowl, combine the garlic, onion, celery seeds, poultry seasoning, paprika, oregano, and pepper. Sprinkle half of the combined seasonings over the cavity of each split half. Cover and refrigerate. Allow the hens to marinate for 2 hours.
3. Transfer the hens in the perforated pan.
4. Select Bake. Set temperature to 350°F (180°C) and set time to 90 minutes. Press Start to begin preheating.
5. Once preheated, place the pan into the Vortex.
6. Remove the panpan from the Vortex halfway through the baking, turn breast side up, and remove the skin. Pour the remaining ½ cup of wine over the top, and sprinkle with the remaining seasonings.
7. When cooking is complete, the inner temperature of the hens should be at least 165°F (74°C). Transfer the hens to a serving platter and serve hot.

Vinegary Chicken with Pineapple
Prep time: 10 minutes | Cook time: 10 minutes | Serves 6

1½ pounds (680 g) boneless, skinless chicken breasts, cut into 1-inch chunks
¾ cup soy sauce
2 tablespoons ketchup
2 tablespoons brown sugar
2 tablespoons rice vinegar
1 green bell pepper, cut into 1-inch chunks
6 scallions, cut into 1-inch pieces
1 cup (¾-inch chunks) fresh pineapple, rinsed and drained
Cooking spray

1. Place the chicken in a large bowl. Add the soy sauce, ketchup, brown sugar, vinegar, red and green peppers, and scallions. Toss to coat.
2. Spritz a baking pan with cooking spray and place the chicken and vegetables on the pan.
3. Select Roast. Set temperature to 375°F (190°C) and set time to 10 minutes. Press Start to begin preheating.
4. Once preheated, place the pan into the Vortex.
5. After 6 minutes, remove the pan from the Vortex. Add the pineapple chunks to the pan and stir. Return the pan to the Vortex and continue cooking.
6. When cooking is complete, remove the pan from the Vortex. Serve with steamed rice, if desired.

Peach Chicken with Dark Cherry
Prep time: 8 minutes | Cook time: 15 minutes | Serves 4

⅓ cup peach preserves
1 teaspoon ground rosemary
½ teaspoon black pepper
½ teaspoon salt
½ teaspoon marjoram
1 teaspoon light olive oil
1 pound (454 g) boneless chicken breasts, cut in 1½-inch chunks
1 (10-ounce / 284-g) package frozen dark cherries, thawed and drained
Cooking spray

1. In a medium bowl, mix peach preserves, rosemary, pepper, salt, marjoram, and olive oil.
2. Stir in chicken chunks and toss to coat well with the preserve mixture.
3. Spritz the perforated pan with cooking spray and lay chicken chunks in the perforated pan.
4. Select Bake. set temperature to 400°F (205°C) and set time to 15 minutes. Press Start to begin preheating.
5. Once preheated, place the pan into the Vortex.
6. After 7 minutes, remove the pan from the Vortex. Flip the chicken chunks. Return the pan to the Vortex and continue cooking.
7. When cooking is complete, the chicken should no longer pink and the juices should run clear.
8. Scatter the cherries over and cook for an additional minute to heat cherries.
9. Serve immediately.

Turkey Meatloaves with Onion
Prep time: 6 minutes | Cook time: 24 minutes | Serves 4

¼ cup grated carrot
2 garlic cloves, minced
2 tablespoons ground almonds
⅓ cup minced onion
2 teaspoons olive oil
1 teaspoon dried marjoram
1 egg white
¾ pound (340 g) ground turkey breast

1. In a medium bowl, stir together the carrot, garlic, almonds, onion, olive oil, marjoram, and egg white.
2. Add the ground turkey. Mix until combined.
3. Double 16 foil muffin cup liners to make 8 cups. Divide the turkey mixture evenly among the liners.
4. Select Bake. Set temperature to 400°F (205°C) and set time to 24 minutes. Press Start to begin preheating.
5. Once preheated, place the muffin cups into the Vortex.
6. When cooking is complete, the meatloaves should reach an internal temperature of 165°F (74°C) on a meat thermometer.
7. Serve immediately.

Paprika Hens with Creole Seasoning
Prep time: 10 minutes | Cook time: 40 minutes | Serves 4

½ tablespoon Creole seasoning
½ tablespoon garlic powder
½ tablespoon onion powder
½ tablespoon freshly ground black pepper
½ tablespoon paprika
2 tablespoons olive oil
2 Cornish hens
Cooking spray

1. Spritz the perforated pan with cooking spray.
2. In a small bowl, mix the Creole seasoning, garlic powder, onion powder, pepper, and paprika.
3. Pat the Cornish hens dry and brush each hen all over with the olive oil. Rub each hen with the seasoning mixture. Place the Cornish hens in the perforated pan.
4. Select Air Fry. Set temperature to 375°F (190°C) and set time to 30 minutes. Press Start to begin preheating.
5. Once preheated, place the pan into the Vortex.
6. After 15 minutes, remove the pan from the Vortex. Flip the hens over and baste it with any drippings collected in the bottom drawer of the Vortex. Return the pan to the Vortex and continue cooking.
7. When cooking is complete, a thermometer inserted into the thickest part of the hens should reach at least 165°F (74°C).
8. Let the hens rest for 10 minutes before carving.

Paprika Whole Chicken Roast
Prep time: 15 minutes | Cook time: 1 hour | Serves 6

1 teaspoon Italian seasoning
½ teaspoon garlic powder
½ teaspoon paprika
1 teaspoon salt
½ teaspoon freshly ground black pepper
½ teaspoon onion powder
2 tablespoons olive oil
1 (3-pound / 1.4-kg) whole chicken, giblets removed, pat dry
Cooking spray

1. Spritz the perforated pan with cooking spray.
2. In a small bowl, mix the Italian seasoning, garlic powder, paprika, salt, pepper, and onion powder.
3. Brush the chicken with the olive oil and rub it with the seasoning mixture.
4. Tie the chicken legs with butcher's twine. Place the chicken in the perforated pan, breast side down.
5. Select Air Fry. Set temperature to 350°F (180°C) and set time to an hour. Press Start to begin preheating.
6. Once preheated, place the pan into the Vortex.
7. After 30 minutes, remove the pan from the Vortex. Flip the chicken over and baste it with any drippings collected in the bottom drawer of the Vortex. Return the pan to the Vortex and continue cooking.
8. When cooking is complete, a thermometer inserted into the thickest part of the thigh should reach at least 165°F (74°C).
9. Let the chicken rest for 10 minutes before carving and serving.

Chicken Drumsticks with Green Beans
Prep time: 5 minutes | Cook time: 25 minutes | Serves 4

8 skin-on chicken drumsticks
1 teaspoon kosher salt, divided
1 pound (454 g) green beans, trimmed
2 garlic cloves, minced
2 tablespoons vegetable oil
⅓ cup Thai sweet chili sauce

1. Salt the drumsticks on all sides with ½ teaspoon of kosher salt. Let sit for a few minutes, then blot dry with a paper towel. Place on a baking pan.
2. Select Roast. Set temperature to 375°F (190°C) and set time to 25 minutes. Press Start to begin preheating.
3. Once preheated, place the pan into the Vortex.
4. While the chicken cooks, place the green beans in a large bowl. Add the remaining kosher salt, the garlic, and oil. Toss to coat.
5. After 15 minutes, remove the pan from the Vortex. Brush the drumsticks with the sweet chili sauce. Place the green beans in the pan. Return the pan to the Vortex and continue cooking.
6. When cooking is complete, the green beans should be sizzling and browned in spots and the chicken cooked through, reading 165°F (74°C) on a meat thermometer. Serve the chicken with the green beans on the side.

Teriyaki Chicken, Pepper, and Pineapple Kebabs
Prep time: 5 minutes | Cook time: 10 minutes | Serves 4

1 pound (454 g) boneless, skinless chicken breasts, cut into 2-inch cubes
1 cup teriyaki sauce, divided
2 green bell peppers, seeded and cut into 1-inch cubes
2 cups fresh pineapple, cut into 1-inch cubes

1. Place the chicken and ½ cup of teriyaki sauce in a large resealable plastic bag or container. Toss to coat evenly. Refrigerate for at least 30 minutes.
2. Insert the Grill Grate and close the hood. Select GRILL, set the temperature to MEDIUM, and set the time to 14 minutes. Select START/STOP to begin preheating.
3. While the unit is preheating, assemble the kebabs by threading the chicken onto the skewers, alternating with the peppers and pineapple. Ensure the ingredients are pushed almost completely down to the end of the skewers.
4. When the unit beeps to signify it has preheated, place the skewers on the Grill Grate. Close the hood and cook for 10 to 14 minutes, occasionally basting the kebabs with the remaining ½ cup of teriyaki sauce while cooking.
5. Cooking is complete when the internal temperature of the chicken reaches 165°F (74°C) on a food thermometer.

Lime Chicken Breast
Prep time: 10 minutes | Cook time: 14 minutes | Serves 4

1½ tablespoons extra-virgin olive oil
3 garlic cloves, minced
¼ teaspoon ground cumin
Sea salt, to taste
Freshly ground black pepper, to taste
Grated zest of 1 lime
Juice of 1 lime
4 boneless, skinless chicken breasts

1. In a large shallow bowl, stir together the oil, garlic, cumin, salt, pepper, zest, and lime juice. Add the chicken breasts and coat well. Cover and marinate in the refrigerator for 30 minutes.
2. Insert the Grill Grate and close the hood. Select GRILL, set the temperature to MEDIUM, and set the time to 18 minutes. Select START/STOP to begin preheating.
3. When the unit has beeped to signify it has preheated, place the chicken breasts on the Grill Grate. Close the hood and cook for 7 minutes. After 7 minutes, flip the chicken, close the hood, and cook for an additional 7 minutes.
4. Check the chicken for doneness. If needed, cook up to 4 minutes more. Cooking is complete when the internal temperature of the chicken reaches at least 165°F (74°C) on a food thermometer.
5. Remove from the grill, and place on a cutting board or platter to rest for 5 minutes. Serve.

Rosemary Chicken Thighs
Prep time: 10 minutes | Cook time: 10 minutes | Serves 4

Grated zest of 2 lemons
Juice of 2 lemons
3 sprigs fresh rosemary, leaves finely chopped
3 sprigs fresh sage, leaves finely chopped
2 garlic cloves, minced
¼ teaspoon red pepper flakes
¼ cup canola oil
Sea salt, to taste
4 (4-to 7-ounce / 113- to 198-g) boneless chicken thighs

1. In a small bowl, whisk together the lemon zest and juice, rosemary, sage, garlic, red pepper flakes, and oil. Season with salt.
2. Place the chicken and lemon-herb mixture in a large resealable plastic bag or container. Toss to coat evenly. Refrigerate the chicken for at least 30 minutes.
3. Insert the Grill Grate and close the hood. Select GRILL, set the temperature to HIGH, and set the time to 13 minutes. Select START/STOP to begin preheating.
4. When the unit beeps to signify it has preheated, place the chicken on the Grill Grate. Close the hood and cook for 10 to 13 minutes.
5. Cooking is complete when the internal temperature of the chicken reaches at least 165°F (74°C) on a food thermometer.

Sriracha-Honey Chicken Thighs
Prep time: 5 minutes | Cook time: 16 minutes | Serves 4

1 cup sriracha
Juice of 2 lemons
¼ cup honey
4 bone-in chicken thighs

1. Place the sriracha, lemon juice, and honey in a large resealable plastic bag or container. Add the chicken thighs and toss to coat evenly. Refrigerate for 30 minutes.
2. Insert the Grill Grate and close the hood. Select GRILL, set the temperature to MEDIUM, and set the time to 14 minutes. Select START/STOP to begin preheating.
3. When the unit beeps to signify it has preheated, place the chicken thighs onto the Grill Grate, gently pressing them down to maximize grill marks. Close the hood and cook for 7 minutes.
4. After 7 minutes, flip the chicken thighs using tongs. Close the hood and cook for 7 minutes more.
5. Cooking is complete when the internal temperature of the meat reaches at least 165°F (74°C) on a food thermometer. If necessary, close the hood and continue cooking for 2 to 3 minutes more.
6. When cooking is complete, remove the chicken from the grill, and let it rest for 5 minutes before serving.

Breaded Chicken Cutlets
Prep time: 10 minutes | Cook time: 9 minutes | Serves 2

½ pound (227 g) boneless, skinless chicken breasts, horizontally sliced in half, into cutlets
½ tablespoon extra-virgin olive oil
⅛ cup bread crumbs
¼ teaspoon sea salt
¼ teaspoon freshly ground black pepper
¼ teaspoon paprika
¼ teaspoon garlic powder
⅛ teaspoon onion powder

1. Insert the Crisper Basket and close the hood. Select AIR CRISP, set the temperature to 375°F (190°C), and set the time to 11 minutes. Select START/STOP to begin preheating.
2. Brush each side of the chicken cutlets with the oil.
3. Combine the bread crumbs, salt, pepper, paprika, garlic powder, and onion powder in a medium shallow bowl. Dredge the chicken cutlets in the bread crumb mixture, turning several times, to ensure the chicken is fully coated.
4. When the unit beeps to signify it has preheated, place the chicken in the basket. Close the hood and cook for 9 minutes. Cooking is complete when the internal temperature of the meat reaches at least 165°F (74°C) on a food thermometer. If needed, cook for up to 2 minutes more.
5. Remove the chicken cutlets and serve immediately.

Air Fried Chicken Wings with Buffalo Sauce
Prep time: 10 minutes | Cook time: 20 minutes | Serves 6

16 chicken drumettes (party wings)
Chicken seasoning or rub, to taste
1 teaspoon garlic powder
Ground black pepper, to taste
¼ cup buffalo wings sauce
Cooking spray

1. Spritz the air fry basket with cooking spray.
2. Rub the chicken wings with chicken seasoning, garlic powder, and ground black pepper on a clean work surface.
3. Arrange the chicken wings in the air fry basket. Spritz with cooking spray.
4. Select Air Fry, Super Convection. Set temperature to 400°F (205°C) and set time to 10 minutes. Press Start/Stop to begin preheating.
5. Once preheated, place the basket on the air fry position. Flip the chicken wings halfway through.
6. When cooking is complete, the chicken wings should be lightly browned.
7. Transfer the chicken wings in a large bowl, then pour in the buffalo wings sauce and toss to coat well.
8. Put the wings back to the Vortex and set time to 7 minutes. Flip the wings halfway through.
9. When cooking is complete, the wings should be heated through. Serve immediately.

Bacon-Wrapped and Cheese-Stuffed Chicken
Prep time: 10 minutes | Cook time: 20 minutes | Serves 4

4 (5-ounce / 142-g) boneless, skinless chicken breasts, pounded to ¼ inch thick
1 cup cream cheese
2 tablespoons chopped fresh chives
8 slices thin-cut bacon
Sprig of fresh cilantro, for garnish
Cooking spray

1. Spritz the air fry basket with cooking spray.
2. On a clean work surface, slice the chicken horizontally to make a 1-inch incision on top of each chicken breast with a knife, then cut into the chicken to make a pocket. Leave a ½-inch border along the sides and bottom.
3. Combine the cream cheese and chives in a bowl. Stir to mix well, then gently pour the mixture into the chicken pockets.
4. Wrap each stuffed chicken breast with 2 bacon slices, then secure the ends with toothpicks.
5. Arrange them in the air fry basket.
6. Select Air Fry, Super Convection. Set temperature to 400°F (205°C) and set time to 20 minutes. Press Start/Stop to begin preheating.
7. Once preheated, place the basket on the air fry position. Flip the bacon-wrapped chicken halfway through the cooking time.
8. When cooking is complete, the bacon should be browned and crispy.
9. Transfer them on a large plate and serve with cilantro on top.

Bell Pepper Stuffed Chicken Roll-Ups
Prep time: 10 minutes | Cook time: 12 minutes | Serves 4

2 (4-ounce / 113-g) boneless, skinless chicken breasts, slice in half horizontally
1 tablespoon olive oil
Juice of ½ lime
2 tablespoons taco seasoning
½ green bell pepper, cut into strips
½ red bell pepper, cut into strips
¼ onion, sliced

1. Unfold the chicken breast slices on a clean work surface. Rub with olive oil, then drizzle with lime juice and sprinkle with taco seasoning.
2. Top the chicken slices with equal amount of bell peppers and onion. Roll them up and secure with toothpicks.
3. Arrange the chicken roll-ups in the air fry basket.
4. Select Air Fry, Super Convection. Set temperature to 400°F (205°C) and set time to 12 minutes. Press Start/Stop to begin preheating.
5. Once preheated, place the basket on the air fry position. Flip the chicken roll-ups halfway through.
6. When cooking is complete, the internal temperature of the chicken should reach at least 165°F (74°C).
7. Remove the chicken from the Vortex. Discard the toothpicks and serve immediately.

Bruschetta Chicken

Prep time: 10 minutes | Cook time: 10 minutes | Serves 4

Bruschetta Stuffing:
1 tomato, diced
3 tablespoons balsamic vinegar
1 teaspoon Italian seasoning
2 tablespoons chopped fresh basil
3 garlic cloves, minced
Chicken:
4 (4-ounce / 113-g) boneless, skinless chicken breasts, cut 4 slits each
1 teaspoon Italian seasoning
Chicken seasoning or rub, to taste
Cooking spray

1. Spritz the air fry basket with cooking spray.
2. Combine the ingredients for the bruschetta stuffing in a bowl. Stir to mix well. Set aside.
3. Rub the chicken breasts with Italian seasoning and chicken seasoning on a clean work surface.
4. Arrange the chicken breasts, slits side up, in the air fry basket and spritz with cooking spray.
5. Select Air Fry, Super Convection. Set temperature to 370°F (188°C) and set time to 10 minutes. Press Start/Stop to begin preheating.
6. Once preheated, place the basket on the air fry position. Flip the breast and fill the slits with the bruschetta stuffing halfway through.
7. When cooking is complete, the chicken should be well browned.
8. Serve immediately.

Cheese-Encrusted Chicken Tenderloins with Peanuts

Prep time: 10 minutes | Cook time: 12 minutes | Serves 4

½ cup grated Parmesan cheese
½ teaspoon garlic powder
1 teaspoon red pepper flakes
Sea salt and ground black pepper, to taste
2 tablespoons peanut oil
1½ pounds (680 g) chicken tenderloins
2 tablespoons peanuts, roasted and roughly chopped
Cooking spray

1. Spritz the air fry basket with cooking spray.
2. Combine the Parmesan cheese, garlic powder, red pepper flakes, salt, black pepper, and peanut oil in a large bow. Stir to mix well.
3. Dip the chicken tenderloins in the cheese mixture, then press to coat well. Shake the excess off.
4. Transfer the chicken tenderloins in the air fry basket.
5. Select Air Fry, Super Convection. Set temperature to 360°F (182°C) and set time to 12 minutes. Press Start/Stop to begin preheating.
6. Once preheated, place the basket on the air fry position. Flip the tenderloin halfway through.
7. When cooking is complete, the tenderloin should be well browned.
8. Transfer the chicken tenderloins on a large plate and top with roasted peanuts before serving.

Air Fried Chicken Potatoes with Sun-Dried Tomato

Prep time: 15 minutes | Cook time: 25 minutes | Serves 2

2 teaspoons minced fresh oregano, divided
2 teaspoons minced fresh thyme, divided
2 teaspoons extra-virgin olive oil, plus extra as needed
1 pound (454 g) fingerling potatoes, unpeeled
2 (12-ounce / 340-g) bone-in split chicken breasts, trimmed
1 garlic clove, minced
¼ cup oil-packed sun-dried tomatoes, patted dry and chopped
1½ tablespoons red wine vinegar
1 tablespoon capers, rinsed and minced
1 small shallot, minced
Salt and ground black pepper, to taste

1. Combine 1 teaspoon of oregano, 1 teaspoon of thyme, ¼ teaspoon of salt, ¼ teaspoon of ground black pepper, 1 teaspoons of olive oil in a large bowl. Add the potatoes and toss to coat well.
2. Combine the chicken with remaining thyme, oregano, and olive oil. Sprinkle with garlic, salt, and pepper. Toss to coat well.
3. Place the potatoes in the air fry basket, then arrange the chicken on top of the potatoes.
4. Select Air Fry, Super Convection. Set temperature to 350°F (180°C) and set time to 25 minutes. Press Start/Stop to begin preheating.
5. Once preheated, place the basket on the air fry position. Flip the chicken and potatoes halfway through.
6. When cooking is complete, the internal temperature of the chicken should reach at least 165°F (74°C) and the potatoes should be wilted.
7. Meanwhile, combine the sun-dried tomatoes, vinegar, capers, and shallot in a separate large bowl. Sprinkle with salt and ground black pepper. Toss to mix well.
8. Remove the chicken and potatoes from the Vortex and allow to cool for 10 minutes. Serve with the sun-dried tomato mix.

Cheesy Pepperoni and Chicken Pizza

Prep time: 15 minutes | Cook time: 15 minutes | Serves 6

2 cups cooked chicken, cubed
1 cup pizza sauce
20 slices pepperoni
¼ cup grated Parmesan cheese
1 cup shredded Mozzarella cheese
Cooking spray

1. Spritz a baking pan with cooking spray.
2. Arrange the chicken cubes in the prepared baking pan, then top the cubes with pizza sauce and pepperoni. Stir to coat the cubes and pepperoni with sauce. Scatter the cheeses on top.
3. Select Air Fry, Super Convection. Set temperature to 375°F (190°C) and set time to 15 minutes. Press Start/Stop to begin preheating.
4. Once preheated, place the pan into the Vortex.
5. When cooking is complete, the pizza should be frothy and the cheeses should be melted.
6. Serve immediately.

Drumsticks with Barbecue-Honey Sauce

Prep time: 5 minutes | Cook time: 18 minutes | Serves 5

1 tablespoon olive oil
10 chicken drumsticks
Chicken seasoning or rub, to taste
Salt and ground black pepper, to taste
1 cup barbecue sauce
¼ cup honey

1. Grease the air fry basket with olive oil.
2. Rub the chicken drumsticks with chicken seasoning or rub, salt and ground black pepper on a clean work surface.
3. Arrange the chicken drumsticks in the air fry basket.
4. Select Air Fry, Super Convection. Set temperature to 390°F (199°C) and set time to 18 minutes. Press Start/Stop to begin preheating.
5. Once preheated, place the basket on the air fry position. Flip the drumsticks halfway through.
6. When cooking is complete, the drumsticks should be lightly browned.
7. Meanwhile, combine the barbecue sauce and honey in a small bowl. Stir to mix well.
8. Remove the drumsticks from the Vortex and baste with the sauce mixture to serve.

Easy Chicken Fingers

Prep time: 20 minutes | Cook time: 10 minutes | Makes 12 chicken fingers

½ cup all-purpose flour
2 cups panko bread crumbs
2 tablespoons canola oil
1 large egg
3 boneless and skinless chicken breasts, each cut into 4 strips
Kosher salt and freshly ground black pepper, to taste
Cooking spray

1. Spritz the air fry basket with cooking spray.
2. Pour the flour in a large bowl. Combine the panko and canola oil on a shallow dish. Whisk the egg in a separate bowl.
3. Rub the chicken strips with salt and ground black pepper on a clean work surface, then dip the chicken in the bowl of flour. Shake the excess off and dunk the chicken strips in the bowl of whisked egg, then roll the strips over the panko to coat well.
4. Arrange the strips in the air fry basket.
5. Select Air Fry, Super Convection. Set temperature to 360°F (182°C) and set time to 10 minutes. Press Start/Stop to begin preheating.
6. Once preheated, place the basket on the air fry position. Flip the strips halfway through.
7. When cooking is complete, the strips should be crunchy and lightly browned.
8. Serve immediately.

Chicken Schnitzel

Prep time: 15 minutes | Cook time: 5 minutes | Serves 4

½ cup all-purpose flour
1 teaspoon marjoram
½ teaspoon thyme
1 teaspoon dried parsley flakes
½ teaspoon salt
1 egg
1 teaspoon lemon juice
1 teaspoon water
1 cup bread crumbs
4 chicken tenders, pounded thin, cut in half lengthwise
Cooking spray

1. Spritz the air fry basket with cooking spray.
2. Combine the flour, marjoram, thyme, parsley, and salt in a shallow dish. Stir to mix well.
3. Whisk the egg with lemon juice and water in a large bowl. Pour the bread crumbs in a separate shallow dish.
4. Roll the chicken halves in the flour mixture first, then in the egg mixture, and then roll over the bread crumbs to coat well. Shake the excess off.
5. Arrange the chicken halves in the air fry basket and spritz with cooking spray on both sides.
6. Once preheated, place the basket on the air fry position. Flip the halves halfway through.
7. When cooking is complete, the chicken halves should be golden brown and crispy.
8. Serve immediately.

Crispy Chicken Skin
Prep time: 5 minutes | Cook time: 6 minutes | Serves 4

1 pound (454 g) chicken skin, cut into slices
1 teaspoon melted butter
½ teaspoon crushed chili flakes
1 teaspoon dried dill
Salt and ground black pepper, to taste

1. Combine all the ingredients in a large bowl. Toss to coat the chicken skin well.
2. Transfer the skin in the air fry basket.
3. Select Air Fry, Super Convection. Set temperature to 360°F (182°C) and set time to 6 minutes. Press Start/Stop to begin preheating.
4. Once preheated, place the basket on the air fry position. Stir the skin halfway through.
5. When cooking is complete, the skin should be crispy.
6. Serve immediately.

Gold Livers
Prep time: 10 minutes | Cook time: 10 minutes | Serves 4

2 eggs
2 tablespoons water
¾ cup flour
2 cups panko bread crumbs
1 teaspoon salt
½ teaspoon ground black pepper
20 ounces (567 g) chicken livers
Cooking spray

1. Spritz the air fry basket with cooking spray.
2. Whisk the eggs with water in a large bowl. Pour the flour in a separate bowl. Pour the panko on a shallow dish and sprinkle with salt and pepper.
3. Dredge the chicken livers in the flour. Shake the excess off, then dunk the livers in the whisked eggs, and then roll the livers over the panko to coat well.
4. Arrange the livers in the air fry basket and spritz with cooking spray.
5. Select Air Fry, Super Convection. Set temperature to 390°F (199°C) and set time to 10 minutes. Press Start/Stop to begin preheating.
6. Once preheated, place the basket on the air fry position. Flip the livers halfway through.
7. When cooking is complete, the livers should be golden and crispy.
8. Serve immediately.

Hawaiian Chicken Bites
Prep time: 15 minutes | Cook time: 15 minutes | Serves 4

½ cup pineapple juice
2 tablespoons apple cider vinegar
½ tablespoon minced ginger
½ cup ketchup
2 garlic cloves, minced
½ cup brown sugar
2 tablespoons sherry
½ cup soy sauce
4 chicken breasts, cubed
Cooking spray

1. Combine the pineapple juice, cider vinegar, ginger, ketchup, garlic, and sugar in a saucepan. Stir to mix well. Heat over low heat for 5 minutes or until thickened. Fold in the sherry and soy sauce.
2. Dunk the chicken cubes in the mixture. Press to submerge. Wrap the bowl in plastic and refrigerate to marinate for at least an hour.
3. Spritz the air fry basket with cooking spray.
4. Remove the chicken cubes from the marinade. Shake the excess off and put in the air fry basket. Spritz with cooking spray.
5. Select Air Fry, Super Convection. Set temperature to 360°F (182°C) and set time to 15 minutes. Press Start/Stop to begin preheating.
6. Once preheated, place the basket on the air fry position. Flip the chicken cubes at least three times during the air frying.
7. When cooking is complete, the chicken cubes should be glazed and well browned.
8. Serve immediately.

Easy Cajun Chicken Drumsticks
Prep time: 5 minutes | Cook time: 18 minutes | Serves 5

1 tablespoon olive oil
10 chicken drumsticks
1½ tablespoons Cajun seasoning
Salt and ground black pepper, to taste

1. Grease the air fry basket with olive oil.
2. On a clean work surface, rub the chicken drumsticks with Cajun seasoning, salt, and ground black pepper.
3. Arrange the seasoned chicken drumsticks in the air fry basket.
4. Select Air Fry, Super Convection. Set temperature to 390°F (199°C) and set time to 18 minutes. Press Start/Stop to begin preheating.
5. Once preheated, place the basket on the air fry position. Flip the drumsticks halfway through.
6. When cooking is complete, the drumsticks should be lightly browned.
7. Remove the chicken drumsticks from the Vortex. Serve immediately.

Honey Glazed Chicken Breasts

Prep time: 5 minutes | Cook time: 10 minutes | Serves 4

4 (4-ounce / 113-g) boneless, skinless chicken breasts
Chicken seasoning or rub, to taste
Salt and ground black pepper, to taste
¼ cup honey
2 tablespoons soy sauce
2 teaspoons grated fresh ginger
2 garlic cloves, minced
Cooking spray

1. Spritz the air fry basket with cooking spray.
2. Rub the chicken breasts with chicken seasoning, salt, and black pepper on a clean work surface.
3. Arrange the chicken breasts in the air fry basket and spritz with cooking spray.
4. Select Air Fry, Super Convection. Set temperature to 400°F (205°C) and set time to 10 minutes. Press Start/Stop to begin preheating.
5. Once preheated, place the basket on the air fry position. Flip the chicken breasts halfway through.
6. When cooking is complete, the internal temperature of the thickest part of the chicken should reach at least 165°F (74°C).
7. Meanwhile, combine the honey, soy sauce, ginger, and garlic in a saucepan and heat over medium-high heat for 3 minutes or until thickened. Stir constantly.
8. Remove the chicken from the Vortex and serve with the honey glaze.

Golden Chicken Cutlets

Prep time: 15 minutes | Cook time: 15 minutes | Serves 4

2 tablespoons panko bread crumbs
¼ cup grated Parmesan cheese
⅛ tablespoon paprika
½ tablespoon garlic powder
2 large eggs
4 chicken cutlets
1 tablespoon parsley
Salt and ground black pepper, to taste
Cooking spray

1. Spritz the air fry basket with cooking spray.
2. Combine the bread crumbs, Parmesan, paprika, garlic powder, salt, and ground black pepper in a large bowl. Stir to mix well. Beat the eggs in a separate bowl.
3. Dredge the chicken cutlets in the beaten eggs, then roll over the bread crumbs mixture to coat well. Shake the excess off.
4. Transfer the chicken cutlets in the air fry basket and spritz with cooking spray.
5. Select Air Fry, Super Convection. Set temperature to 400°F (205°C) and set time to 15 minutes. Press Start/Stop to begin preheating.
6. Once preheated, place the basket on the air fry position. Flip the cutlets halfway through.
7. When cooking is complete, the cutlets should be crispy and golden brown.
8. Serve with parsley on top.

Spicy Tandoori Chicken Drumsticks

Prep time: 70 minutes | Cook time: 14 minutes | Serves 4

8 (4- to 5-ounce / 113- to 142-g) skinless bone-in chicken drumsticks
½ cup plain full-fat or low-fat yogurt
¼ cup buttermilk
2 teaspoons minced garlic
2 teaspoons minced fresh ginger
2 teaspoons ground cinnamon
2 teaspoons ground coriander
2 teaspoons mild paprika
1 teaspoon salt
1 teaspoon Tabasco hot red pepper sauce

1. In a large bowl, stir together all the ingredients except for chicken drumsticks until well combined. Add the chicken drumsticks to the bowl and toss until well coated. Cover in plastic and set in the refrigerator to marinate for 1 hour, tossing once.
2. Arrange the marinated drumsticks in the air fry basket, leaving enough space between them.
3. Select Air Fry, Super Convection. Set temperature to 375°F (190°C) and set time to 14 minutes. Press Start/Stop to begin preheating.
4. Once preheated, place the basket on the air fry position. Flip the drumsticks once halfway through to ensure even cooking.
5. When cooking is complete, the internal temperature of the chicken drumsticks should reach 160°F (71°C) on a meat thermometer.
6. Transfer the drumsticks to plates. Rest for 5 minutes before serving.

Lime Chicken with Cilantro

Prep time: 35 minutes | Cook time: 10 minutes | Serves 4

4 (4-ounce / 113-g) boneless, skinless chicken breasts
½ cup chopped fresh cilantro
Juice of 1 lime
Chicken seasoning or rub, to taste
Salt and ground black pepper, to taste
Cooking spray

1. Put the chicken breasts in the large bowl, then add the cilantro, lime juice, chicken seasoning, salt, and black pepper. Toss to coat well.
2. Wrap the bowl in plastic and refrigerate to marinate for at least 30 minutes.
3. Spritz the air fry basket with cooking spray.
4. Remove the marinated chicken breasts from the bowl and place in the air fry basket. Spritz with cooking spray.
5. Select Air Fry, Super Convection. Set temperature to 400°F (205°C) and set time to 10 minutes. Press Start/Stop to begin preheating.
6. Once preheated, place the basket on the air fry position. Flip the breasts halfway through.
7. When cooking is complete, the internal temperature of the chicken should reach at least 165°F (74°C).
8. Serve immediately.

Nice Goulash
Prep time: 5 minutes | Cook time: 17 minutes | Serves 2

2 red bell peppers, chopped
1 pound (454 g) ground chicken
2 medium tomatoes, diced
½ cup chicken broth
Salt and ground black pepper, to taste
Cooking spray

1. Spritz a baking pan with cooking spray.
2. Set the bell pepper in the baking pan.
3. Select Broil, Super Convection, set temperature to 365°F (185°C) and set time to 5 minutes. Press Start/Stop to begin preheating.
4. Once preheated, place the pan on the broil position. Stir the bell pepper halfway through.
5. When broiling is complete, the bell pepper should be tender.
6. Add the ground chicken and diced tomatoes in the baking pan and stir to mix well.
7. Set the time of oven to 12 minutes. Press Start/Stop. Stir the mixture and mix in the chicken broth, salt and ground black pepper halfway through.
8. When cooking is complete, the chicken should be well browned.
9. Serve immediately.

Simple Chicken Nuggets
Prep time: 10 minutes | Cook time: 8 minutes | Serves 4

1 pound (454 g) boneless, skinless chicken breasts, cut into 1-inch pieces
2 tablespoons panko bread crumbs
6 tablespoons bread crumbs
Chicken seasoning or rub, to taste
Salt and ground black pepper, to taste
2 eggs
Cooking spray

1. Spritz the air fry basket with cooking spray.
2. Combine the bread crumbs, chicken seasoning, salt, and black pepper in a large bowl. Stir to mix well. Whisk the eggs in a separate bowl.
3. Dunk the chicken pieces in the egg mixture, then in the bread crumb mixture. Shake the excess off.
4. Arrange the well-coated chicken pieces in the air fry basket. Spritz with cooking spray.
5. Select Air Fry, Super Convection. Set temperature to 400°F (205°C) and set time to 8 minutes. Press Start/Stop to begin preheating.
6. Once preheated, place the basket on the air fry position. Flip the chicken halfway through.
7. When cooking is complete, the chicken should be crispy and golden brown.
8. Serve immediately.

Simple Whole Chicken Bake
Prep time: 10 minutes | Cook time: 1 hour | Serves 2 to 4

½ cup melted butter
3 tablespoons garlic, minced
Salt, to taste
1 teaspoon ground black pepper
1 (1-pound / 454-g) whole chicken

1. Combine the butter with garlic, salt, and ground black pepper in a small bowl.
2. Brush the butter mixture over the whole chicken, then place the chicken in the air fry basket, skin side down.
3. Select Bake, Super Convection, set temperature to 350°F (180°C) and set time to 60 minutes. Press Start/Stop to begin preheating.
4. Once preheated, place the basket on the bake position. Flip the chicken halfway through.
5. When cooking is complete, an instant-read thermometer inserted in the thickest part of the chicken should register at least 165°F (74°C).
6. Remove the chicken from the Vortex and allow to cool for 15 minutes before serving.

Simple Air Fried Chicken Wings
Prep time: 10 minutes | Cook time: 15 minutes | Serves 4

1 tablespoon olive oil
8 whole chicken wings
Chicken seasoning or rub, to taste
1 teaspoon garlic powder
Freshly ground black pepper, to taste

1. Grease the air fry basket with olive oil.
2. On a clean work surface, rub the chicken wings with chicken seasoning and rub, garlic powder, and ground black pepper.
3. Arrange the well-coated chicken wings in the air fry basket.
4. Select Air Fry, Super Convection. Set temperature to 400°F (205°C) and set time to 15 minutes. Press Start/Stop to begin preheating.
5. Once preheated, place the basket on the air fry position. Flip the chicken wings halfway through.
6. When cooking is complete, the internal temperature of the chicken wings should reach at least 165°F (74°C).
7. Remove the chicken wings from the Vortex. Serve immediately.

Spanish Chicken and Pepper Baguette
Prep time: 10 minutes | Cook time: 20 minutes | Serves 2

1¼ pounds (567 g) assorted small chicken parts, breasts cut into halves
¼ teaspoon salt
¼ teaspoon ground black pepper
2 teaspoons olive oil
½ pound (227 g) mini sweet peppers
¼ cup light mayonnaise
¼ teaspoon smoked paprika
½ clove garlic, crushed
Baguette, for serving
Cooking spray

1. Spritz the air fry basket with cooking spray.
2. Toss the chicken with salt, ground black pepper, and olive oil in a large bowl.
3. Arrange the sweet peppers and chicken in the air fry basket.
4. Select Air Fry, Super Convection. Set temperature to 375°F (190°C) and set time to 20 minutes. Press Start/Stop to begin preheating.
5. Once preheated, place the basket on the air fry position. Flip the chicken and transfer the peppers on a plate halfway through.
6. Meanwhile, combine the mayo, paprika, and garlic in a small bowl. Stir to mix well.
7. Assemble the baguette with chicken and sweet pepper, then spread with mayo mixture and serve.

Sweet-and-Sour Chicken Nuggets
Prep time: 15 minutes | Cook time: 15 minutes | Serves 4

1 cup cornstarch
Chicken seasoning or rub, to taste
Salt and ground black pepper, to taste
2 eggs
2 (4-ounce/ 113-g) boneless, skinless chicken breasts, cut into 1-inch pieces
1½ cups sweet-and-sour sauce
Cooking spray

1. Spritz the air fry basket with cooking spray.
2. Combine the cornstarch, chicken seasoning, salt, and pepper in a large bowl. Stir to mix well. Whisk the eggs in a separate bowl.
3. Dredge the chicken pieces in the bowl of cornstarch mixture first, then in the bowl of whisked eggs, and then in the cornstarch mixture again.
4. Arrange the well-coated chicken pieces in the air fry basket. Spritz with cooking spray.
5. Select Air Fry, Super Convection. Set temperature to 360°F (182°C) and set time to 15 minutes. Press Start/Stop to begin preheating.
6. Once preheated, place the basket on the air fry position. Flip the chicken halfway through.
7. When cooking is complete, the chicken should be golden brown and crispy.
8. Transfer the chicken pieces on a large serving plate, then baste with sweet-and-sour sauce before serving.

China Spicy Turkey Thighs
Prep time: 10 minutes | Cook time: 25 minutes | Serves 6

2 pounds (907 g) turkey thighs
1 teaspoon Chinese five-spice powder
¼ teaspoon Sichuan pepper
1 teaspoon pink Himalayan salt
1 tablespoon Chinese rice vinegar
1 tablespoon mustard
1 tablespoon chili sauce
2 tablespoons soy sauce
Cooking spray

1. Spritz the air fry basket with cooking spray.
2. Rub the turkey thighs with five-spice powder, Sichuan pepper, and salt on a clean work surface.
3. Put the turkey thighs in the air fry basket and spritz with cooking spray.
4. Select Air Fry, Super Convection. Set temperature to 360°F (182°C) and set time to 22 minutes. Press Start/Stop to begin preheating.
5. Once preheated, place the basket on the air fry position. Flip the thighs at least three times during the cooking.
6. When cooking is complete, the thighs should be well browned.
7. Meanwhile, heat the remaining ingredients in a saucepan over medium-high heat. Cook for 3 minutes or until the sauce is thickened and reduces to two thirds.
8. Transfer the thighs onto a plate and baste with sauce before serving.

Strawberry-Glazed Turkey
Prep time: 15 minutes | Cook time: 37 minutes | Serves 2

2 pounds (907 g) turkey breast
1 tablespoon olive oil
Salt and ground black pepper, to taste
1 cup fresh strawberries

1. Rub the turkey bread with olive oil on a clean work surface, then sprinkle with salt and ground black pepper.
2. Transfer the turkey in the air fry basket and spritz with cooking spray.
3. Select Air Fry, Super Convection. Set temperature to 375°F (190°C) and set time to 30 minutes. Press Start/Stop to begin preheating.
4. Once preheated, place the basket on the air fry position. Flip the turkey breast halfway through.
5. Meanwhile, put the strawberries in a food processor and pulse until smooth.
6. When cooking is complete, spread the puréed strawberries over the turkey and fry for 7 more minutes.
7. Serve immediately.

Turkey and Cauliflower Meatloaf

Prep time: 15 minutes | Cook time: 50 minutes | Serves 6

2 pounds (907 g) lean ground turkey
1⅓ cups riced cauliflower
2 large eggs, lightly beaten
¼ cup almond flour
⅔ cup chopped yellow or white onion
1 teaspoon ground dried turmeric
1 teaspoon ground cumin
1 teaspoon ground coriander
1 tablespoon minced garlic
1 teaspoon salt
1 teaspoon ground black pepper
Cooking spray

1. Spritz a loaf pan with cooking spray.
2. Combine all the ingredients in a large bowl. Stir to mix well. Pour half of the mixture in the prepared loaf pan and press with a spatula to coat the bottom evenly. Spritz the mixture with cooking spray.
3. Select Bake, Super Convection, set temperature to 350°F (180°C) and set time to 25 minutes. Press Start/Stop to begin preheating.
4. Once preheated, place the pan on the bake position.
5. When cooking is complete, the meat should be well browned and the internal temperature should reach at least 165°F (74°C).
6. Remove the loaf pan from the Vortex and serve immediately.

Deep Fried Duck Leg Quarters

Prep time: 5 minutes | Cook time: 45 minutes | Serves 4

4 (½-pound / 227-g) skin-on duck leg quarters
2 medium garlic cloves, minced
½ teaspoon salt
½ teaspoon ground black pepper

1. Spritz the air fry basket with cooking spray.
2. On a clean work surface, rub the duck leg quarters with garlic, salt, and black pepper.
3. Arrange the leg quarters in the air fry basket and spritz with cooking spray.
4. Select Air Fry, Super Convection. Set temperature to 300°F (150°C) and set time to 30 minutes. Press Start/Stop to begin preheating.
5. Once preheated, place the basket on the air fry position.
6. After 30 minutes, remove the basket from the Vortex. Flip the leg quarters. Increase temperature to 375°F (190°C) and set time to 15 minutes. Return the basket to the Vortex and continue cooking.
7. When cooking is complete, the leg quarters should be well browned and crispy.
8. Remove the duck leg quarters from the Vortex and allow to cool for 10 minutes before serving.

Duck Breasts with Marmalade Balsamic Glaze

Prep time: 5 minutes | Cook time: 13 minutes | Serves 4

4 (6-ounce / 170-g) skin-on duck breasts
1 teaspoon salt
¼ cup orange marmalade
1 tablespoon white balsamic vinegar
¾ teaspoon ground black pepper

1. Cut 10 slits into the skin of the duck breasts, then sprinkle with salt on both sides.
2. Place the breasts in the air fry basket, skin side up.
3. Select Air Fry, Super Convection. Set temperature to 400°F (205°C) and set time to 10 minutes. Press Start/Stop to begin preheating.
4. Once preheated, place the basket on the air fry position.
5. Meanwhile, combine the remaining ingredients in a small bowl. Stir to mix well.
6. When cooking is complete, brush the duck skin with the marmalade mixture. Flip the breast and air fry for 3 more minutes or until the skin is crispy and the breast is well browned.
7. Serve immediately.

Rosemary Turkey Scotch Eggs

Prep time: 15 minutes | Cook time: 12 minutes | Serves 4

1 egg
1 cup panko bread crumbs
½ teaspoon rosemary
1 pound (454 g) ground turkey
4 hard-boiled eggs, peeled
Salt and ground black pepper, to taste
Cooking spray

1. Spritz the air fry basket with cooking spray.
2. Whisk the egg with salt in a bowl. Combine the bread crumbs with rosemary in a shallow dish.
3. Stir the ground turkey with salt and ground black pepper in a separate large bowl, then divide the ground turkey into four portions.
4. Wrap each hard-boiled egg with a portion of ground turkey. Dredge in the whisked egg, then roll over the bread crumb mixture.
5. Place the wrapped eggs in the air fry basket and spritz with cooking spray.
6. Select Air Fry, Super Convection. Set temperature to 400°F (205°C) and set time to 12 minutes. Press Start/Stop to begin preheating.
7. Once preheated, place the basket on the air fry position. Flip the eggs halfway through.
8. When cooking is complete, the scotch eggs should be golden brown and crunchy.
9. Serve immediately.

Chapter 9
Pizza

Simple Pizza Dough
Prep time: 15 minutes | Cook time: 0 minutes | Makes 2 (12- to 14-inch) pizzas

1 package active dry yeast
1½ cups warm water (about 110º F)
2 tablespoons extra-virgin olive oil
4 cups all-purpose flour, plus more for dusting
1½ teaspoons salt

1. In a medium bowl, add the yeast to the warm water and let bloom for about 10 minutes. Add the olive oil.
2. In a food processor or standing mixer fitted with a paddle attachment, pulse to blend the flour and salt. With the machine running, add the yeast mixture in a slow, steady stream, mixing just until the dough comes together. Turn the dough out onto a well-floured board, and with lightly floured hands, knead the dough using the heels of your hands, pushing the dough and then folding it over. Shape it into a ball, then cut it into 2 or 4 equal pieces.
3. Place the balls of dough on a lightly floured baking sheet and cover with a clean dishtowel. Let them rise in a warm, draft-free spot until they are doubled in size, about 45 minutes.
4. Proceed with the desired recipe.

No-Knead Pan Pizza Dough
Prep time: 5 minutes | Cook time: 0 minutes | Makes 2 (13-by-18-inch) pizzas

3½ cups bread flour, plus more for dusting
¼ teaspoon active dry yeast
1 teaspoon kosher salt
¾ teaspoon sugar
1⅓ cups warm water
Extra-virgin olive oil, for drizzling

1. In the bowl of a standing mixer fitted with the paddle attachment, combine the flour, yeast, salt, and sugar. With the mixer on low, add the water and mix just until combined, about 3 minutes.
2. Cover the bowl with a towel and let the mixture rise at room temperature for 8 to 18 hours, or until it is doubled in volume.
3. Turn the dough onto a well-floured board and divide in half. Lightly drizzle two large (13-by-18-inch) sheet pans with olive oil, and spread to cover with a thin, even coating.
4. Stretch one piece of dough to the length of the pan, then place it in the center of one pan. Gently pull and stretch the dough to fit the width. If it resists, refrigerate the dough for 10 minutes. When the dough fits the pan, cover the pan with a damp kitchen towel and let it rest for 30 minutes at room temperature. Repeat with the second piece of dough and the second sheet pan.
5. Proceed with the desired recipe.

Pro Dough
Prep time: 40 minutes | Cook time: 0 minutes | Makes 2 (12- to 14-inch) pizzas

¼ teaspoon active dry yeast
1½ cups warm water
4 cups "00" flour or all-purpose flour, plus more for dusting
2 teaspoons salt
Extra-virgin olive oil, for greasing

1. In a medium bowl, add the yeast to the warm water and let it stand for 10 minutes. While the yeast is blooming, rinse the bowl of a standing mixer with hot water and dry thoroughly. It should be warm to the touch. In the warm mixing bowl, combine the flour and salt. Add the yeast mixture and mix on low speed with a dough hook for 2 minutes. Raise the speed to medium-low and continue to mix for about 10 minutes, until the dough is cohesive and smooth and has pulled away from the sides of the bowl.
2. Knead again on medium-low speed for an additional 10 minutes, or until the dough is soft and warm to the touch.
3. Transfer the dough to a large, lightly oiled bowl, rolling the dough to coat it on all sides. Cover with plastic wrap and refrigerate overnight.
4. The next day, transfer the dough to a lightly floured board and punch it down. Cut it into 2 or 4 equal pieces and shape into smooth balls. Lightly flour the balls, place them on a baking tray, and cover with a damp kitchen towel. Let the dough rise again in the refrigerator for at least 4 hours or overnight.
5. Remove the dough from the refrigerator, place on a lightly floured baking sheet, and cover with a damp kitchen towel. Let it rise for 1½ to 2 hours, until it is doubled in size.
6. Proceed with the desired recipe.

Garlic Tomato Pizza Sauce
Prep time: 10 minutes | Cook time: 25 minutes | Makes 1 quart

2 tablespoons extra-virgin olive oil
1 small yellow onion, chopped (½ cup)
3 garlic cloves, smashed
1 (28-ounce / 794-g) can whole peeled San Marzano tomatoes, undrained
1 teaspoon fine sea salt
⅛ teaspoon freshly ground black pepper
1 to 2 tablespoons sugar

1. In a large saucepan over medium-high heat, heat the olive oil until it shimmers. Reduce the heat to medium and add the chopped onion. Cook, stirring occasionally, for 5 minutes. Add the garlic and continue to cook for 2 to 3 minutes more, until the onion is translucent and the garlic is aromatic.
2. Add the tomatoes and their juice, and bring to a simmer, stirring occasionally with a wooden spoon to break them apart. Simmer for 10 to 15 minutes, until the sauce has thickened.
3. Using an immersion blender or food processor, pulse until the sauce is smooth. Season with the salt, pepper, and sugar.

Pepperoni Pizza with Mozzarella
Prep time: 5 minutes | Cook time: 20 minutes | Makes 2 (12-inch) pizzas

Extra-virgin olive oil, for brushing
Simple Pizza Dough
1 cup Garlic Tomato Pizza Sauce
1 cup grated Mozzarella cheese
6 ounces (170 g) pepperoni, sliced thin
¼ teaspoon salt

1. Brush two baking sheets with olive oil.
2. Roll out one of the dough balls and place it on the prepared baking sheet.
3. Leaving a 1-inch border, spread half of the sauce evenly over the dough. Top with half the Mozzarella and then half the pepperoni. Sprinkle with half the salt.
4. Slide the baking sheet into the air fryer oven. Press the Power Button. Cook at 400°F (205°C) for 10 minutes, until the crust is golden and the cheese has melted,.
5. Remove the pizza from the air fryer oven and transfer it to a cutting board. Let it rest for 5 minutes, then slice and serve.
6. Repeat with the remaining dough ball and toppings.

Ham and Pineapple Pizza
Prep time: 10 minutes | Cook time: 25 minutes | Makes 2 (12- to 14-inch) pizzas

Extra-virgin olive oil, for brushing
4 slices center-cut bacon
Simple Pizza Dough or Pro Dough
1 cup Garlic Tomato Pizza Sauce
1 cup grated Mozzarella cheese
¼ pound (113 g) smoked ham, cut into ½-inch dice
1 cup diced fresh pineapple
2 tablespoons grated Parmesan cheese

1. Brush two baking sheets with olive oil.
2. In a medium skillet over medium heat, cook the bacon until crisp, 2 to 3 minutes per side. Transfer to a paper towel–lined plate to cool. Cut into bits.
3. Roll out one of the dough balls to the desired size and place it on the prepared baking sheet.
4. Leaving a 1-inch border, spread half of the sauce evenly onto the dough. Sprinkle on half of the Mozzarella, followed by half of the ham, chopped bacon, pineapple, and grated Parmesan cheese.
5. Slide the baking sheet into the air fryer oven. Press the Power Button. Cook at 400°F (205°C) for 10 minutes, until the crust is golden and the cheese has melted.
6. Remove the pizza from the air fryer oven and transfer it to a cutting board. Let it rest for 5 minutes, then slice and serve.
7. Repeat with the remaining dough ball and toppings.

Pear Pizza with Basil
Prep time: 15 minutes | Cook time: 25 minutes | Makes 1 (12- to 14-inch) pizza

½ recipe Simple Pizza Dough
4 Bosc pears
½ lemon
Zest of 1 orange
1 tablespoon chopped fresh basil leaves
1 teaspoon chopped fresh rosemary leaves
2 tablespoons sugar
⅛ teaspoon freshly ground black pepper
2 tablespoons extra-virgin olive oil

1. On a baking sheet, roll out the pizza dough to form a 12- to 14-inch disc.
2. Peel, halve, and cut away the core of the pears. Slice each pear half into thin wedges. Squeeze lemon juice over the pears.
3. Arrange the pears, starting at the outer edge of the crust (leaving no border), in a spiral toward the center. Sprinkle the orange zest, basil, rosemary, sugar, and pepper over the pears. Drizzle with the olive oil.
4. Slide the baking sheet into the air fryer oven. Press the Power Button. Cook at 400°F (205°C) for 25 minutes, until the pizza appears golden and crisp.
5. Remove the pizza from the air fryer oven and let sit for 5 minutes. Slice and serve warm or at room temperature.

Cheese Tomato Pizza with Basil

Prep time: 15 minutes | Cook time: 20 minutes | Makes 2 (12- to 14-inch) pizzas

Extra-virgin olive oil, for brushing
Simple Pizza Dough
1 cup Garlic Tomato Pizza Sauce
¾ cup grated Mozzarella
¾ cup grated fontina cheese
2 plum tomatoes, sliced thin
⅓ cup crumbled goat cheese
½ cup Parmesan cheese
8 fresh basil leaves, torn or roughly chopped
1 tablespoon chopped fresh parsley
⅛ teaspoon freshly ground black pepper

1. Brush two baking sheets with olive oil.
2. Roll out one of the dough balls to the desired size, and place it on the prepared baking sheet.
3. Leaving a 1-inch border, spread half of the sauce evenly over the dough. Sprinkle on half of the Mozzarella and fontina. Arrange half of the tomato slices on top, and finish with half of the goat cheese and Parmesan.
4. Slide the baking sheet into the air fryer oven. Press the Power Button. Cook at 400°F (205°C) for 10 minutes, until the crust is golden and the cheese has melted.
5. Remove the pizza from the air fryer oven and transfer it to a cutting board. Let it rest for 5 minutes, then top with half of the basil and parsley and season with half of the salt and pepper. Slice and serve.
6. Repeat with the remaining dough ball and toppings.

Arugula and Prosciutto Pizza

Prep time: 10 minutes | Cook time: 20 minutes | Makes 2 (12- to 14-inch) pizzas

2 tablespoons extra-virgin olive oil, plus more for brushing
Simple Pizza Dough or Pro Dough
1 cup Garlic Tomato Pizza Sauce
8 slices prosciutto
6 ounces (170 g) fresh Mozzarella cheese, sliced or shredded
3 cups arugula
¼ teaspoon salt
⅛ teaspoon freshly ground black pepper
3 ounces (85 g) Parmesan cheese, shaved with a vegetable peeler

1. Brush two baking sheets with olive oil.
2. Roll out one of the dough balls to the desired size, and place it on the prepared baking sheet.
3. Leaving a 1-inch border, spread half of the sauce evenly onto the dough. Lay half of the prosciutto slices on top, then finish with half of the Mozzarella.
4. Slide the baking sheet into the air fryer oven. Press the Power Button. Cook at 400°F (205°C) for 10 minutes, until the crust is golden and the cheese has melted.
5. Remove the pizza from the air fryer oven and transfer it to a cutting board. Let it rest for 5 minutes, then top with half of the arugula, olive oil, salt, pepper, and Parmesan. Slice and serve.
6. Repeat with the remaining dough ball and toppings.

Prosciutto and Fig Pizza

Prep time: 10 minutes | Cook time: 20 minutes | Makes 2 (12- to 14-inch) pizzas

2 tablespoons extra-virgin olive oil, plus more for brushing
Simple Pizza Dough or Pro Dough
¼ cup fig jam
½ cup shredded Mozzarella cheese
½ cup crumbled goat cheese
8 slices prosciutto
8 figs, stemmed and quartered
4 fresh thyme sprigs, stemmed
¼ teaspoon fine sea salt
⅛ teaspoon freshly ground black pepper

1. Brush two baking sheets with olive oil.
2. Roll out one of the dough balls to the desired size, and place it on the prepared baking sheet.
3. Leaving a 1-inch border, spoon half of the fig jam evenly onto the dough. Top with half of the Mozzarella, goat cheese, and prosciutto. Arrange half of the figs on the pizza, sprinkle on half of the thyme, and season with half of the salt and pepper.
4. Slide the baking sheet into the air fryer oven. Press the Power Button. Cook at 400°F (205°C) for 10 minutes, until the crust is golden and the cheese has melted.
5. Remove the pizza from the air fryer oven and transfer it to a cutting board. Let it rest for 5 minutes, then drizzle with half of the olive oil. Slice and serve.
6. Repeat with the remaining dough ball and toppings.

Ricotta Margherita with Basil

Prep time: 10 minutes | Cook time: 20 minutes | Makes 2 (12- to 14-inch) pizzas

1 tablespoon extra-virgin olive oil, plus more for brushing
Simple Pizza Dough or Pro Dough
1 cup Garlic Tomato Pizza Sauce
1 teaspoon dried oregano
½ cup fresh ricotta cheese
6 ounces (170 g) fresh Mozzarella cheese, sliced thin
¼ teaspoon fine sea salt
⅛ teaspoon freshly ground black pepper
8 fresh basil leaves, torn

1. Brush two baking sheets with olive oil.
2. Roll out one of the dough balls to the desired size, and place it on the prepared baking sheet.
3. Leaving a 1-inch border, spoon half of the sauce onto the dough, spreading it evenly. Sprinkle on half of the oregano.
4. Spoon half of the ricotta cheese in small dollops all over the pizza, then arrange half of the Mozzarella slices on top. Season with half of the salt and pepper, and scatter on half of the torn basil leaves.
5. Slide the baking sheet into the air fryer oven. Press the Power Button. Cook at 400°F (205°C) for 10 minutes, until the crust is golden and the cheese has melted.
6. Remove the pizza from the air fryer oven and transfer it to a cutting board. Let it rest for 5 minutes. Slice and serve.
7. Repeat with the remaining dough ball and toppings.

Spring Pea Pizza with Ramps
Prep time: 10 minutes | Cook time: 25 minutes | Makes 2 (12- to 14-inch) pizzas

2 tablespoons extra-virgin olive oil, plus more for brushing
½ cup shelled fresh English peas (or frozen and thawed peas)
10 ramps
¼ teaspoon fine sea salt
Simple Pizza Dough or Pro Dough
¾ cup ricotta cheese
2 tablespoons chopped fresh mint

1. Brush two baking sheets with olive oil.
2. If using fresh peas, bring a large pot of salted water to a boil. Fill a large bowl with ice water. Blanch the peas for 1 minute then, using a slotted spoon, transfer them to the ice water. Drain and set aside.
3. Spread the ramps on a baking sheet, drizzle with the olive oil, and sprinkle with the salt. Press the Power Button. Cook at 400°F (205°C) for 5 minutes to wilt. Transfer to a cutting board and cut into thirds.
4. Roll out one of the dough balls to the desired size, and place it on the prepared baking sheet.
5. Spoon half of the ricotta in dollops all over the dough. Scatter on half of the peas, ramps, and mint.
6. Slide the baking sheet into the air fryer oven. Press the Power Button. Cook at 400°F (205°C) for 10 minutes, until the crust is golden.
7. Remove the pizza from the air fryer oven, transfer it to a cutting board, and let it sit for 5 minutes. Slice and serve.
8. Repeat with the remaining dough ball and toppings.

Escarole and Radicchio Pizza with Walnuts
Prep time: 10 minutes | Cook time: 25 minutes | Makes 1 pan pizza

1 head escarole, cored, center ribs removed, leaves chopped
½ head radicchio, sliced
1 small red onion, sliced thin
1 tablespoon extra-virgin olive oil
¼ teaspoon fine sea salt
Pinch red pepper flakes
No-Knead Pan Pizza Dough
6 slices provolone cheese
½ cup grated pecorino romano cheese
¼ cup walnuts, toasted

1. Toss the escarole, radicchio, and red onion slices in a bowl with the olive oil. Season with the salt and red pepper flakes. Cover the dough with the slices of provolone. Top the pizza with the escarole mixture, spreading it into a thin, even layer. Sprinkle with the pecorino.
2. Slide the baking sheet into the air fryer oven. Press the Power Button. Cook at 400°F (205°C) for 25 minutes, until the crust is golden.
3. Remove the pizza from the air fryer oven and use a spatula to transfer it to a cutting board. Let it sit for 5 minutes. Top the pizza with a drizzle of olive oil and the toasted walnuts. Slice and serve.

Zucchini Pizza with Pistachios
Prep time: 15 minutes | Cook time: 30 minutes | Makes 2 (12- to 14-inch) pizzas

2 tablespoons extra-virgin olive oil, plus more for brushing
1 medium green zucchini, halved lengthwise and cut thinly into half-moons
1 medium yellow summer squash, halved lengthwise and cut thinly into half-moons
¼ teaspoon salt
Simple Pizza Dough
1 medium red onion, sliced thin
1 teaspoon fresh thyme leaves
¼ teaspoon red pepper flakes
1 teaspoon freshly squeezed lemon juice
¼ cup shelled pistachios, toasted

1. Brush two baking sheets with olive oil.
2. In a large strainer set over a large bowl, toss the zucchini and summer squash well with the salt, and let it sit for about 5 minutes. Use a kitchen towel to press and squeeze the liquid from the squash mixture, removing as much moisture as possible.
3. Roll out one of the dough balls to the desired size, and place it on the prepared baking sheet.
4. In a large mixing bowl, toss together the drained squash mixture, onion, thyme, red pepper flakes, olive oil, and lemon juice. Arrange half of the vegetables on the dough.
5. Slide the baking sheet into the air fryer oven. Press the Power Button. Cook at 400°F (205°C) for 10 minutes, until the crust is golden and the cheese has melted.
6. Remove the pizza from the air fryer oven and transfer it to a cutting board. Let it rest for 5 minutes, then garnish with half of the toasted pistachios. Slice and serve.
7. Repeat with the remaining dough ball and toppings.

Mozzarella Brussels Sprout Pizza

Prep time: 10 minutes | **Cook time:** 30 minutes | **Makes 2 (12- to 14-inch) pizzas**

2 tablespoons extra-virgin olive oil, plus more for brushing and drizzling
1 red onion, sliced
½ teaspoon fine sea salt, divided
⅛ teaspoon freshly ground black pepper
Simple Pizza Dough or Pro Dough
6 ounces (170 g) fresh Mozzarella cheese, shredded
12 Brussels sprouts, shredded or finely sliced
8 sage leaves, rolled and sliced thin
¼ cup grated Parmesan cheese
2 pinches red pepper flakes

1. Brush two baking sheets with olive oil.
2. Spread the onion on a sheet tray, drizzle with the olive oil, and toss to coat. Season with ¼ teaspoon of salt, and the pepper. Transfer the baking sheet to the air fryer oven and Press the Power Button. Cook at 400°F (205°C) for 12 minutes, or until the onions are caramelized. Remove from the air fryer oven and set aside.
3. Roll out one of the dough balls to the desired size, and place it on the prepared baking sheet.
4. Top the dough with half of the Mozzarella, Brussels sprouts, and cooked red onion. Sprinkle on the remaining ¼ teaspoon of salt, half of the sage, and half of the Parmesan, followed by a drizzle of olive oil and a pinch of red pepper flakes.
5. Slide the baking sheet into the air fryer oven. Press the Power Button. Cook at 400°F (205°C) for 10 minutes, until the crust is golden and the cheese has melted.
6. Remove the pizza from the air fryer oven and transfer it to a cutting board. Let it rest for 5 minutes. Slice and serve.
7. Repeat with the remaining dough ball and toppings.

Strawberry Pizza

Prep time: 10 minutes | **Cook time:** 10 minutes | **Serves 4**

2 tablespoons all-purpose flour, plus more as needed
½ store-bought pizza dough (about 8 ounces / 227 g)
1 tablespoon canola oil
1 cup sliced fresh strawberries
1 tablespoon sugar
½ cup chocolate-hazelnut spread

1. Dust a clean work surface with the flour. Place the dough on the floured surface, and roll it out to a 9-inch round of even thickness. Dust your rolling pin and work surface with additional flour, as needed, to ensure the dough does not stick.
2. Brush the surface of the rolled-out dough evenly with half the oil. Flip the dough over, and brush with the remaining oil. Poke the dough with a fork 5 or 6 times across its surface to prevent air pockets from forming during cooking.
3. Place the dough on a greased baking sheet. Slide the baking sheet into the air fryer oven. Press the Power Button. Cook at 400°F (205°C) for 10 minutes.
4. After 5 minutes, flip the dough. Continue cooking for the remaining 5 minutes.
5. Meanwhile, in a medium mixing bowl, combine the strawberries and sugar.
6. Transfer the pizza to a cutting board and let cool. Top with the chocolate-hazelnut spread and strawberries. Cut into pieces and serve.

Zucchini and Onion Pizza

Prep time: 10 minutes | **Cook time:** 10 minutes | **Serves 2**

2 tablespoons all-purpose flour, plus more as needed
½ store-bought pizza dough (about 8 ounces / 227 g)
1 tablespoon canola oil, divided
½ cup pizza sauce
1 cup shredded Mozzarella cheese
½ zucchini, thinly sliced
½ red onion, sliced
½ red bell pepper, seeded and thinly sliced

1. Dust a clean work surface with the flour.
2. Place the dough on the floured surface and roll it into a 9-inch round of even thickness. Dust your rolling pin and work surface with additional flour, as needed, to ensure the dough does not stick.
3. Evenly brush the surface of the rolled-out dough with ½ tablespoon of oil. Flip the dough over and brush the other side with the remaining ½ tablespoon of oil. Poke the dough with a fork 5 or 6 times across its surface to prevent air pockets from forming while it cooks.
4. Place the dough on a greased baking sheet. Slide the baking sheet into the air fryer oven. Press the Power Button. Cook at 400°F (205°C) for 10 minutes.
5. After 5 minutes, flip the dough, then spread the pizza sauce evenly over it. Sprinkle with the cheese, and top with the zucchini, onion, and pepper.
6. Continue cooking for the remaining 5 minutes until the cheese is melted and the veggie slices begin to crisp.
7. When cooking is complete, let cool slightly before slicing.

Chapter 10
Casseroles, Frittatas, and Quiches

Cheddar Chicken Sausage Casserole
Prep time: 10 minutes | Cook time: 20 minutes | Serves 8

10 eggs
1 cup Cheddar cheese, shredded and divided
¾ cup heavy whipping cream
1 (12-ounce / 340-g) package cooked chicken sausage
1 cup broccoli, chopped
2 cloves garlic, minced
½ tablespoon salt
¼ tablespoon ground black pepper
Cooking spray

1. Spritz a baking pan with cooking spray.
2. Whisk the eggs with Cheddar and cream in a large bowl to mix well.
3. Combine the cooked sausage, broccoli, garlic, salt, and ground black pepper in a separate bowl. Stir to mix well.
4. Pour the sausage mixture into the baking pan, then spread the egg mixture over to cover.
5. Select Bake. Set temperature to 400°F (205°C) and set time to 20 minutes. Press Start to begin preheating.
6. Once preheated, place the pan into the Vortex.
7. When cooking is complete, the egg should be set and a toothpick inserted in the center should come out clean.
8. Serve immediately.

Corn Casserole with Bell Pepper
Prep time: 10 minutes | Cook time: 20 minutes | Serves 4

1 cup corn kernels
¼ cup bell pepper, finely chopped
½ cup low-fat milk
1 large egg, beaten
½ cup yellow cornmeal
½ cup all-purpose flour
½ teaspoon baking powder
2 tablespoons melted unsalted butter
1 tablespoon granulated sugar
Pinch of cayenne pepper
¼ teaspoon kosher salt
Cooking spray

1. Spritz a baking pan with cooking spray.
2. Combine all the ingredients in a large bowl. Stir to mix well. Pour the mixture into the baking pan.
3. Select Bake. Set temperature to 330°F (166°C) and set time to 20 minutes. Press Start to begin preheating.
4. Once preheated, place the pan into the Vortex.
5. When cooking is complete, the casserole should be lightly browned and set.
6. Remove the baking pan from the Vortex and serve immediately.

Asparagus Casserole with Grits
Prep time: 5 minutes | Cook time: 30 minutes | Serves 4

10 fresh asparagus spears, cut into 1-inch pieces
2 cups cooked grits, cooled to room temperature
2 teaspoons Worcestershire sauce
1 egg, beaten
½ teaspoon garlic powder
¼ teaspoon salt
2 slices provolone cheese, crushed
Cooking spray

1. Spritz a baking pan with cooking spray.
2. Set the asparagus in the perforated pan. Spritz the asparagus with cooking spray.
3. Select Air Fry. Set temperature to 390°F (199°C) and set time to 5 minutes. Press Start to begin preheating.
4. Once preheated, place the pan into the Vortex. Flip the asparagus halfway through.
5. When cooking is complete, the asparagus should be lightly browned and crispy.
6. Meanwhile, combine the grits, Worcestershire sauce, egg, garlic powder, and salt in a bowl. Stir to mix well.
7. Pour half of the grits mixture in the prepared baking pan, then spread with fried asparagus.
8. Spread the cheese over the asparagus and pour the remaining grits over.
9. Select Bake. Set time to 25 minutes. Place the pan into the Vortex.
10. When cooking is complete, the egg should be set.
11. Serve immediately.

Parmesan Green Bean Casserole
Prep time: 4 minutes | Cook time: 6 minutes | Serves 4

1 tablespoon melted butter
1 cup green beans
6 ounces (170 g) Cheddar cheese, shredded
7 ounces (198 g) Parmesan cheese, shredded
¼ cup heavy cream
Sea salt, to taste

1. Grease a baking pan with the melted butter.
2. Add the green beans, Cheddar, salt, and black pepper to the prepared baking pan. Stir to mix well, then spread the Parmesan and cream on top.
3. Select Bake. Set temperature to 400°F (205°C) and set time to 6 minutes. Press Start to begin preheating.
4. Once preheated, place the pan into the Vortex.
5. When cooking is complete, the beans should be tender and the cheese should be melted.
6. Serve immediately.

Cheddar Pastrami Casserole
Prep time: 10 minutes | Cook time: 8 minutes | Serves 2

1 cup pastrami, sliced
1 bell pepper, chopped
¼ cup Greek yogurt
2 spring onions, chopped
½ cup Cheddar cheese, grated
4 eggs
¼ teaspoon ground black pepper
Sea salt, to taste
Cooking spray

1. Spritz a baking pan with cooking spray.
2. Whisk together all the ingredients in a large bowl. Stir to mix well. Pour the mixture into the baking pan.
3. Select Bake. Set temperature to 330°F (166°C) and set time to 8 minutes. Press Start to begin preheating.
4. Once preheated, place the pan into the Vortex.
5. When cooking is complete, the eggs should be set and the casserole edges should be lightly browned.
6. Remove the baking pan from the Vortex and allow to cool for 10 minutes before serving.

Spinach and Mushroom Frittata
Prep time: 7 minutes | Cook time: 8 minutes | Serves 2

1 cup chopped mushrooms
2 cups spinach, chopped
4 eggs, lightly beaten
3 ounces (85 g) feta cheese, crumbled
2 tablespoons heavy cream
A handful of fresh parsley, chopped
Salt and ground black pepper, to taste
Cooking spray

1. Spritz a baking pan with cooking spray.
2. Whisk together all the ingredients in a large bowl. Stir to mix well.
3. Pour the mixture in the prepared baking pan.
4. Select Bake. Set temperature to 350°F (180°C) and set time to 8 minutes. Press Start to begin preheating.
5. Once preheated, place the pan into the Vortex. Stir the mixture halfway through.
6. When cooking is complete, the eggs should be set.
7. Serve immediately.

Mushroom and Beef Casserole
Prep time: 10 minutes | Cook time: 25 minutes | Serves 4

1½ pounds (680 g) beef steak
1 ounce (28 g) dry onion soup mix
2 cups sliced mushrooms
1 (14.5-ounce / 411-g) can cream of mushroom soup
½ cup beef broth
¼ cup red wine
3 garlic cloves, minced
1 whole onion, chopped

1. Put the beef steak in a large bowl, then sprinkle with dry onion soup mix. Toss to coat well.
2. Combine the mushrooms with mushroom soup, beef broth, red wine, garlic, and onion in a large bowl. Stir to mix well.
3. Transfer the beef steak in a baking pan, then pour in the mushroom mixture.
4. Select Bake. Set temperature to 360°F (182°C) and set time to 25 minutes. Press Start to begin preheating.
5. Once preheated, place the pan into the Vortex.
6. When cooking is complete, the mushrooms should be soft and the beef should be well browned.
7. Remove the baking pan from the Vortex and serve immediately.

Beef and Bean Casserole
Prep time: 15 minutes | Cook time: 31 minutes | Serves 4

1 tablespoon olive oil
½ cup finely chopped bell pepper
½ cup chopped celery
1 onion, chopped
2 garlic cloves, minced
1 pound (454 g) ground beef
1 can diced tomatoes
½ teaspoon parsley
½ tablespoon chili powder
1 teaspoon chopped cilantro
1½ cups vegetable broth
1 (8-ounce / 227-g) can cannellini beans
Salt and ground black pepper, to taste

1. Heat the olive oil in a nonstick skillet over medium heat until shimmering.
2. Add the bell pepper, celery, onion, and garlic to the skillet and sauté for 5 minutes or until the onion is translucent.
3. Add the ground beef and sauté for an additional 6 minutes or until lightly browned.
4. Mix in the tomatoes, parsley, chili powder, cilantro and vegetable broth, then cook for 10 more minutes. Stir constantly.
5. Pour them in a baking pan, then mix in the beans and sprinkle with salt and ground black pepper.
6. Select Bake. Set temperature to 350°F (180°C) and set time to 10 minutes. Press Start to begin preheating.
7. Once preheated, place the pan into the Vortex.
8. When cooking is complete, the vegetables should be tender and the beef should be well browned.
9. Remove the baking pan from the Vortex and serve immediately.

Cheddar Broccoli Casserole
Prep time: 5 minutes | Cook time: 30 minutes | Serves 6

4 cups broccoli florets
¼ cup heavy whipping cream
½ cup sharp Cheddar cheese, shredded
¼ cup ranch dressing
Kosher salt and ground black pepper, to taste

1. Combine all the ingredients in a large bowl. Toss to coat well broccoli well.
2. Pour the mixture into a baking pan.
3. Select Bake. Set temperature to 375°F (190°C) and set time to 30 minutes. Press Start to begin preheating.
4. Once preheated, place the pan into the Vortex.
5. When cooking is complete, the broccoli should be tender.
6. Remove the baking pan from the Vortex and serve immediately.

Cauliflower and Okra Casserole
Prep time: 8 minutes | Cook time: 12 minutes | Serves 4

1 head cauliflower, cut into florets
1 cup okra, chopped
1 yellow bell pepper, chopped
2 eggs, beaten
½ cup chopped onion
1 tablespoon soy sauce
2 tablespoons olive oil
Salt and ground black pepper, to taste

1. Spritz a baking pan with cooking spray.
2. Put the cauliflower in a food processor and pulse to rice the cauliflower.
3. Pour the cauliflower rice in the baking pan and add the remaining ingredients. Stir to mix well.
4. Select Bake. Set temperature to 380°F (193°C) and set time to 12 minutes. Press Start to begin preheating.
5. Once preheated, place the pan into the Vortex.
6. When cooking is complete, the eggs should be set.
7. Remove the baking pan from the Vortex and serve immediately.

Turkey Casserole with Almond Mayo
Prep time: 5 minutes | Cook time: 32 minutes | Serves 4

1 pound (454 g) turkey breasts
1 tablespoon olive oil
2 boiled eggs, chopped
2 tablespoons chopped pimentos
¼ cup slivered almonds, chopped
¼ cup mayonnaise
½ cup diced celery
2 tablespoons chopped green onion
¼ cup cream of chicken soup
¼ cup bread crumbs
Salt and ground black pepper, to taste

1. Put the turkey breasts in a large bowl. Sprinkle with salt and ground black pepper and drizzle with olive oil. Toss to coat well.
2. Transfer the turkey in the perforated pan.
3. Select Air Fry. Set temperature to 390°F (199°C) and set time to 12 minutes. Press Start to begin preheating.
4. Once preheated, place the pan into the Vortex. Flip the turkey halfway through.
5. When cooking is complete, the turkey should be well browned.
6. Remove the turkey breasts from the Vortex and cut into cubes, then combine the chicken cubes with eggs, pimentos, almonds, mayo, celery, green onions, and chicken soup in a large bowl. Stir to mix.
7. Pour the mixture into a baking pan, then spread with bread crumbs.
8. When cooking is complete, the eggs should be set.
9. Remove the baking pan from the Vortex and serve immediately.

Tilapia and Rockfish Casserole
Prep time: 8 minutes | Cook time: 22 minutes | Serves 2

1 tablespoon olive oil
1 small yellow onion, chopped
2 garlic cloves, minced
4 ounces (113 g) tilapia pieces
4 ounces (113 g) rockfish pieces
½ teaspoon dried basil
Salt and ground white pepper, to taste
4 eggs, lightly beaten
1 tablespoon dry sherry
4 tablespoons cheese, shredded

1. Heat the olive oil in a nonstick skillet over medium-high heat until shimmering.
2. Add the onion and garlic and sauté for 2 minutes or until fragrant.
3. Add the tilapia, rockfish, basil, salt, and white pepper to the skillet. Sauté to combine well and transfer them on a baking pan.
4. Combine the eggs, sherry and cheese in a large bowl. Stir to mix well. Pour the mixture in the baking pan over the fish mixture.
5. Select Bake. Set temperature to 360°F (182°C) and set time to 20 minutes. Press Start to begin preheating.
6. Once preheated, place the pan into the Vortex.
7. When cooking is complete, the eggs should be set and the casserole edges should be lightly browned.
8. Serve immediately.

Cheddar and Egg Frittata with Parsley
Prep time: 10 minutes | Cook time: 20 minutes | Serves 4

½ cup shredded Cheddar cheese
½ cup half-and-half
4 large eggs
2 tablespoons chopped scallion greens
2 tablespoons chopped fresh parsley
½ teaspoon kosher salt
½ teaspoon ground black pepper
Cooking spray

1. Spritz a baking pan with cooking spray.
2. Whisk together all the ingredients in a large bowl, then pour the mixture into the prepared baking pan.
3. Select Bake. Set temperature to 300°F (150°C) and set time to 20 minutes. Press Start to begin preheating.
4. Once preheated, place the pan into the Vortex. Stir the mixture halfway through.
5. When cooking is complete, the eggs should be set.
6. Serve immediately.

Peppery Sausage Casserole with Cheddar
Prep time: 15 minutes | Cook time: 25 minutes | Serves 6

1 pound (454 g) minced breakfast sausage
1 yellow pepper, diced
1 red pepper, diced
1 green pepper, diced
1 sweet onion, diced
2 cups Cheddar cheese, shredded
6 eggs
Salt and freshly ground black pepper, to taste
Fresh parsley, for garnish

1. Cook the sausage in a nonstick skillet over medium heat for 10 minutes or until well browned. Stir constantly.
2. When the cooking is finished, transfer the cooked sausage to a baking pan and add the peppers and onion. Scatter with Cheddar cheese.
3. Whisk the eggs with salt and ground black pepper in a large bowl, then pour the mixture into the baking pan.
4. Select Bake. Set temperature to 360°F (182°C) and set time to 15 minutes. Press Start to begin preheating.
5. Once preheated, place the pan into the Vortex.
6. When cooking is complete, the egg should be set and the edges of the casserole should be lightly browned.
7. Remove the baking pan from the Vortex and top with fresh parsley before serving.

Chickpea and Spinach Casserole
Prep time: 10 minutes | Cook time: 21 to 22 minutes | Serves 4

2 tablespoons olive oil
2 garlic cloves, minced
1 tablespoon ginger, minced
1 onion, chopped
1 chili pepper, minced
Salt and ground black pepper, to taste
1 pound (454 g) spinach
1 can coconut milk
½ cup dried tomatoes, chopped
1 (14-ounce / 397-g) can chickpeas, drained

1. Heat the olive oil in a saucepan over medium heat. Sauté the garlic and ginger in the olive oil for 1 minute, or until fragrant.
2. Add the onion, chili pepper, salt and pepper to the saucepan. Sauté for 3 minutes.
3. Mix in the spinach and sauté for 3 to 4 minutes or until the vegetables become soft. Remove from heat.
4. Pour the vegetable mixture into a baking pan. Stir in coconut milk, dried tomatoes and chickpeas until well blended.
5. Select Bake. Set temperature to 370°F (188°C) and set time to 15 minutes. Press Start to begin preheating.
6. Once preheated, place the pan into the Vortex.
7. When cooking is complete, transfer the casserole to a serving dish. Let cool for 5 minutes before serving.

Cheddar Chicken and Broccoli Divan
Prep time: 5 minutes | Cook time: 24 minutes | Serves 4

4 chicken breasts
Salt and ground black pepper, to taste
1 head broccoli, cut into florets
½ cup cream of mushroom soup
1 cup shredded Cheddar cheese
½ cup croutons
Cooking spray

1. Spritz the perforated pan with cooking spray.
2. Put the chicken breasts in the perforated pan and sprinkle with salt and ground black pepper.
3. Select Air Fry. Set temperature to 390°F (199°C) and set time to 14 minutes. Press Start to begin preheating.
4. Once preheated, place the pan into the Vortex. Flip the breasts halfway through the cooking time.
5. When cooking is complete, the breasts should be well browned and tender.
6. Remove the breasts from the Vortex and allow to cool for a few minutes on a plate, then cut the breasts into bite-size pieces.
7. Combine the chicken, broccoli, mushroom soup, and Cheddar cheese in a large bowl. Stir to mix well.
8. Spritz a baking pan with cooking spray. Pour the chicken mixture into the pan. Spread the croutons over the mixture.
9. When cooking is complete, the croutons should be lightly browned and the mixture should be set.
10. Remove the baking pan from the Vortex and serve immediately.

Kale and Egg Frittata with Feta
Prep time: 5 minutes | Cook time: 10 minutes | Serves 2

1 cup kale, chopped
1 teaspoon olive oil
4 large eggs, beaten
Kosher salt, to taste
2 tablespoons water
3 tablespoons crumbled feta
Cooking spray

1. Spritz a baking pan with cooking spray.
2. Add the kale to the baking pan and drizzle with olive oil.
3. Select Broil. Set temperature to 400°F (205°C) and set time to 2 minutes. Press Start to begin preheating.
4. Once preheated, place the pan into the Vortex. Stir the kale halfway through.
5. When cooking is complete, the kale should be wilted.
6. Meanwhile, combine the eggs with salt and water in a large bowl. Stir to mix well.
7. Make the frittata: When broiling is complete, pour the eggs into the baking pan and spread with feta cheese.
8. Select Bake. Set temperature to 300°F (150°C) and set time to 8 minutes. Place the pan into the Vortex.
9. When cooking is complete, the eggs should be set and the cheese should be melted.
10. Remove the baking pan from the Vortex and serve the frittata immediately.

Swiss Chicken and Ham Casserole
Prep time: 15 minutes | Cook time: 15 minutes | Serves 4 to 6

2 cups diced cooked chicken
1 cup diced ham
¼ teaspoon ground nutmeg
½ cup half-and-half
½ teaspoon ground black pepper
6 slices Swiss cheese
Cooking spray

1. Spritz a baking pan with cooking spray.
2. Combine the chicken, ham, nutmeg, half-and-half, and ground black pepper in a large bowl. Stir to mix well.
3. Pour half of the mixture into the baking pan, then top the mixture with 3 slices of Swiss cheese, then pour in the remaining mixture and top with remaining cheese slices.
4. Select Bake. Set temperature to 350°F (180°C) and set time to 15 minutes. Press Start to begin preheating.
5. Once preheated, place the pan into the Vortex.
6. When cooking is complete, the egg should be set and the cheese should be melted.
7. Serve immediately.

Smoked Trout Frittata with Dill
Prep time: 8 minutes | Cook time: 17 minutes | Serves 4

2 tablespoons olive oil
1 onion, sliced
1 egg, beaten
½ tablespoon horseradish sauce
6 tablespoons crème fraiche
1 cup diced smoked trout
2 tablespoons chopped fresh dill
Cooking spray

1. Spritz a baking pan with cooking spray.
2. Heat the olive oil in a nonstick skillet over medium heat until shimmering.
3. Add the onion and sauté for 3 minutes or until translucent.
4. Combine the egg, horseradish sauce, and crème fraiche in a large bowl. Stir to mix well, then mix in the sautéed onion, smoked trout, and dill.
5. Pour the mixture in the prepared baking pan.
6. Select Bake. Set temperature to 350°F (180°C) and set time to 14 minutes. Press Start to begin preheating.
7. Once preheated, place the pan into the Vortex. Stir the mixture halfway through.
8. When cooking is complete, the egg should be set and the edges should be lightly browned.
9. Serve immediately.

Cheddar Broccoli and Carrot Quiche
Prep time: 6 minutes | Cook time: 14 minutes | Serves 4

4 eggs
1 teaspoon dried thyme
1 cup whole milk
1 steamed carrots, diced
2 cups steamed broccoli florets
2 medium tomatoes, diced
¼ cup crumbled feta cheese
1 cup grated Cheddar cheese
1 teaspoon chopped parsley
Salt and ground black pepper, to taste
Cooking spray

1. Spritz a baking pan with cooking spray.
2. Whisk together the eggs, thyme, salt, and ground black pepper in a bowl and fold in the milk while mixing.
3. Put the carrots, broccoli, and tomatoes in the prepared baking pan, then spread with feta cheese and ½ cup Cheddar cheese. Pour the egg mixture over, then scatter with remaining Cheddar on top.
4. Select Bake. Set temperature to 350°F (180°C) and set time to 14 minutes. Press Start to begin preheating.
5. Once preheated, place the pan into the Vortex.
6. When cooking is complete, the egg should be set and the quiche should be puffed.
7. Remove the quiche from the Vortex and top with chopped parsley, then slice to serve.

Ricotta Pork Gratin with Mustard
Prep time: 15 minutes | Cook time: 21 minutes | Serves 4

2 tablespoons olive oil
2 pounds (907 g) pork tenderloin, cut into serving-size pieces
1 teaspoon dried marjoram
¼ teaspoon chili powder
1 teaspoon coarse sea salt
½ teaspoon freshly ground black pepper
1 cup Ricotta cheese
1½ cups chicken broth
1 tablespoon mustard
Cooking spray

1. Spritz a baking pan with cooking spray.
2. Heat the olive oil in a nonstick skillet over medium-high heat until shimmering.
3. Add the pork and sauté for 6 minutes or until lightly browned.
4. Transfer the pork to the prepared baking pan and sprinkle with marjoram, chili powder, salt, and ground black pepper.
5. Combine the remaining ingredients in a large bowl. Stir to mix well. Pour the mixture over the pork in the pan.
6. Select Bake. Set temperature to 350°F (180°C) and set time to 15 minutes. Press Start to begin preheating.
7. Once preheated, place the pan into the Vortex. Stir the mixture halfway through.
8. When cooking is complete, the mixture should be frothy and the cheese should be melted.
9. Serve immediately.

Mexican Beef and Chile Casserole
Prep time: 10 minutes | Cook time: 15 minutes | Serves 4

1 pound (454 g) 85% lean ground beef
1 tablespoon taco seasoning
1 (7-ounce / 198-g) can diced mild green chiles
½ cup milk
2 large eggs
1 cup shredded Mexican cheese blend
2 tablespoons all-purpose flour
½ teaspoon kosher salt
Cooking spray

1. Spritz a baking pan with cooking spray.
2. Toss the ground beef with taco seasoning in a large bowl to mix well. Pour the seasoned ground beef in the prepared baking pan.
3. Combing the remaining ingredients in a medium bowl. Whisk to mix well, then pour the mixture over the ground beef.
4. Select Bake. Set temperature to 350°F (180°C) and set time to 15 minutes. Press Start to begin preheating.
5. Once preheated, place the pan into the Vortex.
6. When cooking is complete, a toothpick inserted in the center should come out clean.
7. Remove the casserole from the Vortex and allow to cool for 5 minutes, then slice to serve.

Tomato and Olive Quiche
Prep time: 10 minutes | Cook time: 30 minutes | Serves 4

4 eggs
¼ cup chopped Kalamata olives
½ cup chopped tomatoes
¼ cup chopped onion
½ cup milk
1 cup crumbled feta cheese
½ tablespoon chopped oregano
½ tablespoon chopped basil
Salt and ground black pepper, to taste
Cooking spray

1. Spritz a baking pan with cooking spray.
2. Whisk the eggs with remaining ingredients in a large bowl. Stir to mix well.
3. Pour the mixture into the prepared baking pan.
4. Select Bake. Set temperature to 340°F (171°C) and set time to 30 minutes. Press Start to begin preheating.
5. Once preheated, place the pan into the Vortex.
6. When cooking is complete, the eggs should be set and a toothpick inserted in the center should come out clean.
7. Serve immediately.

Potato and Chorizo Frittata
Prep time: 8 minutes | Cook time: 12 minutes | Serves 4

2 tablespoons olive oil
1 chorizo, sliced
4 eggs
½ cup corn
1 large potato, boiled and cubed
1 tablespoon chopped parsley
½ cup feta cheese, crumbled
Salt and ground black pepper, to taste

1. Heat the olive oil in a nonstick skillet over medium heat until shimmering.
2. Add the chorizo and cook for 4 minutes or until golden brown.
3. Whisk the eggs in a bowl, then sprinkle with salt and ground black pepper.
4. Mix the remaining ingredients in the egg mixture, then pour the chorizo and its fat into a baking pan. Pour in the egg mixture.
5. Select Bake. Set temperature to 330°F (166°C) and set time to 8 minutes. Press Start to begin preheating.
6. Once preheated, place the pan into the Vortex. Stir the mixture halfway through.
7. When cooking is complete, the eggs should be set.
8. Serve immediately.

Asparagus Frittata with Goat Cheese
Prep time: 5 minutes | Cook time: 25 minutes | Serves 2 to 4

1 cup asparagus spears, cut into 1-inch pieces
1 teaspoon vegetable oil
1 tablespoon milk
6 eggs, beaten
2 ounces (57 g) goat cheese, crumbled
1 tablespoon minced chives, optional
Kosher salt and pepper, to taste

1. Add the asparagus spears to a small bowl and drizzle with the vegetable oil. Toss until well coated and transfer to the perforated pan.
2. Select Air Fry. Set temperature to 400°F (205°C) and set time to 5 minutes. Press Start to begin preheating.
3. Once preheated, place the pan into the Vortex. Flip the asparagus halfway through.
4. When cooking is complete, the asparagus should be tender and slightly wilted.
5. Remove the asparagus from the Vortex to a baking pan.
6. Stir together the milk and eggs in a medium bowl. Pour the mixture over the asparagus in the pan. Sprinkle with the goat cheese and the chives (if using) over the eggs. Season with salt and pepper.
7. Select Bake. Set temperature to 320°F (160°C) and set time to 20 minutes. Place the pan into the Vortex
8. When cooking is complete, the top should be golden and the eggs should be set.
9. Transfer to a serving dish. Slice and serve.

Spinach and Shrimp Frittata
Prep time: 6 minutes | Cook time: 14 minutes | Serves 4

4 whole eggs
1 teaspoon dried basil
½ cup shrimp, cooked and chopped
½ cup baby spinach
½ cup rice, cooked
½ cup Monterey Jack cheese, grated
Salt, to taste
Cooking spray

1. Spritz a baking pan with cooking spray.
2. Whisk the eggs with basil and salt in a large bowl until bubbly, then mix in the shrimp, spinach, rice, and cheese.
3. Pour the mixture into the baking pan.
4. Select Bake. Set temperature to 360°F (182°C) and set time to 14 minutes. Press Start to begin preheating.
5. Once preheated, place the pan into the Vortex. Stir the mixture halfway through.
6. When cooking is complete, the eggs should be set and the frittata should be golden brown.
7. Slice to serve.

Zucchini and Spinach Frittata
Prep time: 15 minutes | Cook time: 20 minutes | Serves 2

4 eggs
⅓ cup milk
2 teaspoons olive oil
1 large zucchini, sliced
2 asparagus, sliced thinly
⅓ cup sliced mushrooms
1 cup baby spinach
1 small red onion, sliced
⅓ cup crumbled feta cheese
⅓ cup grated Cheddar cheese
¼ cup chopped chives
Salt and ground black pepper, to taste

1. Line a baking pan with parchment paper.
2. Whisk together the eggs, milk, salt, and ground black pepper in a large bowl. Set aside.
3. Heat the olive oil in a nonstick skillet over medium heat until shimmering.
4. Add the zucchini, asparagus, mushrooms, spinach, and onion to the skillet and sauté for 5 minutes or until tender.
5. Pour the sautéed vegetables into the prepared baking pan, then spread the egg mixture over and scatter with cheeses.
6. Select Bake. Set temperature to 380°F (193°C) and set time to 15 minutes. Press Start to begin preheating.
7. Once preheated, place the pan into the Vortex. Stir the mixture halfway through.
8. When cooking is complete, the egg should be set and the edges should be lightly browned.
9. Remove the frittata from the Vortex and sprinkle with chives before serving.

Chapter 11
Wraps and Sandwiches

Curried Shrimp and Zucchini Potstickers

Prep time: 35 minutes | Cook time: 5 minutes | Serves 10

½ pound (227 g) peeled and deveined shrimp, finely chopped
1 medium zucchini, coarsely grated
1 tablespoon fish sauce
1 tablespoon green curry paste
2 scallions, thinly sliced
¼ cup basil, chopped
30 round dumpling wrappers
Cooking spray

1. Combine the chopped shrimp, zucchini, fish sauce, curry paste, scallions, and basil in a large bowl. Stir to mix well.
2. Unfold the dumpling wrappers on a clean work surface, dab a little water around the edges of each wrapper, then scoop up 1 teaspoon of filling in the middle of each wrapper.
3. Make the potstickers: Fold the wrappers in half and press the edges to seal.
4. Spritz the perforated pan with cooking spray.
5. Transfer the potstickers to the pan and spritz with cooking spray.
6. Select Air Fry. Set temperature to 350°F (180°C) and set time to 5 minutes. Press Start to begin preheating.
7. Once preheated, place the pan into the Vortex. Flip the potstickers halfway through the cooking time.
8. When cooking is complete, the potstickers should be crunchy and lightly browned.
9. Serve immediately.

Ricotta Spinach and Basil Pockets

Prep time: 20 minutes | Cook time: 10 minutes | Makes 8 pockets

2 large eggs, divided
1 tablespoon water
1 cup baby spinach, roughly chopped
¼ cup sun-dried tomatoes, finely chopped
1 cup ricotta cheese
1 cup basil, chopped
¼ teaspoon red pepper flakes
¼ teaspoon kosher salt
2 refrigerated rolled pie crusts
2 tablespoons sesame seeds

1. Spritz the perforated pan with cooking spray.
2. Whisk an egg with water in a small bowl.
3. Combine the spinach, tomatoes, the other egg, ricotta cheese, basil, red pepper flakes, and salt in a large bowl. Whisk to mix well.
4. Unfold the pie crusts on a clean work surface and slice each crust into 4 wedges. Scoop up 3 tablespoons of the spinach mixture on each crust and leave ½ inch space from edges.
5. Fold the crust wedges in half to wrap the filling and press the edges with a fork to seal.
6. Arrange the wraps in the pan and spritz with cooking spray. Sprinkle with sesame seeds.
7. Select Air Fry. Set temperature to 380°F (193°C) and set time to 10 minutes. Press Start to begin preheating.
8. Once the Vortex has preheated, place the pan into the Vortex. Flip the wraps halfway through the cooking time.
9. When cooked, the wraps will be crispy and golden.
10. Serve immediately.

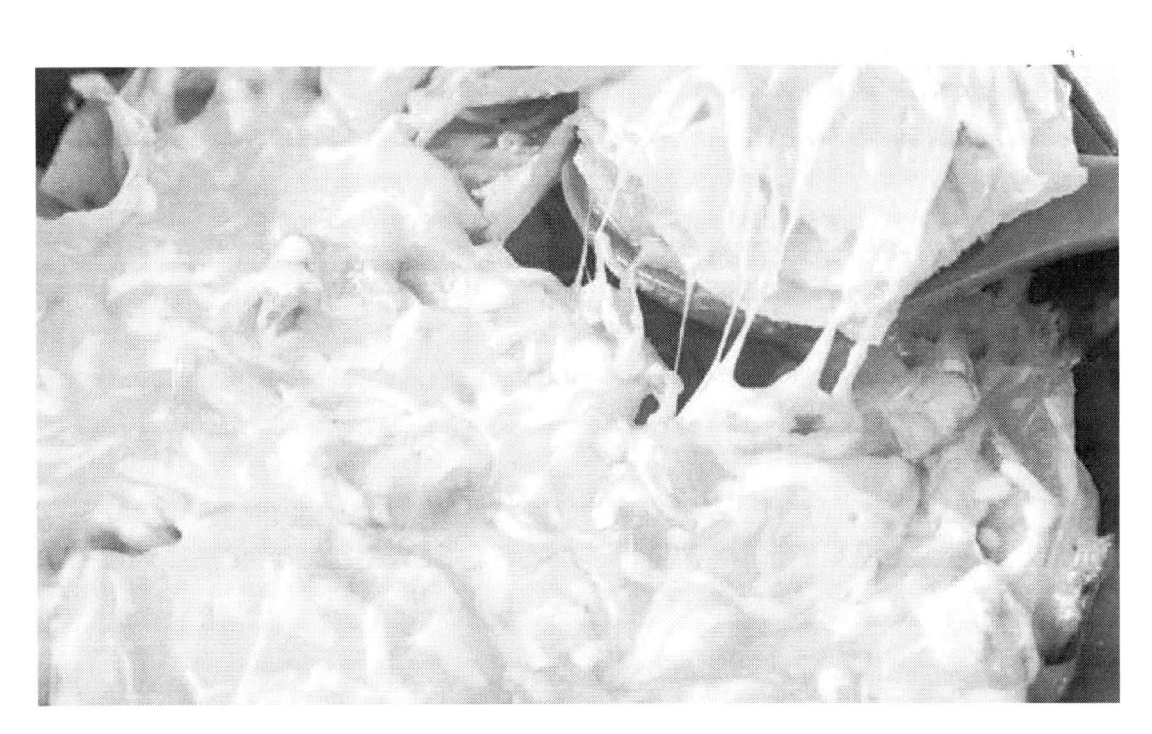

Carrot and Mushroom Spring Rolls
Prep time: 10 minutes | Cook time: 18 minutes | Serves 4

4 spring roll wrappers
½ cup cooked vermicelli noodles
1 teaspoon sesame oil
1 tablespoon freshly minced ginger
1 tablespoon soy sauce
1 clove garlic, minced
½ red bell pepper, deseeded and chopped
½ cup chopped carrot
½ cup chopped mushrooms
¼ cup chopped scallions
Cooking spray

1. Spritz the perforated pan with cooking spray and set aside.
2. Heat the sesame oil in a saucepan on medium heat. Sauté the ginger and garlic in the sesame oil for 1 minute, or until fragrant. Add soy sauce, red bell pepper, carrot, mushrooms and scallions. Sauté for 5 minutes or until the vegetables become tender. Mix in vermicelli noodles. Turn off the heat and remove them from the saucepan. Allow to cool for 10 minutes.
3. Lay out one spring roll wrapper with a corner pointed toward you. Scoop the noodle mixture on spring roll wrapper and fold corner up over the mixture. Fold left and right corners toward the center and continue to roll to make firmly sealed rolls.
4. Arrange the spring rolls in the pan and spritz with cooking spray.
5. Select Air Fry. Set temperature to 340°F (171°C) and set time to 12 minutes. Press Start to begin preheating.
6. Once the Vortex has preheated, place the pan into the Vortex. Flip the spring rolls halfway through the cooking time.
7. Serve warm.

Crispy Cream Cheese Wontons
Prep time: 5 minutes | Cook time: 6 minutes | Serves 4

2 ounces (57 g) cream cheese, softened
1 tablespoon sugar
16 square wonton wrappers
Cooking spray

1. Spritz the perforated pan with cooking spray.
2. In a mixing bowl, stir together the cream cheese and sugar until well mixed. Prepare a small bowl of water alongside.
3. On a clean work surface, lay the wonton wrappers. Scoop ¼ teaspoon of cream cheese in the center of each wonton wrapper. Dab the water over the wrapper edges. Fold each wonton wrapper diagonally in half over the filling to form a triangle.
4. Arrange the wontons in the pan. Spritz the wontons with cooking spray.
5. Select Air Fry. Set temperature to 350°F (180°C) and set time to 6 minutes. Press Start to begin preheating.
6. Once preheated, place the pan into the Vortex. Flip the wontons halfway through the cooking time.
7. When cooking is complete, the wontons will be golden brown and crispy.
8. Divide the wontons among four plates. Let rest for 5 minutes before serving.

Chicken Wraps with Ricotta Cheese
Prep time: 30 minutes | Cook time: 5 minutes | Serves 12

2 large-sized chicken breasts, cooked and shredded
2 spring onions, chopped
10 ounces (284 g) Ricotta cheese
1 tablespoon rice vinegar
1 tablespoon molasses
1 teaspoon grated fresh ginger
¼ cup soy sauce
⅓ teaspoon sea salt
¼ teaspoon ground black pepper, or more to taste
48 wonton wrappers
Cooking spray

1. Spritz the perforated pan with cooking spray.
2. Combine all the ingredients, except for the wrappers in a large bowl. Toss to mix well.
3. Unfold the wrappers on a clean work surface, then divide and spoon the mixture in the middle of the wrappers.
4. Dab a little water on the edges of the wrappers, then fold the edge close to you over the filling. Tuck the edge under the filling and roll up to seal.
5. Arrange the wraps in the pan.
6. Select Air Fry. Set temperature to 375°F (190°C) and set time to 5 minutes. Press Start to begin preheating.
7. Once preheated, place the pan into the Vortex. Flip the wraps halfway through the cooking time.
8. When cooking is complete, the wraps should be lightly browned.
9. Serve immediately.

Avocado and Tomato Wraps
Prep time: 10 minutes | Cook time: 5 minutes | Serves 5

10 egg roll wrappers
3 avocados, peeled and pitted
1 tomato, diced
Salt and ground black pepper, to taste
Cooking spray

1. Spritz the perforated pan with cooking spray.
2. Put the tomato and avocados in a food processor. Sprinkle with salt and ground black pepper. Pulse to mix and coarsely mash until smooth.
3. Unfold the wrappers on a clean work surface, then divide the mixture in the center of each wrapper. Roll the wrapper up and press to seal.
4. Transfer the rolls to the pan and spritz with cooking spray.
5. Select Air Fry. Set temperature to 350°F (180°C) and set time to 5 minutes. Press Start to begin preheating.
6. Once the Vortex has preheated, place the pan into the Vortex. Flip the rolls halfway through the cooking time.
7. When cooked, the rolls should be golden brown.
8. Serve immediately.

Chicken and Cabbage Wraps
Prep time: 10 minutes | Cook time: 23 to 24 minutes | Serves 4

1 pound (454 g) ground chicken
2 teaspoons olive oil
2 garlic cloves, minced
1 teaspoon grated fresh ginger
2 cups white cabbage, shredded
1 onion, chopped
¼ cup soy sauce
8 egg roll wrappers
1 egg, beaten
Cooking spray

1. Spritz the perforated pan with cooking spray.
2. Heat olive oil in a saucepan over medium heat. Sauté the garlic and ginger in the olive oil for 1 minute, or until fragrant. Add the ground chicken to the saucepan. Sauté for 5 minutes, or until the chicken is cooked through. Add the cabbage, onion and soy sauce and sauté for 5 to 6 minutes, or until the vegetables become soft. Remove the saucepan from the heat.
3. Unfold the egg roll wrappers on a clean work surface. Divide the chicken mixture among the wrappers and brush the edges of the wrappers with the beaten egg. Tightly roll up the egg rolls, enclosing the filling. Arrange the rolls in the pan.
4. Select Air Fry. Set temperature to 370°F (188°C) and set time to 12 minutes. Press Start to begin preheating.
5. Once the Vortex has preheated, place the pan into the Vortex. Flip the rolls halfway through the cooking time.
6. When cooked, the rolls will be crispy and golden brown.
7. Transfer to a platter and let cool for 5 minutes before serving.

Parmesan Eggplant Hoagies
Prep time: 15 minutes | Cook time: 12 minutes | Makes 3 hoagies

6 peeled eggplant slices (about ½ inch thick and 3 inches in diameter)
¼ cup jarred pizza sauce
6 tablespoons grated Parmesan cheese
3 Italian sub rolls, split open lengthwise, warmed
Cooking spray

1. Spritz the perforated pan with cooking spray.
2. Arrange the eggplant slices in the pan and spritz with cooking spray.
3. Select Air Fry. Set temperature to 350°F (180°C) and set time to 10 minutes. Press Start to begin preheating.
4. Once the Vortex has preheated, place the pan into the Vortex. Flip the slices halfway through the cooking time.
5. When cooked, the eggplant slices should be lightly wilted and tender.
6. Divide and spread the pizza sauce and cheese on top of the eggplant slice
7. Select Air Fry. Set temperature to 375°F (190°C) and set time to 2 minutes. place the pan into the Vortex. When cooked, the cheese will be melted.
8. Assemble each sub roll with two slices of eggplant and serve immediately.

Cream Cheese and Crab Wontons
Prep time: 10 minutes | Cook time: 10 minutes | Serves 6 to 8

24 wonton wrappers, thawed if frozen
Cooking spray
Filling:
5 ounces (142 g) lump crabmeat, drained and patted dry
4 ounces (113 g) cream cheese, at room temperature
2 scallions, sliced
1½ teaspoons toasted sesame oil
1 teaspoon Worcestershire sauce
Kosher salt and ground black pepper, to taste

1. Spritz the perforated pan with cooking spray.
2. In a medium-size bowl, place all the ingredients for the filling and stir until well mixed. Prepare a small bowl of water alongside.
3. On a clean work surface, lay the wonton wrappers. Scoop 1 teaspoon of the filling in the center of each wrapper. Wet the edges with a touch of water. Fold each wonton wrapper diagonally in half over the filling to form a triangle.
4. Arrange the wontons in the pan. Spritz the wontons with cooking spray.
5. Select Air Fry. Set temperature to 350°F (180°C) and set time to 10 minutes. Press Start to begin preheating.
6. Once preheated, place the pan into the Vortex. Flip the wontons halfway through the cooking time.
7. When cooking is complete, the wontons will be crispy and golden brown.
8. Serve immediately.

Bacon and Egg Wraps with Salsa
Prep time: 15 minutes | Cook time: 10 minutes | Serves 3

3 corn tortillas
3 slices bacon, cut into strips
2 scrambled eggs
3 tablespoons salsa
1 cup grated Pepper Jack cheese
3 tablespoons cream cheese, divided
Cooking spray

1. Spritz the perforated pan with cooking spray.
2. Unfold the tortillas on a clean work surface, divide the bacon and eggs in the middle of the tortillas, then spread with salsa and scatter with cheeses. Fold the tortillas over.
3. Arrange the tortillas in the pan.
4. Select Air Fry. Set temperature to 390°F (199°C) and set time to 10 minutes. Press Start to begin preheating.
5. Once the Vortex has preheated, place the pan into the Vortex. Flip the tortillas halfway through the cooking time.
6. When cooking is complete, the cheeses will be melted and the tortillas will be lightly browned.
7. Serve immediately.

Cajun Beef and Bell Pepper Fajitas
Prep time: 15 minutes | Cook time: 10 minutes | Serves 4

1 pound (454 g) beef sirloin steak, cut into strips
2 shallots, sliced
1 orange bell pepper, sliced
1 red bell pepper, sliced
2 garlic cloves, minced
2 tablespoons Cajun seasoning
1 tablespoon paprika
Salt and ground black pepper, to taste
4 corn tortillas
½ cup shredded Cheddar cheese
Cooking spray

1. Spritz the perforated pan with cooking spray.
2. Combine all the ingredients, except for the tortillas and cheese, in a large bowl. Toss to coat well.
3. Pour the beef and vegetables in the pan and spritz with cooking spray.
4. Select Air Fry. Set temperature to 360°F (182°C) and set time to 10 minutes. Press Start to begin preheating.
5. Once preheated, place the pan into the Vortex. Stir the beef and vegetables halfway through the cooking time.
6. When cooking is complete, the meat will be browned and the vegetables will be soft and lightly wilted.
7. Unfold the tortillas on a clean work surface and spread the cooked beef and vegetables on top. Scatter with cheese and fold to serve.

Potato Taquitos with Mexican Cheese
Prep time: 5 minutes | Cook time: 6 minutes | Makes 12 taquitos

2 cups mashed potatoes
½ cup shredded Mexican cheese
12 corn tortillas
Cooking spray

1. Line a baking pan with parchment paper.
2. In a bowl, combine the potatoes and cheese until well mixed. Microwave the tortillas on high heat for 30 seconds, or until softened. Add some water to another bowl and set alongside.
3. On a clean work surface, lay the tortillas. Scoop 3 tablespoons of the potato mixture in the center of each tortilla. Roll up tightly and secure with toothpicks if necessary.
4. Arrange the filled tortillas, seam side down, in the prepared baking pan. Spritz the tortillas with cooking spray.
5. Select Air Fry. Set temperature to 400°F (205°C) and set time to 6 minutes. Press Start to begin preheating.
6. Once preheated, place the pan into the Vortex. Flip the tortillas halfway through the cooking time.
7. When cooked, the tortillas should be crispy and golden brown.
8. Serve hot.

Chickpea and Mushroom Wraps
Prep time: 15 minutes | Cook time: 9 minutes | Serves 4

8 ounces (227 g) green beans
2 portobello mushroom caps, sliced
1 large red pepper, sliced
2 tablespoons olive oil, divided
¼ teaspoon salt
1 (15-ounce / 425-g) can chickpeas, drained
3 tablespoons lemon juice
¼ teaspoon ground black pepper
4 (6-inch) whole-grain wraps
4 ounces (113 g) fresh herb or garlic goat cheese, crumbled
1 lemon, cut into wedges

1. Add the green beans, mushrooms, red pepper to a large bowl. Drizzle with 1 tablespoon olive oil and season with salt. Toss until well coated.
2. Transfer the vegetable mixture to a baking pan.
3. Select Air Fry. Set temperature to 400°F (205°C) and set time to 9 minutes. Press Start to begin preheating.
4. Once preheated, slide the pan into the Vortex. Stir the vegetable mixture three times during cooking.
5. When cooked, the vegetables should be tender.
6. Meanwhile, mash the chickpeas with lemon juice, pepper and the remaining 1 tablespoon oil until well blended
7. Unfold the wraps on a clean work surface. Spoon the chickpea mash on the wraps and spread all over.
8. Divide the cooked veggies among wraps. Sprinkle 1 ounce crumbled goat cheese on top of each wrap. Fold to wrap. Squeeze the lemon wedges on top and serve.

Mozzarella Chicken Taquitos
Prep time: 15 minutes | Cook time: 12 minutes | Serves 4

1 cup cooked chicken, shredded
¼ cup Greek yogurt
¼ cup salsa
1 cup shredded Mozzarella cheese
Salt and ground black pepper, to taste
4 flour tortillas
Cooking spray

1. Spritz the perforated pan with cooking spray.
2. Combine all the ingredients, except for the tortillas, in a large bowl. Stir to mix well.
3. Make the taquitos: Unfold the tortillas on a clean work surface, then scoop up 2 tablespoons of the chicken mixture in the middle of each tortilla. Roll the tortillas up to wrap the filling.
4. Arrange the taquitos in the pan and spritz with cooking spray.
5. Select Air Fry. Set temperature to 380°F (193°C) and set time to 12 minutes. Press Start to begin preheating.
6. Once preheated, place the pan into the Vortex. Flip the taquitos halfway through the cooking time.
7. When cooked, the taquitos should be golden brown and the cheese should be melted.
8. Serve immediately.

Lamb Hamburgers with Feta Cheese
Prep time: 15 minutes | Cook time: 16 minutes | Makes 4 burgers

1½ pounds (680 g) ground lamb
¼ cup crumbled feta
1½ teaspoons tomato paste
1½ teaspoons minced garlic
1 teaspoon ground dried ginger
1 teaspoon ground coriander
¼ teaspoon salt
¼ teaspoon cayenne pepper
4 kaiser rolls or hamburger buns, split open lengthwise, warmed
Cooking spray

1. Spritz the perforated pan with cooking spray.
2. Combine all the ingredients, except for the buns, in a large bowl. Coarsely stir to mix well.
3. Shape the mixture into four balls, then pound the balls into four 5-inch diameter patties.
4. Arrange the patties in the pan and spritz with cooking spray.
5. Select Air Fry. Set temperature to 375°F (190°C) and set time to 16 minutes. Press Start to begin preheating.
6. Once preheated, place the pan into the Vortex. Flip the patties halfway through the cooking time.
7. When cooking is complete, the patties should be well browned.
8. Assemble the buns with patties to make the burgers and serve immediately.

Curried Pork Sliders
Prep time: 10 minutes | Cook time: 14 minutes | Makes 6 sliders

1 pound (454 g) ground pork
1 tablespoon Thai curry paste
1½ tablespoons fish sauce
¼ cup thinly sliced scallions, white and green parts
2 tablespoons minced peeled fresh ginger
1 tablespoon light brown sugar
1 teaspoon ground black pepper
6 slider buns, split open lengthwise, warmed
Cooking spray

1. Spritz the perforated pan with cooking spray.
2. Combine all the ingredients, except for the buns in a large bowl. Stir to mix well.
3. Divide and shape the mixture into six balls, then bash the balls into six 3-inch-diameter patties.
4. Arrange the patties in the pan and spritz with cooking spray.
5. Select Air Fry. Set temperature to 375°F (190°C) and set time to 14 minutes. Press Start to begin preheating.
6. Once the Vortex has preheated, place the pan into the Vortex. Flip the patties halfway through the cooking time.
7. When cooked, the patties should be well browned.
8. Assemble the buns with patties to make the sliders and serve immediately.

Pork Momos with Carrot
Prep time: 20 minutes | Cook time: 20 minutes | Serves 4

2 tablespoons olive oil
1 pound (454 g) ground pork
1 shredded carrot
1 onion, chopped
1 teaspoon soy sauce
16 wonton wrappers
Salt and ground black pepper, to taste
Cooking spray

1. Heat the olive oil in a nonstick skillet over medium heat until shimmering.
2. Add the ground pork, carrot, onion, soy sauce, salt, and ground black pepper and sauté for 10 minutes or until the pork is well browned and carrots are tender.
3. Unfold the wrappers on a clean work surface, then divide the cooked pork and vegetables on the wrappers. Fold the edges around the filling to form momos. Nip the top to seal the momos.
4. Arrange the momos in the perforated pan and spritz with cooking spray.
5. Select Air Fry. Set temperature to 320°F (160°C) and set time to 10 minutes. Press Start to begin preheating.
6. Once the Vortex has preheated, place the pan into the Vortex.
7. Serve immediately.

Pork and Cabbage Gyoza
Prep time: 10 minutes | Cook time: 10 minutes | Makes 48 gyozas

1 pound (454 g) ground pork
1 head Napa cabbage (about 1 pound / 454 g) sliced thinly and minced
½ cup minced scallions
1 teaspoon minced fresh chives
1 teaspoon soy sauce
1 teaspoon minced fresh ginger
1 tablespoon minced garlic
1 teaspoon granulated sugar
2 teaspoons kosher salt
48 to 50 wonton or dumpling wrappers
Cooking spray

1. Spritz the perforated pan with cooking spray. Set aside.
2. Make the filling: Combine all the ingredients, except for the wrappers in a large bowl. Stir to mix well.
3. Unfold a wrapper on a clean work surface, then dab the edges with a little water. Scoop up 2 teaspoons of the filling mixture in the center.
4. Make the gyoza: Fold the wrapper over to filling and press the edges to seal. Pleat the edges if desired. Repeat with remaining wrappers and fillings.
5. Arrange the gyozas in the pan and spritz with cooking spray.
6. Select Air Fry. Set temperature to 360°F (182°C) and set time to 10 minutes. Press Start to begin preheating.
7. Once preheated, place the pan into the Vortex. Flip the gyozas halfway through the cooking time.
8. When cooked, the gyozas will be golden brown.
9. Serve immediately.

Turkey and Pepper Hamburger

Prep time: 10 minutes | Cook time: 20 minutes | Serves 4

1 cup leftover turkey, cut into bite-sized chunks
1 leek, sliced
1 Serrano pepper, seeded and chopped
2 bell peppers, seeded and chopped
2 tablespoons Tabasco sauce
½ cup sour cream
1 teaspoon hot paprika
¾ teaspoon kosher salt
½ teaspoon ground black pepper
4 hamburger buns
Cooking spray

1. Spritz a baking pan with cooking spray.
2. Mix all the ingredients, except for the buns, in a large bowl. Toss to combine well.
3. Pour the mixture in the baking pan.
4. Select Bake. Set temperature to 385°F (196°C) and set time to 20 minutes. Press Start to begin preheating.
5. Once preheated, place the pan into the Vortex.
6. When done, the turkey will be well browned and the leek will be tender.
7. Assemble the hamburger buns with the turkey mixture and serve immediately.

Beef Burgers with Seeds

Prep time: 15 minutes | Cook time: 10 minutes | Serves 4

1 teaspoon cumin seeds
1 teaspoon mustard seeds
1 teaspoon coriander seeds
1 teaspoon dried minced garlic
1 teaspoon dried red pepper flakes
1 teaspoon kosher salt
2 teaspoons ground black pepper
1 pound (454 g) 85% lean ground beef
2 tablespoons Worcestershire sauce
4 hamburger buns
Mayonnaise, for serving
Cooking spray

1. Spritz the perforated pan with cooking spray.
2. Put the seeds, garlic, red pepper flakes, salt, and ground black pepper in a food processor. Pulse to coarsely ground the mixture.
3. Put the ground beef in a large bowl. Pour in the seed mixture and drizzle with Worcestershire sauce. Stir to mix well.
4. Divide the mixture into four parts and shape each part into a ball, then bash each ball into a patty. Arrange the patties in the pan.
5. Select Air Fry. Set temperature to 350°F (180°C) and set time to 10 minutes. Press Start to begin preheating.
6. Once the Vortex has preheated, place the pan into the Vortex. Flip the patties with tongs halfway through the cooking time.
7. When cooked, the patties will be well browned.
8. Assemble the buns with the patties, then drizzle the mayo over the patties to make the burgers. Serve immediately.

Cheesy Bacon and Egg Wraps

Prep time: 15 minutes | Cook time: 10 minutes | Serves 3

3 corn tortillas
3 slices bacon, cut into strips
2 scrambled eggs
3 tablespoons salsa
1 cup grated Pepper Jack cheese
3 tablespoons cream cheese, divided
Cooking spray

1. Spritz the air fry basket with cooking spray.
2. Unfold the tortillas on a clean work surface, divide the bacon and eggs in the middle of the tortillas, then spread with salsa and scatter with cheeses. Fold the tortillas over.
3. Arrange the tortillas in the basket.
4. Select Air Fry, Super Convection, set temperature to 390°F (199°C) and set time to 10 minutes. Select Start/Stop to begin preheating.
5. Once the Vortex has preheated, place the basket on the air fry position. Flip the tortillas halfway through the cooking time.
6. When cooking is complete, the cheeses will be melted and the tortillas will be lightly browned.
7. Serve immediately.

Cheesy Spring Chicken Wraps

Prep time: 30 minutes | Cook time: 5 minutes | Serves 12

2 large-sized chicken breasts, cooked and shredded
2 spring onions, chopped
10 ounces (284 g) Ricotta cheese
1 tablespoon rice vinegar
1 tablespoon molasses
1 teaspoon grated fresh ginger
¼ cup soy sauce
⅓ teaspoon sea salt
¼ teaspoon ground black pepper, or more to taste
48 wonton wrappers
Cooking spray

1. Spritz the air fry basket with cooking spray.
2. Combine all the ingredients, except for the wrappers in a large bowl. Toss to mix well.
3. Unfold the wrappers on a clean work surface, then divide and spoon the mixture in the middle of the wrappers.
4. Dab a little water on the edges of the wrappers, then fold the edge close to you over the filling. Tuck the edge under the filling and roll up to seal.
5. Arrange the wraps in the basket.
6. Select Air Fry, Super Convection, set temperature to 375°F (190°C) and set time to 5 minutes. Select Start/Stop to begin preheating.
7. Once preheated, place the basket on the air fry position. Flip the wraps halfway through the cooking time.
8. When cooking is complete, the wraps should be lightly browned.
9. Serve immediately.

Avocado and Tomato Egg Rolls

Prep time: 10 minutes | Cook time: 5 minutes | Serves 5

10 egg roll wrappers
3 avocados, peeled and pitted
1 tomato, diced
Salt and ground black pepper, to taste
Cooking spray

1. Spritz the air fry basket with cooking spray.
2. Put the tomato and avocados in a food processor. Sprinkle with salt and ground black pepper. Pulse to mix and coarsely mash until smooth.
3. Unfold the wrappers on a clean work surface, then divide the mixture in the center of each wrapper. Roll the wrapper up and press to seal.
4. Transfer the rolls to the basket and spritz with cooking spray.
5. Select Air Fry, Super Convection, set temperature to 350°F (180°C) and set time to 5 minutes. Select Start/Stop to begin preheating.
6. Once the Vortex has preheated, place the basket on the air fry position. Flip the rolls halfway through the cooking time.
7. When cooked, the rolls should be golden brown.
8. Serve immediately.

Crispy Chicken Egg Rolls

Prep time: 10 minutes | Cook time: 23 to 24 minutes | Serves 4

1 pound (454 g) ground chicken
2 teaspoons olive oil
2 garlic cloves, minced
1 teaspoon grated fresh ginger
2 cups white cabbage, shredded
1 onion, chopped
¼ cup soy sauce
8 egg roll wrappers
1 egg, beaten
Cooking spray

1. Spritz the air fry basket with cooking spray.
2. Heat olive oil in a saucepan over medium heat. Sauté the garlic and ginger in the olive oil for 1 minute, or until fragrant. Add the ground chicken to the saucepan. Sauté for 5 minutes, or until the chicken is cooked through. Add the cabbage, onion and soy sauce and sauté for 5 to 6 minutes, or until the vegetables become soft. Remove the saucepan from the heat.
3. Unfold the egg roll wrappers on a clean work surface. Divide the chicken mixture among the wrappers and brush the edges of the wrappers with the beaten egg. Tightly roll up the egg rolls, enclosing the filling. Arrange the rolls in the basket.
4. Select Air Fry, Super Convection, set temperature to 370°F (188°C) and set time to 12 minutes. Select Start/Stop to begin preheating.
5. Once the Vortex has preheated, place the basket on the air fry position. Flip the rolls halfway through the cooking time.
6. When cooked, the rolls will be crispy and golden brown.
7. Transfer to a platter and let cool for 5 minutes before serving.

Beef and Bell Pepper Fajitas

Prep time: 15 minutes | Cook time: 10 minutes | Serves 4

1 pound (454 g) beef sirloin steak, cut into strips
2 shallots, sliced
1 orange bell pepper, sliced
1 red bell pepper, sliced
2 garlic cloves, minced
2 tablespoons Cajun seasoning
1 tablespoon paprika
Salt and ground black pepper, to taste
4 corn tortillas
½ cup shredded Cheddar cheese
Cooking spray

1. Spritz the air fry basket with cooking spray.
2. Combine all the ingredients, except for the tortillas and cheese, in a large bowl. Toss to coat well.
3. Pour the beef and vegetables in the basket and spritz with cooking spray.
4. Select Air Fry, Super Convection, set temperature to 360°F (182°C) and set time to 10 minutes. Select Start/Stop to begin preheating.
5. Once preheated, place the basket on the air fry position. Stir the beef and vegetables halfway through the cooking time.
6. When cooking is complete, the meat will be browned and the vegetables will be soft and lightly wilted.
7. Unfold the tortillas on a clean work surface and spread the cooked beef and vegetables on top. Scatter with cheese and fold to serve.

Cheesy Potato Taquitos

Prep time: 5 minutes | Cook time: 6 minutes | Makes 12 taquitos

2 cups mashed potatoes
½ cup shredded Mexican cheese
12 corn tortillas
Cooking spray

1. Line a baking pan with parchment paper.
2. In a bowl, combine the potatoes and cheese until well mixed. Microwave the tortillas on high heat for 30 seconds, or until softened. Add some water to another bowl and set alongside.
3. On a clean work surface, lay the tortillas. Scoop 3 tablespoons of the potato mixture in the center of each tortilla. Roll up tightly and secure with toothpicks if necessary.
4. Arrange the filled tortillas, seam side down, in the prepared baking pan. Spritz the tortillas with cooking spray.
5. Select Air Fry, Super Convection, set temperature to 400°F (205°C) and set time to 6 minutes. Select Start/Stop to begin preheating.
6. Once preheated, place the pan into the Vortex. Flip the tortillas halfway through the cooking time.
7. When cooked, the tortillas should be crispy and golden brown.
8. Serve hot.

Eggplant Hoagies

Prep time: 15 minutes | Cook time: 12 minutes | Makes 3 hoagies

6 peeled eggplant slices (about ½ inch thick and 3 inches in diameter)
¼ cup jarred pizza sauce
6 tablespoons grated Parmesan cheese
3 Italian sub rolls, split open lengthwise, warmed
Cooking spray

1. Spritz the air fry basket with cooking spray.
2. Arrange the eggplant slices in the basket and spritz with cooking spray.
3. Select Air Fry, Super Convection, set temperature to 350°F (180°C) and set time to 10 minutes. Select Start/Stop to begin preheating.
4. Once the Vortex has preheated, place the basket on the air fry position. Flip the slices halfway through the cooking time.
5. When cooked, the eggplant slices should be lightly wilted and tender.
6. Divide and spread the pizza sauce and cheese on top of the eggplant slice
7. Select Air Fry, Super Convection, set temperature to 375°F (190°C) and set time to 2 minutes. Place the basket on the air fry position. When cooked, the cheese will be melted.
8. Assemble each sub roll with two slices of eggplant and serve immediately.

Chicken and Yogurt Taquitos

Prep time: 15 minutes | Cook time: 12 minutes | Serves 4

1 cup cooked chicken, shredded
¼ cup Greek yogurt
¼ cup salsa
1 cup shredded Mozzarella cheese
Salt and ground black pepper, to taste
4 flour tortillas
Cooking spray

1. Spritz the air fry basket with cooking spray.
2. Combine all the ingredients, except for the tortillas, in a large bowl. Stir to mix well.
3. Make the taquitos: Unfold the tortillas on a clean work surface, then scoop up 2 tablespoons of the chicken mixture in the middle of each tortilla. Roll the tortillas up to wrap the filling.
4. Arrange the taquitos in the basket and spritz with cooking spray.
5. Select Air Fry, Super Convection, set temperature to 380°F (193°C) and set time to 12 minutes. Select Start/Stop to begin preheating.
6. Once preheated, place the basket on the air fry position. Flip the taquitos halfway through the cooking time.
7. When cooked, the taquitos should be golden brown and the cheese should be melted.
8. Serve immediately.

Thai Pork Sliders

Prep time: 10 minutes | Cook time: 14 minutes | Makes 6 sliders

1 pound (454 g) ground pork
1 tablespoon Thai curry paste
1½ tablespoons fish sauce
¼ cup thinly sliced scallions, white and green parts
2 tablespoons minced peeled fresh ginger
1 tablespoon light brown sugar
1 teaspoon ground black pepper
6 slider buns, split open lengthwise, warmed
Cooking spray

1. Spritz the air fry basket with cooking spray.
2. Combine all the ingredients, except for the buns in a large bowl. Stir to mix well.
3. Divide and shape the mixture into six balls, then bash the balls into six 3-inch-diameter patties.
4. Arrange the patties in the basket and spritz with cooking spray.
5. Select Air Fry, Super Convection, set temperature to 375°F (190°C) and set time to 14 minutes. Select Start/Stop to begin preheating.
6. Once the Vortex has preheated, place the basket on the air fry position. Flip the patties halfway through the cooking time.
7. When cooked, the patties should be well browned.
8. Assemble the buns with patties to make the sliders and serve immediately.

Lamb and Feta Hamburgers

Prep time: 15 minutes | Cook time: 16 minutes | Makes 4 burgers

1½ pounds (680 g) ground lamb
¼ cup crumbled feta
1½ teaspoons tomato paste
1½ teaspoons minced garlic
1 teaspoon ground dried ginger
1 teaspoon ground coriander
¼ teaspoon salt
¼ teaspoon cayenne pepper
4 kaiser rolls or hamburger buns, split open lengthwise, warmed
Cooking spray

1. Spritz the air fry basket with cooking spray.
2. Combine all the ingredients, except for the buns, in a large bowl. Coarsely stir to mix well.
3. Shape the mixture into four balls, then pound the balls into four 5-inch diameter patties.
4. Arrange the patties in the basket and spritz with cooking spray.
5. Select Air Fry, Super Convection, set temperature to 375°F (190°C) and set time to 16 minutes. Select Start/Stop to begin preheating.
6. Once preheated, place the basket on the air fry position. Flip the patties halfway through the cooking time.
7. When cooking is complete, the patties should be well browned.
8. Assemble the buns with patties to make the burgers and serve immediately.

Chapter 12
Holiday Specials

Balsamic Cherry Tomatoes

Prep time: 5 minutes | Cook time: 10 minutes | Serves 4 to 6

2 pounds (907 g) cherry tomatoes
2 tablespoons olive oil
2 teaspoons balsamic vinegar
½ teaspoon salt
½ teaspoon ground black pepper

1. Toss the cherry tomatoes with olive oil in a large bowl to coat well. Pour the tomatoes in a baking pan.
2. Select Air Fry. Set temperature to 400°F (205°C) and set time to 10 minutes. Press Start to begin preheating.
3. Once preheated, slide the pan into the Vortex. Stir the tomatoes halfway through the cooking time.
4. When cooking is complete, the tomatoes will be blistered and lightly wilted.
5. Transfer the blistered tomatoes to a large bowl and toss with balsamic vinegar, salt, and black pepper before serving.

Vanilla Butter Cake

Prep time: 25 minutes | Cook time: 20 minutes | Serves 8

1 cup all-purpose flour
1¼ teaspoons baking powder
¼ teaspoon salt
½ cup plus 1½ tablespoons granulated white sugar
9½ tablespoons butter, at room temperature
2 large eggs
1 large egg yolk
2½ tablespoons milk
1 teaspoon vanilla extract
Cooking spray

1. Spritz a baking pan with cooking spray.
2. Combine the flour, baking powder, and salt in a large bowl. Stir to mix well.
3. Whip the sugar and butter in a separate bowl with a hand mixer on medium speed for 3 minutes.
4. Whip the eggs, egg yolk, milk, and vanilla extract into the sugar and butter mix with a hand mixer.
5. Pour in the flour mixture and whip with hand mixer until sanity and smooth.
6. Scrape the batter into the baking pan and level the batter with a spatula.
7. Select Bake. Set temperature to 325°F (163°C) and set time to 20 minutes. Press Start to begin preheating.
8. Once the Vortex has preheated, place the pan into the Vortex.
9. After 15 minutes, remove the pan from the Vortex. Check the doneness. Return the pan to the Vortex and continue cooking.
10. When done, a toothpick inserted in the center should come out clean.
11. Invert the cake on a cooling rack and allow to cool for 15 minutes before slicing to serve.

Chocolate Macaroons with Coconut

Prep time: 10 minutes | Cook time: 8 minutes | Makes 24 macaroons

3 large egg whites, at room temperature
¼ teaspoon salt
¾ cup granulated white sugar
4½ tablespoons unsweetened cocoa powder
2¼ cups unsweetened shredded coconut

1. Line the perforated pan with parchment paper.
2. Whisk the egg whites with salt in a large bowl with a hand mixer on high speed until stiff peaks form.
3. Whisk in the sugar with the hand mixer on high speed until the mixture is thick. Mix in the cocoa powder and coconut.
4. Scoop 2 tablespoons of the mixture and shape the mixture in a ball. Repeat with remaining mixture to make 24 balls in total.
5. Arrange the balls in a single layer in the perforated pan and leave a little space between each two balls.
6. Select Air Fry. Set temperature to 375°F (190°C) and set time to 8 minutes. Press Start to begin preheating.
7. Once the Vortex has preheated, place the pan into the Vortex.
8. When cooking is complete, the balls should be golden brown.
9. Serve immediately.

Pigs in a Blanket with Sesame Seeds

Prep time: 10 minutes | Cook time: 8 minutes | Makes 16 rolls

1 can refrigerated crescent roll dough
1 small package mini smoked sausages, patted dry
2 tablespoons melted butter
2 teaspoons sesame seeds
1 teaspoon onion powder

1. Place the crescent roll dough on a clean work surface and separate into 8 pieces. Cut each piece in half and you will have 16 triangles.
2. Make the pigs in the blanket: Arrange each sausage on each dough triangle, then roll the sausages up.
3. Brush the pigs with melted butter and place of the pigs in the blanket in the perforated pan. Sprinkle with sesame seeds and onion powder.
4. Select Bake. Set temperature to 330°F (166°C) and set time to 8 minutes. Press Start to begin preheating.
5. Once the Vortex has preheated, place the pan into the Vortex. Flip the pigs halfway through the cooking time.
6. When cooking is complete, the pigs should be fluffy and golden brown.
7. Serve immediately.

Cream-Glazed Cinnamon Rolls

Prep time: 2 hours 15 minutes | Cook time: 5 minutes | Serves 8

1 pound (454 g) frozen bread dough, thawed
2 tablespoons melted butter
1½ tablespoons cinnamon
¾ cup brown sugar
Cooking spray
Cream Glaze:
4 ounces (113 g) softened cream cheese
½ teaspoon vanilla extract
2 tablespoons melted butter
1¼ cups powdered erythritol

1. Place the bread dough on a clean work surface, then roll the dough out into a rectangle with a rolling pin.
2. Brush the top of the dough with melted butter and leave 1-inch edges uncovered.
3. Combine the cinnamon and sugar in a small bowl, then sprinkle the dough with the cinnamon mixture.
4. Roll the dough over tightly, then cut the dough log into 8 portions. Wrap the portions in plastic, better separately, and let sit to rise for 1 or 2 hours.
5. Meanwhile, combine the ingredients for the glaze in a separate small bowl. Stir to mix well.
6. Spritz the perforated pan with cooking spray. Transfer the risen rolls to the perforated pan.
7. Select Air Fry. Set temperature to 350°F (180°C) and set time to 5 minutes. Press Start to begin preheating.
8. Once the Vortex has preheated, place the pan into the Vortex. Flip the rolls halfway through the cooking time.
9. When cooking is complete, the rolls will be golden brown.
10. Serve the rolls with the glaze.

Mozzarella Rice Arancini

Prep time: 5 minutes | Cook time: 30 minutes | Makes 10 arancini

⅔ cup raw white Arborio rice
2 teaspoons butter
½ teaspoon salt
1⅓ cups water
2 large eggs, well beaten
1¼ cups seasoned Italian-style dried bread crumbs
10 ¾-inch semi-firm Mozzarella cubes
Cooking spray

1. Pour the rice, butter, salt, and water in a pot. Stir to mix well and bring a boil over medium-high heat. Keep stirring.
2. Reduce the heat to low and cover the pot. Simmer for 20 minutes or until the rice is tender.
3. Turn off the heat and let sit, covered, for 10 minutes, then open the lid and fluffy the rice with a fork. Allow to cool for 10 more minutes.
4. Pour the beaten eggs in a bowl, then pour the bread crumbs in a separate bowl.
5. Scoop 2 tablespoons of the cooked rice up and form it into a ball, then press the Mozzarella into the ball and wrap.
6. Dredge the ball in the eggs first, then shake the excess off the dunk the ball in the bread crumbs. Roll to coat evenly. Repeat to make 10 balls in total with remaining rice.
7. Transfer the balls in the perforated pan and spritz with cooking spray.
8. Select Air Fry. Set temperature to 375°F (190°C) and set time to 10 minutes. Press Start to begin preheating.
9. Once preheated, place the pan into the Vortex.
10. When cooking is complete, the balls should be lightly browned and crispy.
11. Remove the balls from the Vortex and allow to cool before serving.

Buttermilk Chocolate Cake
Prep time: 20 minutes | Cook time: 20 minutes | Serves 8

1 cup all-purpose flour
⅔ cup granulated white sugar
¼ cup unsweetened cocoa powder
¾ teaspoon baking soda
¼ teaspoon salt
⅔ cup buttermilk
2 tablespoons plus 2 teaspoons vegetable oil
1 teaspoon vanilla extract
Cooking spray

1. Spritz a baking pan with cooking spray.
2. Combine the flour, cocoa powder, baking soda, sugar, and salt in a large bowl. Stir to mix well.
3. Mix in the buttermilk, vanilla, and vegetable oil. Keep stirring until it forms a grainy and thick dough.
4. Scrape the chocolate batter from the bowl and transfer to the pan, level the batter in an even layer with a spatula.
5. Select Bake. Set temperature to 325°F (163°C) and set time to 20 minutes. Press Start to begin preheating.
6. Once preheated, place the pan into the Vortex.
7. After 15 minutes, remove the pan from the Vortex. Check the doneness. Return the pan to the Vortex and continue cooking.
8. When done, a toothpick inserted in the center should come out clean.
9. Invert the cake on a cooling rack and allow to cool for 15 minutes before slicing to serve.

Teriyaki-Marinated Shrimp Skewers
Prep time: 10 minutes | Cook time: 6 minutes | Makes 12 skewered shrimp

1½ tablespoons mirin
1½ teaspoons ginger juice
1½ tablespoons soy sauce
12 large shrimp (about 20 shrimps per pound) peeled and deveined
1 large egg
¾ cup panko bread crumbs
Cooking spray

1. Combine the mirin, ginger juice, and soy sauce in a large bowl. Stir to mix well.
2. Dunk the shrimp in the bowl of mirin mixture, then wrap the bowl in plastic and refrigerate for 1 hour to marinate.
3. Spritz the perforated pan with cooking spray.
4. Run twelve 4-inch skewers through each shrimp.
5. Whisk the egg in the bowl of marinade to combine well. Pour the bread crumbs on a plate.
6. Dredge the shrimp skewers in the egg mixture, then shake the excess off and roll over the bread crumbs to coat well.
7. Arrange the shrimp skewers in the perforated pan and spritz with cooking spray.
8. Select Air Fry. Set temperature to 400°F (205°C) and set time to 6 minutes. Press Start to begin preheating.
9. Once preheated, place the pan into the Vortex. Flip the shrimp skewers halfway through the cooking time.
10. When done, the shrimp will be opaque and firm.
11. Serve immediately.

Garlic Nuggets
Prep time: 15 minutes | Cook time: 4 minutes | Makes 20 nuggets

1 cup all-purpose flour, plus more for dusting
1 teaspoon baking powder
½ teaspoon butter, at room temperature, plus more for brushing
¼ teaspoon salt
¼ cup water
⅛ teaspoon onion powder
¼ teaspoon garlic powder
⅛ teaspoon seasoning salt
Cooking spray

1. Line the perforated pan with parchment paper.
2. Mix the flour, baking powder, butter, and salt in a large bowl. Stir to mix well. Gradually whisk in the water until a sanity dough forms.
3. Put the dough on a lightly floured work surface, then roll it out into a ½-inch thick rectangle with a rolling pin.
4. Cut the dough into about twenty 1- or 2-inch squares, then arrange the squares in a single layer in the perforated pan. Spritz with cooking spray.
5. Combine onion powder, garlic powder, and seasoning salt in a small bowl. Stir to mix well, then sprinkle the squares with the powder mixture.
6. Select Air Fry. Set temperature to 370°F (188°C) and set time to 4 minutes. Press Start to begin preheating.
7. Once the Vortex has preheated, place the pan into the Vortex. Flip the squares halfway through the cooking time.
8. When cooked, the dough squares should be golden brown.
9. Remove the golden nuggets from the Vortex and brush with more butter immediately. Serve warm.

Vanilla Cheese Blintzes
Prep time: 5 minutes | Cook time: 10 minutes | Makes 8 blintzes

2 (7½-ounce / 213-g) packages farmer cheese, mashed
¼ cup cream cheese
¼ teaspoon vanilla extract
¼ cup granulated white sugar
8 egg roll wrappers
4 tablespoons butter, melted

1. Combine the farmer cheese, cream cheese, vanilla extract, and sugar in a bowl. Stir to mix well.
2. Unfold the egg roll wrappers on a clean work surface, spread ¼ cup of the filling at the edge of each wrapper and leave a ½-inch edge uncovering.
3. Wet the edges of the wrappers with water and fold the uncovered edge over the filling. Fold the left and right sides in the center, then tuck the edge under the filling and fold to wrap the filling.
4. Brush the wrappers with melted butter, then arrange the wrappers in a single layer in the perforated pan, seam side down. Leave a little space between each two wrappers.
5. Select Air Fry. Set temperature to 375°F (190°C) and set time to 10 minutes. Press Start to begin preheating.
6. Once preheated, place the pan into the Vortex.
7. When cooking is complete, the wrappers will be golden brown.
8. Serve immediately.

Asiago Balls
Prep time: 37 minutes | Cook time: 12 minutes | Makes 12 balls

2 tablespoons butter, plus more for greasing
½ cup milk
1½ cups tapioca flour
½ teaspoon salt
1 large egg
⅔ cup finely grated aged Asiago cheese

1. Put the butter in a saucepan and pour in the milk, heat over medium heat until the liquid boils. Keep stirring.
2. Turn off the heat and mix in the tapioca flour and salt to form a soft dough. Transfer the dough in a large bowl, then wrap the bowl in plastic and let sit for 15 minutes.
3. Break the egg in the bowl of dough and whisk with a hand mixer for 2 minutes or until a sanity dough forms. Fold the cheese in the dough. Cover the bowl in plastic again and let sit for 10 more minutes.
4. Grease a baking pan with butter.
5. Select Bake. Set temperature to 375°F (190°C) and set time to 12 minutes. Press Start to begin preheating.
6. Once preheated, place the pan into the Vortex. Flip the balls halfway through the cooking time.
7. When cooking is complete, the balls should be golden brown and fluffy.
8. Remove the balls from the Vortex and allow to cool for 5 minutes before serving.

Sriracha Shrimp with Mayo
Prep time: 15 minutes | Cook time: 10 minutes | Serves 4

1 tablespoon Sriracha sauce
1 teaspoon Worcestershire sauce
2 tablespoons sweet chili sauce
¾ cup mayonnaise
1 egg, beaten
1 cup panko bread crumbs
1 pound (454 g) raw shrimp, shelled and deveined, rinsed and drained
Lime wedges, for serving
Cooking spray

1. Spritz the perforated pan with cooking spray.
2. Combine the Sriracha sauce, Worcestershire sauce, chili sauce, and mayo in a bowl. Stir to mix well. Reserve ⅓ cup of the mixture as the dipping sauce.
3. Combine the remaining sauce mixture with the beaten egg. Stir to mix well. Put the panko in a separate bowl.
4. Dredge the shrimp in the sauce mixture first, then into the panko. Roll the shrimp to coat well. Shake the excess off.
5. Place the shrimp in the perforated pan, then spritz with cooking spray.
6. Select Air Fry. Set temperature to 360°F (182°C) and set time to 10 minutes. Press Start to begin preheating.
7. Once preheated, place the pan into the Vortex. Flip the shrimp halfway through the cooking time.
8. When cooking is complete, the shrimp should be opaque.
9. Remove the shrimp from the Vortex and serve with reserve sauce mixture and squeeze the lime wedges over

Chapter 13
Rotisserie Recipes

Chicken Roast with Mustard Paste
Prep time: 5 minutes | Cook time: 1 hour | Serves 4

1 (4-pound / 1.8-kg) chicken
Mustard Paste:
¼ cup Dijon mustard
1 tablespoon kosher salt
1 tablespoon Herbes de Provence
1 teaspoon freshly ground black pepper

1. Mix the mustard paste ingredients in a small bowl. Rub the chicken with the mustard paste, inside and out. Gently work your fingers under the skin on the breast, then rub some of the paste directly onto the breast meat. Refrigerate for at least two hours, preferably overnight.
2. One hour before cooking, remove the chicken from the refrigerator. Fold the wingtips under the wings and truss the chicken. Skewer the chicken on the rotisserie spit, securing it with the rotisserie forks. Let the chicken rest at room temperature.
3. Select Roast, set temperature to 400°F (205°C), Rotate, and set time to 1 hour. Select Start to begin preheating.
4. Once preheated, place the prepared chicken with rotisserie spit into the Vortex. Set a drip tray underneath. Roast until the chicken reaches 160°F (70°C) in the thickest part of the breast.
5. When cooking is complete, remove the chicken using the rotisserie lift. Remove the chicken from the rotisserie spit and remove the twine trussing the chicken. Be careful - the spit and forks are blazing hot. Let the chicken rest for 15 minutes, then carve and serve.

Mustard Lamb Shoulder
Prep time: 5 minutes | Cook time: 2 hours | Serves 4

1 (4-pound / 1.8-kg) boneless lamb shoulder roast
Mustard Herb Paste:
¼ cup whole grain mustard
1 tablespoon kosher salt
1 tablespoon minced fresh thyme
1 teaspoon minced fresh oregano
1 teaspoon minced fresh rosemary
1 teaspoon fresh ground black pepper

1. Mix the paste ingredients in a small bowl. Open up the lamb like a book, then rub all over with the paste, working it into any natural seams in the meat. Refrigerate for at least two hours, preferably overnight.
2. One hour before cooking, remove the lamb from the refrigerator. Fold the lamb into its original shape, truss the lamb, and skewer it on the rotisserie spit, securing it with the rotisserie forks. Let the lamb rest at room temperature until the air fryer oven is ready.
3. Select Roast, set temperature to 375°F (190°C), Rotate, and set time to 2 hours. Select Start to begin preheating.
4. Once preheated, place the prepared lamb with rotisserie spit into the Vortex. Set a drip tray underneath. Roast the lamb until it reaches 190°F (88°C) in its thickest part.
5. When cooking is complete, remove the lamb shoulder using the rotisserie lift. Remove the lamb shoulder from the rotisserie spit and remove the twine trussing the roast. Be careful - the spit and forks are blazing hot. Let the lamb rest for 15 minutes, then carve and serve.

Feta Stuffed Lamb Leg
Prep time: 5 minutes | Cook time: 1 hour | Serves 3

1 (2½-pound / 1.1-kg) boneless leg of lamb roast
2 teaspoons kosher salt
Feta Stuffing:
2 ounces crumbled feta cheese
1 teaspoon minced fresh rosemary
1 teaspoon minced fresh thyme
Zest of ½ lemon

1. Season the leg of lamb with the salt, then refrigerate for at least two hours, preferably overnight.
2. One hour before cooking, remove the lamb from the refrigerator. Just before heating the air fryer oven, mix the stuffing ingredients. Open up the lamb like a book, then spread the stuffing over the cut side of the lamb. Fold the roast back into its original shape. Truss the lamb, then skewer it on the rotisserie spit, securing it with the rotisserie forks. (You're going to lose a little of the stuffing when you tie down the trussing twine; that's OK.) Let the lamb rest at room temperature until the air fryer oven is ready.
3. Select Roast, set temperature to 400°F (205°C), Rotate, and set time to 1 hour. Select Start to begin preheating.
4. Once preheated, place the prepared lamb with rotisserie spit into the Vortex. Set a drip tray underneath. Roast until it reaches 130°F (54°C) in its thickest part for medium. (Cook to 115°F (46°C) for rare, 120°F (49°C) for medium-rare.)
5. When cooking is complete, remove the lamb using the rotisserie lift. Remove the lamb from the rotisserie spit and remove the twine trussing the roast. Be careful - the spit and forks are blazing hot. Let the lamb rest for 15 minutes, then carve and serve.

Teriyaki Chicken

Prep time: 5 minutes | Cook time: 1 hour 10 minutes | Serves 4

1 (4-pound / 1.8-kg) chicken
1 tablespoon kosher salt
Teriyaki Sauce:
¼ cup soy sauce
¼ cup mirin
¼ cup honey (or sugar)
¼ inch slice of ginger, smashed

1. Season the chicken with the salt, inside and out. Gently work your fingers under the skin on the breast, then rub some of the salt directly onto the breast meat. Fold the wingtips under the wings and truss the chicken. Skewer the chicken on the rotisserie spit, securing it with the rotisserie forks. Let the chicken rest at room temperature.
2. Select Roast, set temperature to 400°F (205°C), Rotate, and set time to 1 hour. Select Start to begin preheating.
3. While the air fryer oven is preheating, combine the soy sauce, mirin, honey, and ginger in a saucepan. Bring to a boil over medium-high heat, stirring often, then decrease the heat to low and simmer for 10 minutes, until the liquid is reduced by half.
4. Once preheated, place the prepared chicken with rotisserie spit into the Vortex. Set a drip tray underneath. Roast until the chicken reaches 160°F (70°C) in the thickest part of the breast. During the last 15 minutes of cooking, brush the chicken with the teriyaki sauce every five minutes.
5. When cooking is complete, remove the chicken using the rotisserie lift. Remove the chicken from the rotisserie spit and transfer to a platter. Be careful - the spit and forks are blazing hot. Remove the trussing twine, then brush the chicken one last time with the teriyaki sauce. Let the chicken rest for 15 minutes, then carve and serve, passing any remaining teriyaki sauce at the table.

Chicken with Brown Sugar Brine

Prep time: 5 minutes | Cook time: 1 hour | Serves 4

1 (4-pound / 1.8-kg) chicken
Brine:
2 quarts cold water
½ cup table salt (or 1 cup kosher salt)
¼ cup brown sugar
½ head of garlic (6 to 8 cloves), skin on, crushed
3 bay leaves, crumbled
1 tablespoon peppercorns, crushed or coarsely ground

1. Combine the brine ingredients in large container, and stir until the salt and sugar dissolve. Submerge the chicken in the brine. Store in the refrigerator for at least one hour, preferably four hours, no longer than eight hours.
2. Remove the chicken from the brine and pat dry with paper towels, picking off any pieces of bay leaves or garlic that stick to the chicken. Fold the wingtips underneath the wings, then truss the chicken. Skewer the chicken on the rotisserie spit, securing it with the rotisserie forks. Let the chicken rest at room temperature.
3. Select Roast, set temperature to 400°F (205°C), Rotate, and set time to 1 hour. Select Start to begin preheating.
4. Once preheated, place the prepared chicken with rotisserie spit into the Vortex. Set a drip tray underneath. Roast until the chicken reaches 160°F (70°C) in the thickest part of the breast.
5. When cooking is complete, remove the chicken using the rotisserie lift. Remove the chicken from the rotisserie spit and remove the twine trussing the chicken. Be careful - the spit and forks are blazing hot. Let the chicken rest for 15 minutes, then carve and serve.

Turkey with Thyme-Sage Brine

Prep time: 5 minutes | Cook time: 2½ hours | Serves 12 to 14

1 (12- to 14-pound / 5.4- to 6.3-kg) turkey
Dry Brine:
¼ cup kosher salt
1 tablespoon minced fresh sage
1 tablespoon minced fresh thyme
1 teaspoon fresh ground black pepper
Fist sized chunk of smoking wood (or 1 cup wood chips)

1. Mix the dry brine ingredients in a small bowl. Sprinkle the turkey with the dry brine, inside and out. Gently work your fingers under the skin on the breast, then rub some of the dry brine directly onto the breast meat. Refrigerate at least overnight, preferably two to three days. If dry brining more than a day in advance, cover the turkey with plastic wrap until the night before cooking, then remove the plastic wrap to let the skin dry out overnight.
2. Two hours before cooking, remove the turkey from the refrigerator. Fold the wingtips underneath the wings, then truss the turkey. Skewer the turkey on the rotisserie spit, securing it with the rotisserie forks. Let the turkey rest at room temperature. Submerge the smoking wood in water and let it soak until the air fryer oven is ready.
3. Select Roast, set temperature to 375°F (190°C), Rotate, and set time to 2½ hours. Select Start to begin preheating.
4. Once preheated, place the prepared turkey with rotisserie spit into the Vortex. Set a drip tray underneath. Roast until the turkey reaches 155°F (68°C) in the thickest part of the breast.
5. When cooking is complete, remove the turkey using the rotisserie lift. Remove the turkey from the rotisserie spit and remove the twine trussing the turkey. Be very careful - the spit and forks are blazing hot. Let the turkey rest for 15 to 30 minutes, then carve and serve.

Dried Fruit Stuffed Pork Loin

Prep time: 10 minutes | Cook time: 1 hour | Serves 4

2 (2-pound / 907-g) boneless pork loin roasts
Apple Cider Brine:
2 quarts apple cider
1 quart water
½ cup table salt
Dried Fruit Stuffing:
2 cups mixed dried fruit, chopped (apples, apricots, cranberries and raisins)
1 teaspoon fresh ground black pepper
½ teaspoon dried ginger

1. Combine the brine ingredients in a large container and stir until the salt and sugar dissolve. Roll cut the pork roasts to open them up like a book. Set a roast with the fat cap facing down. Make a cut length of the roast, one third of the way from the bottom, which goes almost all the way to the other side of the roast but not through. Open the roast up like a book along that cut, then make another cut halfway up the opened part of the roast, almost all the way to the other side, and open up the roast again. Submerge the pork roasts in the brine. Store in the refrigerator for one to four hours.
2. One hour before cooking, remove the pork from the brine and pat dry with paper towels. Open up the pork with the cut side facing up, and sprinkle evenly with the chopped fruit, ginger, and pepper. Carefully roll the pork back into a cylinder, then truss each roast at the edges to hold the cylinder shape. Truss the roasts together with the fat caps facing out, then skewer on the rotisserie spit, running the spit between the roasts and securing them with the rotisserie forks. Let the pork rest at room temperature.
3. Select Roast, set temperature to 400°F (205°C), Rotate, and set time to 1 hour. Select Start to begin preheating.
4. Once preheated, place the prepared pork with rotisserie spit into the Vortex. Set a drip tray underneath. Roast until it reaches 135°F (57°C) in its thickest part.
5. When cooking is complete, remove the pork using the rotisserie lift. Remove the pork from the rotisserie spit and remove the twine trussing the roast. Be careful - the spit and forks are blazing hot. Let the pork rest for 15 minutes, then slice into ½ inch thick rounds and serve.

Bacon-Wrapped Sirloin Roast

Prep time: 5 minutes | Cook time: 1 hour | Serves 4

1 (4-pound / 1.8-kg) sirloin roast
1 tablespoon kosher salt
4 slices bacon

1. Season the sirloin roast with the salt, then refrigerate for at least two hours, preferably overnight.
2. One hour before cooking, remove the sirloin roast from the refrigerator. Cut the butcher's twine and lay the strings on a platter, spaced where you want to tie the sirloin roast. Put two slices of bacon on top of the string, with a gap between them. Put the sirloin roast on top of the bacon, then lay the last two pieces of bacon on top of the sirloin roast. Tie the twine to truss the sirloin roast and the bacon. Trim off any loose ends of bacon so they don't burn in the air fryer oven. Skewer the sirloin roast on the rotisserie spit, securing it with the rotisserie forks. Let the beef rest at room temperature until the air fryer oven is ready.
3. Select Roast, set temperature to 400°F (205°C), Rotate, and set time to 1 hour. Select Start to begin preheating.
4. Once preheated, place the prepared sirloin roast with rotisserie spit into the Vortex. Set a drip tray underneath. Roast until it reaches 120°F (49°C) in its thickest part for medium-rare. (Cook to 115°F (46°C) for rare, 130°F (54°C) for medium.)
5. When cooking is complete, remove the sirloin roast using the rotisserie lift. Remove the sirloin roast from the rotisserie spit and remove the twine trussing the roast, leaving as much bacon behind as possible. Be careful - the spit and forks are blazing hot. Let the beef rest for 15 minutes, then carve into thin slices and serve.

Chapter 14
Appetizers and Snacks

Sausage and Onion Rolls with Mustard
Prep time: 15 minutes | Cook time: 15 minutes | Serves 12

1 pound (454 g) bulk breakfast sausage
½ cup finely chopped onion
½ cup fresh bread crumbs
½ teaspoon dried mustard
½ teaspoon dried sage
¼ teaspoon cayenne pepper
1 large egg, beaten
1 garlic clove, minced
2 sheets (1 package) frozen puff pastry, thawed
All-purpose flour, for dusting

1. In a medium bowl, break up the sausage. Stir in the onion, bread crumbs, mustard, sage, cayenne pepper, egg and garlic. Divide the sausage mixture in half and tightly wrap each half in plastic wrap. Refrigerate for 5 to 10 minutes.
2. Lay the pastry sheets on a lightly floured work surface. Using a rolling pin, lightly roll out the pastry to smooth out the dough. Take out one of the sausage packages and form the sausage into a long roll. Remove the plastic wrap and place the sausage on top of the puff pastry about 1 inch from one of the long edges. Roll the pastry around the sausage and pinch the edges of the dough together to seal. Repeat with the other pastry sheet and sausage.
3. Slice the logs into lengths about 1½ inches long. Place the sausage rolls on the sheet pan, cut-side down.
4. Select Roast. Set temperature to 350°F (180°C) and set time to 15 minutes. Press Start to begin preheating.
5. Once the unit has preheated, place the pan into the Vortex.
6. After 7 or 8 minutes, rotate the pan and continue cooking.
7. When cooking is complete, the rolls will be golden brown and sizzling. Remove the pan from the Vortex and let cool for 5 minutes.

Parmesan Cauliflower with Turmeric
Prep time: 15 minutes | Cook time: 15 minutes | Makes 5 cups

8 cups small cauliflower florets (about 1¼ pounds / 567 g)
3 tablespoons olive oil
1 teaspoon garlic powder
½ teaspoon salt
½ teaspoon turmeric
¼ cup shredded Parmesan cheese

1. In a bowl, combine the cauliflower florets, olive oil, garlic powder, salt, and turmeric and toss to coat. Transfer to the perforated pan.
2. Select Air Fry. Set temperature to 390°F (199°C) and set time to 15 minutes. Press Start to begin preheating.
3. Once preheated, place the pan into the Vortex.
4. After 5 minutes, remove from the Vortex and stir the cauliflower florets. Return the pan to the Vortex and continue cooking.
5. After 6 minutes, remove from the Vortex and stir the cauliflower. Return the pan to the Vortex and continue cooking for 4 minutes. The cauliflower florets should be crisp-tender.
6. When cooking is complete, remove from the Vortex to a plate. Sprinkle with the shredded Parmesan cheese and toss well. Serve warm.

Roasted Mushrooms with Garlic
Prep time: 5 minutes | Cook time: 27 minutes | Serves 4

16 garlic cloves, peeled
2 teaspoons olive oil, divided
16 button mushrooms
½ teaspoon dried marjoram
⅛ teaspoon freshly ground black pepper
1 tablespoon white wine

1. Place the garlic cloves on the sheet pan and drizzle with 1 teaspoon of the olive oil. Toss to coat well.
2. Select Roast. Set temperature to 350°F (180°C) and set time to 12 minutes. Press Start to begin preheating.
3. Once the unit has preheated, place the pan into the Vortex.
4. When cooking is complete, remove the pan from the Vortex. Stir in the mushrooms, marjoram and pepper. Drizzle with the remaining 1 teaspoon of the olive oil and the white wine. Toss to coat well. Return the pan to the Vortex.
5. Select Roast. Set temperature to 350°F (180°C) and set time to 15 minutes. place the pan into the Vortex.
6. Once done, the mushrooms and garlic cloves will be softened. Remove the pan from the Vortex.
7. Serve warm.

Cheddar Mushrooms with Pimientos
Prep time: 10 minutes | Cook time: 18 minutes | Serves 12

24 medium raw white button mushrooms, rinsed and drained
4 ounces (113 g) shredded extra-sharp Cheddar cheese
2 ounces (57 g) cream cheese, at room temperature
1 ounce (28 g) chopped jarred pimientos
2 tablespoons grated onion
⅛ teaspoon smoked paprika
⅛ teaspoon hot sauce
2 tablespoons butter, melted, divided
⅓ cup panko bread crumbs
2 tablespoons grated Parmesan cheese

1. Gently pull out the stems of the mushrooms and discard. Set aside.
2. In a medium bowl, stir together the Cheddar cheese, cream cheese, pimientos, onion, paprika and hot sauce.
3. Brush the sheet pan with 1 tablespoon of the melted butter. Arrange the mushrooms evenly on the pan, hollow-side up.
4. Place the cheese mixture into a large heavy plastic bag and cut off the end. Fill the mushrooms with the cheese mixture.
5. In a small bowl, whisk together the remaining 1 tablespoon of the melted butter, bread crumbs and Parmesan cheese. Sprinkle the panko mixture over each mushroom.
6. Select Roast. Set temperature to 350°F (180°C) and set time to 18 minutes. Press Start to begin preheating.
7. When the unit has preheated, place the pan into the Vortex.
8. After about 9 minutes, rotate the pan and continue cooking.
9. When cooking is complete, let the stuffed mushrooms rest for 2 minutes before serving.

Jalapeño Poppers with Cheddar
Prep time: 10 minutes | Cook time: 15 minutes | Serves 8

6 ounces (170 g) cream cheese, at room temperature
4 ounces (113 g) shredded Cheddar cheese
1 teaspoon chili powder
12 large jalapeño peppers, deseeded and sliced in half lengthwise
2 slices cooked bacon, chopped
¼ cup panko bread crumbs
1 tablespoon butter, melted

1. In a medium bowl, whisk together the cream cheese, Cheddar cheese and chili powder. Spoon the cheese mixture into the jalapeño halves and arrange them on the sheet pan.
2. In a small bowl, stir together the bacon, bread crumbs and butter. Sprinkle the mixture over the jalapeño halves.
3. Select Roast. Set temperature to 375°F (190°C) and set time to 15 minutes. Press Start to begin preheating.
4. When the unit has preheated, place the pan into the Vortex.
5. After 7 or 8 minutes, rotate the pan and continue cooking until the peppers are softened, the filling is bubbling and the bread crumbs are browned.
6. When cooking is complete, remove the pan from the Vortex. Let the poppers cool for 5 minutes before serving.

Green Chiles and Cheese Nachos
Prep time: 10 minutes | Cook time: 10 minutes | Serves 6

8 ounces (227 g) tortilla chips
3 cups shredded Monterey Jack cheese, divided
2 (7-ounce / 198-g) cans chopped green chiles, drained
1 (8-ounce / 227-g) can tomato sauce
¼ teaspoon dried oregano
¼ teaspoon granulated garlic
¼ teaspoon freshly ground black pepper
Pinch cinnamon
Pinch cayenne pepper

1. Arrange the tortilla chips close together in a single layer on the sheet pan. Sprinkle 1½ cups of the cheese over the chips. Arrange the green chiles over the cheese as evenly as possible. Top with the remaining 1½ cups of the cheese.
2. Select Roast. Set temperature to 375°F (190°C) and set time to 10 minutes. Press Start to begin preheating.
3. When the unit has preheated, place the pan into the Vortex.
4. After 5 minutes, rotate the pan and continue cooking.
5. Meanwhile, stir together the remaining ingredients in a bowl.
6. When cooking is complete, the cheese will be melted and starting to crisp around the edges of the pan. Remove the pan from the Vortex. Drizzle the sauce over the nachos and serve warm.

Pepperoni Pizza Bites with Marinara
Prep time: 5 minutes | Cook time: 12 minutes | Serves 8

1 cup finely shredded Mozzarella cheese
½ cup chopped pepperoni
¼ cup Marinara sauce
1 (8-ounce / 227-g) can crescent roll dough
All-purpose flour, for dusting

1. In a small bowl, stir together the cheese, pepperoni and Marinara sauce.
2. Lay the dough on a lightly floured work surface. Separate it into 4 rectangles. Firmly pinch the perforations together and pat the dough pieces flat.
3. Divide the cheese mixture evenly between the rectangles and spread it out over the dough, leaving a ¼-inch border. Roll a rectangle up tightly, starting with the short end. Pinch the edge down to seal the roll. Repeat with the remaining rolls.
4. Slice the rolls into 4 or 5 even slices. Place the slices on the sheet pan, leaving a few inches between each slice.
5. Select Roast. Set temperature to 350°F (180°C) and set time to 12 minutes. Press Start to begin preheating.
6. Once the unit has preheated, place the pan into the Vortex.
7. After 6 minutes, rotate the pan and continue cooking.
8. When cooking is complete, the rolls will be golden brown with crisp edges. Remove the pan from the Vortex. Serve hot.

Cheddar Baked Potatoes with Chives
Prep time: 5 minutes | Cook time: 20 minutes | Serves 6

12 small red potatoes
1 teaspoon kosher salt, divided
1 tablespoon extra-virgin olive oil
¼ cup grated sharp Cheddar cheese
¼ cup sour cream
2 tablespoons chopped chives
2 tablespoons grated Parmesan cheese

1. Add the potatoes to a large bowl. Sprinkle with the ½ teaspoon of the salt and drizzle with the olive oil. Toss to coat. Place the potatoes in the sheet pan.
2. Select Roast. Set temperature to 375°F (190°C) and set time to 15 minutes. Press Start to begin preheating.
3. When the unit has preheated, place the pan into the Vortex.
4. After 10 minutes, rotate the pan and continue cooking.
5. When cooking is complete, remove the pan and let the potatoes rest for 5 minutes. Halve the potatoes lengthwise. Using a spoon, scoop the flesh into a bowl, leaving a thin shell of skin. Arrange the potato halves on the sheet pan.
6. Mash the potato flesh until smooth. Stir in the remaining ½ teaspoon of the salt, Cheddar cheese, sour cream and chives. Transfer the filling into a pastry bag with one corner snipped off. Pipe the filling into the potato shells, mounding up slightly. Sprinkle with the Parmesan cheese.
7. Select Roast. Set temperature to 375°F (190°C) and set time to 5 minutes. Place the pan into the Vortex.
8. When cooking is complete, the tops should be browning slightly. Remove the pan from the Vortex and let the potatoes cool slightly before serving.

Honey Roasted Grapes with Basil
Prep time: 5 minutes | Cook time: 10 minutes | Serves 6

2 cups seedless red grapes, rinsed and patted dry
1 tablespoon apple cider vinegar
1 tablespoon honey
1 cup low-fat Greek yogurt
2 tablespoons 2 percent milk
2 tablespoons minced fresh basil

1. Spread the red grapes in the perforated pan and drizzle with the cider vinegar and honey. Lightly toss to coat.
2. Select Roast. Set temperature to 380°F (193°C) and set time to 10 minutes. Press Start to begin preheating.
3. Once the unit has preheated, place the pan into the Vortex.
4. When cooking is complete, the grapes will be wilted but still soft. Remove the pan from the Vortex.
5. In a medium bowl, whisk together the yogurt and milk. Gently fold in the grapes and basil.
6. Serve immediately.

Lemon-Pepper Chicken Wings
Prep time: 5 minutes | Cook time: 24 minutes | Serves 10

2 pounds (907 g) chicken wings
4½ teaspoons salt-free lemon pepper seasoning
1½ teaspoons baking powder
1½ teaspoons kosher salt

1. In a large bowl, toss together all the ingredients until well coated. Place the wings on the sheet pan, making sure they don't crowd each other too much.
2. Select Air Fry. Set temperature to 375°F (190°C) and set time to 24 minutes. Press Start to begin preheating.
3. Once preheated, slide the pan into the Vortex.
4. After 12 minutes, remove the pan from the Vortex. Use tongs to turn the wings over. Rotate the pan and return the pan to the Vortex to continue cooking.
5. When cooking is complete, the wings should be dark golden brown and a bit charred in places. Remove the pan from the Vortex and let rest for 5 minutes before serving.

Cheddar Sausage Balls
Prep time: 10 minutes | Cook time: 10 minutes | Serves 8

12 ounces (340 g) mild ground sausage
1½ cups baking mix
1 cup shredded mild Cheddar cheese
3 ounces (85 g) cream cheese, at room temperature
1 to 2 tablespoons olive oil

1. Line the perforated pan with parchment paper. Set aside.
2. Mix together the ground sausage, baking mix, Cheddar cheese, and cream cheese in a large bowl and stir to incorporate.
3. Divide the sausage mixture into 16 equal portions and roll them into 1-inch balls with your hands. Arrange the sausage balls on the parchment, leaving space between each ball. Brush the sausage balls with the olive oil.
4. Select Air Fry. Set temperature to 325°F (163°C) and set time to 10 minutes. Press Start to begin preheating.
5. Once preheated, place the pan into the Vortex. Flip the balls halfway through the cooking time.
6. When cooking is complete, the balls should be firm and lightly browned on both sides. Remove from the Vortex to a plate and serve warm.

Sugar Roasted Walnuts

Prep time: 5 minutes | Cook time: 15 minutes | Makes 4 cups

1 pound (454 g) walnut halves and pieces
½ cup granulated sugar
3 tablespoons vegetable oil
1 teaspoon cayenne pepper
½ teaspoon fine salt

1. Soak the walnuts in a large bowl with boiling water for a minute or two. Drain the walnuts. Stir in the sugar, oil and cayenne pepper to coat well. Spread the walnuts in a single layer on the sheet pan.
2. Select Roast. Set temperature to 325°F (163°C) and set time to 15 minutes. Press Start to begin preheating.
3. When the unit has preheated, place the pan into the Vortex.
4. After 7 or 8 minutes, remove the pan from the Vortex. Stir the nuts. Return the pan to the Vortex and continue cooking, check frequently.
5. When cooking is complete, the walnuts should be dark golden brown. Remove the pan from the Vortex. Sprinkle the nuts with the salt and let cool. Serve.

Balsamic Prosciutto-Wrapped Pears

Prep time: 12 minutes | Cook time: 6 minutes | Serves 8

2 large, ripe Anjou pears
4 thin slices Parma prosciutto
2 teaspoons aged balsamic vinegar

1. Peel the pears. Slice into 8 wedges and cut out the core from each wedge.
2. Cut the prosciutto into 8 long strips. Wrap each pear wedge with a strip of prosciutto. Place the wrapped pears in the sheet pan.
3. Select Broil. Set temperature to 400°F (205°C) and set time to 6 minutes. Press Start to begin preheating.
4. When the unit has preheated, place the pan into the Vortex.
5. After 2 or 3 minutes, check the pears. The pears should be turned over if the prosciutto is beginning to crisp up and brown. Return the pan to the Vortex and continue cooking.
6. When cooking is complete, remove the pan from the Vortex. Drizzle the pears with the balsamic vinegar and serve warm.

Breaded Zucchini Tots

Prep time: 15 minutes | Cook time: 6 minutes | Serves 8

2 medium zucchini (about 12 ounces / 340 g) shredded
1 large egg, whisked
½ cup grated pecorino romano cheese
½ cup panko bread crumbs
¼ teaspoon black pepper
1 clove garlic, minced
Cooking spray

1. Using your hands, squeeze out as much liquid from the zucchini as possible. In a large bowl, mix the zucchini with the remaining ingredients except the oil until well incorporated.
2. Make the zucchini tots: Use a spoon or cookie scoop to place tablespoonfuls of the zucchini mixture onto a lightly floured cutting board and form into 1-inch logs.
3. Spritz the perforated pan with cooking spray. Place the zucchini tots in the pan.
4. Select Air Fry. Set temperature to 375°F (190°C) and set time to 6 minutes. Press Start to begin preheating.
5. Once preheated, place the pan into the Vortex.
6. When cooking is complete, the tots should be golden brown. Remove from the Vortex to a serving plate and serve warm.

Ginger Shrimp with Sesame Seeds
Prep time: 15 minutes | Cook time: 8 minutes | Serves 4 to 6

½ pound (227 g) raw shrimp, peeled and deveined
1 egg, beaten
2 scallions, chopped, plus more for garnish
2 tablespoons chopped fresh cilantro
2 teaspoons grated fresh ginger
1 to 2 teaspoons sriracha sauce
1 teaspoon soy sauce
½ teaspoon toasted sesame oil
6 slices thinly sliced white sandwich bread
½ cup sesame seeds
Cooking spray
Thai chili sauce, for serving

1. In a food processor, add the shrimp, egg, scallions, cilantro, ginger, sriracha sauce, soy sauce and sesame oil, and pulse until chopped finely. You'll need to stop the food processor occasionally to scrape down the sides. Transfer the shrimp mixture to a bowl.
2. On a clean work surface, cut the crusts off the sandwich bread. Using a brush, generously brush one side of each slice of bread with shrimp mixture.
3. Place the sesame seeds on a plate. Press bread slices, shrimp-side down, into sesame seeds to coat evenly. Cut each slice diagonally into quarters.
4. Spritz the perforated pan with cooking spray. Spread the coated slices in a single layer in the perforated pan.
5. Select Air Fry. Set temperature to 400°F (205°C) and set time to 8 minutes. Press Start to begin preheating.
6. Once preheated, place the pan into the Vortex. Flip the bread slices halfway through.
7. When cooking is complete, they should be golden and crispy. Remove from the Vortex to a plate and let cool for 5 minutes. Top with the chopped scallions and serve warm with Thai chili sauce.

Tuna Melts with Mayo
Prep time: 10 minutes | Cook time: 6 minutes | Serves 6

2 (5- to 6-ounce / 142- to 170-g) cans oil-packed tuna, drained
1 large scallion, chopped
1 small stalk celery, chopped
⅓ cup mayonnaise
1 tablespoon chopped fresh dill
1 tablespoon capers, drained
¼ teaspoon celery salt
12 slices cocktail rye bread
2 tablespoons butter, melted
6 slices sharp Cheddar cheese

1. In a medium bowl, stir together the tuna, scallion, celery, mayonnaise, dill, capers and celery salt.
2. Brush one side of the bread slices with the butter. Arrange the bread slices on the sheet pan, buttered-side down. Scoop a heaping tablespoon of the tuna mixture on each slice of bread, spreading it out evenly to the edges.
3. Cut the cheese slices to fit the dimensions of the bread and place a cheese slice on each piece.
4. Select Roast. Set temperature to 375°F (190°C) and set time to 6 minutes. Press Start to begin preheating.
5. Once the unit has preheated, place the pan into the Vortex.
6. After 4 minutes, remove the pan from the Vortex and check the tuna melts. The tuna melts are done when the cheese has melted and the tuna is heated through. If needed, continue cooking.
7. When cooking is complete, remove the pan from the Vortex. Use a spatula to transfer the tuna melts to a clean work surface and slice each one in half diagonally. Serve warm.

Paprika Polenta Fries with Chili-Lime Mayo
Prep time: 10 minutes | Cook time: 28 minutes | Serves 4

Polenta Fries:
2 teaspoons vegetable or olive oil
¼ teaspoon paprika
1 pound (454 g) prepared polenta, cut into 3-inch × ½-inch strips
Salt and freshly ground black pepper, to taste
Chili-Lime Mayo:
½ cup mayonnaise
1 teaspoon chili powder
1 teaspoon chopped fresh cilantro
¼ teaspoon ground cumin
Juice of ½ lime
Salt and freshly ground black pepper, to taste

1. Mix the oil and paprika in a bowl. Add the polenta strips and toss until evenly coated. Transfer the polenta strips to the perforated pan.
2. Select Air Fry. Set temperature to 400°F (205°C) and set time to 28 minutes. Press Start to begin preheating.
3. Once preheated, place the pan into the Vortex. Stir the polenta strips halfway through the cooking time.
4. Meanwhile, whisk together all the ingredients for the chili-lime mayo in a small bowl.
5. When cooking is complete, remove the polenta fries from the Vortex to a plate. Season as desired with salt and pepper. Serve alongside the chili-lime mayo as a dipping sauce.

Lemon Ricotta with Capers
Prep time: 10 minutes | Cook time: 8 minutes | Serves 4 to 6

1½ cups whole milk ricotta cheese
2 tablespoons extra-virgin olive oil
2 tablespoons capers, rinsed
Zest of 1 lemon, plus more for garnish
1 teaspoon finely chopped fresh rosemary
Pinch crushed red pepper flakes
Salt and freshly ground black pepper, to taste
1 tablespoon grated Parmesan cheese

1. In a mixing bowl, stir together the ricotta cheese, olive oil, capers, lemon zest, rosemary, red pepper flakes, salt, and pepper until well combined.
2. Spread the mixture evenly in a baking dish.
3. Select Air Fry. Set temperature to 380°F (193°C) and set time to 8 minutes. Press Start to begin preheating.
4. Once preheated, place the baking dish in the Vortex.
5. When cooking is complete, the top should be nicely browned. Remove from the Vortex and top with a sprinkle of grated Parmesan cheese. Garnish with the lemon zest and serve warm.

Fried Pickle Spears with Chili
Prep time: 5 minutes | Cook time: 15 minutes | Serves 6

2 jars sweet and sour pickle spears, patted dry
2 medium-sized eggs
⅓ cup milk
1 teaspoon garlic powder
1 teaspoon sea salt
½ teaspoon shallot powder
⅓ teaspoon chili powder
⅓ cup all-purpose flour
Cooking spray

1. Spritz the perforated pan with cooking spray.
2. In a bowl, beat together the eggs with milk. In another bowl, combine garlic powder, sea salt, shallot powder, chili powder and all-purpose flour until well blended.
3. One by one, roll the pickle spears in the powder mixture, then dredge them in the egg mixture. Dip them in the powder mixture a second time for additional coating.
4. Place the coated pickles in the perforated pan.
5. Select Air Fry. Set temperature to 385°F (196°C) and set time to 15 minutes. Press Start to begin preheating.
6. Once preheated, place the pan into the Vortex. Stir the pickles halfway through the cooking time.
7. When cooking is complete, they should be golden and crispy. Transfer to a plate and let cool for 5 minutes before serving.

Honey Snack Mix
Prep time: 5 minutes | Cook time: 10 minutes | Makes about 10 cups

3 tablespoons butter, melted
½ cup honey
1 teaspoon salt
2 cups granola
2 cups sesame sticks
2 cups crispy corn puff cereal
2 cups mini pretzel crisps
1 cup cashews
1 cup pepitas
1 cup dried cherries

1. In a small mixing bowl, mix together the butter, honey, and salt until well incorporated.
2. In a large bowl, combine the granola, sesame sticks, corn puff cereal and pretzel crisps, cashews, and pepitas. Drizzle with the butter mixture and toss until evenly coated. Transfer the snack mix to a sheet pan.
3. Select Air Fry. Set temperature to 370°F (188°C) and set time to 10 minutes. Press Start to begin preheating.
4. Once preheated, slide the pan into the Vortex. Stir the snack mix halfway through the cooking time.
5. When cooking is complete, they should be lightly toasted. Remove from the Vortex and allow to cool completely. Scatter with the dried cherries and mix well. Serve immediately.

Parmesan Snack Mix

Prep time: 5 minutes | Cook time: 6 minutes | Makes 6 cups

2 cups oyster crackers
2 cups Chex rice
1 cup sesame sticks
⅔ cup finely grated Parmesan cheese
8 tablespoons unsalted butter, melted
1½ teaspoons granulated garlic
½ teaspoon kosher salt

1. Toss together all the ingredients in a large bowl until well coated. Spread the mixture on the sheet pan in an even layer.
2. Select Roast. Set temperature to 350°F (180°C) and set time to 6 minutes. Press Start to begin preheating.
3. When the unit has preheated, place the pan into the Vortex.
4. After 3 minutes, remove the pan and stir the mixture. Return the pan to the Vortex and continue cooking.
5. When cooking is complete, the mixture should be lightly browned and fragrant. Let cool before serving.

Paprika Potato Chips

Prep time: 5 minutes | Cook time: 22 minutes | Serves 3

2 medium potatoes, preferably Yukon Gold, scrubbed
Cooking spray
2 teaspoons olive oil
½ teaspoon garlic granules
¼ teaspoon paprika
¼ teaspoon plus ⅛ teaspoon sea salt
¼ teaspoon freshly ground black pepper
Ketchup or hot sauce, for serving

1. Spritz the perforated pan with cooking spray.
2. On a flat work surface, cut the potatoes into ¼-inch-thick slices. Transfer the potato slices to a medium bowl, along with the olive oil, garlic granules, paprika, salt, and pepper and toss to coat well. Transfer the potato slices to the perforated pan.
3. Select Air Fry. Set temperature to 392°F (200°C) and set time to 22 minutes. Press Start to begin preheating.
4. Once preheated, place the pan into the Vortex. Stir the potato slices twice during the cooking process.
5. When cooking is complete, the potato chips should be tender and nicely browned. Remove from the Vortex and serve alongside the ketchup for dipping.

Hush Puppies with Jalapeño

Prep time: 45 minutes | Cook time: 10 minutes | Serves 12

1 cup self-rising yellow cornmeal
½ cup all-purpose flour
1 teaspoon sugar
1 teaspoon salt
1 teaspoon freshly ground black pepper
1 large egg
⅓ cup canned creamed corn
1 cup minced onion
2 teaspoons minced jalapeño pepper
2 tablespoons olive oil, divided

1. Thoroughly combine the cornmeal, flour, sugar, salt, and pepper in a large bowl.
2. Whisk together the egg and corn in a small bowl. Pour the egg mixture into the bowl of cornmeal mixture and stir to combine. Stir in the minced onion and jalapeño. Cover the bowl with plastic wrap and place in the refrigerator for 30 minutes.
3. Line the perforated pan with parchment paper and lightly brush it with 1 tablespoon of olive oil.
4. Scoop out the cornmeal mixture and form into 24 balls, about 1 inch.
5. Arrange the balls on the parchment, leaving space between each ball.
6. Select Air Fry. Set temperature to 375°F (190°C) and set time to 10 minutes. Press Start to begin preheating.
7. Once preheated, place the pan into the Vortex.
8. After 5 minutes, remove the pan from the Vortex. Flip the balls and brush them with the remaining 1 tablespoon of olive oil. Return to the Vortex and continue cooking for 5 minutes until golden brown.
9. When cooking is complete, remove the balls (hush puppies) from the Vortex and serve on a plate.

Cinnamon Apple Chips

Prep time: 10 minutes | Cook time: 10 minutes | Serves 4

2 apples, cored and cut into thin slices
2 heaped teaspoons ground cinnamon
Cooking spray

1. Spritz the perforated pan with cooking spray.
2. In a medium bowl, sprinkle the apple slices with the cinnamon. Toss until evenly coated. Spread the coated apple slices on the pan in a single layer.
3. Select Air Fry. Set temperature to 350°F (180°C) and set time to 10 minutes. Press Start to begin preheating.
4. Once preheated, place the pan into the Vortex.
5. After 5 minutes, remove the pan from the Vortex. Stir the apple slices and return the pan to the Vortex to continue cooking.
6. When cooking is complete, the slices should be until crispy Remove the pan from the Vortex and let rest for 5 minutes before serving.

Avocado Chips with Lime
Prep time: 15 minutes | Cook time: 10 minutes | Serves 4

1 egg
1 tablespoon lime juice
⅛ teaspoon hot sauce
2 tablespoons flour
¾ cup panko bread crumbs
¼ cup cornmeal
¼ teaspoon salt
1 large avocado, pitted, peeled, and cut into ½-inch slices
Cooking spray

1. Whisk together the egg, lime juice, and hot sauce in a small bowl.
2. On a sheet of wax paper, place the flour. In a separate sheet of wax paper, combine the bread crumbs, cornmeal, and salt.
3. Dredge the avocado slices one at a time in the flour, then in the egg mixture, finally roll them in the bread crumb mixture to coat well.
4. Place the breaded avocado slices in the perforated pan and mist them with cooking spray.
5. Select Air Fry. Set temperature to 390°F (199°C) and set time to 10 minutes. Press Start to begin preheating.
6. Once preheated, place the pan into the Vortex.
7. When cooking is complete, the slices should be nicely browned and crispy. Transfer the avocado slices to a plate and serve.

Ginger Apple Wedges
Prep time: 10 minutes | Cook time: 12 minutes | Serves 4

2 medium apples, cored and sliced into ¼-inch wedges
1 teaspoon canola oil
2 teaspoons peeled and grated fresh ginger
½ teaspoon ground cinnamon
½ cup low-fat Greek vanilla yogurt, for serving

1. In a large bowl, toss the apple wedges with the canola oil, ginger, and cinnamon until evenly coated. Put the apple wedges in the perforated pan.
2. Select Air Fry. Set temperature to 360°F (182°C) and set time to 12 minutes. Press Start to begin preheating.
3. Once preheated, place the pan into the Vortex.
4. When cooking is complete, the apple wedges should be crisp-tender. Remove the apple wedges from the Vortex and serve drizzled with the yogurt.

Cumin Tortilla Chips
Prep time: 5 minutes | Cook time: 5 minutes | Serves 4

½ teaspoon ground cumin
½ teaspoon paprika
½ teaspoon chili powder
½ teaspoon salt
Pinch cayenne pepper
8 (6-inch) corn tortillas, each cut into 6 wedges
Cooking spray

1. Lightly spritz the perforated pan with cooking spray.
2. Stir together the cumin, paprika, chili powder, salt, and pepper in a small bowl.
3. Place the tortilla wedges in the perforated pan in a single layer. Lightly mist them with cooking spray. Sprinkle the seasoning mixture on top of the tortilla wedges.
4. Select Air Fry. Set temperature to 375°F (190°C) and set time to 5 minutes. Press Start to begin preheating.
5. Once preheated, place the pan into the Vortex. Stir the tortilla wedges halfway through the cooking time.
6. When cooking is complete, the chips should be lightly browned and crunchy. Remove the pan from the Vortex. Let the tortilla chips cool for 5 minutes and serve.

Old Bay Fried Chicken Wings
Prep time: 10 minutes | Cook time: 13 minutes | Serves 4

2 tablespoons Old Bay seasoning
2 teaspoons baking powder
2 teaspoons salt
2 pounds (907 g) chicken wings, patted dry
Cooking spray

1. Combine the Old Bay seasoning, baking powder, and salt in a large zip-top plastic bag. Add the chicken wings, seal, and shake until the wings are thoroughly coated in the seasoning mixture.
2. Lightly spray the perforated pan with cooking spray. Lay the chicken wings in the perforated pan in a single layer and lightly mist them with cooking spray.
3. Select Air Fry. Set temperature to 400°F (205°C) and set time to 13 minutes. Press Start to begin preheating.
4. Once preheated, place the pan into the Vortex. Flip the wings halfway through the cooking time.
5. When cooking is complete, the wings should reach an internal temperature of 165°F (74°C) on a meat thermometer. Remove from the Vortex to a plate and serve hot.

Carrot Chips

Prep time: 15 minutes | Cook time: 10 minutes | Serves 4

4 to 5 medium carrots, trimmed and thinly sliced
1 tablespoon olive oil, plus more for greasing
1 teaspoon seasoned salt

1. Toss the carrot slices with 1 tablespoon of olive oil and salt in a medium bowl until thoroughly coated.
2. Grease the perforated pan with the olive oil. Place the carrot slices in the greased pan.
3. Select Air Fry. Set temperature to 390°F (199°C) and set time to 10 minutes. Press Start to begin preheating.
4. Once preheated, place the pan into the Vortex. Stir the carrot slices halfway through the cooking time.
5. When cooking is complete, the chips should be crisp-tender. Remove the pan from the Vortex and allow to cool for 5 minutes before serving.

Deviled Eggs with Mayo

Prep time: 20 minutes | Cook time: 16 minutes | Serves 12

3 cups ice
12 large eggs
½ cup mayonnaise
10 hamburger dill pickle chips, diced
¼ cup diced onion
2 teaspoons salt
2 teaspoons yellow mustard
1 teaspoon freshly ground black pepper
½ teaspoon paprika

1. Put the ice in a large bowl and set aside. Carefully place the eggs in the perforated pan.
2. Select Bake. Set temperature to 250°F (121°C) and set time to 16 minutes. Press Start to begin preheating.
3. Once preheated, place the pan into the Vortex.
4. When cooking is complete, transfer the eggs to the large bowl of ice to cool.
5. When cool enough to handle, peel the eggs. Slice them in half lengthwise and scoop out yolks into a small bowl. Stir in the mayonnaise, pickles, onion, salt, mustard, and pepper. Mash the mixture with a fork until well combined.
6. Fill each egg white half with 1 to 2 teaspoons of the egg yolk mixture.
7. Sprinkle the paprika on top and serve immediately.

Mushroom and Sausage Empanadas

Prep time: 5 minutes | Cook time: 12 minutes | Serves 4

½ pound (227 g) Kielbasa smoked sausage, chopped
4 chopped canned mushrooms
2 tablespoons chopped onion
½ teaspoon ground cumin
¼ teaspoon paprika
Salt and black pepper, to taste
½ package puff pastry dough, at room temperature
1 egg, beaten
Cooking spray

1. Combine the sausage, mushrooms, onion, cumin, paprika, salt, and pepper in a bowl and stir to mix well.
2. Make the empanadas: Place the puff pastry dough on a lightly floured surface. Cut circles into the dough with a glass. Place 1 tablespoon of the sausage mixture into the center of each pastry circle. Fold each in half and pinch the edges to seal. Using a fork, crimp the edges. Brush them with the beaten egg and mist with cooking spray.
3. Spritz the perforated pan with cooking spray. Place the empanadas in the perforated pan.
4. Select Air Fry. Set temperature to 360°F (182°C) and set time to 12 minutes. Press Start to begin preheating.
5. Once preheated, place the pan into the Vortex. Flip the empanadas halfway through the cooking time.
6. When cooking is complete, the empanadas should be golden brown. Remove the pan from the Vortex. Allow them to cool for 5 minutes and serve hot.

Cumin Fried Chickpeas

Prep time: 5 minutes | Cook time: 18 minutes | Serves 4

½ teaspoon chili powder
½ teaspoon ground cumin
¼ teaspoon cayenne pepper
¼ teaspoon salt
1 (19-ounce / 539-g) can chickpeas, drained and rinsed
Cooking spray

1. Lina the perforated pan with parchment paper and lightly spritz with cooking spray.
2. Mix the chili powder, cumin, cayenne pepper, and salt in a small bowl.
3. Place the chickpeas in a medium bowl and lightly mist with cooking spray.
4. Add the spice mixture to the chickpeas and toss until evenly coated. Transfer the chickpeas to the parchment.
5. Select Air Fry. Set temperature to 390°F (199°C) and set time to 18 minutes. Press Start to begin preheating.
6. Once preheated, place the pan into the Vortex. Stir the chickpeas twice during cooking.
7. When cooking is complete, the chickpeas should be crunchy. Remove the pan from the Vortex. Let the chickpeas cool for 5 minutes before serving.

Paprika Nut Mix
Prep time: 5 minutes | Cook time: 20 minutes | Serves 6

2 cups mixed nuts (walnuts, pecans, and almonds)
2 tablespoons egg white
2 tablespoons sugar
1 teaspoon paprika
1 teaspoon ground cinnamon
Cooking spray

1. Line the perforated pan with parchment paper and spray with cooking spray.
2. Stir together the mixed nuts, egg white, sugar, paprika, and cinnamon in a small bowl until the nuts are fully coated. Place the nuts in the perforated pan.
3. Select Roast. Set temperature to 300°F (150°C) and set time to 20 minutes. Press Start to begin preheating.
4. Once preheated, place the pan into the Vortex. Stir the nuts halfway through the cooking time.
5. When cooking is complete, remove the pan from the Vortex. Transfer the nuts to a bowl and serve warm.

Garlic Fried Edamame
Prep time: 5 minutes | Cook time: 9 minutes | Serves 4

1 (16-ounce / 454-g) bag frozen edamame in pods
2 tablespoon olive oil, divided
½ teaspoon garlic salt
½ teaspoon salt
¼ teaspoon freshly ground black pepper
½ teaspoon red pepper flakes (optional)

1. Place the edamame in a medium bowl and drizzle with 1 tablespoon of olive oil. Toss to coat well.
2. Stir together the garlic salt, salt, pepper, and red pepper flakes (if desired) in a small bowl. Pour the mixture into the bowl of edamame and toss until the edamame is fully coated.
3. Grease the perforated pan with the remaining 1 tablespoon of olive oil.
4. Place the edamame in the greased pan.
5. Select Air Fry. Set temperature to 375°F (190°C) and set time to 9 minutes. Press Start to begin preheating.
6. Once preheated, place the pan into the Vortex. Stir the edamame once halfway through the cooking time.
7. When cooking is complete, the edamame should be crisp. Remove from the Vortex to a plate and serve warm.

Nutmeg Apple Chips
Prep time: 10 minutes | Cook time: 10 minutes | Serves 4

4 medium apples (any type will work) cored and thinly sliced
¼ teaspoon nutmeg
¼ teaspoon cinnamon
Cooking spray

1. Place the apple slices in a large bowl and sprinkle the spices on top. Toss to coat.
2. Put the apple slices in the perforated pan in a single layer and spray them with cooking spray.
3. Select Air Fry. Set temperature to 360°F (182°C) and set time to 10 minutes. Press Start to begin preheating.
4. Once preheated, place the pan into the Vortex. Stir the apple slices halfway through.
5. When cooking is complete, the apple chips should be crispy. Transfer the apple chips to a paper towel-lined plate and rest for 5 minutes before serving.

Brie Pear Sandwiches
Prep time: 10 minutes | Cook time: 6 minutes | Serves 4 to 8

8 ounces (227 g) Brie
8 slices oat nut bread
1 large ripe pear, cored and cut into ½-inch-thick slices
2 tablespoons butter, melted

1. Make the sandwiches: Spread each of 4 slices of bread with ¼ of the Brie. Top the Brie with the pear slices and remaining 4 bread slices.
2. Brush the melted butter lightly on both sides of each sandwich.
3. Arrange the sandwiches in the perforated pan.
4. Select Bake. Set temperature to 360°F (182°C) and set time to 6 minutes. Press Start to begin preheating.
5. Once preheated, place the pan into the Vortex.
6. When cooking is complete, the cheese should be melted. Remove the pan from the Vortex and serve warm.

Parmesan Bruschetta with Tomato
Prep time: 5 minutes | Cook time: 3 minutes | Serves 6

4 tomatoes, diced
⅓ cup shredded fresh basil
¼ cup shredded Parmesan cheese
1 tablespoon balsamic vinegar
1 tablespoon minced garlic
1 teaspoon olive oil
1 teaspoon salt
1 teaspoon freshly ground black pepper
1 loaf French bread, cut into 1-inch-thick slices
Cooking spray

1. Mix together the tomatoes and basil in a medium bowl. Add the cheese, vinegar, garlic, olive oil, salt, and pepper and stir until well incorporated. Set aside.
2. Spritz the perforated pan with cooking spray and lay the bread slices in the pan in a single layer. Spray the slices with cooking spray.
3. Select Bake. Set temperature to 250°F (121°C) and set time to 3 minutes. Press Start to begin preheating.
4. Once preheated, place the pan into the Vortex.
5. When cooking is complete, remove from the Vortex to a plate. Top each slice with a generous spoonful of the tomato mixture and serve.

Cheddar Black Bean and Corn Salsa
Prep time: 10 minutes | Cook time: 10 minutes | Serves 4

½ (15-ounce / 425-g) can corn, drained and rinsed
½ (15-ounce / 425-g) can black beans, drained and rinsed
¼ cup chunky salsa
2 ounces (57 g) reduced-fat cream cheese, softened
¼ cup shredded reduced-fat Cheddar cheese
½ teaspoon paprika
½ teaspoon ground cumin
Salt and freshly ground black pepper, to taste

1. Combine the corn, black beans, salsa, cream cheese, Cheddar cheese, paprika, and cumin in a medium bowl. Sprinkle with salt and pepper and stir until well blended.
2. Pour the mixture into a baking dish.
3. Select Air Fry. Set temperature to 325°F (163°C) and set time to 10 minutes. Press Start to begin preheating.
4. Once preheated, place the baking dish in the Vortex.
5. When cooking is complete, the mixture should be heated through. Rest for 5 minutes and serve warm.

Italian Rice Balls with Olives
Prep time: 20 minutes | Cook time: 10 minutes | Makes 8 rice balls

1½ cups cooked sticky rice
½ teaspoon Italian seasoning blend
¾ teaspoon salt, divided
8 black olives, pitted
1 ounce (28 g) Mozzarella cheese, cut into tiny pieces (small enough to stuff into olives)
2 eggs
⅓ cup Italian bread crumbs
¾ cup panko bread crumbs
Cooking spray

1. Stuff each black olive with a piece of Mozzarella cheese.
2. In a bowl, combine the cooked sticky rice, Italian seasoning blend, and ½ teaspoon of salt and stir to mix well. Form the rice mixture into a log with your hands and divide it into 8 equal portions. Mold each portion around a black olive and roll into a ball.
3. Transfer to the freezer to chill for 10 to 15 minutes until firm.
4. In a shallow dish, place the Italian bread crumbs. In a separate shallow dish, whisk the eggs. In a third shallow dish, combine the panko bread crumbs and remaining salt.
5. One by one, roll the rice balls in the Italian bread crumbs, then dip in the whisked eggs, finally coat them with the panko bread crumbs.
6. Arrange the rice balls in the perforated pan and spritz both sides with cooking spray.
7. Select Air Fry. Set temperature to 390°F (199°C) and set time to 10 minutes. Press Start to begin preheating.
8. Once preheated, place the pan into the Vortex. Flip the balls halfway through the cooking time.
9. When cooking is complete, the rice balls should be golden brown. Remove from the Vortex and serve warm.

Buttermilk-Marinated Chicken Wings
Prep time: 20 minutes | Cook time: 18 minutes | Serves 4

2 pounds (907 g) chicken wings
Cooking spray
Marinade:
1 cup buttermilk
½ teaspoon salt
½ teaspoon black pepper
Coating:
1 cup flour
1 cup panko bread crumbs
2 tablespoons poultry seasoning
2 teaspoons salt

1. Whisk together all the ingredients for the marinade in a large bowl.
2. Add the chicken wings to the marinade and toss well. Transfer to the refrigerator to marinate for at least an hour.
3. Spritz the perforated pan with cooking spray. Set aside.
4. Thoroughly combine all the ingredients for the coating in a shallow bowl.
5. Remove the chicken wings from the marinade and shake off any excess. Roll them in the coating mixture.
6. Place the chicken wings in the perforated pan in a single layer. Mist the wings with cooking spray.
7. Select Air Fry. Set temperature to 360°F (182°C) and set time to 18 minutes. Press Start to begin preheating.
8. Once preheated, place the pan into the Vortex. Flip the wings halfway through the cooking time.
9. When cooking is complete, the wings should be crisp and golden brown on the outside. Remove from the Vortex to a plate and serve hot.

Cinnamon Peach Wedges
Prep time: 10 minutes | Cook time: 10 to 13 minutes | Serves 4

2 tablespoons sugar
¼ teaspoon ground cinnamon
4 peaches, cut into wedges
Cooking spray

1. Toss the peaches with the sugar and cinnamon in a medium bowl until evenly coated.
2. Lightly spray the perforated pan with cooking spray. Place the peaches in the perforated pan in a single layer. Lightly mist the peaches with cooking spray.
3. Select Air Fry. Set temperature to 350°F (180°C) and set time to 10 minutes. Press Start to begin preheating.
4. Once preheated, place the pan into the Vortex.
5. After 5 minutes, remove from the Vortex and flip the peaches. Return to the Vortex and continue cooking for 5 minutes.
6. When cooking is complete, the peaches should be caramelized. If necessary, continue cooking for 3 minutes. Remove the pan from the Vortex. Let the peaches cool for 5 minutes and serve warm.

BBQ Cheese Chicken Pizza
Prep time: 5 minutes | Cook time: 8 minutes | Serves 1

1 piece naan bread
¼ cup Barbecue sauce
¼ cup shredded Monterrey Jack cheese
¼ cup shredded Mozzarella cheese
½ chicken herby sausage, sliced
2 tablespoons red onion, thinly sliced
Chopped cilantro or parsley, for garnish
Cooking spray

1. Spritz the bottom of naan bread with cooking spray, then transfer to the perforated pan.
2. Brush with the Barbecue sauce. Top with the cheeses, sausage, and finish with the red onion.
3. Select Air Fry. Set temperature to 400°F (205°C) and set time to 8 minutes. Press Start to begin preheating.
4. Once preheated, place the pan into the Vortex.
5. When cooking is complete, the cheese should be melted. Remove the pan from the Vortex. Garnish with the chopped cilantro or parsley before slicing to serve.

Breaded Artichoke Bites
Prep time: 10 minutes | Cook time: 8 minutes | Serves 4

14 whole artichoke hearts packed in water
½ cup all-purpose flour
1 egg
⅓ cup panko bread crumbs
1 teaspoon Italian seasoning
Cooking spray

1. Drain the artichoke hearts and dry thoroughly with paper towels.
2. Place the flour on a plate. Beat the egg in a shallow bowl until frothy. Thoroughly combine the bread crumbs and Italian seasoning in a separate shallow bowl.
3. Dredge the artichoke hearts in the flour, then in the beaten egg, and finally roll in the bread crumb mixture until evenly coated.
4. Place the artichoke hearts in the perforated pan and mist them with cooking spray.
5. Select Air Fry. Set temperature to 375°F (190°C) and set time to 8 minutes. Press Start to begin preheating.
6. Once preheated, place the pan into the Vortex. Flip the artichoke hearts halfway through the cooking time.
7. When cooking is complete, the artichoke hearts should start to brown and the edges should be crispy. Remove the pan from the Vortex. Let the artichoke hearts sit for 5 minutes before serving.

Parmesan Crab Toasts

Prep time: 10 minutes | Cook time: 5 minutes | Makes 15 to 18 toasts

1 (6-ounce / 170-g) can flaked crab meat, well drained
3 tablespoons light mayonnaise
¼ cup shredded Parmesan cheese
¼ cup shredded Cheddar cheese
1 teaspoon Worcestershire sauce
½ teaspoon lemon juice
1 loaf artisan bread, French bread, or baguette, cut into ⅜-inch-thick slices

1. In a large bowl, stir together all the ingredients except the bread slices.
2. On a clean work surface, lay the bread slices. Spread ½ tablespoon of crab mixture onto each slice of bread.
3. Arrange the bread slices in the perforated pan in a single layer.
4. Select Bake. Set temperature to 360°F (182°C) and set time to 5 minutes. Press Start to begin preheating.
5. Once preheated, place the pan into the Vortex.
6. When cooking is complete, the tops should be lightly browned. Remove the pan from the Vortex. Serve warm.

Pork and Turkey Sandwiches

Prep time: 20 minutes | Cook time: 8 minutes | Makes 4 sandwiches

8 slices ciabatta bread, about ¼-inch thick
Cooking spray
1 tablespoon brown mustard
Toppings:
6 to 8 ounces (170 to 227 g) thinly sliced leftover roast pork
4 ounces (113 g) thinly sliced deli turkey
⅓ cup bread and butter pickle slices
2 to 3 ounces (57 to 85 g) Pepper Jack cheese slices

1. On a clean work surface, spray one side of each slice of bread with cooking spray. Spread the other side of each slice of bread evenly with brown mustard.
2. Top 4 of the bread slices with the roast pork, turkey, pickle slices, cheese, and finish with remaining bread slices. Transfer to the perforated pan.
3. Select Air Fry. Set temperature to 390°F (199°C) and set time to 8 minutes. Press Start to begin preheating.
4. Once preheated, place the pan into the Vortex.
5. When cooking is complete, remove the pan from the Vortex. Cool for 5 minutes and serve warm.

Turkey-Wrapped Dates and Almonds

Prep time: 10 minutes | Cook time: 6 minutes | Makes 16 appetizers

16 whole dates, pitted
16 whole almonds
6 to 8 strips turkey bacon, cut in half

Special Equipment:
16 toothpicks, soaked in water for at least 30 minutes

1. On a flat work surface, stuff each pitted date with a whole almond.
2. Wrap half slice of bacon around each date and secure it with a toothpick.
3. Place the bacon-wrapped dates in the perforated pan.
4. Select Air Fry. Set temperature to 390°F (199°C) and set time to 6 minutes. Press Start to begin preheating.
5. Once preheated, place the pan into the Vortex.
6. When cooking is complete, transfer the dates to a paper towel-lined plate to drain. Serve hot.

Muffuletta Sliders with Olive Mix

Prep time: 10 minutes | Cook time: 6 minutes | Makes 8 sliders

¼ pound (113 g) thinly sliced deli ham
¼ pound (113 g) thinly sliced pastrami
4 ounces (113 g) low-fat Mozzarella cheese, grated
8 slider buns, split in half
Cooking spray
1 tablespoon sesame seeds
Olive Mix:
½ cup sliced green olives with pimentos
¼ cup sliced black olives
¼ cup chopped kalamata olives
1 teaspoon red wine vinegar
¼ teaspoon basil
⅛ teaspoon garlic powder

1. Combine all the ingredients for the olive mix in a small bowl and stir well.
2. Stir together the ham, pastrami, and cheese in a medium bowl and divide the mixture into 8 equal portions.
3. Assemble the sliders: Top each bottom bun with 1 portion of meat and cheese, 2 tablespoons of olive mix, finished by the remaining buns. Lightly spritz the tops with cooking spray. Scatter the sesame seeds on top.
4. Arrange the sliders in the perforated pan.
5. Select Bake. Set temperature to 360°F (182°C) and set time to 6 minutes. Press Start to begin preheating.
6. Once preheated, place the pan into the Vortex.
7. When cooking is complete, the cheese should be melted. Remove the pan from the Vortex and serve.

Ham and Cheese Stuffed Peppers
Prep time: 5 minutes | Cook time: 7 minutes | Serves 4

8 Serrano peppers
4 ounces (113 g) ham cubes
4 ounces (113 g) goat cheese, crumbled

1. Start by preheating the air fryer to 370°F (188°C).
2. Stuff the peppers with ham and cheese; transfer them to a lightly oiled crisper tray.
3. Place the crisper tray in the corresponding position in the air fryer. Select Air Fry and cook the peppers for about 7 minutes or until golden brown.
4. Bon appétit!

Cheese Stuffed Mushrooms
Prep time: 10 minutes | Cook time: 7 minutes | Serves 4

1 tablespoon butter
6 ounces (170 g) Pecorino Romano cheese, grated
2 tablespoons chopped chives
1 tablespoon minced garlic
½ teaspoon cayenne pepper
Sea salt and ground black pepper, to taste
1 pound (454 g) button mushrooms, stems removed

1. Start by preheating the air fryer to 400°F (205°C).
2. In a mixing bowl, thoroughly combine the butter, cheese, chives, garlic, cayenne pepper, salt, and black pepper.
3. Divide the filling between the mushrooms. Arrange the mushrooms in the crisper tray.
4. Place the crisper tray in the corresponding position in the air fryer. Select Air Fry and cook the mushrooms for about 7 minutes, shaking the crisper tray halfway through the cooking time.
5. Bon appétit!

Cheesy Broccoli Bites
Prep time: 5 minutes | Cook time: 10 minutes | Serves 4

1 pound (454 g) broccoli florets
1 teaspoon granulated garlic
1 tablespoon dried onion flakes
1 teaspoon crushed red pepper flakes
2 tablespoons olive oil
½ cup grated Pecorino Romano cheese

1. Start by preheating the air fryer to 370°F (188°C).
2. Toss all ingredients in a lightly oiled crisper tray.
3. Place the crisper tray in the corresponding position in the air fryer. Select Air Fry and cook the broccoli florets for about 10 minutes, shaking the crisper tray halfway through the cooking time.
4. Enjoy!

Green Beans with Cheese
Prep time: 5 minutes | Cook time: 6 minutes | Serves 4

1 pound (454 g) green beans
4 tablespoons all-purpose flour
2 eggs, whisked
½ cup bread crumbs
½ cup grated Parmesan cheese
1 teaspoon cayenne pepper
½ teaspoon mustard seeds
1 teaspoon garlic powder
Sea salt and ground black pepper, to taste

1. Start by preheating the air fryer to 390°F (199°C).
2. In a shallow bowl, thoroughly combine the flour and eggs; mix to combine well.
3. Then, in another bowl, mix the remaining ingredients.
4. Dip the green beans in the egg mixture, then, in the bread crumb mixture. Transfer to the crisper tray.
5. Place the crisper tray in the corresponding position in the air fryer. Select Air Fry and cook the green beans for about 6 minutes, tossing the crisper tray halfway through the cooking time.
6. Enjoy!

Cauliflower with Cheese
Prep time: 5 minutes | Cook time: 15 minutes | Serves 4

½ cup milk
1 cup all-purpose flour
1 teaspoon garlic powder
1 teaspoon onion powder
1 teaspoon hot paprika
Sea salt and ground black pepper, to taste
2 tablespoons olive oil
1 pound (454 g) cauliflower florets
4 ounces (113 g) Parmesan cheese, preferably freshly grated

1. Start by preheating the air fryer to 350°F (180°C).
2. In a mixing bowl, thoroughly combine the milk, flour, spices, and olive oil.
3. Dip the cauliflower florets in the flour mixture. Transfer to the crisper tray.
4. Place the crisper tray in the corresponding position in the air fryer. Select Air Fry and cook the cauliflower florets for about 10 minutes, turning them over halfway through the cooking time.
5. Top the cauliflower florets with cheese and continue to cook an additional 5 minutes.
6. Bon appétit!

Brussels Sprouts with Cheese
Prep time: 10 minutes | Cook time: 10 minutes | Serves 4

1 pound (454 g) Brussels sprouts, trimmed
2 tablespoons butter, melted
Sea salt and freshly ground black pepper, to taste
1 teaspoon minced garlic
2 tablespoons red wine vinegar
2 ounces (57 g) Cheddar cheese, shredded

1. Start by preheating the air fryer to 380°F (193°C).
2. Toss the Brussels sprouts with the remaining ingredients; then, arrange the Brussels sprouts in the crisper tray.
3. Place the crisper tray in the corresponding position in the air fryer. Select Air Fry and cook the Brussels sprouts for 10 minutes, shaking the crisper tray halfway through the cooking time.
4. Serve warm and enjoy!

Chile Pork Ribs
Prep time: 5 minutes | Cook time: 35 minutes | Serves 4

1½ pounds (680 g) spare ribs
Kosher salt and ground black pepper, to taste
2 teaspoons brown sugar
1 teaspoon paprika
1 teaspoon chile powder
1 teaspoon garlic powder

1. Start by preheating the air fryer to 350°F (180°C).
2. Toss all the ingredients in a lightly greased crisper tray.
3. Place the crisper tray in the corresponding position in the air fryer. Select Air Fry and cook the pork ribs for 35 minutes, turning them over halfway through the cooking time.
4. Bon appétit!

Carrot with Butter
Prep time: 5 minutes | Cook time: 15 minutes | Serves 4

1 pound (454 g) baby carrots
2 tablespoons butter
Kosher salt and ground white pepper, to taste
1 teaspoon paprika
1 teaspoon dried oregano

1. Start by preheating the air fryer to 380°F (193°C).
2. Toss the carrots with the remaining ingredients; then, arrange the carrots in the crisper tray.
3. Place the crisper tray in the corresponding position in the air fryer. Select Air Fry and cook the carrots for 15 minutes, shaking the crisper tray halfway through the cooking time.
4. Bon appétit!

Syrupy Chicken Wings
Prep time: 6 minutes | Cook time: 18 minutes | Serves 5

2 pounds (907 g) chicken wings
¼ cup agave syrup
2 tablespoons soy sauce
2 tablespoons chopped scallions
2 tablespoons olive oil
1 teaspoon peeled and grated ginger
2 cloves garlic, minced
Sea salt and ground black pepper, to taste

1. Start by preheating the air fryer to 380°F (193°C).
2. Toss the chicken wings with the remaining ingredients. Transfer to the crisper tray.
3. Place the crisper tray in the corresponding position in the air fryer. Select Roast and cook the chicken wings for 18 minutes, turning them over halfway through the cooking time.
4. Bon appétit!

Air Fried Yam Sticks
Prep time: 10 minutes | Cook time: 15 minutes | Serves 2

1 large-sized yam, peeled and cut into ¼-inch sticks
1 tablespoon olive oil
Kosher salt and red pepper, to taste

1. Start by preheating the air fryer to 360°F (182°C).
2. Toss the yam with the remaining ingredients and place them in the crisper tray.
3. Place the crisper tray in the corresponding position in the air fryer. Select Air Fry and cook the yam sticks for 15 minutes, tossing halfway through the cooking time and working in batches.
4. Enjoy!

Potato Chips with Peppercorns
Prep time: 10 minutes | Cook time: 16 minutes | Serves 3

2 large-sized potatoes, peeled and thinly sliced
2 tablespoons olive oil
1 teaspoon Sichuan peppercorns
1 teaspoon garlic powder
½ teaspoon Chinese five-spice powder
Sea salt, to taste

1. Start by preheating the air fryer to 360°F (182°C).
2. Toss the potatoes with the remaining ingredients and place them in the crisper tray.
3. Place the crisper tray in the corresponding position in the air fryer. Select Air Fry and cook the potato chips for 16 minutes, shaking the crisper tray halfway through the cooking time and working in batches.
4. Enjoy!

Zucchini with Cheese
Prep time: 10 minutes | Cook time: 10 minutes | Serves 4

1 pound (454 g) zucchini, cut into sticks
1 egg, whisked
¼ cup grated Parmesan cheese
½ cup bread crumbs
1 teaspoon garlic powder
½ teaspoon onion powder
Sea salt and ground black pepper, to taste

1. Start by preheating the air fryer to 390°F (199°C).
2. Toss the zucchini sticks with the remaining ingredients and arrange them in a single layer in the crisper tray.
3. Place the crisper tray in the corresponding position in the air fryer. Select Air Fry and cook the zucchini sticks for about 10 minutes, shaking the crisper tray halfway through the cooking time. Work in batches.
4. Bon appétit!

Chicken Wings with Sriracha Sauce
Prep time: 5 minutes | Cook time: 18 minutes | Serves 4

2 pounds (907 g) chicken wings
1 tablespoon white vinegar
Sea salt and ground black pepper, to taste
1 teaspoon cayenne pepper
1 teaspoon garlic powder
½ teaspoon onion powder
4 tablespoons butter, room temperature
¼ cup Sriracha sauce

1. Start by preheating the air fryer to 380°F (193°C).
2. Toss the chicken wings with the remaining ingredients. Transfer to the crisper tray.
3. Place the crisper tray in the corresponding position in the air fryer. Select Roast and cook the chicken wings for 18 minutes, turning them over halfway through the cooking time.
4. Bon appétit!

Wax Beans with Cumin
Prep time: 6 minutes | Cook time: 6 minutes | Serves 4

1 pound (454 g) fresh wax beans, trimmed
2 teaspoons olive oil
½ teaspoon onion powder
1 teaspoon garlic powder
½ teaspoon cumin powder
Sea salt and ground black pepper, to taste

1. Start by preheating the air fryer to 390°F (199°C).
2. Toss the wax beans with the remaining ingredients. Transfer to the crisper tray.
3. Place the crisper tray in the corresponding position in the air fryer. Select Air Fry and cook the wax beans for about 6 minutes, tossing the crisper tray halfway through the cooking time.
4. Enjoy!

Eggplant with Paprika
Prep time: 5 minutes | Cook time: 15 minutes | Serves 3

¾ pound (340 g) eggplant
Sea salt and ground black pepper, to taste
½ teaspoon paprika
2 tablespoons olive oil
2 tablespoons balsamic vinegar

1. Start by preheating the air fryer to 400°F (205°C).
2. Toss the eggplant pieces with the remaining ingredients until they are well coated on all sides.
3. Arrange the eggplant in the crisper tray.
4. Place the crisper tray in the corresponding position in the air fryer. Select Air Fry and cook the eggplant for about 15 minutes, shaking the crisper tray halfway through the cooking time.
5. Bon appétit!

Tomato Chips with Cheese
Prep time: 5 minutes | Cook time: 15 minutes | Serves 3

1 large-sized beefsteak tomatoes
2 tablespoons olive oil
½ teaspoon paprika
Sea salt, to taste
1 teaspoon garlic powder
1 tablespoon chopped fresh cilantro
4 tablespoons grated Pecorino cheese

1. Start by preheating the air fryer to 360°F (182°C).
2. Toss the tomato slices with the olive oil and spices until they are well coated on all sides.
3. Arrange the tomato slices in the crisper tray.
4. Place the crisper tray in the corresponding position in the air fryer. Select Air Fry and cook the tomato slices for about 10 minutes.
5. Reduce the temperature to 330°F (166°C). Top the tomato slices with the cheese and continue to cook for a further 5 minutes.
6. Bon appétit!

Cinnamon Mixed Nuts
Prep time: 5 minutes | Cook time: 6 minutes | Serves 4

1 egg white, lightly beaten
½ cup pecan halves
½ cup almonds
½ cup walnuts
Sea salt and cayenne pepper, to taste
1 teaspoon chili powder
½ teaspoon ground cinnamon
½ teaspoon ground allspice

1. Start by preheating the air fryer to 330°F (166°C).
2. Mix the nuts with the rest of the ingredients and place them in the crisper tray.
3. Place the crisper tray in the corresponding position in the air fryer. Select Air Fry and cook the nuts for 6 minutes, shaking the crisper tray halfway through the cooking time and working in batches.
4. Enjoy!

Paprika Beet Chips
Prep time: 10 minutes | Cook time: 30 minutes | Serves 2

½ pound (227 g) golden beets, peeled and thinly sliced
Kosher salt and ground black pepper, to taste
1 teaspoon paprika
2 tablespoons olive oil
½ teaspoon garlic powder
1 teaspoon ground turmeric

1. Start by preheating the air fryer to 330°F (166°C).
2. Toss the beets with the remaining ingredients and place them in the crisper tray.
3. Place the crisper tray in the corresponding position in the air fryer. Select Air Fry and cook the chips for 30 minutes, shaking the crisper tray occasionally and working in batches.
4. Enjoy!

Lime Avocado Chips
Prep time: 15 minutes | Cook time: 10 minutes | Serves 4

1 egg
1 tablespoon lime juice
⅛ teaspoon hot sauce
2 tablespoons flour
¾ cup panko bread crumbs
¼ cup cornmeal
¼ teaspoon salt
1 large avocado, pitted, peeled, and cut into ½-inch slices
Cooking spray

1. Whisk together the egg, lime juice, and hot sauce in a small bowl.
2. On a sheet of wax paper, place the flour. In a separate sheet of wax paper, combine the bread crumbs, cornmeal, and salt.
3. Dredge the avocado slices one at a time in the flour, then in the egg mixture, finally roll them in the bread crumb mixture to coat well.
4. Place the breaded avocado slices in the air fry basket and mist them with cooking spray.
5. Select Air Fry, Super Convection, set temperature to 390°F (199°C), and set time to 10 minutes. Select Start/Stop to begin preheating.
6. Once preheated, place the basket on the air fry position.
7. When cooking is complete, the slices should be nicely browned and crispy. Transfer the avocado slices to a plate and serve.

Sweet and Spicy Roasted Walnuts
Prep time: 5 minutes | Cook time: 15 minutes | Makes 4 cups

1 pound (454 g) walnut halves and pieces
½ cup granulated sugar
3 tablespoons vegetable oil
1 teaspoon cayenne pepper
½ teaspoon fine salt

1. Soak the walnuts in a large bowl with boiling water for a minute or two. Drain the walnuts. Stir in the sugar, oil and cayenne pepper to coat well. Spread the walnuts in a single layer on the sheet pan.
2. Select Roast, Super Convection, set temperature to 325°F (163°C) and set time to 15 minutes. Select Start/Stop to begin preheating.
3. When the unit has preheated, place the pan on the roast position.
4. After 7 or 8 minutes, remove the pan from the Vortex. Stir the nuts. Return the pan to the Vortex and continue cooking, check frequently.
5. When cooking is complete, the walnuts should be dark golden brown. Remove the pan from the Vortex. Sprinkle the nuts with the salt and let cool. Serve.

Parma Prosciutto-Wrapped Pears
Prep time: 5 minutes | Cook time: 6 minutes | Serves 8

2 large, ripe Anjou pears
4 thin slices Parma prosciutto
2 teaspoons aged balsamic vinegar

1. Peel the pears. Slice into 8 wedges and cut out the core from each wedge.
2. Cut the prosciutto into 8 long strips. Wrap each pear wedge with a strip of prosciutto. Place the wrapped pears in the sheet pan.
3. Select Broil, Super Convection, set temperature to High and set time to 6 minutes. Select Start/Stop to begin preheating.
4. When the unit has preheated, place the pan on the broil position.
5. After 2 or 3 minutes, check the pears. The pears should be turned over if the prosciutto is beginning to crisp up and brown. Return the pan to the Vortex and continue cooking.
6. When cooking is complete, remove the pan from the Vortex. Drizzle the pears with the balsamic vinegar and serve warm.

Ricotta Capers with Lemon Zest
Prep time: 10 minutes | Cook time: 8 minutes | Serves 4 to 6

1½ cups whole milk ricotta cheese
2 tablespoons extra-virgin olive oil
2 tablespoons capers, rinsed
Zest of 1 lemon, plus more for garnish
1 teaspoon finely chopped fresh rosemary
Pinch crushed red pepper flakes
Salt and freshly ground black pepper, to taste
1 tablespoon grated Parmesan cheese

1. In a mixing bowl, stir together the ricotta cheese, olive oil, capers, lemon zest, rosemary, red pepper flakes, salt, and pepper until well combined.
2. Spread the mixture evenly in a baking dish.
3. Select Air Fry, Super Convection, set temperature to 380°F (193°C), and set time to 8 minutes. Select Start/Stop to begin preheating.
4. Once preheated, place the baking dish in the Vortex.
5. When cooking is complete, the top should be nicely browned. Remove from the Vortex and top with a sprinkle of grated Parmesan cheese. Garnish with the lemon zest and serve warm.

Parmesan Ranch Snack Mix
Prep time: 5 minutes | Cook time: 6 minutes | Makes 6 cups

2 cups oyster crackers
2 cups Chex rice
1 cup sesame sticks
⅔ cup finely grated Parmesan cheese
8 tablespoons unsalted butter, melted
1½ teaspoons granulated garlic
½ teaspoon kosher salt

1. Toss together all the ingredients in a large bowl until well coated. Spread the mixture on the sheet pan in an even layer.
2. Select Roast, Super Convection, set temperature to 350°F (180°C) and set time to 6 minutes. Select Start/Stop to begin preheating.
3. When the unit has preheated, place the pan on the roast position.
4. After 3 minutes, remove the pan and stir the mixture. Return the pan to the Vortex and continue cooking.
5. When cooking is complete, the mixture should be lightly browned and fragrant. Let cool before serving.

Homemade Potato Chips
Prep time: 5 minutes | Cook time: 22 minutes | Serves 3

2 medium potatoes, preferably Yukon Gold, scrubbed
Cooking spray
2 teaspoons olive oil
½ teaspoon garlic granules
¼ teaspoon paprika
¼ teaspoon plus ⅛ teaspoon sea salt
¼ teaspoon freshly ground black pepper
Ketchup or hot sauce, for serving

1. Spritz the air fry basket with cooking spray.
2. On a flat work surface, cut the potatoes into ¼-inch-thick slices. Transfer the potato slices to a medium bowl, along with the olive oil, garlic granules, paprika, salt, and pepper and toss to coat well. Transfer the potato slices to the air fry basket.
3. Select Air Fry, Super Convection, set temperature to 392°F (200°C), and set time to 22 minutes. Select Start/Stop to begin preheating.
4. Once preheated, place the basket on the air fry position. Stir the potato slices twice during the cooking process.
5. When cooking is complete, the potato chips should be tender and nicely browned. Remove from the Vortex and serve alongside the ketchup for dipping.

Cinnamon Apple Wedges with Yogurt
Prep time: 5 minutes | Cook time: 12 minutes | Serves 4

2 medium apples, cored and sliced into ¼-inch wedges
1 teaspoon canola oil
2 teaspoons peeled and grated fresh ginger
½ teaspoon ground cinnamon
½ cup low-fat Greek vanilla yogurt, for serving

1. In a large bowl, toss the apple wedges with the canola oil, ginger, and cinnamon until evenly coated. Put the apple wedges in the air fry basket.
2. Select Air Fry, Super Convection, set temperature to 360°F (182°C), and set time to 12 minutes. Select Start/Stop to begin preheating.
3. Once preheated, place the basket on the air fry position.
4. When cooking is complete, the apple wedges should be crisp-tender. Remove the apple wedges from the Vortex and serve drizzled with the yogurt.

Air-Fried Old Bay Chicken Wings
Prep time: 5 minutes | Cook time: 13 minutes | Serves 4

2 tablespoons Old Bay seasoning
2 teaspoons baking powder
2 teaspoons salt
2 pounds (907 g) chicken wings, patted dry
Cooking spray

1. Combine the Old Bay seasoning, baking powder, and salt in a large zip-top plastic bag. Add the chicken wings, seal, and shake until the wings are thoroughly coated in the seasoning mixture.
2. Lightly spray the air fry basket with cooking spray. Lay the chicken wings in the air fry basket in a single layer and lightly mist them with cooking spray.
3. Select Air Fry, Super Convection, set temperature to 400°F (205°C), and set time to 13 minutes. Select Start/Stop to begin preheating.
4. Once preheated, place the basket on the air fry position. Flip the wings halfway through the cooking time.
5. When cooking is complete, the wings should reach an internal temperature of 165°F (74°C) on a meat thermometer. Remove from the Vortex to a plate and serve hot.

Simple Carrot Chips
Prep time: 5 minutes | Cook time: 10 minutes | Serves 4

4 to 5 medium carrots, trimmed and thinly sliced
1 tablespoon olive oil, plus more for greasing
1 teaspoon seasoned salt

1. Toss the carrot slices with 1 tablespoon of olive oil and salt in a medium bowl until thoroughly coated.
2. Grease the air fry basket with the olive oil. Place the carrot slices in the greased pan.
3. Select Air Fry, Super Convection, set temperature to 390°F (199°C), and set time to 10 minutes. Select Start/Stop to begin preheating.
4. Once preheated, place the basket on the air fry position. Stir the carrot slices halfway through the cooking time.
5. When cooking is complete, the chips should be crisp-tender. Remove the basket from the Vortex and allow to cool for 5 minutes before serving.

Sesame Kale Chips
Prep time: 15 minutes | Cook time: 8 minutes | Serves 5

8 cups deribbed kale leaves, torn into 2-inch pieces
1½ tablespoons olive oil
¾ teaspoon chili powder
¼ teaspoon garlic powder
½ teaspoon paprika
2 teaspoons sesame seeds

1. In a large bowl, toss the kale with the olive oil, chili powder, garlic powder, paprika, and sesame seeds until well coated.
2. Transfer the kale to the air fry basket.
3. Select Air Fry, Super Convection, set temperature to 350°F (180°C), and set time to 8 minutes. Select Start/Stop to begin preheating.
4. Once preheated, place the basket on the air fry position. Flip the kale twice during cooking.
5. When cooking is complete, the kale should be crispy. Remove from the Vortex and serve warm.

Chapter 15
Desserts

Rum-Plums with Brown Sugar Cream
Prep time: 10 minutes | Cook time: 20 minutes | Serves 6

For the Cream:
¾ cup plus 2 tablespoons heavy cream
⅔ cup Greek yogurt
3 to 4 heaping tablespoons dark brown sugar
For the Plums:
1¾ pounds (793 g) plums (preferably crimson-fleshed), halved and pitted
2 slices of crystallized ginger, very finely chopped
½ cup light brown sugar
½ teaspoon ground ginger
3 broad strips of lime zest, plus juice of 1 lime
⅔ cup dark rum, plus 3 tablespoons

1. Make the cream about 12 hours before you want to serve it. Lightly whip the heavy cream, then fold in the yogurt. Put this in a bowl and sprinkle evenly with the sugar. Cover with plastic wrap and refrigerate. The sugar will become soft and molasses-like.
2. Put the plums into a baking pan in a single layer. Arrange the fruits so they are cut sides up. Scatter the crystallized ginger around the plums. Mix the sugar with the ground ginger and sprinkle it over the top. Squeeze the lime juice over and tuck the pieces of lime zest under the fruits, then pour the ⅔ cup rum around them.
3. Select Bake. Set temperature to 375°F (190°C) and set time to 20 minutes. Select Start to begin preheating.
4. Once preheated, slide the pan into the Vortex.
5. When done, the fruit should be tender when pierced with a sharp knife, but not collapsing. Leave to cool completely; the juices should thicken as they cool. If they aren't thick enough, drain off the juices and boil them in a saucepan until they become more syrupy. Add the remaining 3 tablespoons of rum. Serve the plums, at room temperature, with the brown sugar cream.

Rhubarb with Sloe Gin and Rosemary
Prep time: 10 minutes | Cook time: 30 minutes | Serves 44

1½ pounds (680 g) hothouse or main crop rhubarb stalks, all about the same thickness
½ cup granulated sugar
Finely grated zest of ½ orange
7 tablespoons sloe gin
3 tablespoons orange juice
2 rosemary sprigs, bruised
Whipped cream or heavy cream, to serve

1. Remove any leaves from the rhubarb and trim the bottoms. Cut into 1¼in lengths and put them into a large ovenproof baking dish. Scatter the sugar and zest on top and turn it all over with your hands, then pour in the sloe gin, orange juice, and 2 tablespoons of water, and finally tuck the rosemary sprigs under the rhubarb. Cover tightly with foil.
2. Select Bake. Set temperature to 350°F (180°C) and set time to 30 minutes. Select Start to begin preheating.
3. Once preheated, slide the baking dish into the Vortex.
4. When done, the rhubarb should be tender, but holding its shape and not collapsing.
5. Remove from the Vortex and leave to cool a bit in the dish. Eat warm, at room temperature, or chilled, with whipped cream or heavy cream.

Easy Nutmeg Butter Cookies
Prep time: 10 minutes | Cook time: 11 minutes | Makes 4 dozen

½ cup (1 stick) unsalted butter, melted
1 cup sugar
1 teaspoon vanilla extract
¼ teaspoon kosher salt
1 large egg
1 cup all-purpose flour
1½ teaspoons freshly grated nutmeg

1. Line two sheet pans with silicone baking mats (or use one sheet pan and bake in batches).
2. In a large bowl, mix together the butter and sugar. Stir in the vanilla and salt. Add the egg and beat until the mixture is smooth.
3. In a small bowl, whisk together the flour and nutmeg. Stir the flour mixture into the sugar and butter mixture just until blended.
4. Drop the batter by level teaspoons onto the prepared pans, leaving about 2 inches around the dough balls.
5. Select Bake. Set temperature to 350°F (180°C) and set time to 11 minutes. Select Start to begin preheating.
6. Once preheated, slide the pans into the Vortex.
7. When done, the cookies will spread, the edges will be golden brown, and the tops will start to collapse. Let cool on the pans for a few minutes, then transfer to a rack to cool completely.

Vanilla Coconut Cookies with Pecans
Prep time: 10 minutes | Cook time: 25 minutes | Serves 10

1½ cups coconut flour
1½ cups extra-fine almond flour
½ teaspoon baking powder
⅓ teaspoon baking soda
3 eggs plus an egg yolk, beaten
¾ cup coconut oil, at room temperature
1 cup unsalted pecan nuts, roughly chopped
¾ cup monk fruit
¼ teaspoon freshly grated nutmeg
⅓ teaspoon ground cloves
½ teaspoon pure vanilla extract
½ teaspoon pure coconut extract
⅛ teaspoon fine sea salt

1. Line the perforated pan with parchment paper.
2. Mix the coconut flour, almond flour, baking powder, and baking soda in a large mixing bowl.
3. In another mixing bowl, stir together the eggs and coconut oil. Add the wet mixture to the dry mixture.
4. Mix in the remaining ingredients and stir until a soft dough forms.
5. Drop about 2 tablespoons of dough on the parchment paper for each cookie and flatten each biscuit until it's 1 inch thick.
6. Select Bake. Set temperature to 370°F (188°C) and set time to 25 minutes. Press Start to begin preheating.
7. Once the Vortex has preheated, place the pan into the Vortex.
8. When cooking is complete, the cookies should be golden and firm to the touch.
9. Remove from the Vortex to a plate. Let the cookies cool to room temperature and serve.

Peach and Apple Crisp with Oatmeal
Prep time: 10 minutes | Cook time: 10 to 12 minutes | Serves 4

2 peaches, peeled, pitted, and chopped
1 apple, peeled and chopped
2 tablespoons honey
3 tablespoons packed brown sugar
2 tablespoons unsalted butter, at room temperature
½ cup quick-cooking oatmeal
⅓ cup whole-wheat pastry flour
½ teaspoon ground cinnamon

1. Place the peaches, apple, and honey in a baking pan and toss until thoroughly combined.
2. Mix together the brown sugar, butter, oatmeal, pastry flour, and cinnamon in a medium bowl and stir until crumbly. Sprinkle this mixture generously on top of the peaches and apples.
3. Select Bake. Set temperature to 380°F (193°C) and set time to 10 minutes. Press Start to begin preheating.
4. Once the unit has preheated, place the pan into the Vortex.
5. Bake until the fruit is bubbling and the topping is golden brown.
6. Once cooking is complete, remove the pan from the Vortex and allow to cool for 5 minutes before serving.

Vanilla Walnuts Tart with Cloves
Prep time: 5 minutes | Cook time: 13 minutes | Serves 6

1 cup coconut milk
½ cup walnuts, ground
½ cup Swerve
½ cup almond flour
½ stick butter, at room temperature
2 eggs
1 teaspoon vanilla essence
¼ teaspoon ground cardamom
¼ teaspoon ground cloves
Cooking spray

1. Coat a baking pan with cooking spray.
2. Combine all the ingredients except the oil in a large bowl and stir until well blended. Spoon the batter mixture into the baking pan.
3. Select Bake. Set temperature to 360°F (182°C) and set time to 13 minutes. Press Start to begin preheating.
4. Once the Vortex has preheated, place the pan into the Vortex.
5. When cooking is complete, a toothpick inserted into the center of the tart should come out clean.
6. Remove from the Vortex and place on a wire rack to cool. Serve immediately.

Mixed Berry Bake with Almond Topping
Prep time: 5 minutes | Cook time: 17 minutes | Serves 3

½ cup mixed berries
Cooking spray
Topping:
1 egg, beaten
3 tablespoons almonds, slivered
3 tablespoons chopped pecans
2 tablespoons chopped walnuts
3 tablespoons granulated Swerve
2 tablespoons cold salted butter, cut into pieces
½ teaspoon ground cinnamon

1. Lightly spray a baking dish with cooking spray.
2. Make the topping: In a medium bowl, stir together the beaten egg, nuts, Swerve, butter, and cinnamon until well blended.
3. Put the mixed berries in the bottom of the baking dish and spread the topping over the top.
4. Select Bake. Set temperature to 340°F (171°C) and set time to 17 minutes. Press Start to begin preheating.
5. Once the Vortex has preheated, place the baking dish into the Vortex.
6. When cooking is complete, the fruit should be bubbly and topping should be golden brown.
7. Allow to cool for 5 to 10 minutes before serving.

Peach and Blueberry Galette
Prep time: 10 minutes | Cook time: 20 minutes | Serves 6

1 pint blueberries, rinsed and picked through (about 2 cups)
2 large peaches or nectarines, peeled and cut into ½-inch slices (about 2 cups)
⅓ cup plus 2 tablespoons granulated sugar, divided
2 tablespoons unbleached all-purpose flour
½ teaspoon grated lemon zest (optional)
¼ teaspoon ground allspice or cinnamon
Pinch kosher or fine salt
1 (9-inch) refrigerated piecrust (or use homemade)
2 teaspoons unsalted butter, cut into pea-size pieces
1 large egg, beaten

1. Mix together the blueberries, peaches, ⅓ cup of sugar, flour, lemon zest (if desired) allspice, and salt in a medium bowl.
2. Unroll the crust on the sheet pan, patching any tears if needed. Place the fruit in the center of the crust, leaving about 1½ inches of space around the edges. Scatter the butter pieces over the fruit. Fold the outside edge of the crust over the outer circle of the fruit, making pleats as needed.
3. Brush the egg over the crust. Sprinkle the crust and fruit with the remaining 2 tablespoons of sugar.
4. Select Bake. Set temperature to 350°F (180°C) and set time to 20 minutes. Press Start to begin preheating.
5. Once the unit has preheated, place the pan into the Vortex.
6. After about 15 minutes, check the galette, rotating the pan if the crust is not browning evenly. Continue cooking until the crust is deep golden brown and the fruit is bubbling.
7. When cooking is complete, remove the pan from the Vortex and allow to cool for 10 minutes before slicing and serving.

Chocolate Blueberry Cupcakes
Prep time: 5 minutes | Cook time: 15 minutes | Serves 6

¾ cup granulated erythritol
1¼ cups almond flour
1 teaspoon unsweetened baking powder
3 teaspoons cocoa powder
½ teaspoon baking soda
½ teaspoon ground cinnamon
¼ teaspoon grated nutmeg
⅛ teaspoon salt
½ cup milk
1 stick butter, at room temperature
3 eggs, whisked
1 teaspoon pure rum extract
½ cup blueberries
Cooking spray

1. Spray a 6-cup muffin tin with cooking spray.
2. In a mixing bowl, combine the erythritol, almond flour, baking powder, cocoa powder, baking soda, cinnamon, nutmeg, and salt and stir until well blended.
3. In another mixing bowl, mix together the milk, butter, egg, and rum extract until thoroughly combined. Slowly and carefully pour this mixture into the bowl of dry mixture. Stir in the blueberries.
1. Spoon the batter into the greased muffin cups, filling each about three-quarters full.
4. Select Bake. Set temperature to 345°F (174°C) and set time to 15 minutes. Press Start to begin preheating.
5. Once the Vortex has preheated, place the muffin tin into the Vortex.
6. When done, the center should be springy and a toothpick inserted in the middle should come out clean.
7. Remove from the Vortex and place on a wire rack to cool. Serve immediately.

Vanilla Chocolate Cake
Prep time: 5 minutes | Cook time: 15 minutes | Serves 6

½ cup unsweetened chocolate, chopped
½ stick butter, at room temperature
1 tablespoon liquid stevia
1½ cups coconut flour
2 eggs, whisked
½ teaspoon vanilla extract
A pinch of fine sea salt
Cooking spray

1. Place the chocolate, butter, and stevia in a microwave-safe bowl. Microwave for about 30 seconds until melted.
2. Let the chocolate mixture cool for 5 to 10 minutes.
3. Add the remaining ingredients to the bowl of chocolate mixture and whisk to incorporate.
4. Lightly spray a baking pan with cooking spray.
5. Scrape the chocolate mixture into the prepared baking pan.
6. Select Bake. Set temperature to 330°F (166°C) and set time to 15 minutes. Press Start to begin preheating.
7. Once the Vortex has preheated, place the pan into the Vortex.
8. When cooking is complete, the top should spring back lightly when gently pressed with your fingers.
9. Let the cake cool for 5 minutes and serve.

Coconut Orange Cake
Prep time: 5 minutes | Cook time: 17 minutes | Serves 6

1 stick butter, melted
¾ cup granulated Swerve
2 eggs, beaten
¾ cup coconut flour
¼ teaspoon salt
⅓ teaspoon grated nutmeg
⅓ cup coconut milk
1¼ cups almond flour
½ teaspoon baking powder
2 tablespoons unsweetened orange jam
Cooking spray

1. Coat a baking pan with cooking spray. Set aside.
2. In a large mixing bowl, whisk together the melted butter and granulated Swerve until fluffy.
3. Mix in the beaten eggs and whisk again until smooth. Stir in the coconut flour, salt, and nutmeg and gradually pour in the coconut milk. Add the remaining ingredients and stir until well incorporated.
4. Scrape the batter into the baking pan.
5. Select Bake. Set temperature to 355°F (179°C) and set time to 17 minutes. Press Start to begin preheating.
6. Once the Vortex has preheated, place the pan into the Vortex.
7. When cooking is complete, the top of the cake should spring back when gently pressed with your fingers.
8. Remove from the Vortex to a wire rack to cool. Serve chilled.

Honey Apple-Peach Crumble
Prep time: 10 minutes | Cook time: 11 minutes | Serves 4

1 apple, peeled and chopped
2 peaches, peeled, pitted, and chopped
2 tablespoons honey
½ cup quick-cooking oatmeal
⅓ cup whole-wheat pastry flour
2 tablespoons unsalted butter, at room temperature
3 tablespoons packed brown sugar
½ teaspoon ground cinnamon

1. Mix together the apple, peaches, and honey in a baking pan until well incorporated.
2. In a bowl, combine the oatmeal, pastry flour, butter, brown sugar, and cinnamon and stir to mix well. Spread this mixture evenly over the fruit.
3. Select Bake. Set temperature to 380°F (193°C) and set time to 11 minutes. Press Start to begin preheating.
4. Once the Vortex has preheated, place the pan into the Vortex.
5. When cooking is complete, the fruit should be bubbling around the edges and the topping should be golden brown.
6. Remove from the Vortex and serve warm.

Honey-Glazed Peach and Plum Kebabs
Prep time: 10 minutes | Cook time: 4 minutes | Serves 4

2 peaches, peeled, pitted, and thickly sliced
3 plums, halved and pitted
3 nectarines, halved and pitted
1 tablespoon honey
½ teaspoon ground cinnamon
¼ teaspoon ground allspice
Pinch cayenne pepper

Special Equipment:
8 metal skewers

1. Thread, alternating peaches, plums, and nectarines onto the metal skewers that fit into the Vortex.
2. Thoroughly combine the honey, cinnamon, allspice, and cayenne in a small bowl. Brush generously the glaze over the fruit skewers.
3. Transfer the fruit skewers to the perforated pan.
4. Select Air Fry. Set temperature to 400°F (205°C) and set time to 4 minutes. Press Start to begin preheating.
5. Once the Vortex has preheated, place the pan into the Vortex.
6. When cooking is complete, the fruit should be caramelized.
7. Remove the fruit skewers from the Vortex and let rest for 5 minutes before serving.

Vanilla Chocolate Chip Cookies
Prep time: 10 minutes | Cook time: 20 minutes | Makes 4 dozen (1-by-1½-inch) cookies

1 cup unsalted butter, at room temperature
1 cup dark brown sugar
½ cup granulated sugar
2 large eggs
1 tablespoon vanilla extract
Pinch salt
2 cups old-fashioned rolled oats
1½ cups all-purpose flour
1 teaspoon baking powder
1 teaspoon baking soda
2 cups chocolate chips

1. Stir together the butter, brown sugar, and granulated sugar in a large mixing bowl until smooth and light in color.
2. Crack the eggs into the bowl, one at a time, mixing after each addition. Stir in the vanilla and salt.
3. Mix together the oats, flour, baking powder, and baking soda in a separate bowl. Add the mixture to the butter mixture and stir until mixed. Stir in the chocolate chips.
4. Spread the dough onto the sheet pan in an even layer.
5. Select Bake. Set temperature to 350°F (180°C) and set time to 20 minutes. Press Start to begin preheating.
6. Once the unit has preheated, place the pan into the Vortex.
7. After 15 minutes, check the cookie, rotating the pan if the crust is not browning evenly. Continue cooking for a total of 18 to 20 minutes or until golden brown.
8. When cooking is complete, remove the pan from the Vortex and allow to cool completely before slicing and serving.

Pineapple Sticks with Coconut
Prep time: 10 minutes | Cook time: 10 minutes | Serves 4

½ fresh pineapple, cut into sticks
¼ cup desiccated coconut

1. Place the desiccated coconut on a plate and roll the pineapple sticks in the coconut until well coated.
2. Lay the pineapple sticks in the perforated pan.
3. Select Air Fry. Set temperature to 400°F (205°C) and set time to 10 minutes. Press Start to begin preheating.
4. Once the Vortex has preheated, place the pan into the Vortex.
5. When cooking is complete, the pineapple sticks should be crisp-tender.
6. Serve warm.

Vanilla Pound Cake
Prep time: 5 minutes | Cook time: 30 minutes | Serves 8

1 stick butter, at room temperature
1 cup Swerve
4 eggs
1½ cups coconut flour
½ cup buttermilk
½ teaspoon baking soda
½ teaspoon baking powder
¼ teaspoon salt
1 teaspoon vanilla essence
A pinch of ground star anise
A pinch of freshly grated nutmeg
Cooking spray

1. Spray a baking pan with cooking spray.
2. With an electric mixer or hand mixer, beat the butter and Swerve until creamy. One at a time, mix in the eggs and whisk until fluffy. Add the remaining ingredients and stir to combine.
3. Transfer the batter to the prepared baking pan.
4. Select Bake. Set temperature to 320°F (160°C) and set time to 30 minutes. Press Start to begin preheating.
5. Once the Vortex has preheated, place the pan into the Vortex. Rotate the pan halfway through the cooking time.
6. When cooking is complete, the center of the cake should be springy.
7. Allow the cake to cool in the pan for 10 minutes before removing and serving.

Pumpkin Pudding with Vanilla Wafers
Prep time: 10 minutes | Cook time: 15 minutes | Serves 4

1 cup canned no-salt-added pumpkin purée (not pumpkin pie filling)
¼ cup packed brown sugar
3 tablespoons all-purpose flour
1 egg, whisked
2 tablespoons milk
1 tablespoon unsalted butter, melted
1 teaspoon pure vanilla extract
4 low-fat vanilla wafers, crumbled
Cooking spray

1. Coat a baking pan with cooking spray. Set aside.
2. Mix the pumpkin purée, brown sugar, flour, whisked egg, milk, melted butter, and vanilla in a medium bowl and whisk to combine. Transfer the mixture to the baking pan.
3. Select Bake. Set temperature to 350°F (180°C) and set time to 15 minutes. Press Start to begin preheating.
4. Once the Vortex has preheated, place the pan into the Vortex.
5. When cooking is complete, the pudding should be set.
6. Remove the pudding from the Vortex to a wire rack to cool.
7. Divide the pudding into four bowls and serve with the vanilla wafers sprinkled on top.

Peanut Butter Bread Pudding
Prep time: 10 minutes | Cook time: 10 minutes | Serves 8

1 egg
1 egg yolk
¾ cup chocolate milk
3 tablespoons brown sugar
3 tablespoons peanut butter
2 tablespoons cocoa powder
1 teaspoon vanilla
5 slices firm white bread, cubed
Nonstick cooking spray

1. Spritz a baking pan with nonstick cooking spray.
2. Whisk together the egg, egg yolk, chocolate milk, brown sugar, peanut butter, cocoa powder, and vanilla until well combined.
3. Fold in the bread cubes and stir to mix well. Allow the bread soak for 10 minutes.
4. When ready, transfer the egg mixture to the prepared baking pan.
5. Select Bake. Set temperature to 330°F (166°C) and set time to 10 minutes. Press Start to begin preheating.
6. Once the Vortex has preheated, place the pan into the Vortex.
7. When done, the pudding should be just firm to the touch.
8. Serve at room temperature.

Chocolate Cake with Blackberries
Prep time: 10 minutes | Cook time: 22 minutes | Serves 8

½ cup butter, at room temperature
2 ounces (57 g) Swerve
4 eggs
1 cup almond flour
1 teaspoon baking soda
⅓ teaspoon baking powder
½ cup cocoa powder
1 teaspoon orange zest
⅓ cup fresh blackberries

1. With an electric mixer or hand mixer, beat the butter and Swerve until creamy.
2. One at a time, mix in the eggs and beat again until fluffy.
3. Add the almond flour, baking soda, baking powder, cocoa powder, orange zest and mix well. Add the butter mixture to the almond flour mixture and stir until well blended. Fold in the blackberries.
4. Scrape the batter into a baking pan.
5. Select Bake. Set temperature to 335°F (168°C) and set time to 22 minutes. Press Start to begin preheating.
6. Once the Vortex has preheated, place the pan into the Vortex.
7. When cooking is complete, a toothpick inserted into the center of the cake should come out clean.
8. Allow the cake cool on a wire rack to room temperature. Serve immediately.

Vanilla Ricotta Cake with Lemon
Prep time: 5 minutes | Cook time: 25 minutes | Serves 6

17.5 ounces (496 g) ricotta cheese
5.4 ounces (153 g) sugar
3 eggs, beaten
3 tablespoons flour
1 lemon, juiced and zested
2 teaspoons vanilla extract

1. In a large mixing bowl, stir together all the ingredients until the mixture reaches a creamy consistency.
2. Pour the mixture into a baking pan and place in the Vortex.
3. Select Bake. Set temperature to 320°F (160°C) and set time to 25 minutes. Press Start to begin preheating.
4. Once the Vortex has preheated, place the pan into the Vortex.
5. When cooking is complete, a toothpick inserted in the center should come out clean.
6. Allow to cool for 10 minutes on a wire rack before serving.

Cinnamon Pineapple Rings
Prep time: 5 minutes | Cook time: 7 minutes | Serves 6

1 cup rice milk
⅔ cup flour
½ cup water
¼ cup unsweetened flaked coconut
4 tablespoons sugar
½ teaspoon baking soda
½ teaspoon baking powder
½ teaspoon vanilla essence
½ teaspoon ground cinnamon
¼ teaspoon ground anise star
Pinch of kosher salt
1 medium pineapple, peeled and sliced

1. In a large bowl, stir together all the ingredients except the pineapple.
2. Dip each pineapple slice into the batter until evenly coated.
3. Arrange the pineapple slices in the perforated pan.
4. Select Air Fry. Set temperature to 380°F (193°C) and set time to 7 minutes. Press Start to begin preheating.
5. Once the Vortex has preheated, place the pan into the Vortex.
6. When cooking is complete, the pineapple rings should be golden brown.
7. Remove from the Vortex to a plate and cool for 5 minutes before serving.

Apple Bake with Cinnamon
Prep time: 15 minutes | Cook time: 12 minutes | Serves 4

1 cup packed light brown sugar
2 teaspoons ground cinnamon
2 medium Granny Smith apples, peeled and diced

1. Thoroughly combine the brown sugar and cinnamon in a medium bowl.
2. Add the apples to the bowl and stir until well coated. Transfer the apples to a baking pan.
3. Select Bake. Set temperature to 350°F (180°C) and set time to 12 minutes. Press Start to begin preheating.
4. Once the Vortex has preheated, place the pan into the Vortex.
5. After about 9 minutes, stir the apples and bake for an additional 3 minutes. When cooking is complete, the apples should be softened.
6. Serve warm.

Vanilla Fudge Pie
Prep time: 15 minutes | Cook time: 26 minutes | Serves 8

1½ cups sugar
½ cup self-rising flour
⅓ cup unsweetened cocoa powder
3 large eggs, beaten
12 tablespoons (1½ sticks) butter, melted
1½ teaspoons vanilla extract
1 (9-inch) unbaked pie crust
¼ cup confectioners' sugar (optional)

1. Thoroughly combine the sugar, flour, and cocoa powder in a medium bowl. Add the beaten eggs and butter and whisk to combine. Stir in the vanilla.
2. Pour the prepared filling into the pie crust and transfer to the perforated pan.
3. Select Bake. Set temperature to 350°F (180°C) and set time to 26 minutes. Press Start to begin preheating.
4. Once the Vortex has preheated, place the pan into the Vortex.
5. When cooking is complete, the pie should be set.
6. Allow the pie to cool for 5 minutes. Sprinkle with the confectioners' sugar, if desired. Serve warm.

Blackberry Cobbler
Prep time: 15 minutes | Cook time: 20 to 25 minutes | Serves 6

3 cups fresh or frozen blackberries
1¾ cups sugar, divided
1 teaspoon vanilla extract
8 tablespoons (1 stick) butter, melted
1 cup self-rising flour
Cooking spray

1. Spritz a baking pan with cooking spray.
2. Mix the blackberries, 1 cup of sugar, and vanilla in a medium bowl and stir to combine.
3. Stir together the melted butter, remaining sugar, and flour in a separate medium bowl.
4. Spread the blackberry mixture evenly in the prepared pan and top with the butter mixture.
5. Select Bake. Set temperature to 350°F (180°C) and set time to 25 minutes. Press Start to begin preheating.
6. Once the Vortex has preheated, place the pan into the Vortex.
7. After about 20 minutes, check if the cobbler has a golden crust and you can't see any batter bubbling while it cooks. If needed, bake for another 5 minutes.
8. Remove from the Vortex and place on a wire rack to cool to room temperature. Serve immediately.

Vanilla Baked Peaches and Blueberries
Prep time: 10 minutes | Cook time: 10 minutes | Serves 6

3 peaches, peeled, halved, and pitted
2 tablespoons packed brown sugar
1 cup plain Greek yogurt
¼ teaspoon ground cinnamon
1 teaspoon pure vanilla extract
1 cup fresh blueberries

1. Arrange the peaches in the perforated pan, cut-side up. Top with a generous sprinkle of brown sugar.
2. Select Bake. Set temperature to 380°F (193°C) and set time to 10 minutes. Press Start to begin preheating.
3. Once the Vortex has preheated, place the pan into the Vortex.
4. Meanwhile, whisk together the yogurt, cinnamon, and vanilla in a small bowl until smooth.
5. When cooking is complete, the peaches should be lightly browned and caramelized.
6. Remove the peaches from the Vortex to a plate. Serve topped with the yogurt mixture and fresh blueberries.

Chocolate Chip Brownies

Prep time: 10 minutes | Cook time: 20 minutes | Makes 1 dozen brownies

1 egg
¼ cup brown sugar
2 tablespoons white sugar
2 tablespoons safflower oil
1 teaspoon vanilla
⅓ cup all-purpose flour
¼ cup cocoa powder
¼ cup white chocolate chips
Nonstick cooking spray

1. Spritz a baking pan with nonstick cooking spray.
2. Whisk together the egg, brown sugar, and white sugar in a medium bowl. Mix in the safflower oil and vanilla and stir to combine.
3. Add the flour and cocoa powder and stir just until incorporated. Fold in the white chocolate chips.
4. Scrape the batter into the prepared baking pan.
5. Select Bake. Set temperature to 340°F (171°C) and set time to 20 minutes. Press Start to begin preheating.
6. Once the Vortex has preheated, place the pan into the Vortex.
7. When done, the brownie should spring back when touched lightly with your fingers.
8. Transfer to a wire rack and let cool for 30 minutes before slicing to serve.

White Chocolate Cookies with Nutmeg

Prep time: 5 minutes | Cook time: 11 minutes | Serves 10

8 ounces (227 g) unsweetened white chocolate
2 eggs, well beaten
¾ cup butter, at room temperature
1⅔ cups almond flour
½ cup coconut flour
¾ cup granulated Swerve
2 tablespoons coconut oil
⅓ teaspoon grated nutmeg
⅓ teaspoon ground allspice
⅓ teaspoon ground anise star
¼ teaspoon fine sea salt

1. Line a baking sheet with parchment paper.
2. Combine all the ingredients in a mixing bowl and knead for about 3 to 4 minutes, or until a soft dough forms. Transfer to the refrigerator to chill for 20 minutes.
3. Make the cookies: Roll the dough into 1-inch balls and transfer to the parchment-lined baking sheet, spacing 2 inches apart. Flatten each with the back of a spoon.
4. Select Bake. Set temperature to 350°F (180°C) and set time to 11 minutes. Press Start to begin preheating.
5. Once the Vortex has preheated, place the baking sheet into the Vortex.
6. When cooking is complete, the cookies should be golden and firm to the touch.
7. Transfer to a wire rack and let the cookies cool completely. Serve immediately.

Mixed Berry Crisp with Cloves

Prep time: 5 minutes | Cook time: 20 minutes | Serves 6

1 tablespoon butter, melted
12 ounces (340 g) mixed berries
⅓ cup granulated Swerve
1 teaspoon pure vanilla extract
½ teaspoon ground cinnamon
¼ teaspoon ground cloves
¼ teaspoon grated nutmeg
½ cup coconut chips, for garnish

1. Coat a baking pan with melted butter.
2. Put the remaining ingredients except the coconut chips in the prepared baking pan.
3. Select Bake. Set temperature to 330°F (166°C) and set time to 20 minutes. Press Start to begin preheating.
4. Once the Vortex has preheated, place the pan into the Vortex.
5. When cooking is complete, remove from the Vortex. Serve garnished with the coconut chips.

Chocolate S'mores

Prep time: 5 minutes | Cook time: 3 minutes | Makes 12 s'mores

12 whole cinnamon graham crackers, halved
2 (1.55-ounce / 44-g) chocolate bars, cut into 12 pieces
12 marshmallows

1. Arrange 12 graham cracker squares in the perforated pan in a single layer.
2. Top each square with a piece of chocolate.
3. Select Bake. Set temperature to 350°F (180°C) and set time to 3 minutes. Press Start to begin preheating.
4. Once the Vortex has preheated, place the pan into the Vortex.
5. After 2 minutes, remove the pan and place a marshmallow on each piece of melted chocolate. Return the pan to the Vortex and continue to cook for another 1 minute.
6. Remove from the Vortex to a serving plate.
7. Serve topped with the remaining graham cracker squares

Pecan Pie with Chocolate Chips
Prep time: 20 minutes | Cook time: 25 minutes | Serves 8

1 (9-inch) unbaked pie crust
Filling:
2 large eggs
⅓ cup butter, melted
1 cup sugar
½ cup all-purpose flour
1 cup milk chocolate chips
1½ cups coarsely chopped pecans
2 tablespoons bourbon

1. Whisk the eggs and melted butter in a large bowl until creamy.
2. Add the sugar and flour and stir to incorporate. Mix in the milk chocolate chips, pecans, and bourbon and stir until well combined.
3. Use a fork to prick holes in the bottom and sides of the pie crust. Pour the prepared filling into the pie crust. Place the pie crust in the perforated pan.
4. Select Bake. Set temperature to 350°F (180°C) and set time to 25 minutes. Press Start to begin preheating.
5. Once the Vortex has preheated, place the pan into the Vortex.
6. When cooking is complete, a toothpick inserted in the center should come out clean.
7. Allow the pie cool for 10 minutes in the pan before serving.

Banana Bread Pudding
Prep time: 5 minutes | Cook time: 50 minutes | Serves 4

½ cup brown sugar
3 eggs
¾ cup half and half
1 teaspoon pure vanilla extract
6 cups cubed Kings Hawaiian bread (½-inch cubes)
2 bananas, sliced
1 cup caramel sauce, plus more for serving

1. Combine the brown sugar, eggs, half and half and vanilla extract in a large bowl, whisking until the sugar has dissolved and the mixture is smooth. Stir in the cubed bread and toss to coat all the cubes evenly. Let the bread sit for 10 minutes to absorb the liquid.
2. Mix the sliced bananas and caramel sauce together in a separate bowl.
3. Fill the bottom of 4 greased ramekins with half the bread cubes. Divide the caramel and bananas between the ramekins, spooning them on top of the bread cubes. Top with the remaining bread cubes and wrap each ramekin with aluminum foil, tenting the foil at the top to leave some room for the bread to puff up during the cooking process.
4. Select the AIR FRY function and cook at 350°F (180°C) for 25 minutes. Air fry two bread puddings at a time. Let the puddings cool a little and serve warm with additional caramel sauce drizzled on top.

Cookie Sundae with Chocolate Chips
Prep time: 15 minutes | Cook time: 12 to 15 minutes | Serves 4

1 stick unsalted butter, softened
3 tablespoons granulated sugar
3 tablespoons brown sugar
1 egg
1 teaspoon vanilla extract
½ cup all-purpose flour
¼ teaspoon baking soda
¼ teaspoon kosher salt
½ cup semisweet chocolate chips
Vegetable oil for spraying
Vanilla ice cream for serving
Hot fudge or caramel sauce for serving

1. In a medium bowl, cream the butter and sugars together using a handheld mixer until light and fluffy. Add the egg and vanilla and mix until combined. In a small bowl, whisk together the flour, baking soda, and salt. Add the dry ingredients to the batter and mix until combined. Add the chocolate chips and mix a final time.
2. Select the BAKE function and preheat VORTEX to 325°F (165°C). Lightly grease a 7-inch pizza pan insert for the air fryer oven. Spread the batter evenly in the pan. Place the pan in the air fryer oven and bake for 12 to 15 minutes, until the top of the cookie is browned and the middle is gooey but cooked. Remove the pan from the air fryer oven.
3. Place 1 to 2 scoops of vanilla ice cream in the center of the cookie and top with hot fudge or caramel sauce, as you prefer. Pass around spoons and eat the cookie sundae right out of the pan.

Pumpkin Pudding
Prep time: 10 minutes | Cook time: 15 minutes | Serves 4

3 cups pumpkin purée
3 tablespoons honey
1 tablespoon ginger
1 tablespoon cinnamon
1 teaspoon clove
1 teaspoon nutmeg
1 cup full-fat cream
2 eggs
1 cup sugar

1. Select the BAKE function and preheat VORTEX to 390°F (199°C).
2. In a bowl, stir all the ingredients together to combine.
3. Scrape the mixture into the a greased dish and transfer to the air fryer oven. Bake for 15 minutes. Serve warm.

Apple Turnovers with Raisins
Prep time: 10 minutes | Cook time: 45 to 50 minutes | Serves 4

3½ ounces (99 g) dried apples
¼ cup golden raisins
1 tablespoon granulated sugar
1 tablespoon freshly squeezed lemon juice
½ teaspoon cinnamon
1 pound (454 g) frozen puff pastry, defrosted
1 egg beaten with 1 tablespoon water
Turbinado or demerara sugar for sprinkling

1. Place the dried apples in a medium saucepan and cover with about 2 cups of water. Bring the mixture to a boil over medium-high heat, then reduce the heat to low, cover, and simmer until the apples have absorbed most of the liquid, about 20 minutes. Remove the apples from the heat and allow to cool. Add the raisins, sugar, lemon juice, and cinnamon to the rehydrated apples and set aside.
2. Select the BAKE function and preheat VORTEX to 325°F (165°C).
3. On a well-floured board, roll the puff pastry out to a 12-inch square. Cut the square into 4 equal quarters. Divide the filling equally among the 4 squares, mounding it in the middle of each square. Brush the edges of each square with water and fold the pastry diagonally over the apple mixture, creating a triangle. Seal the edges by pressing them with the tines of a fork. Transfer the turnovers to a sheet pan lined with parchment paper.
4. Brush the top of 2 turnovers with egg wash and sprinkle with turbinado sugar. Make 2 small slits in the top of the turnovers for venting and bake for 25 to 30 minutes, until the top is browned and puffed and the pastry is cooked through. Remove the cooked turnovers to a cooling rack and repeat with the remaining turnovers. Serve warm or at room temperature.

Brazilian Pineapple Bake
Prep time: 5 minutes | Cook time: 16 minutes | Serves 4

½ cup brown sugar
2 teaspoons ground cinnamon
1 small pineapple, peeled, cored, and cut into spears
3 tablespoons unsalted butter, melted

1. Select the BAKE function and preheat VORTEX to 400°F (204°C).
2. In a small bowl, mix the brown sugar and cinnamon until thoroughly combined.
3. Brush the pineapple spears with the melted butter. Sprinkle the cinnamon-sugar over the spears, pressing lightly to ensure it adheres well.
4. Put the spears in the air fryer basket in a single layer. (Depending on the size of the air fryer oven, you may have to do this in batches.) Bake for 10 minutes for the first batch (6 to 8 minutes for the next batch, as the air fryer oven will be preheated). Halfway through the cooking time, brush the spears with butter.
5. The pineapple spears are done when they are heated through and the sugar is bubbling. Serve hot.

Ricotta Lemon Poppy Seed Cake
Prep time: 15 minutes | Cook time: 55 minutes | Serves 4

Unsalted butter, at room temperature
1 cup almond flour
½ cup sugar
3 large eggs
¼ cup heavy cream
¼ cup full-fat ricotta cheese
¼ cup coconut oil, melted
2 tablespoons poppy seeds
1 teaspoon baking powder
1 teaspoon pure lemon extract
Grated zest and juice of 1 lemon, plus more zest for garnish

1. Select the BAKE function and preheat VORTEX to 325°F (163°C).
2. Generously butter a round baking pan. Line the bottom of the pan with parchment paper cut to fit.
3. In a large bowl, combine the almond flour, sugar, eggs, cream, ricotta, coconut oil, poppy seeds, baking powder, lemon extract, lemon zest, and lemon juice. Beat with a hand mixer on medium speed until well blended and fluffy.
4. Pour the batter into the prepared pan. Cover the pan tightly with aluminum foil. Set the pan in the air fryer basket and bake for 45 minutes. Remove the foil and bake for 10 to 15 minutes more until a knife (do not use a toothpick) inserted into the center of the cake comes out clean.
5. Let the cake cool in the pan on a wire rack for 10 minutes. Remove the cake from pan and let it cool on the rack for 15 minutes before slicing.
6. Top with additional lemon zest, slice and serve.

Cardamom and Vanilla Custard
Prep time: 5 minutes | Cook time: 25 minutes | Serves 2

1 cup whole milk
1 large egg
2 tablespoons plus 1 teaspoon sugar
¼ teaspoon vanilla bean paste or pure vanilla extract
¼ teaspoon ground cardamom, plus more for sprinkling

1. Select the BAKE function and preheat VORTEX to 350°F (177°C).
2. In a medium bowl, beat together the milk, egg, sugar, vanilla, and cardamom.
3. Put two ramekins in the air fryer basket. Divide the mixture between the ramekins. Sprinkle lightly with cardamom. Cover each ramekin tightly with aluminum foil. Bake for 25 minutes, or until a toothpick inserted in the center comes out clean.
4. Let the custards cool on a wire rack for 5 to 10 minutes.
5. Serve warm, or refrigerate until cold and serve chilled.

Chickpea Brownies
Prep time: 10 minutes | Cook time: 20 minutes | Serves 6

Vegetable oil
1 (15-ounce / 425-g) can chickpeas, drained and rinsed
4 large eggs
⅓ cup coconut oil, melted
⅓ cup honey
3 tablespoons unsweetened cocoa powder
1 tablespoon espresso powder (optional)
1 teaspoon baking powder
1 teaspoon baking soda
½ cup chocolate chips

1. Select the BAKE function and preheat VORTEX to 325°F (163°C).
2. Generously grease a baking pan with vegetable oil.
3. In a blender or food processor, combine the chickpeas, eggs, coconut oil, honey, cocoa powder, espresso powder (if using), baking powder, and baking soda. Blend or process until smooth. Transfer to the prepared pan and stir in the chocolate chips by hand.
4. Set the pan in the air fryer basket and bake for 20 minutes, or until a toothpick inserted into the center comes out clean.
5. Let cool in the pan on a wire rack for 30 minutes before cutting into squares.
6. Serve immediately.

Orange Cake
Prep time: 10 minutes | Cook time: 23 minutes | Serves 8

Nonstick baking spray with flour
1¼ cups all-purpose flour
⅓ cup yellow cornmeal
¾ cup white sugar
1 teaspoon baking soda
¼ cup safflower oil
1¼ cups orange juice, divided
1 teaspoon vanilla
¼ cup powdered sugar

1. Select the BAKE function and preheat VORTEX to 350°F (177°C).
2. Spray a baking pan with nonstick spray and set aside.
3. In a medium bowl, combine the flour, cornmeal, sugar, baking soda, safflower oil, 1 cup of the orange juice, and vanilla, and mix well.
4. Pour the batter into the baking pan and place in the air fryer oven. Bake for 23 minutes or until a toothpick inserted in the center of the cake comes out clean.
5. Remove the cake from the basket and place on a cooling rack. Using a toothpick, make about 20 holes in the cake.
6. In a small bowl, combine remaining ¼ cup of orange juice and the powdered sugar and stir well. Drizzle this mixture over the hot cake slowly so the cake absorbs it.
7. Cool completely, then cut into wedges to serve.

Cinnamon Almonds
Prep time: 5 minutes | Cook time: 8 minutes | Serves 4

1 cup whole almonds
2 tablespoons salted butter, melted
1 tablespoon sugar
½ teaspoon ground cinnamon

1. Select the BAKE function and preheat VORTEX to 300°F (149°C).
2. In a medium bowl, combine the almonds, butter, sugar, and cinnamon. Mix well to ensure all the almonds are coated with the spiced butter.
3. Transfer the almonds to the air fryer basket and shake so they are in a single layer. Bake for 8 minutes, stirring the almonds halfway through the cooking time.
4. Let cool completely before serving.

Berry Crumble
Prep time: 10 minutes | Cook time: 15 minutes | Serves 4

For the Filling:
2 cups mixed berries
2 tablespoons sugar
1 tablespoon cornstarch
1 tablespoon fresh lemon juice
For the Topping
¼ cup all-purpose flour
¼ cup rolled oats
1 tablespoon sugar
2 tablespoons cold unsalted butter, cut into small cubes
Whipped cream or ice cream (optional)

1. For the filling: In a round baking pan, gently mix the berries, sugar, cornstarch, and lemon juice until thoroughly combined.
2. For the topping: In a small bowl, combine the flour, oats, and sugar. Stir the butter into the flour mixture until the mixture has the consistency of bread crumbs.
3. Sprinkle the topping over the berries. Put the pan in the air fryer basket.
4. Select the AIR FRY function and cook at 400°F (204°C) for 15 minutes.
5. Let cool for 5 minutes on a wire rack.
6. Serve topped with whipped cream or ice cream, if desired.

Spice Cookies

Prep time: 15 minutes | Cook time: 12 minutes | Serves 4

4 tablespoons (½ stick) unsalted butter, at room temperature
2 tablespoons agave nectar
1 large egg
2 tablespoons water
2½ cups almond flour
½ cup sugar
2 teaspoons ground ginger
1 teaspoon ground cinnamon
½ teaspoon freshly grated nutmeg
1 teaspoon baking soda
¼ teaspoon kosher salt

1. Select the BAKE function and preheat VORTEX to 325°F (163°C).
2. Line the bottom of the air fryer basket with parchment paper cut to fit.
3. In a large bowl using a hand mixer, beat together the butter, agave, egg, and water on medium speed until fluffy.
4. Add the almond flour, sugar, ginger, cinnamon, nutmeg, baking soda, and salt. Beat on low speed until well combined.
5. Roll the dough into 2-tablespoon balls and arrange them on the parchment paper in the basket. (They don't really spread too much, but try to leave a little room between them.) Bake for 12 minutes, or until the tops of cookies are lightly browned.
6. Transfer to a wire rack and let cool completely.
7. Serve immediately

Jelly Doughnuts

Prep time: 5 minutes | Cook time: 5 minutes | Serves 8

1 (16.3-ounce / 462-g) package large refrigerator biscuits
Cooking spray
1¼ cups good-quality raspberry jam
Confectioners' sugar, for dusting

1. Separate biscuits into 8 rounds. Spray both sides of rounds lightly with oil.
2. Spray the basket with oil and place 3 to 4 rounds in the basket.
3. Select the AIR FRY function and cook at 350°F (177°C) for 5 minutes, or until golden brown. Transfer to a wire rack; let cool. Repeat with the remaining rounds.
4. Fill a pastry bag, fitted with small plain tip, with raspberry jam; use tip to poke a small hole in the side of each doughnut, then fill the centers with the jam. Dust doughnuts with confectioners' sugar.
5. Serve immediately.

Chocolate and Peanut Butter Lava Cupcakes

Prep time: 10 minutes | Cook time: 10 to 13 minutes | Serves 8

Nonstick baking spray with flour
1⅓ cups chocolate cake mix
1 egg
1 egg yolk
¼ cup safflower oil
¼ cup hot water
⅓ cup sour cream
3 tablespoons peanut butter
1 tablespoon powdered sugar

1. Select the BAKE function and preheat VORTEX to 350°F (177°C).
2. Double up 16 foil muffin cups to make 8 cups. Spray each lightly with nonstick spray; set aside.
3. In a medium bowl, combine the cake mix, egg, egg yolk, safflower oil, water, and sour cream, and beat until combined.
4. In a small bowl, combine the peanut butter and powdered sugar and mix well. Form this mixture into 8 balls.
5. Spoon about ¼ cup of the chocolate batter into each muffin cup and top with a peanut butter ball. Spoon remaining batter on top of the peanut butter balls to cover them.
6. Arrange the cups in the air fryer basket, leaving some space between each. Bake for 10 to 13 minutes or until the tops look dry and set.
7. Let the cupcakes cool for about 10 minutes, then serve warm.

Honey-Roasted Pears

Prep time: 5 minutes | Cook time: 20 minutes | Serves 4

2 large Bosc pears, halved and deseeded
3 tablespoons honey
1 tablespoon unsalted butter
½ teaspoon ground cinnamon
¼ cup walnuts, chopped
¼ cup part skim low-fat ricotta cheese, divided

1. Select the ROAST function and preheat VORTEX to 350°F (177°C).
2. In a baking pan, place the pears, cut side up.
3. In a small microwave-safe bowl, melt the honey, butter, and cinnamon. Brush this mixture over the cut sides of the pears.
4. Pour 3 tablespoons of water around the pears in the pan. Roast the pears for 20 minutes, or until tender when pierced with a fork and slightly crisp on the edges, basting once with the liquid in the pan.
5. Carefully remove the pears from the pan and place on a serving plate. Drizzle each with some liquid from the pan, sprinkle the walnuts on top, and serve with a spoonful of ricotta cheese.

Chocolate Croissants
Prep time: 5 minutes | Cook time: 24 minutes | Serves 8

1 sheet frozen puff pastry, thawed
⅓ cup chocolate-hazelnut spread
1 large egg, beaten

1. On a lightly floured surface, roll puff pastry into a 14-inch square. Cut pastry into quarters to form 4 squares. Cut each square diagonally to form 8 triangles.
2. Spread 2 teaspoons chocolate-hazelnut spread on each triangle; from wider end, roll up pastry. Brush egg on top of each roll. Place in the air fryer basket.
3. Select the AIR FRY function and cook at 375°F (191°C) for 8 minutes, or until pastry is golden brown. You may need to work in batches.
4. Cool on a wire rack; serve while warm or at room temperature.

Curry Peaches, Pears, and Plums
Prep time: 5 minutes | Cook time: 5 minutes | Serves 6 to 8

2 peaches
2 firm pears
2 plums
2 tablespoons melted butter
1 tablespoon honey
2 to 3 teaspoons curry powder

1. Select the BAKE function and preheat VORTEX to 325°F (163°C).
2. Cut the peaches in half, remove the pits, and cut each half in half again. Cut the pears in half, core them, and remove the stem. Cut each half in half again. Do the same with the plums.
3. Spread a large sheet of heavy-duty foil on the work surface. Arrange the fruit on the foil and drizzle with the butter and honey. Sprinkle with the curry powder.
4. Wrap the fruit in the foil, making sure to leave some air space in the packet.
5. Put the foil package in the basket and bake for 5 to 8 minutes, shaking the basket once during the cooking time, until the fruit is soft.
6. Serve immediately.

Apple, Peach, and Cranberry Crisp
Prep time: 10 minutes | Cook time: 12 minutes | Serves 8

1 apple, peeled and chopped
2 peaches, peeled and chopped
⅓ cup dried cranberries
2 tablespoons honey
⅓ cup brown sugar
¼ cup flour
½ cup oatmeal
3 tablespoons softened butter

1. Select the BAKE function and preheat VORTEX to 370°F (188°C).
2. In a baking pan, combine the apple, peaches, cranberries, and honey, and mix well.
3. In a medium bowl, combine the brown sugar, flour, oatmeal, and butter, and mix until crumbly. Sprinkle this mixture over the fruit in the pan.
4. Bake for 10 to 12 minutes or until the fruit is bubbly and the topping is golden brown. Serve warm.

Pecan and Cherry Stuffed Apples
Prep time: 10 minutes | Cook time: 20 minutes | Serves 4

4 apples (about 1¼ pounds / 567 g)
¼ cup chopped pecans
⅓ cup dried tart cherries
1 tablespoon melted butter
3 tablespoons brown sugar
¼ teaspoon allspice
Pinch salt
Ice cream, for serving

1. Cut off top ½ inch from each apple; reserve tops. With a melon baller, core through stem ends without breaking through the bottom. (Do not trim bases.)
2. Combine pecans, cherries, butter, brown sugar, allspice, and a pinch of salt. Stuff mixture into the hollow centers of the apples. Cover with apple tops. Put in the air fryer basket, using tongs.
3. Select the AIR FRY function and cook at 350°F (177°C) for 20 to 25 minutes, or just until tender.
4. Serve warm with ice cream.

Lemony Blackberry Crisp
Prep time: 5 minutes | Cook time: 20 minutes | Serves 1

2 tablespoons lemon juice
⅓ cup powdered erythritol
¼ teaspoon xantham gum
2 cup blackberries
1 cup crunchy granola

1. Select the BAKE function and preheat VORTEX to 350°F (177°C).
2. In a bowl, combine the lemon juice, erythritol, xantham gum, and blackberries. Transfer to a round baking dish and cover with aluminum foil.
3. Put the dish in the air fryer oven and bake for 12 minutes.
4. Take care when removing the dish from the air fryer oven. Give the blackberries a stir and top with the granola.
5. Return the dish to the air fryer oven and bake for an additional 3 minutes, this time at 320°F (160°C). Serve once the granola has turned brown and enjoy.

Black Forest Pies
Prep time: 10 minutes | Cook time: 15 minutes | Serves 6

3 tablespoons milk or dark chocolate chips
2 tablespoons thick, hot fudge sauce
2 tablespoons chopped dried cherries
1 (10-by-15-inch) sheet frozen puff pastry, thawed
1 egg white, beaten
2 tablespoons sugar
½ teaspoon cinnamon

1. Select the BAKE function and preheat VORTEX to 350°F (177°C).
2. In a small bowl, combine the chocolate chips, fudge sauce, and dried cherries.
3. Roll out the puff pastry on a floured surface. Cut into 6 squares with a sharp knife.
4. Divide the chocolate chip mixture into the center of each puff pastry square. Fold the squares in half to make triangles. Firmly press the edges with the tines of a fork to seal.
5. Brush the triangles on all sides sparingly with the beaten egg white. Sprinkle the tops with sugar and cinnamon.
6. Put in the air fryer basket and bake for 15 minutes or until the triangles are golden brown. The filling will be hot, so cool for at least 20 minutes before serving.

Chapter 16
Staples

Buttery Mushrooms

Prep time: 8 minutes | Cook time: 30 minutes | Makes about 1½ cups

1 pound (454 g) button or cremini mushrooms, washed, stems trimmed, and cut into quarters or thick slices
¼ cup water
1 teaspoon kosher salt or ½ teaspoon fine salt
3 tablespoons unsalted butter, cut into pieces, or extra-virgin olive oil

1. Place a large piece of aluminum foil on the sheet pan. Place the mushroom pieces in the middle of the foil. Spread them out into an even layer. Pour the water over them, season with the salt, and add the butter. Wrap the mushrooms in the foil.
2. Select Roast. Set temperature to 325ºF (163ºC) and set time to 15 minutes. Press Start to begin preheating.
3. Once the unit has preheated, place the pan into the Vortex.
4. After 15 minutes, remove the pan from the Vortex. Transfer the foil packet to a cutting board and carefully unwrap it. Pour the mushrooms and cooking liquid from the foil onto the sheet pan.
5. Select Roast. Set temperature to 350ºF (180ºC) and set time to 15 minutes. place the pan into the Vortex. Press Start to begin preheating.
6. After about 10 minutes, remove the pan from the Vortex and stir the mushrooms. Return the pan to the Vortex and continue cooking for 5 to 15 more minutes, or until the liquid is mostly gone and the mushrooms start to brown.
7. Serve immediately.

Shawarma Seasoning

Prep time: 5 minutes | Cook time: 0 minutes | Makes about 1 tablespoon

1 teaspoon smoked paprika
1 teaspoon cumin
¼ teaspoon turmeric
¼ teaspoon kosher salt or ⅛ teaspoon fine salt
¼ teaspoon cinnamon
¼ teaspoon allspice
¼ teaspoon red pepper flakes
¼ teaspoon freshly ground black pepper

1. Stir together all the ingredients in a small bowl.
2. Use immediately or place in an airtight container in the pantry.

Lemon Anchocy Dressing

Prep time: 5 minutes | Cook time: 0 minutes | Makes about ⅔ cup

½ cup extra-virgin olive oil
2 tablespoons freshly squeezed lemon juice
1 teaspoon anchovy paste
¼ teaspoon kosher salt or ⅛ teaspoon fine salt
¼ teaspoon minced or pressed garlic
1 egg, beaten

1. Add all the ingredients to a tall, narrow container.
2. Purée the mixture with an immersion blender until smooth.
3. Use immediately.

Paprika-Oregano Seasoning

Prep time: 5 minutes | Cook time: 0 minutes | Makes about ¾ cups

3 tablespoons ancho chile powder
3 tablespoons paprika
2 tablespoons dried oregano
2 tablespoons freshly ground black pepper
2 teaspoons cayenne
2 teaspoons cumin
1 tablespoon granulated onion
1 tablespoon granulated garlic

1. Stir together all the ingredients in a small bowl.
2. Use immediately or place in an airtight container in the pantry.

Baked White Rice

Prep time: 3 minutes | Cook time: 35 minutes | Makes about 4 cups

1 cup long-grain white rice, rinsed and drained
1 tablespoon unsalted butter, melted, or 1 tablespoon extra-virgin olive oil
2 cups water
1 teaspoon kosher salt or ½ teaspoon fine salt

1. Add the butter and rice to the baking pan and stir to coat. Pour in the water and sprinkle with the salt. Stir until the salt is dissolved.
2. Select Bake. Set temperature to 325ºF (163ºC) and set time to 35 minutes. Press Start to begin preheating.
3. Once the unit has preheated, place the pan into the Vortex.
4. After 20 minutes, remove the pan from the Vortex. Stir the rice. Transfer the pan back to the Vortex and continue cooking for 10 to 15 minutes, or until the rice is mostly cooked through and the water is absorbed.
5. When done, remove the pan from the Vortex and cover with aluminum foil. Let stand for 10 minutes. Using a fork, gently fluff the rice.
6. Serve immediately.

Ginger-Garlic Dipping Sauce

Prep time: 15 minutes | Cook time: 0 minutes | Makes about 1 cup

¼ cup rice vinegar
¼ cup hoisin sauce
¼ cup low-sodium chicken or vegetable stock
3 tablespoons soy sauce
1 tablespoon minced or grated ginger
1 tablespoon minced or pressed garlic
1 teaspoon chili-garlic sauce or sriracha (or more to taste)

1. Stir together all the ingredients in a small bowl, or place in a jar with a tight-fitting lid and shake until well mixed.
2. Use immediately.

Garlic Tomato Sauce

Prep time: 15 minutes | Cook time: 30 minutes | Makes about 3 cups

¼ cup extra-virgin olive oil
3 garlic cloves, minced
1 small onion, chopped (about ½ cup)
2 tablespoons minced or puréed sun-dried tomatoes (optional)
1 (28-ounce / 794-g) can crushed tomatoes
½ teaspoon dried basil
½ teaspoon dried oregano
¼ teaspoon red pepper flakes
1 teaspoon kosher salt or ½ teaspoon fine salt, plus more as needed

1. Heat the oil in a medium saucepan over medium heat.
2. Add the garlic and onion and sauté for 2 to 3 minutes, or until the onion is softened. Add the sun-dried tomatoes (if desired) and cook for 1 minute until fragrant. Stir in the crushed tomatoes, scraping any brown bits from the bottom of the pot. Fold in the basil, oregano, red pepper flakes, and salt. Stir well.
3. Bring to a simmer. Cook covered for about 30 minutes, stirring occasionally.
4. Turn off the heat and allow the sauce to cool for about 10 minutes.
5. Taste and adjust the seasoning, adding more salt if needed.
6. Use immediately.

Teriyaki Sauce

Prep time: 5 minutes | Cook time: 0 minutes | Makes ¾ cup

½ cup soy sauce
3 tablespoons honey
1 tablespoon rice wine or dry sherry
1 tablespoon rice vinegar
2 teaspoons minced fresh ginger
2 garlic cloves, smashed

1. Beat together all the ingredients in a small bowl.
2. Use immediately.

Creamy Grits

Prep time: 3 minutes | Cook time: 1 hour 5 minutes | Makes about 4 cups

1 cup grits or polenta (not instant or quick cook)
2 cups chicken or vegetable stock
2 cups milk
2 tablespoons unsalted butter, cut into 4 pieces
1 teaspoon kosher salt or ½ teaspoon fine salt

1. Add the grits to the baking pan. Stir in the stock, milk, butter, and salt.
2. Select Bake. set temperature to 325°F (163°C) and set time to 1 hour and 5 minutes. Press Start to begin preheating.
3. Once the unit has preheated, place the pan into the Vortex.
4. After 15 minutes, remove the pan from the Vortex and stir the polenta. Return the pan to the Vortex and continue cooking.
5. After 30 minutes, remove the pan again and stir the polenta again. Return the pan to the Vortex and continue cooking for 15 to 20 minutes, or until the polenta is soft and creamy and the liquid is absorbed.
6. When done, remove the pan from the Vortex.
7. Serve immediately.

Poblano Garlic Sauce

Prep time: 15 minutes | Cook time: 0 minutes | Makes 2 cups

3 large ancho chiles, stems and seeds removed, torn into pieces
1½ cups very hot water
2 garlic cloves, peeled and lightly smashed
2 tablespoons wine vinegar
1½ teaspoons sugar
½ teaspoon dried oregano
½ teaspoon ground cumin
2 teaspoons kosher salt or 1 teaspoon fine salt

1. Mix together the chile pieces and hot water in a bowl and let stand for 10 to 15 minutes.
2. Pour the chiles and water into a blender jar. Fold in the garlic, vinegar, sugar, oregano, cumin, and salt and blend until smooth.
3. Use immediately.

Chapter 17
Dehydrate

Dehydrated Pineapple Slices
Prep time: 10 minutes | Cook time: 12 hours | Serves 6

1 pineapple, peeled, cored and sliced ¼ inch thick
1 tablespoon coconut palm sugar
2 teaspoons ground cinnamon
½ teaspoon ground ginger
½ teaspoon Himalayan pink salt

1. Toss the pineapple slices with the sugar, cinnamon, ginger and salt.
2. Place the pineapple slices in a single layer on three air flow racks. Place the racks on the bottom, middle, and top shelves of the air fryer oven.
3. Press the Power Button. Cook at 120°F (49°C) for 12 hours.

Pork Jerky
Prep time: 10 minutes | Cook time: 3 hours | Makes 35 jerky strips

2 pounds (907 g) ground pork
1 tablespoon sesame oil
1 tablespoon Sriracha
1 tablespoon soy sauce
1 tablespoon rice vinegar
½ teaspoon salt
½ teaspoon black pepper
½ teaspoon onion powder
½ teaspoon pink curing salt

1. Combine ground pork, sesame oil, Sriracha, soy sauce, rice vinegar, salt, black pepper, onion powder, and pink curing salt in a large bowl; mix until evenly combined. Cover and refrigerate for 8 hours.
2. Using a jerky gun, form as many sticks as you can fit on all three air flow racks. They will shrink almost immediately so you can put them close together and utilize the full length of the racks.
3. Slide the racks into the air fryer oven. Press the Power Button. Cook at 160°F (70°C) for 1 hour.
4. Remove racks from the air fryer oven and blot excess moisture with paper towels. Flip each stick and cook for 1 more hour.
5. Repeat step 4 for a total cook time of 3 hours. Transfer jerky sticks to a paper towel-lined baking sheet. Cover with another layer of paper towels and let sit out 8 hours for final drying. Repeat with any remaining jerky mix.
6. Transfer jerky to an airtight container and refrigerate for up to 30 days.

Beef Jerky
Prep time: 10 minutes | Cook time: 3 to 4 hours | Serves 8

12 ounces (340 g) top sirloin beef
1 garlic clove, minced
1 inch piece fresh gingerroot, peeled and grated
2 tablespoons reduced sodium soy sauce
1 tablespoon turbinado sugar
1 tablespoon chili paste (such as Sambal Oelek)
1 tablespoon rice vinegar

1. Using a sharp knife, thinly slice beef and place in a resealable bag.
2. In a bowl, combine garlic, ginger, soy sauce, sugar chili paste and rice vinegar; whisk well.
3. Pour marinade into bag, seal and place in the refrigerator for at least 4 or up to 24 hours.
4. When ready to cook, remove pieces of beef from a marinade and pat dry with a paper towel.
5. Place the beef on three air flow racks. Slide the racks into the air fryer oven. Press the Power Button. Cook at 160°F (70°C) for 3 to 4 hours.
6. Checking the jerky periodically for desired doneness. Allow to cool completely and then store in an airtight container.

Strawberry Roll Ups
Prep time: 10 minutes | Cook time: 9 hours | Serves 2

2 cups fresh strawberries
3 tablespoons Splenda
½ lemon, juiced

1. Blend your strawberries, sugar and lemon juice until smooth.
2. Line the air flow racks with parchment paper.
3. Spread the fruit mixture evenly across the racks.
4. Slide the racks into the air fryer oven. Press the Power Button. Cook at 140°F (60°C) for 9 hours, or until it is no longer sticky.
5. Cut into slices and roll.
6. Store in an air tight container at room temperature for up to a month or in the freezer for up to a year.\

Cinnamon Orange Slices
Prep time: 10 minutes | Cook time: 6 hours | Serves 3

2 large oranges, cut into ⅛-inch-thick slices
½ teaspoon ground star anise
½ teaspoon ground cinnamon
1 tablespoon chocolate hazelnut spread (optional)

1. Sprinkle spices on the orange slices.
2. Place orange slices on the air flow racks. Slide the racks into the air fryer oven. Press the Power Button. Cook at 140°F (60°C) for 6 hours.
3. Remove when done, and if desired serve with chocolate hazelnut spread.

Dehydrated Strawberries
Prep time: 10 minutes | Cook time: 2 hours | Serves 4

1 pound (454 g) fresh strawberries

1. Line three air flow racks with parchment paper.
2. Wash strawberries and cut off stem ends. Cut strawberries into slices, about ⅛ inch thick.
3. Place sliced strawberries on the air flow racks. Space them so the pieces are not touching.
4. Slide the racks into the air fryer oven. Press the Power Button. Cook at 170°F (77°C) for 30 minutes. Use tongs to turn the berries. Cook for another 30 minutes. Repeat this until strawberry slices are leathery.
5. Allow the slices to cool completely. Transfer dried strawberry slices to an airtight container. They will keep up to 5 days.

Peach Fruit Leather
Prep time: 15 minutes | Cook time: 6 hours 15 minutes | Serves 4

4 peaches, pitted and each peach cut into 6 pieces

1. Line three air flow racks with parchment paper. Place peach slices on parchment.
2. Slide the racks into the air fryer oven. Press the Power Button. Cook at 400°F (205°C) for 15 minutes.
3. Transfer the cooked peaches to a blender or food processor and blend until smooth.
4. Line a baking sheet with parchment paper and pour peach purée onto paper, spreading as necessary with a spatula into an even layer.
5. Slide the sheet into the air fryer oven. Press the Power Button. Cook at 130°F (54°C) for 6 hours or until leather is desired consistency.

Dehydrated Zucchini Chips
Prep time: 10 minutes | Cook time: 3 hours | Serves 4

4 to 5 medium zucchini, thinly sliced
2 tablespoons olive oil
Garlic salt and black pepper, to taste

1. Toss the zucchini with the olive oil, garlic salt and pepper.
2. Lay in a single layer on the air flow racks. Slide the racks into the air fryer oven. Press the Power Button. Cook at 170°F (77°C) for 3 hours, until dry and crisp.
3. Store in a plastic container for up to two weeks.

Smoky Venison Jerky
Prep time: 30 minutes | Cook time: 4 hours | Makes 1 to 2 pounds

3 to 5 pounds (1.4 to 2.3 kg) deer roast
Hi-Mountain cure and jerky mix or another brand
3 to 5 teaspoons liquid smoke

1. Start by slicing your roast into thin strips, and removing any silver skin on each piece of the meat.
2. Lay it all out flat, and then mix up your seasoning per the box. Sprinkle on both sides of the meat, massaging it in.
3. Then transfer the meat into a bag and add in the liquid smoke. Massage bag.
4. Store in the fridge for 24 hours to let it marinade and cure.
5. Lay the jerky out on the air flow racks, don't let the pieces touch.
6. Slide the racks into the air fryer oven. Press the Power Button. Cook at 160°F (70°C) for 3 to 4 hours.
7. Make sure to flip and randomly check, and remove the meat when it is cooked to your texture liking.

Dried Mushrooms
Prep time: 30 minutes | Cook time: 4 hours | Makes 2½ quarts

4 to 5 pounds (1.8 to 2.3 kg) fresh mushrooms, washed, rinsed and drained well.

1. Rinse whole mushrooms well under cold running water. Gently scrub any visible dirt away with out damaging the mushroom. Pat dry with paper towels if needed.
2. Break the stem off of each mushroom and slice into ¼ to ½ inch thick slices with a sharp knife.
3. Place the sliced mushrooms on the parchment-lined air flow racks.
4. Slide the racks into the air fryer oven. Press the Power Button. Cook at 170°F (77°C) for 4 hours.
5. Check the mushrooms after 1 hour and flip them over for even drying. Check the mushroom slices every hour.
6. As the mushroom slices dry, remove them from the air fryer oven and allow to cool on the racks or a paper towel.
7. Store dried mushroom slices in an airtight glass container.

Cinnamon Pear Chips
Prep time: 20 minutes | Cook time: 2 hours | Serves 2

2 pears
3 tablespoons cinnamon and sugar mixture

1. Line a baking pan with parchment paper.
2. Slice the pears very thin and lay them on the pan in a single layer.
3. Sprinkle them with the cinnamon and sugar mixture.
4. Slide the pan into the air fryer oven. Press the Power Button. Cook at 170°F (77°C) for 2 hours, turning pears over halfway through.
5. Transfer to wire rack to cool.

Dried Hot Peppers
Prep time: 10 minutes | Cook time: 10 hours | Serves 2

10 hot peppers

1. Place the peppers on the air flow racks.
2. Slide the racks into the air fryer oven. Press the Power Button. Cook at 160°F (70°C) for 8 to 10 hours.
3. They should be very dry.

Lemon-Pepper Salmon Jerky
Prep time: 20 minutes | Cook time: 3 hours | Serves 10

1¾ pounds (794 g) filet wild Alaskan salmon, skin on, bones removed
½ cup low sodium soy sauce
1 tablespoon lemon juice
1 tablespoon brown sugar
2 teaspoons mixed whole peppercorns
1 teaspoon lemon zest
½ teaspoon liquid smoke
½ teaspoon celery seeds
½ teaspoon onion powder
½ teaspoon garlic powder
¼ teaspoon kosher salt

1. Freeze salmon for 1 hour.
2. In the meantime, in a large bowl, combine the soy sauce, lemon juice, sugar, peppercorns, lemon zest, liquid smoke, celery seeds, onion and garlic powders, and salt.
3. Remove the salmon from the freezer and cut it into thin strips (about ½ inch), then place in the marinade. Cover and marinate for 1 to 3 hours in the fridge.
4. Remove strips and place on a plate, patting dry with a paper towel.
5. Place the salmon strips on three air flow racks in a single layer. Slide the racks into the air fryer oven. Press the Power Button. Cook at 170°F (77°C) for 3 hours, flipping over halfway through. Salmon is done when dried all the way through, but slightly chewy.
6. Store in a cool dry place in a sealed container.

Kiwi Chips
Prep time: 15 minutes | Cook time: 6 to 12 hours | Makes 10 to 12 slices

2 kiwis

1. Peel the kiwis, using a paring knife to slice the skin off or a vegetable peeler.
2. Slice the peeled kiwis into ¼ inch slices.
3. Place the kiwi slices on the air flow racks. Slide the racks into the air fryer oven. Press the Power Button. Cook at 135°F (57°C) for 6 to 12 hours.
4. These should be slightly chewy when done.

Dehydrated Onions
Prep time: 15 minutes | Cook time: 9 hours | Makes 6 tablespoons dried minced onions and 1 tablespoon onion powder

1 medium onion

To dry the onions:

1. Prepare your onions by removing the skins, trimming the ends, and slicing into even sized pieces.
2. Separate the onion segments and spread them out evenly on the air flow racks in a single layer.
3. Slide the racks into the air fryer oven. Press the Power Button. Cook at 125°F (52°C) for 3 to 9 hours.
4. The timing will depend on the size of your onion pieces and moisture content. The dehydrated onions should be crisp and snap when your break them.
5. Let the dried onion pieces cool, crush into onion flakes, and package into airtight glass containers or process further into dried onion flakes and onion powder.

Candied Bacon
Prep time: 10 minutes | Cook time: 4 hours | Makes 6 slices

6 slices bacon
3 tablespoons light brown sugar
2 tablespoons rice vinegar
2 tablespoons chilli paste
1 tablespoon soy sauce

1. Mix brown sugar, rice vinegar, chilli paste, and soy sauce in a bowl.
2. Add bacon slices and mix until the slices are evenly coated.
3. Marinate for up to 3 hours or until ready to dehydrate.
4. Discard the marinade, then place the bacon onto the air flow racks.
5. Slide the racks into the air fryer oven. Press the Power Button. Cook at 170°F (77°C) for 4 hours.
6. Remove from the air fryer oven when done and let the bacon cool down for 5 minutes, then serve.

Appendix 1 Measurement Conversion Chart

Volume Equivalents (Dry)	
US STANDARD	METRIC (APPROXIMATE)
1/8 teaspoon	0.5 mL
1/4 teaspoon	1 mL
1/2 teaspoon	2 mL
3/4 teaspoon	4 mL
1 teaspoon	5 mL
1 tablespoon	15 mL
1/4 cup	59 mL
1/2 cup	118 mL
3/4 cup	177 mL
1 cup	235 mL
2 cups	475 mL
3 cups	700 mL
4 cups	1 L

Volume Equivalents (Liquid)		
US STANDARD	US STANDARD (OUNCES)	METRIC (APPROXIMATE)
2 tablespoons	1 fl.oz.	30 mL
1/4 cup	2 fl.oz.	60 mL
1/2 cup	4 fl.oz.	120 mL
1 cup	8 fl.oz.	240 mL
1 1/2 cup	12 fl.oz.	355 mL
2 cups or 1 pint	16 fl.oz.	475 mL
4 cups or 1 quart	32 fl.oz.	1 L
1 gallon	128 fl.oz.	4 L

Temperatures Equivalents	
FAHRENHEIT(F)	CELSIUS(C) APPROXIMATE)
225 °F	107 °C
250 °F	120 ° °C
275 °F	135 °C
300 °F	150 °C
325 °F	160 °C
350 °F	180 °C
375 °F	190 °C
400 °F	205 °C
425 °F	220 °C
450 °F	235 °C
475 °F	245 °C
500 °F	260 °C

Weight Equivalents	
US STANDARD	METRIC (APPROXIMATE)
1 ounce	28 g
2 ounces	57 g
5 ounces	142 g
10 ounces	284 g
15 ounces	425 g
16 ounces (1 pound)	455 g
1.5 pounds	680 g
2 pounds	907 g

Appendix 2: Air Fryer Cooking Chart

Beef

Item	Temp (°F)	Time (mins)	Item	Temp (°F)	Time (mins)
Beef Eye Round Roast (4 lbs.)	400 °F	45 to 55	Meatballs (1-inch)	370 °F	7
Burger Patty (4 oz.)	370 °F	16 to 20	Meatballs (3-inch)	380 °F	10
Filet Mignon (8 oz.)	400 °F	18	Ribeye, bone-in (1-inch, 8 oz)	400 °F	10 to 15
Flank Steak (1.5 lbs.)	400 °F	12	Sirloin steaks (1-inch, 12 oz)	400 °F	9 to 14
Flank Steak (2 lbs.)	400 °F	20 to 28			

Chicken

Item	Temp (°F)	Time (mins)	Item	Temp (°F)	Time (mins)
Breasts, bone in (1 1/4 lb.)	370 °F	25	Legs, bone-in	380 °F	30
Breasts, boneless (4 oz)	380 °F	12	Thighs, boneless (1 1/2 lb.)	380 °F	18 to 20
Drumsticks (2 1/2 lb.)	370 °F	20	Wings (2 lb.)	400 °F	12
Game Hen (halved 2 lb.)	390 °F	20	Whole Chicken	360 °F	75
Thighs, bone-in (2 lb.)	380 °F	22	Tenders	360 °F	8 to 10

Pork & Lamb

Item	Temp (°F)	Time (mins)	Item	Temp (°F)	Time (mins)
Bacon (regular)	400 °F	5 to 7	Pork Tenderloin	370 °F	15
Bacon (thick cut)	400 °F	6 to 10	Sausages	380 °F	15
Pork Loin (2 lb.)	360 °F	55	Lamb Loin Chops (1-inch thick)	400 °F	8 to 12
Pork Chops, bone in (1-inch, 6.5 oz)	400 °F	12	Rack of Lamb (1.5 - 2 lb.)	380 °F	22
Flank Steak (2 lbs.)	400 °F	20 to 28			

Fish & Seafood

Item	Temp (°F)	Time (mins)	Item	Temp (°F)	Time (mins)
Calamari (8 oz)	400 °F	4	Tuna Steak	400 °F	7 to 10
Fish Fillet (1-inch, 8 oz)	400 °F	10	Scallops	400 °F	5 to 7
Salmon, fillet (6 oz)	380 °F	12	Shrimp	400 °F	5
Swordfish steak	400 °F	10			

Vegetables

INGREDIENT	AMOUNT	PREPARATION	OIL	TEMP	COOK TIME
Asparagus	2 bunches	Cut in half, trim stems	2 Tbsp	420°F	12-15 mins
Beets	1 1/2 lbs	Peel, cut in 1/2-inch cubes	1 Tbsp	390°F	28-30 mins
Bell peppers (for roasting)	4 peppers	Cut in quarters, remove seeds	1 Tbsp	400°F	15-20 mins
Broccoli	1 large head	Cut in 1-2-inch florets	1 Tbsp	400°F	15-20 mins
Brussels sprouts	1 lb	Cut in half, remove stems	1 Tbsp	425°F	15-20 mins
Carrots	1 lb	Peel, cut in 1/4-inch rounds	1 Tbsp	425°F	10-15 mins
Cauliflower	1 head	Cut in 1-2-inch florets	2 Tbsp	400°F	20-22 mins
Corn on the cob	7 ears	Whole ears, remove husks	1 Tbps	400°F	14-17 mins
Green beans	1 bag (12 oz)	Trim	1 Tbps	420°F	18-20 mins
Kale (for chips)	4 OZ	Tear into pieces, remove stems	None	325°F	5-8 mins
Mushrooms	16 OZ	Rinse, slice thinly	1 Tbps	390°F	25-30 mins
Potatoes, russet	1 1/2 lbs	Cut in 1-inch wedges	1 Tbps	390°F	25-30 mins
Potatoes, russet	1 lb	Hand-cut fries, soak 30 mins in cold water, then pat dry	1/2-3 Tbps	400F	25-28 mins
Potatoes, sweet	1 lb	Hand-cut fries, soak 30 mins in cold water, then pat dry	1 Tbps	400F	25-28 mins
Zucchini	1 lb	Cut in eighths lengthwise, then cut in half	1 Tbps	400°F	15-20 mins

Appendix 3 The Dirty Dozen and Clean Fifteen

The Environmental Working Group (EWG) is a nonprofit, nonpartisan organization dedicated to protecting human health and the environment Its mission is to empower people to live healthier lives in a healthier environment. This organization publishes an annual list of the twelve kinds of produce, in sequence, that have the highest amount of pesticide residue-the Dirty Dozen-as well as a list of the fifteen kinds ofproduce that have the least amount of pesticide residue-the Clean Fifteen.

THE DIRTY DOZEN

The 2016 Dirty Dozen includes the following produce. These are considered among the year's most important produce to buy organic:

Strawberries	Spinach
Apples	Tomatoes
Nectarines	Bell peppers
Peaches	Cherry tomatoes
Celery	Cucumbers
Grapes	Kale/collard greens
Cherries	Hot peppers

The Dirty Dozen list contains two additional itemskale/collard greens and hot peppers-because they tend to contain trace levels of highly hazardous pesticides.

THE CLEAN FIFTEEN

The least critical to buy organically are the Clean Fifteen list. The following are on the 2016 list:

Avocados	Papayas
Corn	Kiw
Pineapples	Eggplant
Cabbage	Honeydew
Sweet peas	Grapefruit
Onions	Cantaloupe
Asparagus	Cauliflower
Mangos	

Some of the sweet corn sold in the United States are made from genetically engineered (GE) seedstock. Buy organic varieties of these crops to avoid GE produce.

Appendix 4 Index

A-B

Air Fried Beef Ribs	61
Air Fried Chicken Potatoes with Sun-Dried Tomato	89
Air Fried Chicken Wings with Buffalo Sauce	88
Air Fried Green Beans	43
Air Fried Tofu Sticks	29
Air Fried Yam Sticks	145
Air-Fried Avocado Tempura	21
Air-Fried Old Bay Chicken Wings	149
Almond, Coconut, and Apple Granola	10
Apple Bake with Cinnamon	157
Apple Turnovers with Raisins	160
Apple, Peach, and Cranberry Crisp	163
Arugula and Prosciutto Pizza	99
Asiago Balls	123
Asparagus Casserole with Grits	103
Asparagus Frittata with Goat Cheese	109
Asparagus Strata with Havarti Cheese	15
Avocado and Egg Burrito	11
Avocado and Tomato Egg Rolls	117
Avocado and Tomato Wraps	112
Avocado Chips with Lime	137
Avocado, Cauliflower, and Chickpea Mash	43
Bacon and Egg Cup	19
Bacon and Egg Wraps with Salsa	113
Bacon-Wrapped and Cheese-Stuffed Chicken	88
Bacon-Wrapped Herb Rainbow Trout	65
Bacon-Wrapped Jalapeño Poppers	45
Bacon-Wrapped Pork Hot Dogs	53
Bacon-Wrapped Sirloin Roast	128
Baked Avocado with Eggs and Tomato	12
Baked Eggs with Kale Pesto	16
Baked White Rice	166
Balsamic Asparagus	41
Balsamic Cherry Tomatoes	120
Balsamic Chicken Breast with Oregano	85
Balsamic Chickpea and Fig Salad	44
Balsamic Duck Breasts with Orange Marmalade	84
Balsamic Ginger Scallops	75
Balsamic Italian Sausages and Red Grapes	54
Balsamic Prosciutto-Wrapped Pears	133
Balsamic Shrimp with Goat Cheese	76
Balsamic-Glazed Beets	31
Balsamic-Maple Brussels Sprout	42
Banana Bread Pudding	159
Banana Carrot Muffin	17
Banana Chocolate Bread with Walnuts	13
Barbecue Drumsticks with Vegetable	79
Barbecue Pork Ribs	63
Barbecue Turkey Burgers	81
Basil Scallops with Broccoli	75
BBQ Cheese Chicken Pizza	141
BBQ Kielbasa Sausage	53
BBQ Pork Steaks	60
Beef and Bean Casserole	104
Beef and Bell Pepper Fajitas	117
Beef and Cheese Stuffed Peppers	45
Beef Burgers with Seeds	116
Beef Cheeseburger Egg Rolls	59
Beef Chuck Cheeseburgers	60
Beef Chuck with Brussels Sprouts	59
Beef Egg Rolls	59
Beef Hash with Eggs	18
Beef Jerky	169
Beef Meatloaf with Roasted Vegetables	47
Beef Ravioli with Parmesan	56
Bell Pepper and Carrot Frittata	11
Bell Pepper and Sausage Rolls	58
Bell Pepper Stuffed Chicken Roll-Ups	88
Bell Pepper, Onion, and Mushroom Frittata	25
Berry Crumble	161
Black Forest Pies	164
Blackberry Cobbler	157
Blueberries Quesadillas	16
Blueberry Cake with Lemon	18
Bourbon Sirloin Steak	49
Brazilian Pineapple Bake	160
Breaded Artichoke Bites	141
Breaded Asparagus Fries	40
Breaded Avocado	21
Breaded Brussels Sprouts with Paprika	41
Breaded Calf's Liver Strips	55
Breaded Catfish Nuggets	69
Breaded Chicken Cutlets	88
Breaded Crab Cakes	76
Breaded Fish Sticks	69
Breaded Gold Mushrooms	45
Breaded Pork Chops	58
Breaded Pork Loin Chops	52
Breaded Zucchini Chips with Parmesan	34
Breaded Zucchini Tots	133
Breakfast Raisins Bars	11
Breakfast Sausage Quiche	14
Brie Pear Sandwiches	139
British Pumpkin Egg Bake	20
Broccoli and Red Pepper Quiche	12
Broiled Lemony Salmon Steak	66
Brown Rice Porridge with Dates	15
Brown Rice Quiches with Pimiento	16
Brown Sugar Acorn Squash	39
Brown Sugar-Mustard Glazed Ham	49
Bruschetta Chicken	89
Brussels Sprouts with Cheese	144
Buttermilk Chocolate Cake	122
Buttermilk-Marinated Chicken Wings	141
Butternut Squash and Parsnip with Thyme	28
Butternut Squash with Goat Cheese	27
Buttery Mushrooms	166

C-D

Cajun Beef and Bell Pepper Fajitas	114
Cajun Catfish Cakes with Parmesan	71
Cajun Cod Fillets with Lemon Pepper	71
Candied Bacon	171

Cardamom and Vanilla Custard	160
Carrot and Mushroom Spring Rolls	112
Carrot Chips	138
Carrot with Butter	144
Catfish Fillets with Pecan Crust	68
Catfish, Toamto and Onion Kebabs	68
Cauliflower and Okra Casserole	105
Cauliflower with Cheese	143
Cauliflower with Teriyaki Sauce	33
Cayenne Green Beans	30
Cayenne Prawns with Cumin	70
Char Siew	62
Cheddar and Basmati Rice Risotto	43
Cheddar and Egg Frittata with Parsley	106
Cheddar Bacon Burst with Spinach	60
Cheddar Bacon Casserole	13
Cheddar Baked Potatoes with Chives	132
Cheddar Black Bean and Corn Salsa	140
Cheddar Broccoli and Carrot Quiche	107
Cheddar Broccoli Casserole	105
Cheddar Broccoli Gratin	40
Cheddar Chicken and Broccoli Divan	106
Cheddar Chicken Sausage Casserole	103
Cheddar Egg and Bacon Muffins	20
Cheddar Hash Brown Casserole	14
Cheddar Mushrooms with Pimientos	131
Cheddar Pastrami Casserole	104
Cheddar Sausage Balls	132
Cheese and Bacon Muffin Sandwiches	11
Cheese Crusted Chops	61
Cheese Stuffed Mushrooms	143
Cheese Tomato Pizza with Basil	99
Cheese-Encrusted Chicken Tenderloins with Peanuts	89
Cheeseburgers with American Cheese	57
Cheesy Bacon and Egg Wraps	116
Cheesy Broccoli Bites	143
Cheesy Eggplant with Chili Smoked Almonds	27
Cheesy Italian Sausage Egg Muffins	23
Cheesy Onion Omelet	22
Cheesy Pepperoni and Chicken Pizza	90
Cheesy Potato Taquitos	117
Cheesy Spring Chicken Wraps	116
Chia Seeds Oat Porridge	22
Chicken and Cabbage Wraps	113
Chicken and Pepper Baguette with Mayo	83
Chicken and Veggies with 'Nduja	81
Chicken and Yogurt Taquitos	118
Chicken Breakfast Sausage Biscuits	20
Chicken Breakfast Sausages	13
Chicken Breast in Mango Sauce	80
Chicken Drumsticks with Green Beans	86
Chicken Pot Pie	79
Chicken Roast with Mustard Paste	125
Chicken Schnitzel	90
Chicken Thighs with Mirin	83
Chicken Wings with Sriracha Sauce	145
Chicken with Brown Sugar Brine	126
Chicken Wraps with Ricotta Cheese	112
Chicken, Vegetable and Rice Casserole	81
Chickpea and Mushroom Wraps	114
Chickpea and Spinach Casserole	106
Chickpea Brownies	161
Chickpea-Stuffed Bell Peppers	35
Chile Pork Ribs	144
China Spicy Turkey Thighs	94
Chocolate and Peanut Butter Lava Cupcakes	162
Chocolate Blueberry Cupcakes	153
Chocolate Cake with Blackberries	156
Chocolate Chip Brownies	158
Chocolate Croissants	163
Chocolate Macaroons with Coconut	120
Chocolate S'mores	158
Cinnamon Almonds	161
Cinnamon Apple Chips	136
Cinnamon Apple Wedges with Yogurt	148
Cinnamon Mixed Nuts	146
Cinnamon Orange Slices	169
Cinnamon Peach Wedges	141
Cinnamon Pear Chips	171
Cinnamon Pineapple Rings	156
Citrus Carrots with Balsamic Glaze	38
Citrus Pork Loin Roast	63
Citrus Pork Ribs with Oregano	51
Clam Appetizers	68
Coconut Curried Fish with Chilies	71
Coconut Orange Cake	154
Coffee Cake with Pecan	9
Colby Pork Sausage with Cauliflower	54
Cookie Sundae with Chocolate Chips	159
Corn Casserole with Bell Pepper	103
Corn Casserole with Swiss Cheese	38
Corn Frittata with Avocado Dressing	10
Crab Cheese Enchiladas	65
Crab Ratatouille with Thyme	76
Cream Cheese and Crab Wontons	113
Cream-Glazed Cinnamon Rolls	121
Creamy Grits	167
Creamy Sausage and Cauliflower	19
Crispy Cauliflower	45
Crispy Chicken Egg Rolls	117
Crispy Chicken Skin	91
Crispy Cream Cheese Wontons	112
Crispy Fish Fillet	66
Crumbed Golden Filet Mignon	61
Crumbled Tofu with Sweet Potatoes	43
Cumin Fried Chickpeas	138
Cumin Tortilla Chips	137
Curried Cauliflower with Cashews	31
Curried Chicken and Brussels Sprouts	84
Curried Halibut Fillets with Parmesan	67
Curried King Prawns with Cumin	73
Curried Pork Sliders	115
Curried Prawns with Coconut	72
Curried Shrimp and Zucchini Potstickers	111
Curry Peaches, Pears, and Plums	163
Deep Fried Duck Leg Quarters	95
Dehydrated Onions	171
Dehydrated Pineapple Slices	169
Dehydrated Strawberries	170
Dehydrated Zucchini Chips	170
Deviled Eggs with Mayo	138
Dijon Pork Tenderloin	50
Dijon Turkey Breast with Sage	83
Dijon Turkey with Carrots	84

Dijon-Honey Pork Tenderloin	56
Dijon-Rosemary Chicken Breasts	80
Double Cheese Roasted Asparagus	28
Dried Fruit Stuffed Pork Loin	127
Dried Hot Peppers	171
Dried Mushrooms	170
Drumsticks with Barbecue-Honey Sauce	90
Duck Breast with Potato	80
Duck Breasts with Marmalade Balsamic Glaze	95

E-F

Easy Cajun Chicken Drumsticks	91
Easy Chicken Fingers	90
Easy Cinnamon Toasts	23
Easy Nutmeg Butter Cookies	151
Egg in a Hole	10
Eggplant and Sushi Rice Bowl	42
Eggplant Hoagies	118
Eggplant with Paprika	146
Escarole and Radicchio Pizza with Walnuts	100
Feta Stuffed Lamb Leg	125
Fish Fillet with Poblano Sauce	66
Fish Fillet with Sun-Dried Tomato Pesto	67
Five-Spice Turkey Thighs	82
Flounder Fillet and Asparagus Rolls	67
Flounder Fillets with Lemon Pepper	72
French Toast Sticks	20
French Toast Sticks with Strawberries	18
Fried Bacon-Wrapped Scallops	77
Fried Breaded Scallops	75
Fried Pickle Spears with Chili	135
Fried Root Veggies with Thyme	32
Fried Scallops with Thyme	77

G-H

Garlic Bell Peppers with Marjoram	32
Garlic Broccoli with Parmesan	41
Garlic Butternut Squash Croquettes	37
Garlic Calamari Rings	75
Garlic Chicken Wings	82
Garlic Duck Leg Quarters	84
Garlic Eggplant Slices with Parsley	30
Garlic Fried Edamame	139
Garlic Nuggets	122
Garlic Pork Belly with Bay Leaves	51
Garlic Pork Leg Roast with Candy Onions	54
Garlic Potatoes with Heavy Cream	37
Garlic Potatoes with Peppers and Onions	16
Garlic Ratatouille	33
Garlic Tofu with Basil	30
Garlic Tomato Pizza Sauce	98
Garlic Tomato Sauce	167
Garlic Turnip and Zucchini	33
Garlic Zucchini Crisps	38
Garlic Zucchini Sticks	40
Garlic-Lime Shishito Peppers	39
Garlicky Cabbage with Red Pepper	41
Garlicky Whole Chicken Bake	82
Ginger Apple Wedges	137
Ginger Shrimp with Sesame Seeds	134
Ginger-Garlic Dipping Sauce	167
Ginger-Pepper Broccoli	29

Glazed Strawberry Toast	25
Gold Livers	91
Golden Chicken Cutlets	92
Golden Potato, Carrot and Onion	28
Greek Lamb Rack	60
Greek Potatoes with Chives	39
Green Beans with Cheese	143
Green Chiles and Cheese Nachos	131
Half-and-Half Cinnamon Rolls	15
Halloumi Zucchinis and Eggplant	32
Ham and Cheese Stuffed Peppers	143
Ham and Pineapple Pizza	98
Hawaiian Chicken Bites	91
Hoisin Roasted Pork Ribs	48
Hoisin Scallops with Sesame Seeds	73
Homemade Potato Chips	148
Honey Apple-Peach Crumble	154
Honey Baby Carrots with Dill	30
Honey Cashew Granola with Cranberries	19
Honey Glazed Chicken Breasts	92
Honey Halibut Steaks with Parsley	68
Honey Halibut Steaks with Parsley	76
Honey Roasted Grapes with Basil	132
Honey Snack Mix	135
Honey-Glazed Peach and Plum Kebabs	154
Honey-Roasted Pears	162
Hush Puppies with Jalapeño	136

I-J-K

Italian Bacon Hot Dogs	19
Italian Rice Balls with Olives	140
Jalapeño Poppers with Cheddar	131
Jelly Doughnuts	162
Juicy Bacon and Beef Cheeseburgers	47
Jumbo Shrimp with Dijon-Mayo Sauce	74
Kale and Egg Frittata with Feta	107
Kiwi Chips	171

L-M

Lamb and Feta Hamburgers	118
Lamb Chops with Rosemary	58
Lamb Hamburgers with Feta Cheese	115
Lemon Anchocy Dressing	166
Lemon Crab Cakes with Mayo	77
Lemon Pork Loin Chop with Marjoram	52
Lemon Ricotta with Capers	135
Lemon Shrimp with Cumin	73
Lemon Tilapia Fillets with Garlic	69
Lemon-Pepper Chicken Wings	132
Lemon-Pepper Salmon Jerky	171
Lemony Blackberry Crisp	164
Lemony Shrimp with Arugula	66
Lemony-Honey Roasted Radishes	27
Lime Avocado Chips	147
Lime Chicken Breast	87
Lime Chicken with Cilantro	92
Lime Sweet Potatoes with Allspice	37
Lime-Honey Grilled Fruit Salad	25
Low-Fat Buttermilk Biscuits	9
Lush Veggie Omelet	21
Maple Banana Bread Pudding	17
Maple French Toast Casserole	19

Maple Garlic Brussels Sprout	37
Marinated Catfish Fillet	65
Mediterranean Baked Fish Fillet	67
Mediterranean Herbed Zucchini and Parsnip	44
Mexican Beef and Chile Casserole	108
Mexican Pork Chops	61
Mint-Roasted Boneless Lamb Leg	48
Minted-Balsamic Lamb Chops	50
Mixed Berry Bake with Almond Topping	152
Mixed Berry Crisp with Cloves	158
Mozzarella Brussels Sprout Pizza	101
Mozzarella Chicken Taquitos	114
Mozzarella Ham Stromboli	58
Mozzarella Pepperoni Pizza	23
Mozzarella Rice Arancini	121
Mozzarella Sausage Pizza	20
Mozzarella Tomato Salsa Rounds	10
Mozzarella Walnut Stuffed Mushrooms	34
Muffuletta Sliders with Olive Mix	142
Mushroom and Beef Casserole	104
Mushroom and Beef Meatloaf	61
Mushroom and Pepperoni Pizza	45
Mushroom and Sausage Empanadas	138
Mushroom and Spinach Frittata	14
Mushroom and Yellow Squash Toast	22
Mushroom Summer Rolls	42
Mustard Lamb Shoulder	125

N-O

Nice Goulash	93
No-Knead Pan Pizza Dough	97
Nut-Crusted Pork Rack	51
Nutmeg Apple Chips	139
Old Bay Crab Sticks with Mayo Sauce	74
Old Bay Fried Chicken Wings	137
Old Bay Shrimp with Potatoes	71
Onion-Stuffed Mushrooms	33
Orange Cake	161
Orange Pork Tenderloin	62
Orange Scones with Blueberries	18
Orange Shrimp with Cayenne	70
Orange-Glazed Whole Chicken	79
Oyster Mushroom Pizza Squares	42

P-R

Paprika Beet Chips	147
Paprika Hens in Wine	85
Paprika Hens with Creole Seasoning	86
Paprika Lamb Chops with Sage	52
Paprika Nut Mix	139
Paprika Polenta Fries with Chili-Lime Mayo	135
Paprika Potato Chips	136
Paprika Tiger Shrimp	70
Paprika Tilapia with Garlic Aioli	69
Paprika Whole Chicken Roast	86
Paprika-Oregano Seasoning	166
Parma Prosciutto-Wrapped Pears	147
Parmesan Bruschetta with Tomato	140
Parmesan Brussels Sprout	29
Parmesan Cauliflower with Turmeric	130
Parmesan Corn on the Cob	39
Parmesan Crab Toasts	142

Parmesan Eggplant Hoagies	113
Parmesan Fennel with Red Pepper	31
Parmesan Fish Fillets with Tarragon	70
Parmesan Green Bean Casserole	103
Parmesan Ham and Egg Cups	9
Parmesan Ranch Snack Mix	148
Parmesan Snack Mix	136
Parsley Shrimp with Lemon	73
Peach and Apple Crisp with Oatmeal	152
Peach and Blueberry Galette	153
Peach Chicken with Dark Cherry	85
Peach Fruit Leather	170
Peanut Butter Bread Pudding	156
Pear Pizza with Basil	98
Pecan and Cherry Stuffed Apples	163
Pecan Pie with Chocolate Chips	159
Peppercorn Crusted Beef Tenderloin	60
Pepperoni and Bell Pepper Pockets	62
Pepperoni Pizza Bites with Marinara	131
Pepperoni Pizza with Mozzarella	98
Peppery Sausage Casserole with Cheddar	106
Pigs in a Blanket with Sesame Seeds	120
Pineapple Sticks with Coconut	155
Poblano Garlic Sauce	167
Pork and Cabbage Gyoza	115
Pork and Pineapple Kebabs	53
Pork and Turkey Sandwiches	142
Pork and Veggie Kebabs	52
Pork Chop Roast with Worcestershire	55
Pork Chops and Apple Bake	55
Pork Chops with Pickapeppa Sauce	49
Pork Chops with Rinds	59
Pork Jerky	169
Pork Meatballs with Scallions	55
Pork Momos with Carrot	115
Pork Sausage Ratatouille	53
Pork Tenderloin with Potatoes	57
Pork Tenderloin with Rice	56
Potato and Chorizo Frittata	108
Potato and Prosciutto Salad	62
Potato Chips with Peppercorns	145
Potato Shells with Cheddar and Bacon	28
Potato Taquitos with Mexican Cheese	114
Potato, Broccoli, and Zucchini Veg Bowl	44
Pro Dough	97
Prosciutto and Fig Pizza	99
Prosciutto Tart with Asparagus	50
Prosciutto-Wrapped Pork Tenderloin	57
Provolone Stuffed Beef and Pork Meatballs	63
Pumpkin Pudding	159
Pumpkin Pudding with Vanilla Wafers	155
Ranch Risotto with Parmesan Cheese	22
Red Chili Okra	32
Rhubarb with Sloe Gin and Rosemary	151
Rice and Olives Stuffed Peppers	35
Ricotta Capers with Lemon Zest	148
Ricotta Lemon Poppy Seed Cake	160
Ricotta Margherita with Basil	99
Ricotta Pork Gratin with Mustard	108
Ricotta Spinach and Basil Pockets	111
Ricotta Spinach Omelet	24
Roasted Broccoli	45

Entry	Page
Roasted Mushrooms with Garlic	130
Roasted Pork Rib	57
Roasted Potatoes with Rosemary	40
Roasted Veggie Rice with Eggs	29
Rosemary Chicken Thighs	87
Rosemary Turkey Scotch Eggs	95
Rosemary-Balsamic Pork Loin Roast	48
Rum-Plums with Brown Sugar Cream	151
Rump Roast with Bell Peppers	48

S-T

Entry	Page
Salmon Fillet with Spinach, and Beans	65
Sausage and Onion Rolls with Mustard	130
Scotch Eggs	24
Sesame Balsamic Chicken Breast	80
Sesame Green Beans with Sriracha	38
Sesame Kale Chips	149
Shawarma Seasoning	166
Shrimp and Artichoke Paella	74
Shrimp and Spinach Frittata	13
Shrimp and Veggie Patties	74
Shrimp Kebabs with Cherry Tomatoes	72
Shrimp Scampi with Garlic Butter	72
Simple Air Fried Asparagus	44
Simple Air Fried Chicken Wings	93
Simple Blueberry Muffins	23
Simple Carrot Chips	149
Simple Chicken Cordon Bleu	79
Simple Chicken Nuggets	93
Simple Pizza Dough	97
Simple Whole Chicken Bake	93
Smoked Beef	63
Smoked Trout Frittata with Dill	107
Smoky Venison Jerky	170
Spanish Chicken and Pepper Baguette	94
Speedy Coffee Donuts	21
Spice Cookies	162
Spicy Pepper Steak	49
Spicy Tandoori Chicken Drumsticks	92
Spinach and Egg Florentine	17
Spinach and Mushroom Frittata	104
Spinach and Shrimp Frittata	109
Spinach and Tomato with Scrambled Eggs	24
Spinach-Stuffed Beefsteak Tomatoes	34
Spring Pea Pizza with Ramps	100
Sriracha Shrimp with Mayo	123
Sriracha-Honey Chicken Thighs	87
Strawberry Pizza	101
Strawberry Roll Ups	169
Strawberry-Glazed Turkey	94
Stuffed Bell Pepper with Cheddar Bacon	25
Stuffed Bell Peppers with Cream Cheese	35
Stuffed Peppers with Cheese and Basil	27
Sugar Roasted Walnuts	133
Sweet and Spicy Roasted Walnuts	147
Sweet Banana Bread	9
Sweet-and-Sour Chicken Breasts	82
Sweet-and-Sour Chicken Nuggets	94
Swiss Chicken and Ham Casserole	107
Syrupy Chicken Wings	144
Tasty Meat and Vegetable Loaf	81
Teriyaki Chicken	126
Teriyaki Chicken, Pepper, and Pineapple Kebabs	87
Teriyaki Sauce	167
Teriyaki-Glazed Pork Ribs	50
Teriyaki-Marinated Shrimp Skewers	122
Thai Pork Sliders	118
Thyme Pork Chops with Carrots	54
Tilapia and Rockfish Casserole	105
Tomato and Black Bean Chili	44
Tomato and Olive Quiche	108
Tomato Chips with Cheese	146
Tomato-Stuffed Portobello Mushrooms	34
Tuna Melts with Mayo	134
Turkey and Cauliflower Meatloaf	95
Turkey and Pepper Hamburger	116
Turkey Breast with Strawberries	83
Turkey Casserole with Almond Mayo	105
Turkey Meatloaves with Onion	86
Turkey with Thyme-Sage Brine	127
Turkey-Wrapped Dates and Almonds	142

V-W-Z

Entry	Page
Vanilla Baked Peaches and Blueberries	157
Vanilla Banana Bread Pudding	12
Vanilla Blueberry Cobbler	15
Vanilla Butter Cake	120
Vanilla Cheese Blintzes	122
Vanilla Chocolate Cake	154
Vanilla Chocolate Chip Cookies	155
Vanilla Coconut Cookies with Pecans	152
Vanilla Fudge Pie	157
Vanilla Pancake with Mixed Berries	12
Vanilla Pancake with Walnuts	14
Vanilla Pound Cake	155
Vanilla Ricotta Cake with Lemon	156
Vanilla Walnuts Tart with Cloves	152
Vinegary Chicken with Pineapple	85
Vinegary Pork Schnitzel	51
Warm Sourdough Croutons	24
Wax Beans with Cumin	146
White Chocolate Cookies with Nutmeg	158
Whole-Wheat Blueberries Muffins	17
Worcestershire Ribeye Steaks with Garlic	56
Zucchini and Onion Pizza	101
Zucchini and Spinach Frittata	109
Zucchini Pizza with Pistachios	100
Zucchini Quesadilla with Gouda Cheese	31
Zucchini with Cheese	145

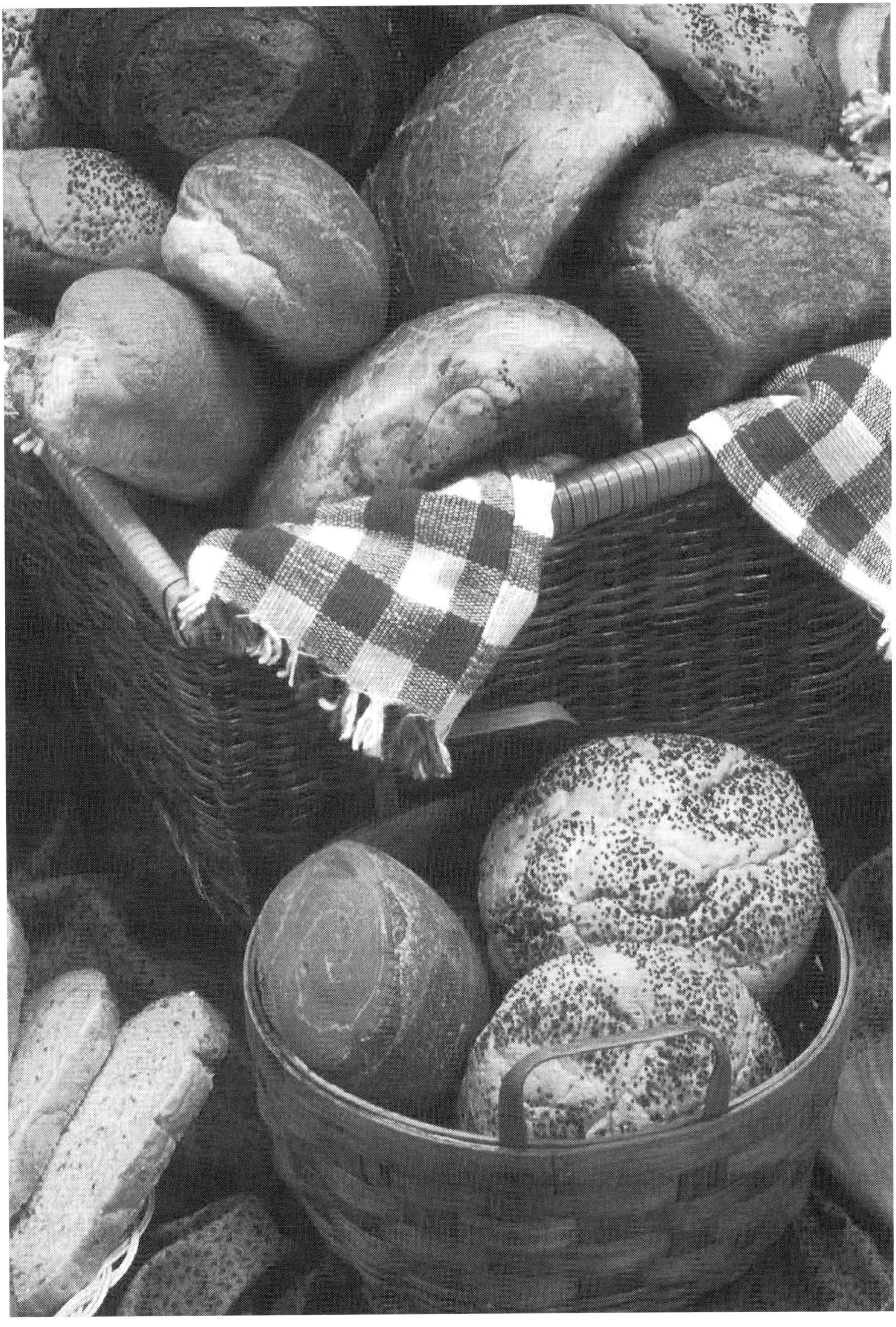

TIFFANY D. MORGAN

Printed in Great Britain
by Amazon